Register for Free Membership to

solutions@syngress.com

Over the last few years, Syngress has published many best-selling and critically acclaimed books, including Tom Shinder's *Configuring ISA Server 2000*, Brian Caswell and Jay Beale's *Snort 2.0 Intrusion Detection*, and Angela Orebaugh and Gilbert Ramirez's *Ethereal Packet Sniffing*. One of the reasons for the success of these books has been our unique **solutions@syngress.com** program. Through this site, we've been able to provide readers a real time extension to the printed book.

As a registered owner of this book, you will qualify for free access to our members-only solutions@syngress.com program. Once you have registered, you will enjoy several benefits, including:

- Four downloadable e-booklets on topics related to the book. Each booklet is approximately 20-30 pages in Adobe PDF format. They have been selected by our editors from other best-selling Syngress books as providing topic coverage that is directly related to the coverage in this book.

- A comprehensive FAQ page that consolidates all of the key points of this book into an easy to search web page, providing you with the concise, easy to access data you need to perform your job.

- A "From the Author" Forum that allows the authors of this book to post timely updates links to related sites, or additional topic coverage that may have been requested by readers.

Just visit us at **www.syngress.com/solutions** and follow the simple registration process. You will need to have this book with you when you register.

Thank you for giving us the opportunity to serve your needs. And be sure to let us know if there is anything else we can do to make your job easier.

D1511673

YNGRESS®

Application Defense
www.appliacationdefense.com

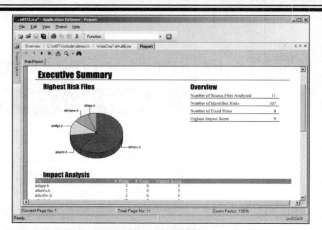

Application Defense Specials

- Free Software with Purchase of Application Security Services Program
- $1,000 Enterprise Language Special Until February 2005 with Proof of Purchase for Ultimate DeskRef.

Business Benefits

- Application Defense Developer Edition, strives to educate individual developers on proper secure programming techniques during the development cycle, thereby saving thousands in post-development consulting
- Developmental education approach on secure development strengthens your business at the core, its people
- Executive-level reporting allows your development team to visually depict trending improvements, vulnerability remediation, and high-risk segments of code
- Distributed Software Architecture permits development teams to review their code centrally by a QA or Auditing team or individually by the developers
- Industry-best multi-language support permits organizations to manage all their software development needs with one application

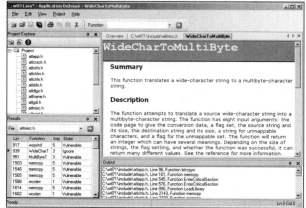

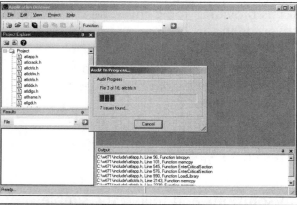

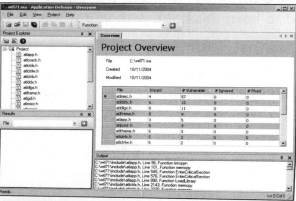

Application Defense Technology Features:

- Industry leading analysis engine can parse and examine entire software code base in under a minute
- Executive, technical, trending reports allow information to be displayed for all audiences
- Flexible XML output allows easy integration with other enterprise applications
- Unique IDE allows you to update results in real-time or in batches to code base – No need to recreate code in multiple locations!
- Custom developer code is analyzed by proprietary artificial intelligence engine
- Project file storage allows developers to save analysis results for later review or to save for continued analysis
- Real-time bug tracking system
- Interactive software interface allows developers to make security decisions during analysis
- Able to input Visual Studio Project files
- Customizable reports allow you to specify company name, application, auditor, and more…

PROGRAMMER'S
Ultimate
Security
DeskRef

James C. Foster
Steven C. Foster

KEY	SERIAL NUMBER
001	HJIRTCV764
002	PO9873D5FG
003	829KM8NJH2
004	JKVBF54KM9
005	CVPLQ6WQ23
006	VBP965T5T5
007	HJJJ863WD3E
008	2987GVTWMK
009	629MP5SDJT
010	IMWQ295T6T

PUBLISHED BY
Syngress Publishing, Inc.
800 Hingham Street
Rockland, MA 02370

Programmer's Ultimate Security DeskRef

Printed in the United States of America
1 2 3 4 5 6 7 8 9 0
ISBN: 1-932266-72-0

Publisher: Andrew Williams	Page Layout and Art: Patricia Lupien
Acquisitions Editor: Jaime Quigley	Copy Editor: Mike McGee
Cover Designer: Michael Kavish	

Distributed by O'Reilly Media, Inc. in the United States and Canada.

For information on rights and translations, contact Matt Pedersen, Director of Sales and Rights, at Syngress Publishing; email matt@syngress.com or fax to 781-681-3585.

For Mom and Dad
and Gabriel...

Acknowledgments

Syngress would like to acknowledge the following people for their kindness and support in making this book possible.

Syngress books are now distributed in the United States and Canada by O'Reilly Media, Inc. The enthusiasm and work ethic at O'Reilly is incredible and we would like to thank everyone there for their time and efforts to bring Syngress books to market: Tim O'Reilly, Laura Baldwin, Mark Brokering, Mike Leonard, Donna Selenko, Bonnie Sheehan, Cindy Davis, Grant Kikkert, Opol Matsutaro, Steve Hazelwood, Mark Wilson, Rick Brown, Leslie Becker, Jill Lothrop, Tim Hinton, Kyle Hart, Sara Winge, C. J. Rayhill, Peter Pardo, Leslie Crandell, Valerie Dow, Regina Aggio, Pascal Honscher, Preston Paull, Susan Thompson, Bruce Stewart, Laura Schmier, Sue Willing, Mark Jacobsen, Betsy Waliszewski, Dawn Mann, Kathryn Barrett, John Chodacki, and Rob Bullington.

The incredibly hard working team at Elsevier Science, including Jonathan Bunkell, Ian Seager, Duncan Enright, David Burton, Rosanna Ramacciotti, Robert Fairbrother, Miguel Sanchez, Klaus Beran, Emma Wyatt, Rosie Moss, Chris Hossack, Mark Hunt, and Krista Leppiko, for making certain that our vision remains worldwide in scope.

David Buckland, Marie Chieng, Lucy Chong, Leslie Lim, Audrey Gan, Pang Ai Hua, and Joseph Chan of STP Distributors for the enthusiasm with which they receive our books.

Kwon Sung June at Acorn Publishing for his support.

David Scott, Tricia Wilden, Marilla Burgess, Annette Scott, Andrew Swaffer, Stephen O'Donoghue, Bec Lowe, and Mark Langley of Woodslane for distributing our books throughout Australia, New Zealand, Papua New Guinea, Fiji Tonga, Solomon Islands, and the Cook Islands.

Winston Lim of Global Publishing for his help and support with distribution of Syngress books in the Philippines.

Author

James C. Foster, Fellow is the Deputy Director of Global Security Solution Development for Computer Sciences Corporation where he is responsible for the vision and development of physical, personnel, and data security solutions. Prior to CSC, Foster was the Director of Research and Development for Foundstone Inc. (acquired by McAfee) and was responsible for all aspects of product, consulting, and corporate R&D initiatives. Prior to joining Foundstone, Foster was an Executive Advisor and Research Scientist with Guardent Inc. (acquired by Verisign) and an adjunct author at Information Security Magazine(acquired by TechTarget), subsequent to working as Security Research Specialist for the Department of Defense. With his core competencies residing in high-tech remote management, international expansion, application security, protocol analysis, and search algorithm technology, Foster has conducted numerous code reviews for commercial OS components, Win32 application assessments, and reviews on commercial-grade cryptography implementations.

Foster is a seasoned speaker and has presented throughout North America at conferences, technology forums, security summits, and research symposiums with highlights at the Microsoft Security Summit, Black Hat USA, Black Hat Windows, MIT Wireless Research Forum, SANS, MilCon, TechGov, InfoSec World 2001, and the Thomson Security Conference. He also is commonly asked to comment on pertinent security issues and has been sited in *USAToday, Information Security Magazine, Baseline, Computer World, Secure Computing,* and the *MIT Technologist.* Foster holds an A.S., B.S., MBA and numerous technology and management certifications and has attended or conducted research at the Yale School of Business, Harvard University, the University of Maryland, and is currently a Fellow at University of Pennsylvania's Wharton School of Business.

Foster is also a well published author with multiple commercial and educational papers; and has authored, contributed, or edited for major publications to include *Snort 2.1 Intrusion Detection* (Syngress Publishing, ISBN: 1-931836-04-3), *Hacking Exposed, Fourth Edition, Anti-Hacker Toolkit, Second Edition, Advanced Intrusion Detection, Hacking the Code: ASP.NET Web Application Security* (Syngress, ISBN: 1-932266-65-8), *Anti-Spam Toolkit,* and the forthcoming *Google Hacking for Penetration Techniques* (Syngress, ISBN: 1-931836-36-1) .

Contributing Author

Steven C. Foster is a graduate student pursuing his Ph.D. in mathematics at the University of North Carolina, Chapel Hill. There, he is studying applied mathematics, most notably computational and geophysical fluid dynamics. He is currently being supported under a grant from the Office of Naval Research, administered by Dr. Christopher K. R. T. Jones in addition to a fellowship from the Statistical and Mathematical Sciences Institute. Steven earned his bachelor of science degree at the University of Maryland, Baltimore County under Dr. Matthias K. Gobbert. He has worked as a computer security consultant at Computer Sciences Corporation, including the development of the Hydra Expert Assessment Technology (HEAT), and as a research mathematician at Northrop Grumman, specializing in the optimization of radar design and signal processing. Steven has also provided his mathematical expertise to Foundstone on their Foundstone Enterprise product and has significant programming experience in C/C++, Perl, Python, HTML, Fortran, and Matlab. Upon finishing his degree at UNC, Steven will pursue a career in computational mathematics and a professional degree in finance.

Area Experts

Kevin Harriford an information security and programming expert, works on the vulnerability assessment team for Computer Sciences Corporation. Mr. Harriford's areas of expertise include C and C++ development, security architectures, and analog network security.

Jeremie Kregelka is a senior distributed applications development engineer at Johns Hopkins University. With numerous development awards on his resume, Jeremie has spent the last decade creating distributed applications in Java, ASP, ColdFusion, and .Net. Jeremie has a B.S. in Software Engineering.

Chad Curtis, a research and development engineer at Foundstone Inc. (acquired by McAfee), is responsible for emerging threat research and Foundstone Enterprise product development. Chad has specialized in custom scripting language development, Microsoft Windows' code development, deep packet inspection, and vulnerability research.

Conrad Smith is a security researcher with expertise in vulnerability testing, software development, application security architecture, and security policies. Conrad has consulted and conducted research for numerous government and private sector organizations in the US and the UK, while working for companies including Exodus Communications, Insight Ltd UK, and most recently Foundstone (acquired by McAfee.)

Michael Prentice, a recent graduate of Cornell University, has extensive experience developing and testing educational and statistics software utilizing both graphical interfaces and client/server architectures. He is currently engaged in freelance web application and database development.

Author's Acknowledgments

First and foremost, I'd like to thank my family for sticking with me and believing in me through the tough times. Mom, Dad: thank you for instilling the importance of a strong work ethic and continuous education. Steve, what can I say—you've always been there for me. You continue to impress me, pushing me forward—thank you.

Jeremie, Kevin, Mike, Conrad, Chad, Johnny, and Mark: Your input, assistance, and knowledge kept this book on the straight and narrow. Keep on rocking the technology world—true experts.

I'd also like to take a well-deserved moment and thank Computer Sciences Corporation for working with me on this publication and ensuring that it saw the light of day. Reg, if it weren't for you this book would still be in the database—a sincere thank you for all of your help. Additionally, I'd like to thank Chris, Jason, Ron, Jen, and Mary.

For those of you in the industry leading interesting and innovative technologies and business models: I salute you.

Last but certainly not least—Syngress you continue to redefine the publishing world and I am truly honored to be part of such a great team and effort. I appreciate your willingness and flexibility to publish a new kind of book in such an accelerated fashion. Andrew and Jaime, I owe you two.

—James Foster

October 8, 2004

About the Book

The goals for this book are simple. Instill the proper programming techniques for the world's most popular and complex languages. Teach those who want to hone in on their technical skills and increase their knowledge and overall marketability in the information security industry by providing the reference for elite programming techniques that are the backbones for the best security professionals in an easy-to-read format. And lastly, to be the sole desk reference required and utilized on a day-by-day basis to ensure that all code making it to production status is **secure**. The personal acquisition of these techniques should be enough to get a promotion just about anywhere or potentially even join the infosec industry from another similar vertical.

Each language covered in this book has received its own chapter. With this said, the C chapter may contain the proper overlap for functions and methods utilized within the complementary C++ and C# chapters. It's imperative that when in search of a C++ or C# reference, you first look at its corresponding chapter before checking to see if it has been included in the C chapter.

Each function or method documented in this book is followed by a series of elements created to help you, the reader, exercise each task responsibly by calling awareness to each function's purpose, risk, origin, resources, and more. Each function may incorporate some or all of the following:

- **Prototype** This is the function's prototype or method's proper implementation usage.

- **Summary** A one-line description of the function or method and its intended use.

- **Description** The descriptions will be one paragraph and contain a detailed explanation of how the function should be used and when it should not be used. It will also contain explanations for any parameters the function or method may accept as input in addition to providing detail on returned values.

- **Risk** The risk description informs the readers of the particular security threat posed when implementing the function or method. In proper cases it recommends more secure alternatives, secure usage, bolt-on alternatives, and other types of clear developer-focused solutions.

- **Note** Any additional comments or notes that pertain to the function.

- **Additional Resources** These resources are included for additional information on the programmatic particulars of the language, function, or method. All resources will consist of web links to educational websites, Microsoft, or other commercial powerhouses.

- **Impact** The impact will be High, Medium or Low, signifying a potential high-level result that a poorly implemented function or method may have on the application.

- **Cross Reference** Cross references are similar functions and methods that are available for use in the language. For example, the C language printf may have cross references of sprintf and snprintf.

The information security industry is in a state of constant evolution with the rate of automated malicious intent, increasing at a faster pace than that of defensive protections and staff. With the release of every new "bleeding edge" bolt-on security product comes the idea that this problem will not only completely secure your organization but it will also be the only product required to accomplish such a task. However, if you have ever spent the money to hire the best security consultants, you'd soon find out that their recommendation would be to layer security protections throughout your environment. Supporting just about every security professional that's been around for the past decade, secure development will eventually supersede all of these other security initiatives. Tackling the source is the key, but until now has been ridiculously difficult of a task. As long as you believe that knowledge is power then the answer has arrived.

—Foster

Contents

Foreword

The software development community by and large understands that it is in midst of a new crisis: our applications are insecure. Viruses, worms, spam, stolen credit card numbers, and leaked personal information; this is a very different situation than the last crisis we faced. Y2K was pervasive, critical, and hard to fix. The security crisis is all that and more. During Y2K we were fighting a natural force: the passage of time. Time is relentless, but measurable and predictable. The people attacking our computers and infrastructure are relentless too, but thus far, they defy our abilities to predict and prepare.

The battle for software security is being fought one small programming detail at a time. Arm yourself.

While the basic outline of the software security crisis is widely agreed upon, there isn't yet a consensus about the solution. Most believe that education has a role to play, but what is it? Should security training be part of a programmer's core education? Certainly, apart from the specifics of any particular programming language, algorithm, or development methodology, programmers are taught to value efficiency, elegance and precision, and they can be taught to value security too. Security training will help developers learn critical security principles to include least privilege, defense in depth, and fail secure. Even though the result will consist of better programmers and therefore better programs, this alone will not resolve the security crisis.

The problem is that good software security means more than just good design. It requires great attention to an enormous number of implementation details. In software, the defender's dilemma is acute. The attacker only needs to find one problem in order to defeat the system, while the defender must guard all fronts. The result is that more than half of all known exploits take advantage of small implementation errors, not design defects.

How does a programmer guard against implementation errors? The traditional answer is testing, but for security purposes, testing is less than ideal. Without a doubt, testing is the way that most bugs are identified in software. Understanding this, most bugs don't make it off of the programmer's desktop. By running simple test cases during the process of development, programmers find and fix most of their own bugs before the rest of the world has a chance to see them. Unfortunately, security is a different beast. Security bugs are less likely to be found during normal testing activities because many security problems don't occur under anything like normal conditions or through "user testing." They require strange sets of characters, strange combinations of boundary conditions, or unusual machine states in order to be activated.

If testing isn't an answer, perhaps we should return again to education. In addition to being trained to think about security at a high level, programmers need to know how to get all of the details right, and that's exactly what the *Ultimate Programmer's Security DeskRef* does. Any function you call may have security implications, and most of them do. Some are obvious (`seteuid`), but many aren't (`vsnprintf`). As you learn more about how to make your software secure, you'll find that you return here more and more often.

—Brian Chess, PhD
Founder & Chief Scientist
Fortify Software

application.lock

Prototype: `Application.Lock`

Summary: This method is used to prevent the modification of variables stored in the `application` object.

Description: The `Lock` method is used to prevent all clients, excluding the current client, from accessing and manipulating variables stored in the `application` object. All variables will remain locked until the corresponding "Unlock" method is called or the session is terminated.

Risk: The `application.lock` method is designed to create file/object locks to system variables. Uncontrolled access to this method creates the ability to lock and unlock resources that may be in use by other processes. This results in corrupted data or denied access to necessary resources.

Additional Resources:
http://msdn.microsoft.com/library/default.asp?url=/library/en-us/cdo/html/_denali_newmail_object_cdonts_library_.asp

Impact: Low

asperror.aspcode

Prototype: `ASPError.ASPCode()`

Summary: This method is used to return an IIS generated error code.

Description: The `aspcode` method returns an IIS generated error code as a string.

Risk: Error codes thrown by the application should be handled within the application and not propagated to the end user. Malicious users can use error codes reference codes to gain additional error descriptions. It is critical to contain and prevent end-user access since error information can result in the disclosure of vital system information including: system configuration, application configuration, memory references, etc.

Additional Resources:

http://msdn.microsoft.com/library/default.asp?url=/library/
en-us/cdo/html/_denali_newmail_object_cdonts_library_.asp

Impact: Low

asperror.aspdescription

Prototype: `ASPError.ASPDescription()`

Summary: This method is used to return a description of the error.

Description: The `aspdescription` method returns a full detailed description of the error generated, if available. This description is returned as a string.

Risk: Error message associated with application functionality should be handled within the application or be developers only. Error messages that are propagated to the end user allow malicious users can further understanding to the internal workings of the application. This allows the attacker an efficient means of analyzing attack vectors for greater results. It is critical to contain and prevent end-user access since error information can result in the disclosure of vital system information including: system configuration, application configuration, memory references, etc.

Additional Resources:

http://msdn.microsoft.com/library/default.asp?url=/library/
en-us/cdo/html/_denali_newmail_object_cdonts_library_.asp

Impact: Low

asperror.category

Prototype: `ASPError.Category()`

Summary: This method is used to return the source of the error.

Description: The category method returns a string that is used to determined whether the error was generated by IIS, scripting, or various components.

Risk: All errors associated with the application should be hidden from the end user. Unnecessary understanding of the applications design and implementation could expose flaws allowing attackers to gain access to sensitive information. Error codes thrown by the application should be handled within the application and not propagated to the end user. It is critical to contain and prevent end-user access since error information can result in the disclosure of vital system information including: system configuration, application configuration, memory references, etc.

Additional Resources:
http://msdn.microsoft.com/library/default.asp?url=/library/en-us/cdo/html/_denali_newmail_object_cdonts_library_.asp

Impact: Low

asperror.description

Prototype: `ASPError.Description()`

Summary: This method is used to return a summary of the description of the error.

Description: The `description` method returns a summary of the description of the error generated, if available. This description is returned as a string.

Risk: A short description of the error being generated by malicious us of an application may lead to further information gathering based on new attack methods. It is vital to contain and prevent end-user access since error information can result in the disclosure of vital system information including: system configuration, application configuration, memory references, etc. Any additional information provided will allow a malicious user to escalate attacks against an application.

ASP

Additional Resources:

http://msdn.microsoft.com/library/default.asp?url=/library/
en-us/cdo/html/_denali_newmail_object_cdonts_library_.asp

Impact: Low

asperror.file

Prototype: `ASPError.File()`

Summary: This method is used the return the file name that generated the error.

Description: The `file` method returns the name and extension of the file that generated the error. This is returned as a string.

Risk: All error messages, including the filename originating the error, should be hidden from the end user. Attackers can use such information to determine reference points in more complex attacks.

Additional Resources:

http://msdn.microsoft.com/library/default.asp?url=/library/
en-us/cdo/html/_denali_newmail_object_cdonts_library_.asp

Impact: Low

asperror.source

Prototype: `ASPError.Source()`

Summary: This method is used to return the code that caused the error.

Description: The `source` method returns the actual line of code that cased the error, if available. This is returned as a string.

Risk: It is critical to contain and prevent end-user access since error information can result in the disclosure of vital system information including: system configuration, application configuration, memory references, etc. Giving the end user access to the code that caused an error allows malicious users to determine memory resources being used by the process and potentially provides access to data.

ASP

Additional Resources:
http://msdn.microsoft.com/library/default.asp?url=/library/
en-us/cdo/html/_denali_newmail_object_cdonts_library_.asp

Impact: Low

attachment.delete

Prototype: `objAttach.Delete()`

Summary: This method is used to remove an attachment.

Description: The `delete` method is used to remove an attachment from the attachment collection. This method requires the `attachment` object.

Risk: When using input from the client to determine which attachments to delete, careful parsing of data should be performed to prevent the accidental or malicious deletion of attachments. File descriptions should be constrained to the commoner file name characters (A–Z, 0–9, -, _, etc.)

Note: ASP CDONTS External Library

Impact: Low

attachment.readfromfile

Prototype: `objAttach.ReadFromFile(fileName)`

Summary: This method is used to read the contents of a file and load them to the output.

Description: The `readfromfile` method is used to read the contents of a file and load them to the output. This method requires the `attachment` object as well as the name of the file to read.

Risk: When using input data to determine files to be read and displayed out put, file names should be carefully parsed to prevent the usage of such conventions as '../../../', also known as dot dot attacks.

Note: ASP CDONTS External Library

Impact: Medium

ASP

attachment.writetofile

Prototype: objAttach.WriteToFile(fileName)

Summary: This method is used to write the attachment to the server.

Description: The writetofile method is used to write the attachment to the server filesystem. If there is currently a file on the file system with a same name as the file you wish to write the file will be over written. This method requires the attachment object as well as the name of the file to read.

Risk: When using input data to determine files to be written to file names should be carefully parsed to prevent the usage of such conventions as '../../../', also known as dot dot attacks. Since the write method will overwrite existing files it becomes especially important to guard against attacks which may overwrite system and application logs.

Note: ASP CDONTS External Library

Impact: Low

attachments.add

Prototype: Set objAttach = collAttachments.Add([name] [, type] [, source] [, ContentLocation] [, ContentBase])

Summary: This method is used to add a new attachment object to the attachments collection.

Description: This method is used to add a new attachment object to the attachments collection. It is possible to add the attachment data at the same time as adding the object to the collection. This method requires the attachment object as well as the name of the file to read.

Risk: To prevent excessive attachments from being posted to the system that may use up system storage resources and cause elevated network usage in transfer, both the files being attached, and the attachment collection should be regulated for size.

Note: ASP CDONTS External Library

ASP

Additional Resources:

http://msdn.microsoft.com/library/default.asp?url=/library/
en-us/iissdk/iis/com_components_for_iis.asp

Impact: Low

attachments.delete

Prototype: `collAttachments.Delete( )`

Summary: This method is used to remove every attachment associated with the attachments collection.

Description: The `delete` method is used to remove every attachment associated with the attachments collection. This is a final process with no recursive action.

Risk: In multiuser applications, it may be possible for an attacker to execute malicious code using the `collAttachments.delete` method to continually flush the attachment collection of end users thus denying the ability to upload files. Usage of the delete method should thus be strictly regulated.

Note: ASP CDONTS External Library

Additional Resources:

http://msdn.microsoft.com/library/default.asp?url=/library/
en-us/iissdk/iis/com_components_for_iis.asp

Impact: Low

message.delete

Prototype: `objMessage.Delete( )`

Summary: This method is used to remove a message.

Description: The `delete` method is used to remove a message from the messages collection. This method requires the `message` object.

Risk: This method can be used by a malicious user and a multiuser application to deny or alter access to the system. For instance, in the case of a chat system a malicious user might delete a certain users input and then use other methods to spoof this users identity providing false information to the chat audience.

ASP

Note: ASP CDONTS External Library

Additional Resources:
http://msdn.microsoft.com/library/default.asp?url=/library
/en-us/iissdk/iis/com_components_for_iis.asp

Impact: Low

message.send

Prototype: `objMessage.Send( )`

Summary: This method is used to send the message to the specified addresses.

Description: This method is used to send the message to the specified addresses through the default messaging service. This method requires the `message` object.

Risk: Unless properly filtered, this method could allow a malicious user to SPAM user consoles with bogus or unrequested information. Additionally creating messages exceeding application capabilities can result in a denial of service on the system. Proper regulation of message distribution should be used to prevent usage abuse.

Note: ASP CDONTS External Library

Additional Resources:
http://msdn.microsoft.com/library/default.asp?url=/library/en-us/iissdk/iis/com_components_for_iis.asp

Impact: Medium

messages.add

Prototype: `Set objMessage = collMessages.Add( [subject] [, text] [, importance] )`

Summary: This method is used to add a new `message` object to the messages collection.

Description: This method is used to add a new `message` object to the messages collection. It is mandatory that all new messages are created in the Outbox of the messaging service. This method requires the `message` object as well as the name of the file to add.

Risk: Origins and content of messages added to the message collection should be checked to ensure invalid or repetitive messages are not occupying the message collection utilizing excess resources, which can lower application performance.

Note: ASP CDONTS External Library

Additional Resources:
http://msdn.microsoft.com/library/default.asp?url=/library/
en-us/iissdk/iis/com_components_for_iis.asp

Impact: Medium

messages.delete

Prototype: `collMessages.Delete( )`

Summary: This method is used to remove every message associated with the messages collection.

Description: The `delete` method is used to remove every message associated with the messages collection. This is a final process with no recursive action.

Risk: This method can be used by a malicious user and a multiuser application to deny or alter access to the system. For instance, in the case of a chat system a malicious user might delete a certain user's input and then use other methods to spoof this user's identity, providing false information to the chat audience.

Note: ASP CDONTS External Library

Additional Resources:
http://msdn.microsoft.com/library/default.asp?url=/library/
en-us/iissdk/iis/com_components_for_iis.asp

Impact: Medium

newmail.attachfile

Prototype: `objNewMail.AttachFile(Source [, FileName] [, EncodingMethod] )`

Summary: This method is used to read a file and add it as the attachment to the message.

ASP

Description: The attachfile method is used to read a file and add it as the attachment to the message. The method requires the NewMail object as well as the name of the file to be attached.

Risk: To prevent excessive attachments from being posted to the system that may use up system storage resources and cause elevated network usage in transfer, both the files being attached, and the attachment collection should be regulated for size.

Note: ASP CDONTS External Library

Additional Resources:
http://msdn.microsoft.com/library/default.asp?url=/library/
en-us/iissdk/iis/com_components_for_iis.asp

Impact: High

newmail.attachurl

Prototype: objNewMail.AttachURL(Source, ContentLocation [, ContentBase] [, EncodingMethod])

Summary: This method is used to associate a URL with the attachment to a message.

Description: The attachurl method is used to associate a URL with the attachment to a message.

Risk: URLs should be stripped of query stings and special characters that could cause the passing of parameters and data to a malicious third-party site.

Note: ASP CDONTS External Library

Additional Resources:
http://msdn.microsoft.com/library/default.asp?url=/library/
en-us/iissdk/iis/com_components_for_iis.asp

Impact: High

newmail.send

Prototype: objNewMail.Send([From] [, To] [, Subject] [, Body]
[, Importance])

Summary: This method is used to send the `NewMail` object to the specified addresses.

Description: The `send` method is used to send the `NewMail` object to the specified addresses.

Risk: Unless properly filtered, this method could allow a malicious user to SPAM user mail with bogus or unrequested information. Additionally creating mail exceeding application capabilities can result in a denial of service on the system by filling quotas and utilizing all of the system resources. Proper regulation of message distribution should be used to prevent usage abuse.

Note: ASP CDONTS External Library

Additional Resources:
http://msdn.microsoft.com/library/default.asp?url=/library/
en-us/iissdk/iis/com_components_for_iis.asp

Impact: Low

newmail.setlocaleids

Prototype: `objNewMail.SetLocaleIDs(CodePageID)`

Summary: This method is used to set the local identifier.

Description: The `setlocaleids` method is used to set the local identifier. It determines various information such as time zone, language, date, or currency.

Risk: When using setlocaleids, input values must be carefully regulated. In the instance of currency, item A might cost 1 dollar, but cost 1.8 euros. If an attacker managed to manipulate the `lcid`, he could then purchase an item for nearly half price. In general input, data should be verified to prevent data manipulation which can occur on the client end.

Note: ASP CDONTS External Library

Additional Resources:
http://msdn.microsoft.com/library/default.asp?url=/library/
en-us/iissdk/iis/com_components_for_iis.asp

Impact: Medium

ASP

recipients.add

Prototype: `Set objRecip = collRecips.Add( [name] [, address] [, type] )`

Summary: This method is used to add a new recipient to the recipients collection.

Description: The `add` method is used to add a new recipient to the recipients collection.

Risk: Inputs to the recipients collection should be regulated to ensure additional users are not added to the collection by mistake. Unintended users receive messages by accident or malicious actions could result in the disclosure of sensitive information.

Note: ASP CDONTS External Library

Additional Resources:
http://msdn.microsoft.com/library/default.asp?url=/library/
en-us/iissdk/iis/com_components_for_iis.asp

Impact: High

recipients.delete

Prototype: `collRecips.Delete( )`

Summary: This method is used to remove every recipient associated with the recipients collection.

Description: The `delete` method is used to remove every recipient associated with the recipients collection.

Risk: On multiuser systems, the delete collection method could cause denial of service on the system by allowing malicious code to continuous remove recipients from the collection preventing the distribution of messages.

Note: ASP CDONTS External Library

Additional Resources:
http://msdn.microsoft.com/library/default.asp?url=/library/
en-us/iissdk/iis/com_components_for_iis.asp

Impact: High

ASP

request.binaryread

Prototype: `Request.BinaryRead(count)`

Summary: This method is used to read the data sent to the server via a post request.

Description: The `BinaryRead` method is used to read the data sent the server from the client via a post request (usually a form). This data is stored in a safe array. `BinaryRead` does require that you tell it how much of the data is to be read (i.e., `Request.TotalBytes`). Once `BinaryRead` is called, any additional calls using `Request.Form` will generate an error.

Risk: Even though the `BinaryRead` method prevents additional posting of information once a transaction is complete, it does not account for transaction hijacking which is unlikely but could still occur during a process. Any information obtained from the `BinaryRead` method should be thoroughly analyzed before usage.

Additional Resources:
http://msdn.microsoft.com/library/default.asp?url=/library/
en-us/cdo/html/_denali_newmail_object_cdonts_library_.asp

Impact: Medium

request.cookiescollection

Prototype: `Response.Cookies(name)[(key)|.attribute]=value`
`variablename=Request.Cookies(name)[(key)|.attribute]`

Summary: The `Cookies collection` contains all cookies sent with a given HTTP request.

Description: The `Cookies collection` is used to create, modify, delete or retrieve a cookie. When a session is created with a server the values stored in a given cookie are read into this collection. This collection holds all the information from the cookies. Just like a form, one cookie can have multiple values stored in key/value pairs.

Risk: This method provides access to all cookies obtained during a particular transaction. A malicious user could use this method to gain access to critical information

ASP

provided in the session. It is a common mistake of Web developers to pass sensitive information to the client via cookies in order to maintain state. Sensitive date should be maintained on the server and never passed to the client where it can be manipulated and fed back to the server.

Additional Resources:

http://msdn.microsoft.com/library/default.asp?url=/library/
en-us/cdo/html/_denali_newmail_object_cdonts_library_.asp

Impact: Medium

request.querystringcollection

Prototype: `Request.QueryString(variable)[(index)|.Count]`

Summary: The `QueryString` collection contains data sent in a request in name/value pairs.

Description: The `QueryString` collection is used to retrieve the values that are given in the HTTP query string. A `QueryString` is the additional information that proceeds a '?' after the file name in the URL box of a browser. These are name/value pairs joined together by an '=' and if multiple pairs are found the groups are separated by an '&'. This data can be retrieved by either specifying the key or a location. The `QueryString collection` is identical to that of the `ServerVariable Query_String`.

Risk: `QueryStrings` are often used by malicious users in attacks such as SQL injections. When using `QueryStrings`, it is important to filter all inputs and ensure parameter integrity. Failure to do so may result in authentication bypass or data compromise.

Additional Resources:

http://msdn.microsoft.com/library/default.asp?url=/library/
en-us/cdo/html/_denali_newmail_object_cdonts_library_.asp

Impact: High

request.servervariablescollection

Prototype: `Request.ServerVariables (server_variable)`

Summary: The `ServerVariables` `collection` contains information about the server.

Description: The `ServerVariables` `collection` is used to retrieve HTTP headers and various pieces of information about the server and the request. These HTTP headers can contain information such as the `Query_string`, referring page, script location, and client operating system. These headers are created every time a request is sent to the Web server.

Risk: The `ServerVariables` method returns HTTP headers, which can contain information such as the `Query_string`, referring page, script location, and client operating system. Interception of this information may result in either server information or client information exposure providing attackers with otherwise restricted information. Additionally malicious users can falsify information disclosed to manipulate application behavior.

Additional Resources:
http://msdn.microsoft.com/library/default.asp?url=/library/
en-us/cdo/html/_denali_newmail_object_cdonts_library_.asp

Impact: High

response.addheader

Prototype: `response.AddHeader name,value`

Summary: This method is used to add or modify an HTTP header

Description: The `addHeader` method is used to add or modify an HTTP header. Once a header has been added it cannot be removed.

Risk: Malicious users can falsify information from the header to manipulate application behavior.

Additional Resources:
http://msdn.microsoft.com/library/default.asp?url=/library/
en-us/cdo/html/_denali_newmail_object_cdonts_library_.asp

Impact: Medium

ASP

response.appendtolog

Prototype: `response.AppendToLog string`

Summary: This method is used to add information to the Web log.

Description: The `AppendtoLog` method is used to add information to the Web log for a given request. This information is usually a string giving more information about the request. You may call this method multiple times in one script, each time adding additional information to the log. This information will be included at the end of the log entry.

Risk: This method should be regulated, otherwise an attacker can overwrite Web logs or write excessive logs to fill file system capacity. This can effectively cause a Denial of Service to an application or a system.

Additional Resources:
http://msdn.microsoft.com/library/default.asp?url=/library/
en-us/cdo/html/_denali_newmail_object_cdonts_library_.asp

Impact: Medium

response.binarywrite

Prototype: `response.BinaryWrite data`

Summary: This method is used to write data directly to the output.

Description: The `BinaryWrite` method is used to write data directly to the out without any type of conversion. This could be useful for storing images in a database or sending data to an image generator. This method does require that you specify the data to be written.

Risk: Usage of `BinaryWrite` should be regulated to ensure malicious users do not write to otherwise restricted data storage areas, or write over data segments without proper privilege levels.

Additional Resources:
http://msdn.microsoft.com/library/default.asp?url=/library/
en-us/cdo/html/_denali_newmail_object_cdonts_library_.asp

Impact: Medium

response.flush

Prototype: `Response.Flush`

Summary: This method is used to immediately output all buffered HTML.

Description: The `Flush` method is used to output all buffered HTML data to the client's screen immediately. This useful if you are trying to output a larger file, the flush method will be able to display data a little at a time. In order to use this method successfully you must set the `response.buffer` = true, otherwise it will generate an error.

Risk: Information contained in the buffer can be flushed to the client at any given time. For this reason no vital data should be stored in buffer errors even for temporary storage.

Additional Resources:
http://msdn.microsoft.com/library/default.asp?url=/library/
en-us/cdo/html/_denali_newmail_object_cdonts_library_.asp

Impact: Low

response.redirect

Prototype: `Response.Redirect URL`

Summary: This method is used to redirect the client to a specified URL.

Description: The `redirect` method is called when you want the server to redirect the client to a different Web page. This method does require that you specify the URL you want to redirect to, this URL can be a relative path (If on the same site) or a fully qualified URL beginning with http:// (if it is on an external site).

Risk: Redirects can be captured by an attacker and forged to force clients into spoofed Web pages creating the potential for clients to disclose sensitive information to malicious sites.

Additional Resources:
http://msdn.microsoft.com/library/default.asp?url=/library/
en-us/cdo/html/_denali_newmail_object_cdonts_library_.asp

Impact: Low

ASP

response.write

Prototype: `Response.Write string`

Summary: This method is used to write a string to the output.

Description: The `write` method is used to write a specified string to the current page. When calling this method, it is required that you specify the string to be written.

Risk: All inputs to this method should be thoroughly parsed to prevent the potential for cross-site scripting attacks. Input parameters should be restricted to alphanumeric characters to prevent command executions during processing.

Additional Resources:

http://msdn.microsoft.com/library/default.asp?url=/library/
en-us/cdo/html/_denali_newmail_object_cdonts_library_.asp

Impact: Medium

server.execute

Prototype: `Server.Execute(path)`

Summary: This method is used to execute other ASP files out side of the current document.

Description: The `Execute` method is used when you need to run another ASP file from within an ASP file. After the outside file has been run to completion the first page will finish executing its own code. This method does require the path to the file that needs to be executed.

Risk: Any instance where an application calls an outside program should be tightly restricted. Allowing execution of programs outside of the application opens the door for malicious code to be executed with system or application privileges which can be further escalated by an attacker.

Additional Resources:

http://msdn.microsoft.com/library/default.asp?url=/library/
en-us/cdo/html/_denali_newmail_object_cdonts_library_.asp

Impact: High

server.getlasterror

Prototype: `Server.GetLastError()`

Summary: This method is used to return an `ASPError` object for an error that just occurred.

Description: The `getlasterror` method is used to return an `ASPError` object for an error that just occurred.

Risk: Gaining access to errors caused by malicious code or queries, can allow the attacker to determine payload information containing such data as system info, application configuration, or memory storage.

Additional Resources:
http://msdn.microsoft.com/library/default.asp?url=/library/
en-us/cdo/html/_denali_newmail_object_cdonts_library_.asp

Impact: Medium

server.htmlencode

Prototype: `Server.HTMLEncode(string)`

Summary: This method applies HTML encoding to a given string.

Description: The `htmlencode` method is used to apply HTML encoding to a given string. This is very useful when trying to output HTML code. This method will encode all special characters that HTML usually interprets as identifiers. This method requires that a string be passed to it.

Risk: Inputs received after encoding may need to be decoded before being processes, otherwise there is the risk that malicious or otherwise invalid strings can be passed through the application.

Additional Resources:
http://msdn.microsoft.com/library/default.asp?url=/library/
en-us/cdo/html/_denali_newmail_object_cdonts_library_.asp

Impact: Medium

ASP

server.urlencode

Prototype: `Server.URLEncode(string)`

Summary: This method applies URL encoding to a given string.

Description: The `urlencode` method is used to apply URL encoding to a given string. This is useful for passing URLs in `query_strings`. It will convert all characters to valid URL characters to ensure data integrity.

Risk: Inputs received after encoding may need to be decoded before being processes, otherwise there is the risk that malicious or otherwise invalid strings can be passed through the application.

Additional Resources:

http://msdn.microsoft.com/library/default.asp?url=/library/
en-us/cdo/html/_denali_newmail_object_cdonts_library_.asp

Impact: Medium

session.lcid

Prototype: `Session.LCID(=LCID)`

Summary: This property is used to set the local identifier.

Description: The `lcid` property is used to set the local identifier. The `lcid` determines various information such as time zone, language, date, or currency. If a location identifier has not been installed, it cannot be set.

Risk: When using `lcid`, input values must be carefully regulated. In the instance of currency, item A might cost 1 dollar, but cost 1.8 euros. If an attacker managed to manipulate the lcid he could then purchase an item for nearly half off. In general, input data should be verified to prevent any data manipulation that might occur on the client end.

Additional Resources:

http://msdn.microsoft.com/library/default.asp?url=/library/en-
us/cdo/html/_denali_newmail_object_cdonts_library_.asp

Impact: High

session.sessionID

Prototype: `Session.SessionID`

Summary: This property is used to return a unique identifier for this session.

Description: The `SessionID` property is a unique identifier that is generated by the server the instant a session is created and is unique to that particular session. This property is read-only.

Risk: Relying solely on the ID for user authentication can lead to spoofed information which may cause data corruption, or unauthorized access to Web content.

Additional Resources:
http://msdn.microsoft.com/library/default.asp?url=/library/en-us/cdo/html/_denali_newmail_object_cdonts_library_.asp

Impact: High

session.session_onend

Prototype: `session.session_onend()`

Summary: This method is called when a session ends.

Description: The `session_onend` method is called every single time a client ends a session. This could be useful in tracking total number of current active sessions and would usually be found in your global.asa file.

Risk: The onend method can be used to close sessions preventing further access to session data. User permissions should be closely regulated to prevent one session from ending another upon exit.

Additional Resources:
http://msdn.microsoft.com/library/default.asp?url=/library/en-us/cdo/html/_denali_newmail_object_cdonts_library_.asp

Impact: Low

session.session_onstart

Prototype: `session.session_onstart()`

Summary: This method is called when a session begins.

Description: The `session_onstart` method is called every single time a client creates a new session. This could be useful in tracking total number of current active sessions and would usually be found in your global.asa file.

Risk: Using the `onstart` method a malicious user could continue to create new sessions until the systems capacity to handle sessions was full. This would in effect deny service to the application. To prevent permanent session locking, timing controls should be established to timeout sessions on inactivity.

Additional Resources:

http://msdn.microsoft.com/library/default.asp?url=/library/
en-us/cdo/html/_denali_newmail_object_cdonts_library_.asp

Impact: Low

Programmer's Ultimate Security DeskRef: C

_cprintf

Prototype: `int _cprintf( const char *format [, argument] ... )`

Summary: This function formats and outputs a string to the console.

Description: Using the input string "`format`" this function will output a string to the console. It uses the inputs to define the format of the output string and the content. The format (and content) is held in the constant string "`format`", and the argument (if any) provides values to variables and additional content. The formatting is similar to that of `printf`. The function returns the number of characters printed to the console.

Risk: This function is potentially vulnerable to a format string attack where an attacker could cause the application to crash unexpected or execute arbitrary code. Format string bugs were discovered in 2000 and the problem is typically spawned from user input that is not properly filtered. Both Microsoft .Net and SPI Dynamics to name two have secure objects that can be implemented to check strings and

23

user input gained from human sources within applications to protect against input-directed vulnerabilities. It is critical that you verify the inputted data have only proper and expected characters in addition to ensuring that your function is properly called. For example, the functions should always utilize their parameters such as `printf("%s", malicious_string)` instead of `printf(malicious_string)`.

Note: At time of publication, this function was designed for Windows compatibility.

Additional Resources:

http://msdn.microsoft.com/library/default.asp?url=/library/en-us/vccore98/html/_crt__cprintf.asp

Impact: Medium

Cross References: _cscanf, fprintf, printf, sprintf, vfprint

_cscanf

Prototype: `int _cscanf( const char *format [, argument] ... )`

Summary: This function reads and assigns formatted data from the console command line.

Description: This function reads incoming formatted data from the console command line. The function input string "`format`" defines the formatting scheme for the data, while the arguments (if any) provide locations for the data assignment. The function returns the number of properly converted and assigned fields. A return value of 0 means that no fields were assigned.

Risk: This function is potentially vulnerable to a format string attack where an attacker could cause the application to crash unexpected or execute arbitrary code. Format string bugs were discovered in 2000 and the problem is typically spawned from user input that is not properly filtered. Both Microsoft .Net and SPI Dynamics to name two have secure objects that can be implemented to check strings and user input gained from human sources within applications to protect against input-directed vulnerabilities. It is critical that you verify the inputted data have only proper and expected characters in addition to ensuring that your function is properly called. For example, the functions should always utilize their parameters such as

printf("%s", malicious_string) instead of
printf(malicious_string).

Note: At time of publication, this function was designed for Windows compatibility.

Additional Resources:
http://msdn.microsoft.com/library/default.asp?url=/library/en-us/
vccore98/html/_crt__cscanf.asp

Impact: Medium

Cross References: _cprintf, fscanf, scanf, sscanf

_execl

Prototype: int _execl(const char *cmdname, const char *arg0,…
const char *argn, NULL)

Summary: This function executes a file from within the current shell.

Description: The function will execute a file pointed to by the argument "cmd-name", which contains the path to file to be executed. The other input arguments (arg0, arg1, …, argN) are command line parameters to be used in the execution of the file. Ideally, the function does not return a value, as it does not return to the calling process. However, upon an error, a value of -1 is returned and the global variable ERRNO is set.

Risk: This function has the ability to execute a file on the local system. Attackers commonly target functions similar to this since they have the ability to launch potentially dangerous or malicious executables with differing privileges. It is imperative that you filter all input and never allow a user direct access to passing variables as the parameters for this function. Ensure that all special characters are stripped before the data is parsed and passed in addition to limiting access to only the desired executables. Lastly, require that all executable output is controlled within a forked or spawned process within the local application to ensure the integrity of the outputted data. If possible, avoid calling dynamic programs from within applications. Static program execution is more secure.

Note: At time of publication, this function was designed for Windows compatibility.

Additional Resources:

http://msdn.microsoft.com/library/default.asp?url=/library/en-us/vccore98/html/_crt__execl.2c_._wexecl.asp

Impact: High

Cross References: abort, atexit, exit, _onexit, _spawn, system, _wexecl

_execle

Prototype: int _execle(const char *cmdname, const char *arg0, ... const char *argn, NULL, const char *const *envp)

Summary: This function executes a file from within the current shell with an additional argument for an array of environment parameters.

Description: The function will execute a file pointed to by the argument "cmd-name", which contains the path to file to be executed. The second set of input arguments (arg0, arg1, ..., argN) are command line parameters to be used in the execution of the file. The final input argument is the array of pointers to environmental parameters needed for file execution. Like _execl, the function does not return a value unless an error occurs, as it does not return to the calling process. However, upon an error, a value of -1 is returned and the global variable ERRNO is set.

Risk: This function has the ability to execute a file on the local system. Attackers commonly target functions similar to this since they have the ability to launch potentially dangerous or malicious executables with differing privileges. It is imperative that you filter all input and never allow a user direct access to passing variables as the parameters for this function. Ensure that all special characters are stripped before the data is parsed and passed in addition to limiting access to only the desired executables. Lastly, require that all executable output is controlled within a forked or spawned process within the local application to ensure the integrity of the outputted data. If possible, avoid calling dynamic programs from within applications. Static program execution is more secure.

Note: At time of publication, this function was designed for Windows compatibility.

Additional Resources:
http://msdn.microsoft.com/library/default.asp?url=/library/en-us/vccore98/html/_crt__execle.2c_._wexecle.asp

Impact: High

Cross References: abort, atexit, exit, _onexit, _spawn, system, _wexecle

_execlp

Prototype: `int _execlp( const char *cmdname, const char *arg0, ... const char *argn, NULL )`

Summary: This function executes a file from within the current shell, searching for it from the PATH environment variable.

Description: The function will execute a file pointed to by the argument "cmdname", searching in the system's PATH for the file. The other input arguments (`arg0, arg1, …, argN`) are command line parameters to be used in the execution of the file. Ideally, the function does not return a value, as it does not return to the calling process. However, upon an error, a value of `-1` is returned and the global variable ERRNO is set.

Risk: This function has the ability to execute a file on the local system. Attackers commonly target functions similar to this since they have the ability to launch potentially dangerous or malicious executables with differing privileges. It is imperative that you filter all input and never allow a user direct access to passing variables as the parameters for this function. Ensure that all special characters are stripped before the data is parsed and passed in addition to limiting access to only the desired executables. Lastly, require that all executable output is controlled within a forked or spawned process within the local application to ensure the integrity of the outputted data. If possible, avoid calling dynamic programs from within applications. Static program execution is more secure.

Note: At time of publication, this function was designed for Windows compatibility.

Additional Resources:
http://msdn.microsoft.com/library/default.asp?url=/library/en-us/vccore98/html/_crt__execlp.2c_._wexeclp.asp

Impact: High

Cross References: abort, atexit, exit, _onexit, _spawn, system, _wexeclp

_execlpe

Prototype: int _execlpe(const char *cmdname, const char *arg0, … const char *argn, NULL, const char *const *envp)

Summary: This function executes a file from within the current shell, searching for it from the PATH environment variable, with a separate input for environmental parameters.

Description: The function will execute a file pointed to by the argument "cmdname", searching for it in the system's PATH environment variable. The next input arguments (arg0, arg1, …, argN) are command line parameters to be used in the execution of the file. The final input argument is the array of pointers to environmental parameters needed for file execution. Ideally, the function does not return a value, as it does not return to the calling process. However, upon an error, a value of -1 is returned and the global variable ERRNO is set.

Risk: This function has the ability to execute a file on the local system. Attackers commonly target functions similar to this since they have the ability to launch potentially dangerous or malicious executables with differing privileges. It is imperative that you filter all input and never allow a user direct access to passing variables as the parameters for this function. Ensure that all special characters are stripped before the data is parsed and passed in addition to limiting access to only the desired executables. Lastly, require that all executable output is controlled within a forked or spawned process within the local application to ensure the integrity of the outputted data. If possible, avoid calling dynamic programs from within applications. Static program execution is more secure.

Note: At time of publication, this function was designed for Windows compatibility.

Additional Resources:

http://msdn.microsoft.com/library/default.asp?url=/library/en-us/vccore98/html/_crt__execlpe.2c_._wexeclpe.asp

Impact: High

Cross References: abort, atexit, exit, _onexit, _spawn, system, _wexeclpe

_execv

Prototype: `int _execv( const char *cmdname, const char *const *argv )`

Summary: This function executes a file with an array of pointers to be passed to the command line.

Description: The function will execute a file pointed to by the argument "`cmd-name`", which contains the path to the file to be executed. The other input argument, "`argv`", is an array command line parameter to be used in the execution of the file. Ideally, the function does not return a value, as it does not return to the calling process. However, upon an error, a value of `-1` is returned and the global variable ERRNO is set.

Risk: This function has the ability to execute a file on the local system. Attackers commonly target functions similar to this since they have the ability to launch potentially dangerous or malicious executables with differing privileges. It is imperative that you filter all input and never allow a user direct access to passing variables as the parameters for this function. Ensure that all special characters are stripped before the data is parsed and passed in addition to limiting access to only the desired executables. Lastly, require that all executable output is controlled within a forked or spawned process within the local application to ensure the integrity of the outputted data. If possible, avoid calling dynamic programs from within applications. Static program execution is more secure.

Note: At time of publication, this function was designed for Windows compatibility.

Additional Resources:
http://msdn.microsoft.com/library/default.asp?url=/library/en-us/vccore98/html/_crt__execv.2c_._wexecv.asp

Impact: High

Cross References: abort, atexit, exit, _onexit, _spawn, system, _wexecv

_execve

Prototype: `int _execve( const char *cmdname, const char *const *argv, const char *const *envp )`

Summary: This function executes a file with an array of pointers to be passed to the command line, keeping control over the environmental parameters.

Description: The function will execute a file pointed to by the argument "cmdname", which contains the path to file to be executed. The next input argument, "argv", is an array of command line parameters to be used in the execution of the file. The final input argument is an array of environmental parameters for file execution. Ideally, the function does not return a value, as it does not return to the calling process. However, upon an error, a value of -1 is returned and the global variable ERRNO is set.

Risk: This function has the ability to execute a file on the local system. Attackers commonly target functions similar to this since they have the ability to launch potentially dangerous or malicious executables with differing privileges. It is imperative that you filter all input and never allow a user direct access to passing variables as the parameters for this function. Ensure that all special characters are stripped before the data is parsed and passed in addition to limiting access to only the desired executables. Lastly, require that all executable output is controlled within a forked or spawned process within the local application to ensure the integrity of the outputted data. If possible, avoid calling dynamic programs from within applications. Static program execution is more secure.

Note: At time of publication, this function was designed for Windows compatibility.

Additional Resources:

http://msdn.microsoft.com/library/default.asp?url=/library/en-us/vccore98/html/_crt__execve.2c_._wexecve.asp

Impact: High

Cross References: `abort`, `atexit`, `exit`, `_onexit`, `_spawn`, `system`, `_wexecve`

_execvp

Prototype: `int _execvp( const char *cmdname, const char *const *argv )`

Summary: This function executes a file with an array of pointers to be passed to the command line using the environment variable PATH to find the file.

Description: The function will execute a file pointed to by the argument "cmdname", searching for it using the environmental variable PATH. The other input argument, "argv", is an array command line parameters to be used in the execution of the file. Ideally, the function does not return a value, as it does not return to the calling process. However, upon an error, a value of -1 is returned and the global variable ERRNO is set.

Risk: This function has the ability to execute a file on the local system. Attackers commonly target functions similar to this since they have the ability to launch potentially dangerous or malicious executables with differing privileges. It is imperative that you filter all input and never allow a user direct access to passing variables as the parameters for this function. Ensure that all special characters are stripped before the data is parsed and passed in addition to limiting access to only the desired executables. Lastly, require that all executable output is controlled within a forked or spawned process within the local application to ensure the integrity of the outputted data. If possible, avoid calling dynamic programs from within applications. Static program execution is more secure.

Note: At time of publication, this function was designed for Windows compatibility.

Additional Resources:
http://msdn.microsoft.com/library/default.asp?url=/library/en-us/vccore98/html/_crt__execvp.2c_._wexecvp.asp

Impact: High

Cross References: `abort`, `atexit`, `exit`, `_onexit`, `_spawn`, `system`, `_wexecvp`

_execvpe

Prototype: `int _execvpe( const char *cmdname, const char *const *argv, const char *const *envp )`

Summary: This function executes a file with an array of pointers to be passed to the command line using the environment variable PATH, as well as another array of pointers containing environmental parameters.

Description: The function will execute a file pointed to by the argument "cmd-name", searching for it using the environmental variable PATH. The next input argument, "argv", is an array command line parameters to be used in the execution of the file. The final input argument is another array of pointers to environmental parameters to be used on execution. Ideally, the function does not return a value, as it does not return to the calling process. However, upon an error, a value of -1 is returned and the global variable ERRNO is set.

Risk: This function has the ability to execute a file on the local system. Attackers commonly target functions similar to this since they have the ability to launch potentially dangerous or malicious executables with differing privileges. It is imperative that you filter all input and never allow a user direct access to passing variables as the parameters for this function. Ensure that all special characters are stripped before the data is parsed and passed in addition to limiting access to only the desired executables. Lastly, require that all executable output is controlled within a forked or spawned process within the local application to ensure the integrity of the outputted data. If possible, avoid calling dynamic programs from within applications. Static program execution is more secure.

Note: At time of publication, this function was designed for Windows compatibility.

Additional Resources:

http://msdn.microsoft.com/library/default.asp?url=/library/en-us/vccore98/html/_crt__execvpe.2c_._wexecvpe.asp

Impact: High

Cross References: abort, atexit, exit, _onexit, _spawn, system, _wexecvpe

_ftprintf

Prototype: `int _ftprintf( FILE *stream, const _tchar *format [, argument ]...)`

Summary: This function prints a string to a file stream.

Description: This function attempts to print a string to a filestream. It has two format input arguments. The first is the filestream to be written to, while the second is the t-character string to write. Informally, the function may have more arguments, as the string could have its own arguments due to formatting. The function returns the number of characters written to the stream. In the event of an error, the function returns a negative value.

Risk: This function is potentially vulnerable to a format string attack where an attacker could cause the application to crash unexpected or execute arbitrary code. Format string bugs were discovered in 2000 and the problem is typically spawned from user input that is not properly filtered. Both Microsoft .Net and SPI Dynamics to name two have secure objects that can be implemented to check strings and user input gained from human sources within applications to protect against input-directed vulnerabilities. It is critical that you verify the inputted data have only proper and expected characters in addition to ensuring that your function is properly called. For example, the functions should always utilize their parameters such as `printf("%s", malicious_string)` instead of `printf(malicious_string)`.

Note: At time of publication, this function was designed for Windows compatibility.

Additional Resources:
www.gnu.org/software/libc/manual/html_node/Formatted-Output-Functions.html#Formatted%20Output%20Functions;
http://msdn.microsoft.com/library/default.asp?url=/library/en-us/vccore98/html/_crt_fprintf.2c_.fwprintf.asp

Impact: Medium

Cross References: `_cprintf, fscanf, sprintf`

_ftscanf

Prototype: `int _ftscanf( FILE *stream, const _tchar *format [, argument ]... )`

Summary: This function reads pre-formatted data from a filestream.

Description: This function attempts to read formatted data from given filestream. The function has two formal arguments: the filestream and the t–character string which will house the new data read into it. The function may have informal arguments due to the formatting of the data, and the requisite arguments needed for compiler clarification in the string. The function will return the number of characters read. However, in the event of an error, it will return a negative number.

Risk: This function is potentially vulnerable to a format string attack where an attacker could cause the application to crash unexpected or execute arbitrary code. Format string bugs were discovered in 2000 and the problem is typically spawned from user input that is not properly filtered. Both Microsoft .Net and SPI Dynamics to name two have secure objects that can be implemented to check strings and user input gained from human sources within applications to protect against input-directed vulnerabilities. It is critical that you verify the inputted data have only proper and expected characters in addition to ensuring that your function is properly called. For example, the functions should always utilize their parameters such as `printf("%s", malicious_string)` instead of `printf(malicious_string)`.

Additional Resources:
www.gnu.org/software/libc/manual/html_node/Formatted-Input-Functions.html#Formatted%20Input%20Functions;
http://msdn.microsoft.com/library/default.asp?url=/library/en-us/vccore98/html/_crt_fscanf.2c_.fwscanf.asp

Impact: Medium

Cross References: `cscanf, fprintf, scanf, sscanf`

_mbscat

Prototype: `unsigned char *_mbscat( unsigned char *destination, const unsigned char *source )`

Summary: This function concatenates the multibyte-character source string onto the multibyte-character destination string

Description: The function concatenates the multibyte-character source string onto the multibyte-character destination string by overwriting the null character of the destination with the first character of the source. It closes off the new string by tacking on a null character to the end of the source string. The function is undefined if the two strings overlap. The returned value is the new destination string, with no defined value if an error occurs.

Risk: Multibyte strings have the potential to be very large strings that can be potentially leveraged in a buffer overflow attack scenario. These strings should restrict characters to include only those that are required by the application to function. Additionally, standard string manipulation functions should be utilized instead of large multibyte strings in all cases possible. Ensure that the destination buffer is of appropriate size and that the source buffer is limited to the size −1.

Note: At time of publication, this function was designed for Windows compatibility.

Additional Resources:
http://msdn.microsoft.com/library/default.asp?url=/library/en-us/vccore98/html/_crt_strcat.2c_.wcscat.2c_._mbscat.asp

Impact: Low

Cross References: `strncat, strncmp, strncpy, _strnicmp, strrchr, strspn, wcscat`

_mbscpy

Prototype: `unsigned char *_mbscpy( unsigned char *destination, const unsigned char *source )`

Summary: This function copies the multibyte-character source string to a multibyte-character destination string.

Description: The function copies the multibyte-character source string into the multibyte-character destination string. It closes off the new string by tacking on a null character to the end of the source string. The function is undefined if the two strings overlap. The returned value is the new destination string, with no defined value if an error occurs.

Risk: Multibyte strings have the potential to be very large strings that can be potentially leveraged in a buffer overflow attack scenario. These strings should restrict characters to include only those that are required by the application to function. Additionally, standard string manipulation functions should be utilized instead of large multibyte strings in all cases possible. Ensure that the destination buffer is of appropriate size and that the source buffer is limited to the size -1.

Note: At time of publication, this function was designed for Windows compatibility.

Additional Resources:
http://msdn.microsoft.com/library/default.asp?url=/library/en-us/vccore98/html/_crt_strcpy.2c_.wcscpy.2c_._mbscpy.asp

Impact: Medium

Cross References: `strcat`, `strcmp`, `strncat`, `strncmp`, `strncpy`, `_strnicmp`, `strrchr`, `strspn`, `wcscpy`

_mbslen

Prototype: `size_t _mbslen( const unsigned char *string )`

Summary: This function reads and returns the length of a multibyte-character string.

Description: This function reads the multibyte-characeter string passed to it in the input argument and returns the number of characters in the string (excluding the null character). The return value is undefined in the case of an error. This function does not do a validation check on the incoming string.

Risk: Multibyte strings have the potential to be very large strings that can be potentially leveraged in a buffer overflow attack scenario. These strings should restrict characters to include only those that are required by the application to function. Additionally, standard string manipulation functions should be utilized instead of large multibyte strings in all cases possible. Ensure that the destination buffer is of appropriate size and that the source buffer is limited to the size -1.

Note: At time of publication, this function was designed for Windows compatibility.

Additional Resources:
http://msdn.microsoft.com/library/default.asp?url=/library/en-us/
vccore98/html/_crt_strlen.2c_.wcslen.2c_._mbslen.2c_._mbstrlen.asp

Impact: Low

Cross References: setlocale, strcat, strcmp, strcoll, strcpy, strrchr, _strset, strspn, wcslen

_mbsnbcat

Prototype: unsigned char *_mbsnbcat(unsigned char *destination, const unsigned char *source, size_t count)

Summary: This function concatenates a multibyte-character string onto a multibyte-character string with a limiting variable.

Description: This function concatenates the multibyte-character string "source" onto the end of "destination", overwriting the null character in "destination" the function proceeds until the lesser of "count" or the length of "source" is reached. It terminates the destination string with a null character. The function returns the string "destination". The return value is not set if an error occurs during string concatenation.

Risk: Multibyte strings have the potential to be very large strings that can be potentially leveraged in a buffer overflow attack scenario. These strings should restrict characters to include only those that are required by the application to function. Additionally, standard string manipulation functions should be utilized instead of large multibyte strings in all cases possible. Ensure that the destination buffer is of appropriate size and that the source buffer is limited to the size -1.

Note: At time of publication, this function was designed for Windows compatibility.

Additional Resources:
http://msdn.microsoft.com/library/default.asp?url=/library/en-us/
vccore98/html/_crt__mbsnbcat.asp

Impact: Low

Cross References: _mbsnbcmp, _mbsnbcnt, _mbsnccnt, _mbsnbcpy, _mbsnbicmp, _mbsnbset, strncat

_mbsnbcpy

Prototype: `unsigned char * _mbsnbcpy( unsigned char *destination, const unsigned char *source, size_t count )`

Summary: This function copies a multibyte-character string into another multibyte-character string with a limiting variable.

Description: This function copies the multibyte-character string "source" into the multibyte-character string "destination". The function proceeds until the lesser of "count" or the length of "source" is reached. It terminates the destination string with a null character. The function returns the string "destination". The return value is not set if an error occurs during string copying.

Risk: Multibyte strings have the potential to be very large strings that can be potentially leveraged in a buffer overflow attack scenario. These strings should restrict characters to include only those that are required by the application to function. Additionally, standard string manipulation functions should be utilized instead of large multibyte strings in all cases possible. Ensure that the destination buffer is of appropriate size and that the source buffer is limited to the size -1.

Note: At time of publication, this function was designed for Windows compatibility.

Additional Resource
http://msdn.microsoft.com/library/default.asp?url=/library/en-us/
vccore98/html/_crt__mbsnbcpy.asp

Impact: Low

Cross References: _mbsnbcat, _mbsnbcmp, _mbsnbcnt, _mbsnccnt, _mbsnbicmp, _mbsnbset, _mbsncpy

_mbsncpy

Prototype: `unsigned char *_mbsncpy( unsigned char *destination, const unsigned char *source, size_t count )`

Summary: This function copies a multibyte-character string into another multibyte-character string with a limiting variable.

Description: This function copies the multibyte-character string "source" into the multibyte-character string "destination". The function proceeds until the lesser of "count" or the length of "source" is reached. It terminates the destination string with a null character. The function returns the string "destination". The return value is not set if an error occurs during string copying.

Risk: Multibyte strings have the potential to be very large strings that can be potentially leveraged in a buffer overflow attack scenario. These strings should restrict characters to include only those that are required by the application to function. Additionally, standard string manipulation functions should be utilized instead of large multibyte strings in all cases possible. Ensure that the destination buffer is of appropriate size and that the source buffer is limited to the size −1.

Note: At time of publication, this function was designed for Windows compatibility.

Additional Resources:
http://msdn.microsoft.com/library/default.asp?url=/library/en-us/vccore98/html/_crt_strncpy.2c_.wcsncpy.2c_._mbsncpy.asp

Impact: Low

Cross References: _mbsnbcpy, strcat, strcmp, strcpy, strncat, strncmp, _strnicmp, strrchr, _strset, strspn

_snprintf

Prototype: `int _snprintf( char *buffer, size_t count, const char *format [, argument] ... )`

Summary: This function prints a predetermined number of characters to a new formatted string.

Description: The function takes the string "`format`" and its arguments, printing the resultant string to "`buffer`". It copies only the number specified by the lesser of "`count`" or the length of the string to be printed. It only appends a null character if "`count`" is less than the length of the string. The function is undefined if overlapping occurs between the "`format`" and "`buffer`" strings. It returns the number of bytes being stored in the string "`buffer`" (excluding the null character, if it exists).

Risk: This function is potentially vulnerable to a format string attack where an attacker could cause the application to crash unexpected or execute arbitrary code. Format string bugs were discovered in 2000 and the problem is typically spawned from user input that is not properly filtered. Both Microsoft .Net and SPI Dynamics to name two have secure objects that can be implemented to check strings and user input gained from human sources within applications to protect against input-directed vulnerabilities. It is critical that you verify the inputted data have only proper and expected characters in addition to ensuring that your function is properly called. For example, the functions should always utilize their parameters such as `printf("%s", malicious_string)` instead of `printf(malicious_string)`.

Note: At time of publication, this function was designed for Windows compatibility.

Additional Resources:
http://msdn.microsoft.com/library/default.asp?url=/library/en-us/vccore98/html/_crt__snprintf.2c_._snwprintf.asp

Impact: Medium

Cross References: sprintf, fprintf, printf, scanf, sscanf, vprintf, _snwprintf

_snwprintf

Prototype: `int _snwprintf( wchar_t *buffer, size_t count, const wchar_t *format [, argument] ... )`

Summary: This function prints a predetermined number of wide characters to a new formatted string.

Description: The function takes the wide-character string "format" and its arguments, printing the resultant wide-character string to "buffer". It copies only the number specified by the lesser of "count" or the length of the string to be printed. It only appends a null character if "count" is less than the length of the string. The function is undefined if overlapping occurs between the "format" and "buffer" strings. It returns the number of wide characters being stored in the string "buffer" (excluding the null character, if it exists).

Risk: This function is potentially vulnerable to a format string attack where an attacker could cause the application to crash unexpected or execute arbitrary code. Format string bugs were discovered in 2000 and the problem is typically spawned from user input that is not properly filtered. Both Microsoft .Net and SPI Dynamics to name two have secure objects that can be implemented to check strings and user input gained from human sources within applications to protect against input-directed vulnerabilities. It is critical that you verify the inputted data have only proper and expected characters in addition to ensuring that your function is properly called. For example, the functions should always utilize their parameters such as printf("%s", malicious_string) instead of printf(malicious_string).

Note: At time of publication, this function was designed for Windows compatibility.

Additional Resources:
http://msdn.microsoft.com/library/default.asp?url=/library/en-us/vccore98/html/_crt__snprintf.2c_._snwprintf.asp

Impact: Medium

Cross References: sprintf, fprintf, printf, scanf, sscanf, vprintf, _snprintf

_spawnl

Prototype: int _spawnl(int mode, const char *cmdname, const char *arg0, const char *arg1, ... const char *argn, NULL)

Summary: This function executes a file with control given over the execution mode.

Description: The function executes the file given by the path `cmdname`. It executes it using the mode determined by `mode`. The remaining input arguments are the parameters to passed to the command line with the execution of the file. The function has two options for its timing, synchronous and asynchronous. The synchronous timing function call returns the exit status of the executed file. The asynchronous timing function call returns the handle of the process associated with the file execution. In the case of an error, the value `errno` will be set accordingly.

Risk: This function has the ability to execute a file on the local system. Attackers commonly target functions similar to this since they have the ability to launch potentially dangerous or malicious executables with differing privileges. It is imperative that you filter all input and never allow a user direct access to passing variables as the parameters for this function. Ensure that all special characters are stripped before the data is parsed and passed in addition to limiting access to only the desired executables. Lastly, require that all executable output is controlled within a forked or spawned process within the local application to ensure the integrity of the outputted data. If possible, avoid calling dynamic programs from within applications. Static program execution is more secure.

Note: At time of publication, this function was designed for Windows compatibility.

Additional Resources:
http://msdn.microsoft.com/library/default.asp?url=/library/en-us/vccore98/html/_crt__spawnl.2c_._wspawnl.asp

Impact: High

Cross References: abort, atexit, _exec, exit, _flushall, _getmbcp, _onexit, _setmbcp, system, _wspawnl

_spawnle

Prototype: int _spawnle(int mode, const char *cmdname, const char *arg0, const char *arg1, ... const char *argn, NULL, const char *const *envp)

Summary: This function executes a file with control given over the execution mode and environmental parameters.

Description: The function executes the file given by the path `cmdname`. It executes it using the mode determined by `mode`. The next input arguments are the parameters to passed to the command line with the execution of the file. The final input arguments are the environmental parameters to be passed. The function has two options for its timing, synchronous and asynchronous. The synchronous timing function call returns the exit status of the executed file. The asynchronous timing function call returns the handle of the process associated with the file execution. In the case of an error, the value `errno` will be set accordingly.

Risk: This function has the ability to execute a file on the local system. Attackers commonly target functions similar to this since they have the ability to launch potentially dangerous or malicious executables with differing privileges. It is imperative that you filter all input and never allow a user direct access to passing variables as the parameters for this function. Ensure that all special characters are stripped before the data is parsed and passed in addition to limiting access to only the desired executables. Lastly, require that all executable output is controlled within a forked or spawned process within the local application to ensure the integrity of the outputted data. If possible, avoid calling dynamic programs from within applications. Static program execution is more secure.

Note: At time of publication, this function was designed for Windows compatibility.

Additional Resources:
http://msdn.microsoft.com/library/default.asp?url=/library/en-us/vccore98/html/_crt__spawnle.2c_._wspawnle.asp

Impact: High

Cross References: abort, atexit, _exec, exit, _flushall, _getmbcp, _onexit, _setmbcp, system, _wspawnle

_spawnlp

Prototype: int _spawnlp(int mode, const char *cmdname, const char *arg0, const char *arg1, ... const char *argn, NULL)

Summary: This function executes a file (in the environment variable PATH) with control given over the execution mode.

Description: The function executes the file given by "cmdname", but that's located in the PATH environment variable. It executes it using the mode determined by "mode". The remaining input arguments are the parameters to passed to the command line with the execution of the file. The function has two options for its timing, synchronous and asynchronous. The synchronous timing function call returns the exit status of the executed file. The asynchronous timing function call returns the handle of the process associated with the file execution. In the case of an error, the value "errno" will be set accordingly.

Risk: This function has the ability to execute a file on the local system. Attackers commonly target functions similar to this since they have the ability to launch potentially dangerous or malicious executables with differing privileges. It is imperative that you filter all input and never allow a user direct access to passing variables as the parameters for this function. Ensure that all special characters are stripped before the data is parsed and passed in addition to limiting access to only the desired executables. Lastly, require that all executable output is controlled within a forked or spawned process within the local application to ensure the integrity of the outputted data. If possible, avoid calling dynamic programs from within applications. Static program execution is more secure.

Note: At time of publication, this function was designed for Windows compatibility.

Additional Resources:
http://msdn.microsoft.com/library/default.asp?url=/library/en-us/vccore98/html/_crt__spawnlp.2c_._wspawnlp.asp

Impact: High

Cross References: abort, atexit, _exec, exit, _flushall, _getmbcp, _onexit, _setmbcp, system, _wspawnlp

_spawnlpe

Prototype: `int _spawnlpe( int mode, const char *cmdname, const char *arg0, const char *arg1, ... const char *argn, NULL, const char *const *envp )`

Summary: This function executes a file (in the environment variable PATH) with control given over the execution mode and the environmental parameters.

Description: The function executes the file given by "`cmdname`" but that's located in the PATH environment variable. It executes it using the mode determined by "`mode`". The next input arguments are the parameters to passed to the command line with the execution of the file. The final input arguments are the environmental parameters to be used during file execution. The function has two options for its timing, synchronous and asynchronous. The synchronous timing function call returns the exit status of the executed file. The asynchronous timing function call returns the handle of the process associated with the file execution. In the case of an error, the value "`errno`" will be set accordingly.

Risk: This function has the ability to execute a file on the local system. Attackers commonly target functions similar to this since they have the ability to launch potentially dangerous or malicious executables with differing privileges. It is imperative that you filter all input and never allow a user direct access to passing variables as the parameters for this function. Ensure that all special characters are stripped before the data is parsed and passed in addition to limiting access to only the desired executables. Lastly, require that all executable output is controlled within a forked or spawned process within the local application to ensure the integrity of the outputted data. If possible, avoid calling dynamic programs from within applications. Static program execution is more secure.

Note: At time of publication, this function was designed for Windows compatibility.

Additional Resources:
http://msdn.microsoft.com/library/default.asp?url=/library/en-us/vccore98/html/_crt__spawnlpe.2c_._wspawnlpe.asp

Impact: High

Cross References: abort, atexit, _exec, exit, _flushall, _getmbcp, _onexit, _setmbcp, system, _wspwanlpe

_spawnv

Prototype: int _spawnv(int mode, const char *cmdname, const char *const *argv)

Summary: This function executes a file with control given over the execution mode.

Description: The function executes the file given by the path "`cmdname`". It executes it using the mode determined by "`mode`". The remaining input argument is a pointer to the parameters to passed to the command line with the execution of the file. The function has two options for its timing, synchronous and asynchronous. The synchronous timing function call returns the exit status of the executed file. The asynchronous timing function call returns the handle of the process associated with the file execution. In the case of an error, the value "`errno`" will be set accordingly.

Risk: This function has the ability to execute a file on the local system. Attackers commonly target functions similar to this since they have the ability to launch potentially dangerous or malicious executables with differing privileges. It is imperative that you filter all input and never allow a user direct access to passing variables as the parameters for this function. Ensure that all special characters are stripped before the data is parsed and passed in addition to limiting access to only the desired executables. Lastly, require that all executable output is controlled within a forked or spawned process within the local application to ensure the integrity of the outputted data. If possible, avoid calling dynamic programs from within applications. Static program execution is more secure.

Note: At time of publication, this function was designed for Windows compatibility.

Additional Resources:

http://msdn.microsoft.com/library/default.asp?url=/library/en-us/
vccore98/html/_crt__spawnv.2c_._wspawnv.asp

Impact: High

Cross References: abort, atexit, _exec, exit, _flushall, _getmbcp, _onexit, _setmbcp, system, _wspawnv

_spawnve

Prototype: int _spawnve(int mode, const char *cmdname, const char *const *argv, const char *const *envp)

Summary: This function executes a file with control given over the execution mode and environmental parameters.

Description: The function executes the file given by the path `cmdname`. It executes it using the mode determined by `mode`. The next input argument is a pointer to the parameters to passed to the command line with the execution of the file. The last input argument is an array of pointers containing the environmental parameters for file execution. The function has two options for its timing, synchronous and asynchronous. The synchronous timing function call returns the exit status of the executed file. The asynchronous timing function call returns the handle of the process associated with the file execution. In the case of an error, the value `errno` will be set accordingly.

Risk: This function has the ability to execute a file on the local system. Attackers commonly target functions similar to this since they have the ability to launch potentially dangerous or malicious executables with differing privileges. It is imperative that you filter all input and never allow a user direct access to passing variables as the parameters for this function. Ensure that all special characters are stripped before the data is parsed and passed in addition to limiting access to only the desired executables. Lastly, require that all executable output is controlled within a forked or spawned process within the local application to ensure the integrity of the outputted data. If possible, avoid calling dynamic programs from within applications. Static program execution is more secure.

Note: At time of publication, this function was designed for Windows compatibility.

Additional Resources:
http://msdn.microsoft.com/library/default.asp?url=/library/en-us/
vccore98/html/_crt__spawnve.2c_._wspawnve.asp

Impact: High

Cross References: abort, atexit, _exec, exit, _flushall, _getmbcp, _onexit, _setmbcp, system, _wspawnve

_spawnvp

Prototype: `int _spawnvp( int mode, const char *cmdname, const char *const *argv )`

Summary: This function executes a file (from within the environmental variable PATH) with control given over the execution mode.

Description: The function executes the file given by "cmdname" but that's located in the PATH environment variable. It executes it using the mode determined by "mode". The remaining input argument is an array containing the parameters to passed to the command line with the execution of the file. The function has two options for its timing, synchronous and asynchronous. The synchronous timing function call returns the exit status of the executed file. The asynchronous timing function call returns the handle of the process associated with the file execution. In the case of an error, the value "errno" will be set accordingly.

Risk: This function has the ability to execute a file on the local system. Attackers commonly target functions similar to this since they have the ability to launch potentially dangerous or malicious executables with differing privileges. It is imperative that you filter all input and never allow a user direct access to passing variables as the parameters for this function. Ensure that all special characters are stripped before the data is parsed and passed in addition to limiting access to only the desired executables. Lastly, require that all executable output is controlled within a forked or spawned process within the local application to ensure the integrity of the outputted data. If possible, avoid calling dynamic programs from within applications. Static program execution is more secure.

Note: At time of publication, this function was designed for Windows compatibility.

Additional Resources:
http://msdn.microsoft.com/library/default.asp?url=/library/
en-us/vccore98/html/_crt__spawnvp.2c_._wspawnvp.asp

Impact: High

Cross References: abort, atexit, _exec, exit, _flushall, _getmbcp, _onexit, _setmbcp, system, _wspawnvp

_spawnvpe

Prototype: `int _spawnvpe( int mode, const char *cmdname, const char *const *argv, const char *const *envp )`

Summary: This function executes a file (from within the environmental variable PATH) with control given over the execution mode and environmental parameters.

Description: The function executes the file given by "cmdname" but that's located in the PATH environment variable. It executes it using the mode determined by "mode". The next input argument is an array containing the parameters to passed to the command line with the execution of the file. The final input argument is another array of pointers, though to the environmental parameters for file execution. The function has two options for its timing, synchronous and asynchronous. The synchronous timing function call returns the exit status of the executed file. The asynchronous timing function call returns the handle of the process associated with the file execution. In the case of an error, the value "errno" will be set accordingly.

Risk: This function has the ability to execute a file on the local system. Attackers commonly target functions similar to this since they have the ability to launch potentially dangerous or malicious executables with differing privileges. It is imperative that you filter all input and never allow a user direct access to passing variables as the parameters for this function. Ensure that all special characters are stripped before the data is parsed and passed in addition to limiting access to only the desired executables. Lastly, require that all executable output is controlled within a forked or spawned process within the local application to ensure the integrity of the outputted data. If possible, avoid calling dynamic programs from within applications. Static program execution is more secure.

Note: At time of publication, this function was designed for Windows compatibility.

Additional Resources:
http://msdn.microsoft.com/library/default.asp?url=/library/
en-us/vccore98/html/_crt__spawnvpe.2c_._wspawnvpe.asp

Impact: High

Cross References: abort, atexit, _exec, exit, _flushall, _getmbcp, _onexit, _setmbcp, system, _wspawnvpe

_stprintf

Prototype: int _stprintf (_tchar *buffer, const _tchar *template)

Summary: This function prints a formatted array of characters to a string.

Description: The function attempts to print a formatted array of t-characters to a string. It has two formal arguments: the new string and the array to be printed. However, as it can be formatted data, there can be subsequent, informal arguments. The function will return the number of t-characters printed. However, in the event of an error, the function returns a negative value.

Risk: This function is potentially vulnerable to a format string attack where an attacker could cause the application to crash unexpected or execute arbitrary code. Format string bugs were discovered in 2000 and the problem is typically spawned from user input that is not properly filtered. Both Microsoft .Net and SPI Dynamics to name two have secure objects that can be implemented to check strings and user input gained from human sources within applications to protect against input-directed vulnerabilities. It is critical that you verify the inputted data have only proper and expected characters in addition to ensuring that your function is properly called. For example, the functions should always utilize their parameters such as `printf("%s", malicious_string)` instead of `printf(malicious_string)`.

Note: At time of publication, this function was designed for Windows compatibility.

Additional Resources:
www.gnu.org/software/libc/manual/html_node/Formatted-Output-Functions.html#Formatted%20Output%20Functions;
http://msdn.microsoft.com/library/default.asp?url=/library/en-us/vccore98/html/_crt_sprintf.2c_.swprintf.asp

Impact: Medium

Cross References: _ftprintf, _tprintf, _tscanf

_stscanf

Prototype: `int _stscanf( const _thar *buffer, const _tchar *format [, argument ] )`

Summary: The function reads a formatted array of characters from a string.

Description: The function attempts to scan a formatted array of t-characters from a string. It has two formal arguments: the string which the function will read and the array to be read in to. However, as it can be formatted data, there can be subsequent, informal arguments. The function will return the number of t-characters read. However, in the event of an error, the function returns a negative value.

Risk: This function is potentially vulnerable to a format string attack where an attacker could cause the application to crash unexpected or execute arbitrary code. Format string bugs were discovered in 2000 and the problem is typically spawned from user input that is not properly filtered. Both Microsoft .Net and SPI Dynamics to name two have secure objects that can be implemented to check strings and user input gained from human sources within applications to protect against input-directed vulnerabilities. It is critical that you verify the inputted data have only proper and expected characters in addition to ensuring that your function is properly called. For example, the functions should always utilize their parameters such as `printf("%s", malicious_string)` instead of `printf(malicious_string)`.

Note: At time of publication, this function was designed for Windows compatibility.

Additional Resources:
www.gnu.org/software/libc/manual/html_node/Formatted-Input-Functions.html#Formatted%20Input%20Functions;
http://msdn.microsoft.com/library/default.asp?url=/library/
en-us/vccore98/html/_crt_sscanf.2c_.swscanf.asp

Impact: Medium

Cross References: _ftscanf, _tscanf, _tsprintf

_tcscat

Prototype: `_tchar *_tcscat( _thar *destination, const _tchar *source )`

Summary: This function concatenates a string onto the end of another.

Description: The function attempts to append one string onto the end of another. It has two input arguments: the source and destination strings. The function will return a pointer to the destination string when finished. In the event of an error, the

C

function can return a NULL pointer. All strings in this function are given as t-character strings.

Risk: Functions that are utilized to copy or concatenate strings are commonly misused and fall victim to buffer overflow attacks. It is critical that you ensure before execution of this function that the destination source is large enough to house the source data. Additionally, limiting the source data memory space will not only make your application more efficient, it will also add another layer of security by relying less on the destination buffer. For example, if X should be copied to Y then ensure that Y's space is less than X-1's total space allocation. It is similar for concatenation functions where as the strings are limited to a total length.

Additional Resources: www.gnu.org/software/libc/manual/html_node/Copying-and-Concatenation.html#Copying%20and%20Concatenation; http://msdn.microsoft.com/library/default.asp?url=/library/en-us/vccore98/html/_crt_strcat.2c_.wcscat.2c_._mbscat.asp

Impact: Medium

Cross References: _tcscpy, _tcslen, _tcsncat, _tcsncpy

_tcscpy

Prototype: `_tchar *_tcscpy( _tchar *destination, const _tchar *source )`

Summary: This function copies a string onto another.

Description: The function attempts to copy one string onto another. It has two input arguments: the source and destination strings. The function will return a pointer to the destination string when finished. In the event of an error, the function can return a NULL pointer. All of the strings in this function are to be given as t-character strings.

Risk: Functions that are utilized to copy or concatenate strings are commonly misused and fall victim to buffer overflow attacks. It is critical that you ensure before execution of this function that the destination source is large enough to house the source data. Additionally, limiting the source data memory space will not only make your application more efficient, it will also add another layer of security by relying

less on the destination buffer. For example, if X should be copied to Y then ensure that Y's space is less than X-1's total space allocation. It is similar for concatenation functions where as the strings are limited to a total length.

Note: At time of publication, this function was designed for Windows compatibility.

Additional Resources: www.gnu.org/software/libc/manual/html_node/Copying-and-Concatenation.html#Copying%20and%20Concatenation; http://msdn.microsoft.com/library/default.asp?url=/library/en-us/vccore98/html/_crt_strcpy.2c_.wcscpy.2c_._mbscpy.asp

Impact: Medium

Cross References: _tcscat, _tcslen, _tcsncat, _tcsncpy

_tcslen

Prototype: `size_t _tcslen( const _tchar *string )`

Summary: This function finds the length of a string.

Description: The function attempts to find the length of the t-character string. It has only one input argument: the string to get the length of. The function will return an integer indicating the length of the string. In the event that the string does not exist or an error occurs, the function can return 0.

Risk: The length of a string is commonly ascertained before it is passed to a function that utilizes it to calculate the space required for a destination buffer. Ensure that human users do not have the ability to modify this number thereby potentially making it smaller than the destination. Calculate the length of the source then add one byte so to avoid off-by-one application buffer overflow attacks.

Note: At time of publication, this function was designed for Windows compatibility.

Additional Resources: www.gnu.org/software/libc/manual/html_node/String-Length.html#String%20Length; http://msdn.microsoft.com/library/default.asp?url=/library/en-us/vccore98/html/_crt_strlen.2c_.wcslen.2c_._mbslen.2c_._mbstrlen.asp

Impact: Low

Cross References: _tcscat, _tcscpy, _tcsncat, _tcsncpy

_tcsncat

Prototype: `_tchar *_tcsncat( _tchar *destination, const _tchar *source, size_t count )`

Summary: This function concatenates a string onto the end of another.

Description: The function attempts to append one t-character string onto the end of another. It has three input arguments: the source and destination strings and the max number oft-characters to concatenate. The function will return a pointer to the destination string when finished. In the event of an error, the function can return a NULL pointer.

Risk: Functions that are utilized to copy or concatenate strings are commonly misused and fall victim to buffer overflow attacks. It is critical that you ensure before execution of this function that the destination source is large enough to house the source data. Additionally, limiting the source data memory space will not only make your application more efficient, it will also add another layer of security by relying less on the destination buffer. For example, if X should be copied to Y then ensure that Y's space is less than X-1's total space allocation. It is similar for concatenation functions where as the strings are limited to a total length.

Note: At time of publication, this function was designed for Windows compatibility.

Additional Resources: www.gnu.org/software/libc/manual/html_node/Copying-and-Concatenation.html#Copying%20and%20Concatenation; http://msdn.microsoft.com/library/default.asp?url=/library/en-us/vccore98/html/_crt_strncat.2c_.wcsncat.2c_._mbsncat.asp

Impact: Medium

Cross References: `_tcscat, _tcscpy, _tcslen, _tcsncpy`

_tcsncpy

Prototype: `_tchar *_tcsncpy( _tchar *destination, const _tchar *source, size_t count )`

Summary: This function copies a string onto another.

Description: The function attempts to copy one t-character string onto another with control over the number of t-characters to copy. It has three input arguments: the source and destination strings and the maximum number of t-characters to copy. The function will return a pointer to the destination string when finished. In the event of an error, the function can return a NULL pointer.

Risk: Functions that are utilized to copy or concatenate strings are commonly misused and fall victim to buffer overflow attacks. It is critical that you ensure before execution of this function that the destination source is large enough to house the source data. Additionally, limiting the source data memory space will not only make your application more efficient, it will also add another layer of security by relying less on the destination buffer. For example, if X should be copied to Y, then ensure that Y's space is less than X-1's total space allocation. It is similar for concatenation functions where as the strings are limited to a total length.

Note: At time of publication, this function was designed for Windows compatibility.

Additional Resources: www.gnu.org/software/libc/manual/html_node/Copying-and-Concatenation.html#Copying%20and%20Concatenation; http://msdn.microsoft.com/library/default.asp?url=/library/en-us/vccore98/html/_crt_strncpy.2c_.wcsncpy.2c_._mbsncpy.asp

Impact: Medium

Cross References: _tcscat, _tcscpy, _tcslen, _tcsncat

_tcsxfrm

Prototype: `size_t strxfrm( _thar *destination, const _tchar *source, size_t count )`

Summary: This function transforms a string based off of the locale.

Description: The function attempts to transform a t-character string based on the locale information of the system. It takes in three input arguments: the source and destination strings and the maximum number of t-characters to put in the destination string. The function will return the length of the string written. In the event of an error, the function returns -1.

Risk: Functions that are utilized to copy or concatenate strings are commonly misused and fall victim to buffer overflow attacks. It is critical that you ensure before execution of this function that the destination source is large enough to house the source data. Additionally, limiting the source data memory space will not only make your application more efficient, it will also add another layer of security by relying less on the destination buffer. For example, if X should be copied to Y then ensure that Y's space is less than X-1's total space allocation. It is similar for concatenation functions where as the strings are limited to a total length.

Note: At time of publication, this function was designed for Windows compatibility.

Additional Resources:

www.gnu.org/software/libc/manual/html_node/Collation-Functions.html#Collation%20Functions;

http://msdn.microsoft.com/library/default.asp?url=/library/en-us/vccore98/html/_crt_strxfrm.2c_.wcsxfrm.asp

Impact: Medium

_texecl

Prototype: `int _texecl( const _tchar *cmdname, const _tchar *arg0, ... const _tchar *argn, NULL )`

Summary: This function executes a file from within the current shell.

Description: The function will execute a file pointed to by the argument "cmdname" which contains the path to file to be executed. The other input arguments (`arg0, arg1, ..., argN`) are command line parameters to be used in the execution of the file. Both of these arguments are given as t-character strings or pointers to strings. Ideally, the function does not return a value, as it does not return to the calling process. However, upon an error, a value of `-1` is returned and the global variable ERRNO is set.

Risk: This function has the ability to execute a file on the local system. Attackers commonly target functions similar to this since they have the ability to launch potentially dangerous or malicious executables with differing privileges. It is imperative that you filter all input and never allow a user direct access to passing variables as the parameters for this function. Ensure that all special characters are stripped before the data is parsed and passed in addition to limiting access to only the desired executables. Lastly, require that all executable output is controlled within a forked or spawned process within the local application to ensure the integrity of the outputted data. If possible, avoid calling dynamic programs from within applications. Static program execution is more secure.

Note: At time of publication, this function was designed for Windows compatibility.

Additional Resources:
http://msdn.microsoft.com/library/default.asp?url=/library/
en-us/vccore98/html/_crt__execl.2c_._wexecl.asp

Impact: High

Cross References: `abort`, `atexit`, `_execl`, `exit`, `_onexit`, `_spawn`, `system`

_texecle

Prototype: `int _texecle( const _tchar *cmdname, const _tchar *arg0, … const _tchar *argn, NULL, const _tchar *envp )`

Summary: This function executes a file from within the current shell with control over the environmental parameters.

Description: The function will execute a file pointed to by the t–character string "`cmdname`" which contains the path to file to be executed. The other input arguments (`arg0`, `arg1`, `…`, `argN`) are command line parameters to be used in the execution of the file (given as t–character strings). Ideally, the function does not return a value, as it does not return to the calling process. However, upon an error, a value of `-1` is returned and the global variable ERRNO is set.

Risk: This function has the ability to execute a file on the local system. Attackers commonly target functions similar to this since they have the ability to launch potentially dangerous or malicious executables with differing privileges. It is imperative that you filter all input and never allow a user direct access to passing variables as the parameters for this function. Ensure that all special characters are stripped before the data is parsed and passed in addition to limiting access to only the desired executables. Lastly, require that all executable output is controlled within a forked or spawned process within the local application to ensure the integrity of the outputted

data. If possible, avoid calling dynamic programs from within applications. Static program execution is more secure.

Note: At time of publication, this function was designed for Windows compatibility.

Additional Resources:
http://msdn.microsoft.com/library/default.asp?url=/library/en-us/vccore98/html/_crt__execle.2c_._wexecle.asp

Impact: High

Cross References: `abort, atexit, _execle, exit, _onexit, _spawn, system`

_texeclp

Prototype: `int _texeclp( const _tchar *cmdname, const _tchar *arg0, … const _tchar *argn, NULL )`

Summary: This function executes a file from within the current shell, searching for it from the PATH environment variable.

Description: The function will execute a file pointed to by the t-character string "cmdname" searching for it in the system's PATH. The other input arguments (`arg0, arg1, …, argN`) are t-character strings containing command line parameters to be used in the execution of the file. Ideally, the function does not return a value, as it does not return to the calling process. However, upon an error, a value of `-1` is returned and the global variable ERRNO is set.

Risk: This function has the ability to execute a file on the local system. Attackers commonly target functions similar to this since they have the ability to launch potentially dangerous or malicious executables with differing privileges. It is imperative that you filter all input and never allow a user direct access to passing variables as the parameters for this function. Ensure that all special characters are stripped before the data is parsed and passed in addition to limiting access to only the desired executables. Lastly, require that all executable output is controlled within a forked or spawned process within the local application to ensure the integrity of the outputted data. If possible, avoid calling dynamic programs from within applications. Static program execution is more secure.

Note: At time of publication, this function was designed for Windows compatibility.

Additional Resources:
http://msdn.microsoft.com/library/default.asp?url=/library/
en-us/vccore98/html/_crt__execlp.2c_._wexeclp.asp

Impact: High

Cross References: `abort`, `atexit`, `_execlp`, `exit`, `_onexit`, `_spawn`, `system`

_texeclpe

Prototype: `int _texeclpe( const _tchar *cmdname, const _tchar *arg0, … const _tchar *argn, NULL, const char *const *envp )`

Summary: This function executes a file from within the current shell, searching for it from the PATH environment variable, with a separate input for environmental parameters.

Description: The function will execute a file pointed to by the t-character string "cmdname" searching for it in the system's PATH environment variable. The next input arguments (`arg0`, `arg1`, …, `argN`) are command line parameters to be used in the execution of the file. The final input argument is the array of pointers to environmental parameters needed for file execution. Ideally, the function does not return a value, as it does not return to the calling process. However, upon an error, a value of `-1` is returned and the global variable ERRNO is set.

Risk: This function has the ability to execute a file on the local system. Attackers commonly target functions similar to this since they have the ability to launch potentially dangerous or malicious executables with differing privileges. It is imperative that you filter all input and never allow a user direct access to passing variables as the parameters for this function. Ensure that all special characters are stripped before the data is parsed and passed in addition to limiting access to only the desired executables. Lastly, require that all executable output is controlled within a forked or spawned process within the local application to ensure the integrity of the outputted data. If possible, avoid calling dynamic programs from within applications. Static program execution is more secure.

Note: At time of publication, this function was designed for Windows compatibility.

Additional Resources:
http://msdn.microsoft.com/library/default.asp?url=/library/
en-us/vccore98/html/_crt__execlpe.2c_._wexeclpe.asp

Impact: High

Cross References: `abort`, `atexit`, `_execlpe`, `exit`, `_onexit`, `_spawn`, `system`

_texecv

Prototype: `int _texecv( const _tchar *cmdname, const _tchar *const *argv )`

Summary: This function executes a file with an array of pointers to be passed to the command line.

Description: The function will execute a file pointed to by the t-character string "`cmdname`" which contains the path to file to be executed. The other input argument, "`argv`", is a t-character array command line parameters to be used in the execution of the file. Ideally, the function does not return a value, as it does not return to the calling process. However, upon an error, a value of `-1` is returned and the global variable ERRNO is set.

Risk: This function has the ability to execute a file on the local system. Attackers commonly target functions similar to this since they have the ability to launch potentially dangerous or malicious executables with differing privileges. It is imperative that you filter all input and never allow a user direct access to passing variables as the parameters for this function. Ensure that all special characters are stripped before the data is parsed and passed in addition to limiting access to only the desired executables. Lastly, require that all executable output is controlled within a forked or spawned process within the local application to ensure the integrity of the outputted data. If possible, avoid calling dynamic programs from within applications. Static program execution is more secure.

Note: At time of publication, this function was designed for Windows compatibility.

Additional Resources:
http://msdn.microsoft.com/library/default.asp?url=/library/
en-us/vccore98/html/_crt__execv.2c_._wexecv.asp

Impact: High

Cross References: `abort, atexit, _execv, exit, _onexit, _spawn, system`

_texecve

Prototype: `int _texecve( const _tchar *cmdname, const _tchar *const *argv, const _tchar *const *envp )`

Summary: This function executes a file with an array of pointers to be passed to the command line, keeping control over the environmental parameters.

Description: The function will execute a file pointed to by the t-character string "cmdname" which contains the path to file to be executed. The next input argument, "argv", is an array of t-character strings containing command line parameters to be used in the execution of the file. The final input argument is an array of t-character strings containing environmental parameters for file execution. Ideally, the function does not return a value, as it does not return to the calling process. However, upon an error, a value of -1 is returned and the global variable ERRNO is set.

Risk: This function has the ability to execute a file on the local system. Attackers commonly target functions similar to this since they have the ability to launch potentially dangerous or malicious executables with differing privileges. It is imperative that you filter all input and never allow a user direct access to passing variables as the parameters for this function. Ensure that all special characters are stripped before the data is parsed and passed in addition to limiting access to only the desired executables. Lastly, require that all executable output is controlled within a forked or spawned process within the local application to ensure the integrity of the outputted data. If possible, avoid calling dynamic programs from within applications. Static program execution is more secure.

Note: At time of publication, this function was designed for Windows compatibility.

C

Additional Resources:

http://msdn.microsoft.com/library/default.asp?url=/library/
en-us/vccore98/html/_crt__execve.2c_._wexecve.asp

Impact: High

Cross References: `abort, atexit, _execve, exit, _onexit, _spawn, system`

_texecvp

Prototype: `int _texecvp( const _tchar *cmdname, const _tchar *const *argv )`

Summary: This function executes a file with an array of pointers to be passed to the command line using the environment variable PATH to find the file.

Description: The function will execute a file pointed to by the t–character string "`cmdname`" searching for it using the environmental variable PATH. The other input argument, "`argv`", is an array of t–character strings containing the command line parameters to be used in the execution of the file. Ideally, the function does not return a value, as it does not return to the calling process. However, upon an error, a value of –1 is returned and the global variable ERRNO is set.

Risk: This function has the ability to execute a file on the local system. Attackers commonly target functions similar to this since they have the ability to launch potentially dangerous or malicious executables with differing privileges. It is imperative that you filter all input and never allow a user direct access to passing variables as the parameters for this function. Ensure that all special characters are stripped before the data is parsed and passed in addition to limiting access to only the desired executables. Lastly, require that all executable output is controlled within a forked or spawned process within the local application to ensure the integrity of the outputted data. If possible, avoid calling dynamic programs from within applications. Static program execution is more secure.

Note: At time of publication, this function was designed for Windows compatibility.

Additional Resources:

http://msdn.microsoft.com/library/default.asp?url=/library/
en-us/vccore98/html/_crt__execvp.2c_._wexecvp.asp

Impact: High

Cross References: abort, atexit, _execvp, exit, _onexit, _spawn, system

_texecvpe

Prototype: int _texecvpe(const _tchar *cmdname, const _tchar *const *argv, const _tchar *const *envp)

Summary: This function executes a file with an array of pointers to be passed to the command line using the environment variable PATH, as well as another array of pointers containing environmental parameters.

Description: The function will execute a file pointed to by the t-character string "cmdname" searching for it using the environmental variable PATH. The next input argument, "argv", is an array of t-character strings containing the command line parameters to be used in the execution of the file. The final input argument is another array of t-character strings with the environmental parameters to be used on execution. Ideally, the function does not return a value, as it does not return to the calling process. However, upon an error, a value of -1 is returned and the global variable ERRNO is set.

Risk: This function has the ability to execute a file on the local system. Attackers commonly target functions similar to this since they have the ability to launch potentially dangerous or malicious executables with differing privileges. It is imperative that you filter all input and never allow a user direct access to passing variables as the parameters for this function. Ensure that all special characters are stripped before the data is parsed and passed in addition to limiting access to only the desired executables. Lastly, require that all executable output is controlled within a forked or spawned process within the local application to ensure the integrity of the outputted data. If possible, avoid calling dynamic programs from within applications. Static program execution is more secure.

Note: At time of publication, this function was designed for Windows compatibility.

Additional Resources:

http://msdn.microsoft.com/library/default.asp?url=/library/
en-us/vccore98/html/_crt__execvpe.2c_._wexecvpe.asp

Impact: High

Cross References: `abort`, `atexit`, `_execvpe`, `exit`, `_onexit`, `_spawn`, `system`

_tprintf

Prototype: `int _tprintf( const _tchar *format [, argument]...)`

Summary: This function prints a formatted array of characters to the I/O stream.

Description: The function attempts to print a formatted array of t–characters to the stream. It has only one formal argument: the array to be printed. However, as it can be formatted data, there can be subsequent, informal arguments. The function will return the number of t–characters printed. However, in the event of an error, the function returns a negative value.

Risk: This function is potentially vulnerable to a format string attack where an attacker could cause the application to crash unexpected or execute arbitrary code. Format string bugs were discovered in 2000 and the problem is typically spawned from user input that is not properly filtered. Both Microsoft .Net and SPI Dynamics to name two have secure objects that can be implemented to check strings and user input gained from human sources within applications to protect against input-directed vulnerabilities. It is critical that you verify the inputted data have only proper and expected characters in addition to ensuring that your function is properly called. For example, the functions should always utilize their parameters such as `printf("%s", malicious_string)` instead of `printf(malicious_string)`.

Note: At time of publication, this function was designed for Windows compatibility.

Additional Resources:
www.gnu.org/software/libc/manual/html_node/Formatted-Output-Functions.html#Formatted%20Output%20Functions;
http://msdn.microsoft.com/library/default.asp?url=/library/en-us/vccore98/html/_crt_printf.2c_.wprintf.asp

Impact: Medium

Cross References: `_fptrintf`, `_stprintf`, `_tscanf`

_tscanf

Prototype: `int _tscanf( const _tchar *format [,argument]... )`

Summary: The function reads a formatted array of characters from the I/O stream.

Description: The function attempts to scan a formatted array of t-characters from the stream. It has only one formal argument: the array to be read in to. However, as it can be formatted data, there can be subsequent, informal arguments. The function will return the number of t-characters read. However, in the event of an error, the function returns a negative value.

Risk: This function is potentially vulnerable to a format string attack where an attacker could cause the application to crash unexpected or execute arbitrary code. Format string bugs were discovered in 2000 and the problem is typically spawned from user input that is not properly filtered. Both Microsoft .Net and SPI Dynamics to name two have secure objects that can be implemented to check strings and user input gained from human sources within applications to protect against input-directed vulnerabilities. It is critical that you verify the inputted data have only proper and expected characters in addition to ensuring that your function is properly called. For example, the functions should always utilize their parameters such as `printf("%s", malicious_string)` instead of `printf(malicious_string)`.

Note: At time of publication, this function was designed for Windows compatibility.

Additional Resources:
www.gnu.org/software/libc/manual/html_node/Formatted-Input-Functions.html#Formatted%20Input%20Functions;
http://msdn.microsoft.com/library/default.asp?url=/library/en-us/vccore98/html/_crt_scanf.2c_.wscanf.asp

Impact: Medium

Cross References: `_ftscanf, _stprintf, _tprintf`

_tspawnl

Prototype: `int _tspawnl( int mode, const _tchar *cmdname, const _tchar *arg0, const _tchar *arg1, … const _tchart *argn, NULL )`

Summary: This function executes a file with control given over the execution mode.

Description: The function executes the file given by the t-character string containing the path to "cmdname". It executes it using the mode determined by "mode". The remaining input arguments are the parameters to passed to the command line (as t-character strings) with the execution of the file. The function has two options for its timing, synchronous and asynchronous. The synchronous timing function call returns the exit status of the executed file. The asynchronous timing function call returns the handle of the process associated with the file execution. In the case of an error, the value "errno" will be set accordingly.

Risk: This function has the ability to execute a file on the local system. Attackers commonly target functions similar to this since they have the ability to launch potentially dangerous or malicious executables with differing privileges. It is imperative that you filter all input and never allow a user direct access to passing variables as the parameters for this function. Ensure that all special characters are stripped before the data is parsed and passed in addition to limiting access to only the desired executables. Lastly, require that all executable output is controlled within a forked or spawned process within the local application to ensure the integrity of the outputted data. If possible, avoid calling dynamic programs from within applications. Static program execution is more secure.

Note: At time of publication, this function was designed for Windows compatibility.

Additional Resources:
http://msdn.microsoft.com/library/default.asp?url=/library/
en-us/vccore98/html/_crt__spawnl.2c_._wspawnl.asp

Impact: High

Cross References: abort, atexit, _exec, exit, _flushall, _getmbcp, _onexit, _setmbcp, _spawnl, system

_tspawnle

Prototype: int _tspawnle(int mode, const _tchar *cmdname, const _tchar *arg0, const _tchar *arg1, ... const _tchar *argn, NULL, const _tchar *const *envp)

Summary: This function executes a file with control given over the execution mode and environmental parameters.

Description: The function executes the file given by the t-character string containing the path of "cmdname". It executes it using the mode determined by "mode". The next input arguments are the parameters to passed to the command line with the execution of the file. The final input arguments are the environmental parameters to be passed. Both are passed as t-character strings or arrays of t-character strings. The function has two options for its timing, synchronous and asynchronous. The synchronous timing function call returns the exit status of the executed file. The asynchronous timing function call returns the handle of the process associated with the file execution. In the case of an error, the value "errno" will be set accordingly.

Risk: This function has the ability to execute a file on the local system. Attackers commonly target functions similar to this since they have the ability to launch potentially dangerous or malicious executables with differing privileges. It is imperative that you filter all input and never allow a user direct access to passing variables as the parameters for this function. Ensure that all special characters are stripped before the data is parsed and passed in addition to limiting access to only the desired executables. Lastly, require that all executable output is controlled within a forked or spawned process within the local application to ensure the integrity of the outputted data. If possible, avoid calling dynamic programs from within applications. Static program execution is more secure.

Note: At time of publication, this function was designed for Windows compatibility.

Additional Resources:
http://msdn.microsoft.com/library/default.asp?url=/library/
en-us/vccore98/html/_crt__spawnle.2c_._wspawnle.asp

Impact: High

Cross References: abort, atexit, _exec, exit, _flushall, _getmbcp, _onexit, _setmbcp, _spawnle, system

_tspawnlp

Prototype: int _tspawnlp(int mode, const _tchar *cmdname, const _tchar *arg0, const _tchar *arg1, ... const _tchar *argn, NULL)

Summary: This function executes a file (in the environment variable PATH) with control given over the execution mode.

Description: The function executes the file given by t-character string "cmd-name" but that's located in the PATH environment variable. It executes it using the mode determined by "mode". The remaining input arguments are the parameters to passed to the command line with the execution of the file. They are passed as t-character strings. The function has two options for its timing, synchronous and asynchronous. The synchronous timing function call returns the exit status of the executed file. The asynchronous timing function call returns the handle of the process associated with the file execution. In the case of an error, the value "errno" will be set accordingly.

Risk: This function has the ability to execute a file on the local system. Attackers commonly target functions similar to this since they have the ability to launch potentially dangerous or malicious executables with differing privileges. It is imperative that you filter all input and never allow a user direct access to passing variables as the parameters for this function. Ensure that all special characters are stripped before the data is parsed and passed in addition to limiting access to only the desired executables. Lastly, require that all executable output is controlled within a forked or spawned process within the local application to ensure the integrity of the outputted data. If possible, avoid calling dynamic programs from within applications. Static program execution is more secure.

Note: At time of publication, this function was designed for Windows compatibility.

Additional Resources:

http://msdn.microsoft.com/library/default.asp?url=/library/en-us/vccore98/html/_crt__spawnlp.2c_._wspawnlp.asp

Impact: High

Cross References: abort, atexit, _exec, exit, _flushall, _getmbcp, _onexit, _setmbcp, _spawnlp, system

_tspawnlpe

Prototype: int _tspawnlpe(int mode, const _tchar *cmdname, const _tchar *arg0, const _tchar *arg1, … const _tchar *argn, NULL, const _tchar *const *envp)

Summary: This function executes a file (in the environment variable PATH) with control given over the execution mode and the environmental parameters.

Description: The function executes the file given by the t-character string "cmd-name", but that's located in the PATH environment variable. It executes it using the mode determined by "mode". The next input arguments are the parameters to passed to the command line with the execution of the file. The final input arguments are the environmental parameters to be used during file execution. Both are passed as t-character strings or arrays of t-character strings. The function has two options for its timing, synchronous and asynchronous. The synchronous timing function call returns the exit status of the executed file. The asynchronous timing function call returns the handle of the process associated with the file execution. In the case of an error, the value "errno" will be set accordingly.

Risk: This function has the ability to execute a file on the local system. Attackers commonly target functions similar to this since they have the ability to launch potentially dangerous or malicious executables with differing privileges. It is imperative that you filter all input and never allow a user direct access to passing variables as the parameters for this function. Ensure that all special characters are stripped before the data is parsed and passed in addition to limiting access to only the desired executables. Lastly, require that all executable output is controlled within a forked or spawned process within the local application to ensure the integrity of the outputted data. If possible, avoid calling dynamic programs from within applications. Static program execution is more secure.

Note: At time of publication, this function was designed for Windows compatibility.

Additional Resources:

http://msdn.microsoft.com/library/default.asp?url=/library/en-us/vccore98/html/_crt__spawnlpe.2c_._wspawnlpe.asp

Impact: High

Cross References: abort, atexit, _exec, exit, _flushall, _getmbcp, _onexit, _setmbcp, _spwanlpe, system

_tspawnv

Prototype: int _tspawnv(int mode, const _tchar *cmdname, const _tchar *const *argv)

Summary: This function executes a file with control given over the execution mode.

Description: The function executes the file given by the t-character string containing the path "cmdname". It executes it using the mode determined by "mode". The remaining input argument is a pointer to an array of t-character strings with the parameters to passed to the command line with the execution of the file. The function has two options for its timing, synchronous and asynchronous. The synchronous timing function call returns the exit status of the executed file. The asynchronous timing function call returns the handle of the process associated with the file execution. In the case of an error, the value "errno" will be set accordingly.

Risk: This function has the ability to execute a file on the local system. Attackers commonly target functions similar to this since they have the ability to launch potentially dangerous or malicious executables with differing privileges. It is imperative that you filter all input and never allow a user direct access to passing variables as the parameters for this function. Ensure that all special characters are stripped before the data is parsed and passed in addition to limiting access to only the desired executables. Lastly, require that all executable output is controlled within a forked or spawned process within the local application to ensure the integrity of the outputted data. If possible, avoid calling dynamic programs from within applications. Static program execution is more secure.

Note: At time of publication, this function was designed for Windows compatibility.

Additional Resources:
http://msdn.microsoft.com/library/default.asp?url=/library/en-us/vccore98/html/_crt__spawnv.2c_._wspawnv.asp

Impact: High

Cross References: abort, atexit, _exec, exit, _flushall, _getmbcp, _onexit, _setmbcp, _spawnv, system

_tspawnve

Prototype: int _tspawnve(int mode, const _tchar *cmdname, const _tchar *const *argv, const _tchar *const *envp)

Summary: This function executes a file with control given over the execution mode and environmental parameters.

Description: The function executes the file given by the t-character string containing the path to "cmdname". It executes it using the mode determined by "mode". The next input argument is a pointer to the t-character string array of parameters to passed to the command line with the execution of the file. The last input argument is an array of pointers to the t-character strings containing environmental parameters for file execution. The function has two options for its timing, synchronous and asynchronous. The synchronous timing function call returns the exit status of the executed file. The asynchronous timing function call returns the handle of the process associated with the file execution. In the case of an error, the value "errno" will be set accordingly.

Risk: This function has the ability to execute a file on the local system. Attackers commonly target functions similar to this since they have the ability to launch potentially dangerous or malicious executables with differing privileges. It is imperative that you filter all input and never allow a user direct access to passing variables as the parameters for this function. Ensure that all special characters are stripped before the data is parsed and passed in addition to limiting access to only the desired executables. Lastly, require that all executable output is controlled within a forked or spawned process within the local application to ensure the integrity of the outputted data. If possible, avoid calling dynamic programs from within applications. Static program execution is more secure.

Note: At time of publication, this function was designed for Windows compatibility.

Additional Resources:

http://msdn.microsoft.com/library/default.asp?url=/library/en-us/vccore98/html/_crt__spawnve.2c_._wspawnve.asp

Impact: High

Cross References: abort, atexit, _exec, exit, _flushall, _getmbcp, _onexit, _setmbcp, _spawnve, system

_tspawnvp

Prototype: int _tspawnvp(int mode, const _tchar *cmdname, const _tchar *const *argv)

Summary: This function executes a file (from within the environmental variable PATH) with control given over the execution mode.

Description: The function executes the file given by the t-character string "cmdname" but that's located in the PATH environment variable. It executes it using the mode determined by "mode". The remaining input argument is an array of t-character strings containing the parameters to passed to the command line with the execution of the file. The function has two options for its timing, synchronous and asynchronous. The synchronous timing function call returns the exit status of the executed file. The asynchronous timing function call returns the handle of the process associated with the file execution. In the case of an error, the value "errno" will be set accordingly.

Risk: This function has the ability to execute a file on the local system. Attackers commonly target functions similar to this since they have the ability to launch potentially dangerous or malicious executables with differing privileges. It is imperative that you filter all input and never allow a user direct access to passing variables as the parameters for this function. Ensure that all special characters are stripped before the data is parsed and passed in addition to limiting access to only the desired executables. Lastly, require that all executable output is controlled within a forked or spawned process within the local application to ensure the integrity of the outputted data. If possible, avoid calling dynamic programs from within applications. Static program execution is more secure.

Note: At time of publication, this function was designed for Windows compatibility.

Additional Resources:
http://msdn.microsoft.com/library/default.asp?url=/library/en-us/vccore98/html/_crt__spawnvp.2c_._wspawnvp.asp

Impact: High

Cross References: abort, atexit, _exec, exit, _flushall, _getmbcp, _onexit, _setmbcp, _spawnvp, system

_tspawnvpe

Prototype: int _tspawnvpe(int mode, const _tchar *cmdname, const _tchar *const *argv, const _tchar *const

Summary: This function executes a file (from within the environmental variable PATH) with control given over the execution mode and environmental parameters.

Description: The function executes the file given by the t-character string "cmd-name" but that's located in the PATH environment variable. It executes it using the mode determined by "mode". The next input argument is an array of t-character strings containing the parameters passed to the command line with the execution of the file. The final input argument is another array of pointers to t-character strings, containing the environmental parameters for file execution. The function has two options for its timing, synchronous and asynchronous. The synchronous timing function call returns the exit status of the executed file. The asynchronous timing function call returns the handle of the process associated with the file execution. In the case of an error, the value "errno" will be set accordingly.

Risk: This function has the ability to execute a file on the local system. Attackers commonly target functions similar to this since they have the ability to launch potentially dangerous or malicious executables with differing privileges. It is imperative that you filter all input and never allow a user direct access to passing variables as the parameters for this function. Ensure that all special characters are stripped before the data is parsed and passed in addition to limiting access to only the desired executables. Lastly, require that all executable output is controlled within a forked or spawned process within the local application to ensure the integrity of the outputted

data. If possible, avoid calling dynamic programs from within applications. Static program execution is more secure.

Note: At time of publication, this function was designed for Windows compatibility.

Additional Resources:

http://msdn.microsoft.com/library/default.asp?url=/library/en-us/vccore98/html/_crt__spawnvpe.2c_._wspawnvpe.asp

Impact: High

Cross References: abort, atexit, _exec, exit, _flushall, _getmbcp, _onexit, _setmbcp, _spawnvpe, system

_vsnprintf

Prototype: int _vsnprintf(char *buffer, size_t count, const char *format, const char *const *argv)

Summary: This function writes a highly formatted string with a pointer to a list of arguments to be used.

Description: This function writes to the string "buffer" using the string "format" as its basis. It will write the lesser of "count" or the length of "buffer". The input argument "argv" is a pointer to a list of arguments to be used for the writing process. The function returns the number of characters written (excluding the null character, if applicable).

Risk: This function is potentially vulnerable to a format string attack where an attacker could cause the application to crash unexpected or execute arbitrary code. Format string bugs were discovered in 2000 and the problem is typically spawned from user input that is not properly filtered. Both Microsoft .Net and SPI Dynamics to name two have secure objects that can be implemented to check strings and user input gained from human sources within applications to protect against input-directed vulnerabilities. It is critical that you verify the inputted data have only proper and expected characters in addition to ensuring that your function is properly called. For example, the functions should always utilize their parameters such as printf("%s", malicious_string) instead of printf(malicious_string).

Note: At time of publication, this function was designed for Windows compatibility.

Additional Resources:
http://msdn.microsoft.com/library/default.asp?url=/library/en-us/vccore98/html/_crt__vsnprintf.2c_._vsnwprintf.asp

Impact: Low

Cross References: `fprintf`, `printf`, `sprintf`, `va_arg`, `_vsnwprintf`

_vsnwprintf

Prototype: `int _vsnwprintf( wchar_t *buffer, size_t count, const wchar_t *format, va_list argptr )`

Summary: This function writes a highly formatted, wide-character string with a pointer to a list of arguments to be used.

Description: This function writes to the wide-character string "`buffer`" using the wide-character string "`format`" as its basis. It will write the lesser of "`count`" or the length of "`buffer`". The input argument "`argv`" is a pointer to a list of arguments to be used for the writing process. The function returns the number of wide-characters written (excluding the null character, if applicable).

Risk: This function is potentially vulnerable to a format string attack where an attacker could cause the application to crash unexpected or execute arbitrary code. Format string bugs were discovered in 2000 and the problem is typically spawned from user input that is not properly filtered. Both Microsoft .Net and SPI Dynamics to name two have secure objects that can be implemented to check strings and user input gained from human sources within applications to protect against input-directed vulnerabilities. It is critical that you verify the inputted data have only proper and expected characters in addition to ensuring that your function is properly called. For example, the functions should always utilize their parameters such as `printf("%s", malicious_string)` instead of `printf(malicious_string)`.

Note: At time of publication, this function was designed for Windows compatibility.

Additional Resources:

http://msdn.microsoft.com/library/default.asp?url=/library/en-us/vccore98/html/_crt__vsnprintf.2c_._vsnwprintf.asp

Impact: Low

Cross References: `fprintf`, `printf`, `sprintf`, `va_arg`, `_vsnprint`

_wexecl

Prototype: `int _wexecl( const wchar_t *cmdname, const wchar_t *arg0, ... const wchar_t *argn, NULL )`

Summary: This function executes a file from within the current shell.

Description: The function will execute a file pointed to by the argument "cmd-name" which contains the path to file to be executed. The other input arguments (`arg0`, `arg1`, …, `argN`) are command line parameters to be used in the execution of the file. Both of these arguments are given as wide-character strings or pointers to strings. Ideally, the function does not return a value, as it does not return to the calling process. However, upon an error, a value of −1 is returned and the global variable ERRNO is set.

Risk: This function has the ability to execute a file on the local system. Attackers commonly target functions similar to this since they have the ability to launch potentially dangerous or malicious executables with differing privileges. It is imperative that you filter all input and never allow a user direct access to passing variables as the parameters for this function. Ensure that all special characters are stripped before the data is parsed and passed in addition to limiting access to only the desired executables. Lastly, require that all executable output is controlled within a forked or spawned process within the local application to ensure the integrity of the outputted data. If possible, avoid calling dynamic programs from within applications. Static program execution is more secure.

Note: At time of publication, this function was designed for Windows compatibility.

Additional Resources:

http://msdn.microsoft.com/library/default.asp?url=/library/en-us/vccore98/html/_crt__execl.2c_._wexecl.asp

Impact: High

Cross References: abort, atexit, _execl, exit, _onexit, _spawn, system

_wexecle

Prototype: `int _wexecle( const wchar_t *cmdname, const wchar_t *arg0, … const wchar_t *argn, NULL, const char *const *envp )`

Summary: This function executes a file from within the current shell with control over the environmental parameters.

Description: The function will execute a file pointed to by the wide-character `string` "cmdname" which contains the path to the file to be executed. The other input arguments (`arg0`, `arg1`, …, `argN`) are command line parameters to be used in the execution of the file (given as wide-character strings). Ideally, the function does not return a value, as it does not return to the calling process. However, upon an error, a value of −1 is returned and the global variable ERRNO is set.

Risk: This function has the ability to execute a file on the local system. Attackers commonly target functions similar to this since they have the ability to launch potentially dangerous or malicious executables with differing privileges. It is imperative that you filter all input and never allow a user direct access to passing variables as the parameters for this function. Ensure that all special characters are stripped before the data is parsed and passed in addition to limiting access to only the desired executables. Lastly, require that all executable output is controlled within a forked or spawned process within the local application to ensure the integrity of the outputted data. If possible, avoid calling dynamic programs from within applications. Static program execution is more secure.

Note: At time of publication, this function was designed for Windows compatibility.

Additional Resources:
http://msdn.microsoft.com/library/default.asp?url=/library/
en-us/vccore98/html/_crt__execle.2c_._wexecle.asp

Impact: High

Cross References: abort, atexit, _execle, exit, _onexit, _spawn, system

_wexeclp

Prototype: `int _wexeclp( const wchar_t *cmdname, const wchar_t *arg0, ... const wchar_t *argn, NULL )`

Summary: This function executes a file from within the current shell, searching for it from the PATH environment variable.

Description: The function will execute a file pointed to by the wide-character string "cmdname" searching for it in the system's PATH. The other input arguments (`arg0`, `arg1`, ..., `argN`) are wide-character strings containing command line parameters to be used in the execution of the file. Ideally, the function does not return a value, as it does not return to the calling process. However, upon an error, a value of `-1` is returned and the global variable ERRNO is set.

Risk: This function has the ability to execute a file on the local system. Attackers commonly target functions similar to this since they have the ability to launch potentially dangerous or malicious executables with differing privileges. It is imperative that you filter all input and never allow a user direct access to passing variables as the parameters for this function. Ensure that all special characters are stripped before the data is parsed and passed in addition to limiting access to only the desired executables. Lastly, require that all executable output is controlled within a forked or spawned process within the local application to ensure the integrity of the outputted data. If possible, avoid calling dynamic programs from within applications. Static program execution is more secure.

Note: At time of publication, this function was designed for Windows compatibility.

Additional Resources:
http://msdn.microsoft.com/library/default.asp?url=/library/
en-us/vccore98/html/_crt__execlp.2c_._wexeclp.asp

Impact: High

Cross References: `abort`, `atexit`, `_execlp`, `exit`, `_onexit`, `_spawn`, `system`

_wexeclpe

Prototype: `int _wexeclpe( const wchar_t *cmdname, const wchar_t *arg0, ... const wchar_t *argn, NULL, const wchar_t *const *envp )`

Summary: This function executes a file from within the current shell, searching for it from the PATH environment variable, with a separate input for environmental parameters.

Description: The function will execute a file pointed to by the wide-character string "cmdname" searching for it in the system's PATH environment variable. The next input arguments (`arg0`, `arg1`, …, `argN`) are command line parameters to be used in the execution of the file. The final input argument is the array of pointers to environmental parameters needed for file execution. Ideally, the function does not return a value, as it does not return to the calling process. However, upon an error, a value of `-1` is returned and the global variable ERRNO is set.

Risk: This function has the ability to execute a file on the local system. Attackers commonly target functions similar to this since they have the ability to launch potentially dangerous or malicious executables with differing privileges. It is imperative that you filter all input and never allow a user direct access to passing variables as the parameters for this function. Ensure that all special characters are stripped before the data is parsed and passed in addition to limiting access to only the desired executables. Lastly, require that all executable output is controlled within a forked or spawned process within the local application to ensure the integrity of the outputted data. If possible, avoid calling dynamic programs from within applications. Static program execution is more secure.

Note: At time of publication, this function was designed for Windows compatibility.

Additional Resources:
http://msdn.microsoft.com/library/default.asp?url=/library/en-us/vccore98/html/_crt__execlpe.2c_._wexeclpe.asp

Impact: High

Cross References: abort, atexit, _execlpe, exit, _onexit, _spawn, system

_wexecv

Prototype: `int _wexecv( const wchar_t *cmdname, const wchar_t *const *argv )`

Summary: This function executes a file with an array of pointers to be passed to the command line.

Description: The function will execute a file pointed to by the wide-character string "cmdname" which contains the path to file to be executed. The other input argument, "argv" is a wide-character array command line parameters to be used in the execution of the file. Ideally, the function does not return a value, as it does not return to the calling process. However, upon an error, a value of –1 is returned and the global variable ERRNO is set.

Risk: This function has the ability to execute a file on the local system. Attackers commonly target functions similar to this since they have the ability to launch potentially dangerous or malicious executables with differing privileges. It is imperative that you filter all input and never allow a user direct access to passing variables as the parameters for this function. Ensure that all special characters are stripped before the data is parsed and passed in addition to limiting access to only the desired executables. Lastly, require that all executable output is controlled within a forked or spawned process within the local application to ensure the integrity of the outputted data. If possible, avoid calling dynamic programs from within applications. Static program execution is more secure.

Note: At time of publication, this function was designed for Windows compatibility.

Additional Resources:
http://msdn.microsoft.com/library/default.asp?url=/library/en-us/vccore98/html/_crt__execv.2c_._wexecv.asp

Impact: High

Cross References: `abort, atexit, _execv, exit, _onexit, _spawn, system`

_wexecve

Prototype: `int _wexecve( const wchar_t *cmdname, const wchar_t *const *argv, const wchar_t *const *envp )`

Summary: This function executes a file with an array of pointers to be passed to the command line, keeping control over the environmental parameters.

Description: The function will execute a file pointed to by the wide-character string "cmdname" which contains the path to file to be executed. The next input argument, "argv" is an array of wide-character strings containing command line parameters to be used in the execution of the file. The final input argument is an array of wide-character strings containing environmental parameters for file execution. Ideally, the function does not return a value, as it does not return to the calling process. However, upon an error, a value of -1 is returned and the global variable ERRNO is set.

Risk: This function has the ability to execute a file on the local system. Attackers commonly target functions similar to this since they have the ability to launch potentially dangerous or malicious executables with differing privileges. It is imperative that you filter all input and never allow a user direct access to passing variables as the parameters for this function. Ensure that all special characters are stripped before the data is parsed and passed in addition to limiting access to only the desired executables. Lastly, require that all executable output is controlled within a forked or spawned process within the local application to ensure the integrity of the outputted data. If possible, avoid calling dynamic programs from within applications. Static program execution is more secure.

Note: At time of publication, this function was designed for Windows compatibility.

Additional Resources:
http://msdn.microsoft.com/library/default.asp?url=/library/en-us/vccore98/html/_crt__execve.2c_._wexecve.asp

Impact: High

Cross References: `abort, atexit, _execve, exit, _onexit, _spawn, system`

_wexecvp

Prototype: `int _wexecvp( const wchar_t *cmdname, const wchar_t *const *argv )`

Summary: This function executes a file with an array of pointers to be passed to the command line using the environment variable PATH to find the file.

Description: The function will execute a file pointed to by the wide-character string "cmdname" searching for it using the environmental variable PATH. The other input argument, "argv", is an array of wide-character strings containing the command line parameters to be used in the execution of the file. Ideally, the function does not return a value, as it does not return to the calling process. However, upon an error, a value of −1 is returned and the global variable ERRNO is set.

Risk: This function has the ability to execute a file on the local system. Attackers commonly target functions similar to this since they have the ability to launch potentially dangerous or malicious executables with differing privileges. It is imperative that you filter all input and never allow a user direct access to passing variables as the parameters for this function. Ensure that all special characters are stripped before the data is parsed and passed in addition to limiting access to only the desired executables. Lastly, require that all executable output is controlled within a forked or spawned process within the local application to ensure the integrity of the outputted data. If possible, avoid calling dynamic programs from within applications. Static program execution is more secure.

Note: At time of publication, this function was designed for Windows compatibility.

Additional Resources:

http://msdn.microsoft.com/library/default.asp?url=/library/en-us/vccore98/html/_crt__execvp.2c_._wexecvp.asp

Impact: High

Cross References: `abort, atexit, _execvp, exit, _onexit, _spawn, system`

_wexecvpe

Prototype: `int _wexecvpe( const wchar_t *cmdname, const wchar_t *const *argv, const wchar_t *const *envp )`

Summary: This function executes a file with an array of pointers to be passed to the command line using the environment variable PATH, as well as another array of pointers containing environmental parameters.

Description: The function will execute a file pointed to by the wide-character string "cmdname" searching for it using the environmental variable PATH. The next input argument, "argv" is an array of wide-character strings containing the command line parameters to be used in the execution of the file. The final input argument is another array of wide-character strings with the environmental parameters to be used on execution. Ideally, the function does not return a value, as it does not return to the calling process. However, upon an error, a value of −1 is returned and the global variable ERRNO is set.

Risk: This function has the ability to execute a file on the local system. Attackers commonly target functions similar to this since they have the ability to launch potentially dangerous or malicious executables with differing privileges. It is imperative that you filter all input and never allow a user direct access to passing variables as the parameters for this function. Ensure that all special characters are stripped before the data is parsed and passed in addition to limiting access to only the desired executables. Lastly, require that all executable output is controlled within a forked or spawned process within the local application to ensure the integrity of the outputted data. If possible, avoid calling dynamic programs from within applications. Static program execution is more secure.

Note: At time of publication, this function was designed for Windows compatibility.

Additional Resources:
http://msdn.microsoft.com/library/default.asp?url=/library/en-us/vccore98/html/_crt__execvpe.2c_._wexecvpe.asp

Impact: High

Cross References: `abort, atexit, _execvpe, exit, _onexit, _spawn, system`

_wspawnl

Prototype: `int _wspawnl( int mode, const wchar_t *cmdname, const wchar_t *arg0, const wchar_t *arg1, ... const wchar_t *argn, NULL )`

Summary: This function executes a file with control given over the execution mode.

Description: The function executes the file given by the wide-character string containing the path to "cmdname". It executes it using the mode determined by "mode". The remaining input arguments are the parameters to passed to the command line (as wide-character strings) with the execution of the file. The function has two options for its timing, synchronous and asynchronous. The synchronous timing function call returns the exit status of the executed file. The asynchronous timing function call returns the handle of the process associated with the file execution. In the case of an error, the value "errno" will be set accordingly.

Risk: This function has the ability to execute a file on the local system. Attackers commonly target functions similar to this since they have the ability to launch potentially dangerous or malicious executables with differing privileges. It is imperative that you filter all input and never allow a user direct access to passing variables as the parameters for this function. Ensure that all special characters are stripped before the data is parsed and passed in addition to limiting access to only the desired executables. Lastly, require that all executable output is controlled within a forked or spawned process within the local application to ensure the integrity of the outputted data. If possible, avoid calling dynamic programs from within applications. Static program execution is more secure.

Note: At time of publication, this function was designed for Windows compatibility.

Additional Resources:

http://msdn.microsoft.com/library/default.asp?url=/library/en-us/vccore98/html/_crt__spawnl.2c_._wspawnl.asp

Impact: High

Cross References: abort, atexit, _exec, exit, _flushall, _getmbcp, _onexit, _setmbcp, _spawnl, system

_wspawnle

Prototype: `int _wspawnle( int mode, const wchar_t *cmdname, const wchar_t *arg0, const wchar_t *arg1, ... const wchar_t *argn, NULL, const wchar_t *const *envp )`

Summary: This function executes a file with control given over the execution mode and environmental parameters.

Description: The function executes the file given by the wide-character string containing the path of "cmdname". It executes it using the mode determined by "mode". The next input arguments are the parameters to passed to the command line with the execution of the file. The final input arguments are the environmental parameters to be passed. Both are passed as wide-character strings or arrays of wide-character strings. The function has two options for its timing, synchronous and asynchronous. The synchronous timing function call returns the exit status of the executed file. The asynchronous timing function call returns the handle of the process associated with the file execution. In the case of an error, the value "errno" will be set accordingly.

Risk: This function has the ability to execute a file on the local system. Attackers commonly target functions similar to this since they have the ability to launch potentially dangerous or malicious executables with differing privileges. It is imperative that you filter all input and never allow a user direct access to passing variables as the parameters for this function. Ensure that all special characters are stripped before the data is parsed and passed in addition to limiting access to only the desired executables. Lastly, require that all executable output is controlled within a forked or spawned process within the local application to ensure the integrity of the outputted data. If possible, avoid calling dynamic programs from within applications. Static program execution is more secure.

Note: At time of publication, this function was designed for Windows compatibility.

Additional Resources:
http://msdn.microsoft.com/library/default.asp?url=/library/en-us/vccore98/html/_crt__spawnle.2c_._wspawnle.asp

Impact: High

Cross References: abort, atexit, _exec, exit, _flushall, _getmbcp, _onexit, _setmbcp, _spawnle, system

_wspawnlp

Prototype: `int _wspawnlp( int mode, const wchar_t *cmdname, const wchar_t *arg0, const wchar_t *arg1, ... const wchar_t *argn, NULL )`

Summary: This function executes a file (in the environment variable PATH) with control given over the execution mode.

Description: The function executes the file given by wide-character string "cmdname" but that's located in the PATH environment variable. It executes it using the mode determined by "mode". The remaining input arguments are the parameters to passed to the command line with the execution of the file. They are passed as wide-character strings. The function has two options for its timing, synchronous and asynchronous. The synchronous timing function call returns the exit status of the executed file. The asynchronous timing function call returns the handle of the process associated with the file execution. In the case of an error, the value "errno" will be set accordingly.

Risk: This function has the ability to execute a file on the local system. Attackers commonly target functions similar to this since they have the ability to launch potentially dangerous or malicious executables with differing privileges. It is imperative that you filter all input and never allow a user direct access to passing variables as the parameters for this function. Ensure that all special characters are stripped before the data is parsed and passed in addition to limiting access to only the desired executables. Lastly, require that all executable output is controlled within a forked or spawned process within the local application to ensure the integrity of the outputted data. If possible, avoid calling dynamic programs from within applications. Static program execution is more secure.

Note: At time of publication, this function was designed for Windows compatibility.

Additional Resources:
http://msdn.microsoft.com/library/default.asp?url=/library/en-us/vccore98/html/_crt__spawnlp.2c_._wspawnlp.asp

Impact: High

Cross References: abort, atexit, _exec, exit, _flushall, _getmbcp, _onexit, _setmbcp, _spawnlp, system

_wspawnlpe

Prototype: int _wspawnlpe(int mode, const wchar_t *cmdname, const wchar_t *arg0, const wchar_t *arg1, ... const wchar_t *argn, NULL, const wchar_t *const *envp)

Summary: This function executes a file (in the environment variable PATH) with control given over the execution mode and the environmental parameters.

Description: The function executes the file given by the wide-character string "cmdname" but that's located in the PATH environment variable. It executes it using the mode determined by "mode". The next input arguments are the parameters to passed to the command line with the execution of the file. The final input arguments are the environmental parameters to be used during file execution. Both are passed as wide-character strings or arrays of wide-character strings. The function has two options for its timing, synchronous and asynchronous. The synchronous timing function call returns the exit status of the executed file. The asynchronous timing function call returns the handle of the process associated with the file execution. In the case of an error, the value "errno" will be set accordingly.

Risk: This function has the ability to execute a file on the local system. Attackers commonly target functions similar to this since they have the ability to launch potentially dangerous or malicious executables with differing privileges. It is imperative that you filter all input and never allow a user direct access to passing variables as the parameters for this function. Ensure that all special characters are stripped before the data is parsed and passed in addition to limiting access to only the desired executables. Lastly, require that all executable output is controlled within a forked or spawned process within the local application to ensure the integrity of the outputted data. If possible, avoid calling dynamic programs from within applications. Static program execution is more secure.

Note: At time of publication, this function was designed for Windows compatibility.

Additional Resources:

http://msdn.microsoft.com/library/default.asp?url=/library/en-us/vccore98/html/_crt__spawnlpe.2c_._wspawnlpe.asp

Impact: High

Cross References: abort, atexit, _exec, exit, _flushall, _getmbcp, _onexit, _setmbcp, _spwanlpe, system

_wspawnv

Prototype: int _wspawnv(int mode, const wchar_t *cmdname, const wchar_t *const *argv)

Summary: This function executes a file with control given over the execution mode.

Description: The function executes the file given by the wide-character string containing the path "cmdname". It executes it using the mode determined by "mode". The remaining input argument is a pointer to an array of wide-character strings with the parameters to passed to the command line with the execution of the file. The function has two options for its timing, synchronous and asynchronous. The synchronous timing function call returns the exit status of the executed file. The asynchronous timing function call returns the handle of the process associated with the file execution. In the case of an error, the value "errno" will be set accordingly.

Risk: This function has the ability to execute a file on the local system. Attackers commonly target functions similar to this since they have the ability to launch potentially dangerous or malicious executables with differing privileges. It is imperative that you filter all input and never allow a user direct access to passing variables as the parameters for this function. Ensure that all special characters are stripped before the data is parsed and passed in addition to limiting access to only the desired executables. Lastly, require that all executable output is controlled within a forked or spawned process within the local application to ensure the integrity of the outputted data. If possible, avoid calling dynamic programs from within applications. Static program execution is more secure.

Note: At time of publication, this function was designed for Windows compatibility.

Additional Resources:
http://msdn.microsoft.com/library/default.asp?url=/library/en-us/vccore98/html/_crt__spawnv.2c_._wspawnv.asp

Impact: High

Cross References: abort, atexit, _exec, exit, _flushall, _getmbcp, _onexit, _setmbcp, _spawnv, system

_wspawnve

Prototype: int _wspawnve(int mode, const wchar_t *cmdname, const wchar_t *const *argv, const wchar_t *const *envp)

Summary: This function executes a file with control given over the execution mode and environmental parameters.

Description: The function executes the file given by the wide-character string containing the path to "cmdname". It executes it using the mode determined by "mode". The next input argument is a pointer to the wide-character string array of parameters to passed to the command line with the execution of the file. The last input argument is an array of pointers to the wide-character strings containing environmental parameters for file execution. The function has two options for its timing, synchronous and asynchronous. The synchronous timing function call returns the exit status of the executed file. The asynchronous timing function call returns the handle of the process associated with the file execution. In the case of an error, the value "errno" will be set accordingly.

Risk: This function has the ability to execute a file on the local system. Attackers commonly target functions similar to this since they have the ability to launch potentially dangerous or malicious executables with differing privileges. It is imperative that you filter all input and never allow a user direct access to passing variables as the parameters for this function. Ensure that all special characters are stripped before the data is parsed and passed in addition to limiting access to only the desired executables. Lastly, require that all executable output is controlled within a forked or spawned process within the local application to ensure the integrity of the outputted data. If possible, avoid calling dynamic programs from within applications. Static program execution is more secure.

Note: At time of publication, this function was designed for Windows compatibility.

Additional Resources:
http://msdn.microsoft.com/library/default.asp?url=/library/en-us/vccore98/html/_crt__spawnve.2c_._wspawnve.asp

Impact: High

Cross References: abort, atexit, _exec, exit, _flushall, _getmbcp, _onexit, _setmbcp, _spawnve, system

_wspawnvp

Prototype: int _wspawnvp(int mode, const wchar_t *cmdname, const wchar_t *const *argv)

Summary: This function executes a file (from within the environmental variable PATH) with control given over the execution mode.

Description: The function executes the file given by the wide-character string "cmdname" but that's located in the PATH environment variable. It executes it using the mode determined by "mode". The remaining input argument is an array of wide-character strings containing the parameters to passed to the command line with the execution of the file. The function has two options for its timing, synchronous and asynchronous. The synchronous timing function call returns the exit status of the executed file. The asynchronous timing function call returns the handle of the process associated with the file execution. In the case of an error, the value "errno" will be set accordingly.

Risk: This function has the ability to execute a file on the local system. Attackers commonly target functions similar to this since they have the ability to launch potentially dangerous or malicious executables with differing privileges. It is imperative that you filter all input and never allow a user direct access to passing variables as the parameters for this function. Ensure that all special characters are stripped before the data is parsed and passed in addition to limiting access to only the desired executables. Lastly, require that all executable output is controlled within a forked or spawned process within the local application to ensure the integrity of the outputted data. If possible, avoid calling dynamic programs from within applications. Static program execution is more secure.

Note: At time of publication, this function was designed for Windows compatibility.

Additional Resources:
http://msdn.microsoft.com/library/default.asp?url=/library/en-us/vccore98/html/_crt__spawnvp.2c_._wspawnvp.asp

Impact: High

Cross References: abort, atexit, _exec, exit, _flushall, _getmbcp, _onexit, _setmbcp, _spawnvp, system

_wspawnvpe

Prototype: int _wspawnvpe(int mode, const wchar_t *cmdname, const wchar_t *const *argv, const wchar_t *const *envp)

Summary: This function executes a file (from within the environmental variable PATH) with control given over the execution mode and environmental parameters.

Description: The function executes the file given by the wide-character string "cmdname" but that's located in the PATH environment variable. It executes it using the mode determined by "mode". The next input argument is an array of wide-character strings containing the parameters to passed to the command line with the execution of the file. The final input argument is another array of pointers to wide-character strings, containing the environmental parameters for file execution. The function has two options for its timing, synchronous and asynchronous. The synchronous timing function call returns the exit status of the executed file. The asynchronous timing function call returns the handle of the process associated with the file execution. In the case of an error, the value "errno" will be set accordingly.

Risk: This function has the ability to execute a file on the local system. Attackers commonly target functions similar to this since they have the ability to launch potentially dangerous or malicious executables with differing privileges. It is imperative that you filter all input and never allow a user direct access to passing variables as the parameters for this function. Ensure that all special characters are stripped before the data is parsed and passed in addition to limiting access to only the desired executables. Lastly, require that all executable output is controlled within a forked or spawned process within the local application to ensure the integrity of the outputted

data. If possible, avoid calling dynamic programs from within applications. Static program execution is more secure.

Note: At time of publication, this function was designed for Windows compatibility.

Additional Resources:

http://msdn.microsoft.com/library/default.asp?url=/library/en-us/vccore98/html/_crt__spawnvpe.2c_._wspawnvpe.asp

Impact: High

Cross References: abort, atexit, _exec, exit, _flushall, _getmbcp, _onexit, _setmbcp, _spawnvpe, system

_wsystem

Prototype: int _wsystem(const wchar_t *command)

Summary: This function calls a system command from within the shell.

Description: The function calls a system command contained in the wide-character string "command". You must either flush or close any open streams before calling the function. The function will return one of several options. If the command interpreter is found in the PATH, then the function will return an arbitrary non-zero integer for an empty "command" string or the value that the system returns from the function call if "command" is not empty. If the command interpreter is not found, then the function returns 0 and sets "errno". If a general error occurs, then the function returns -1 and sets the variable "errno".

Risk: This function is utilized to execute system-level commands from within an application. Executing system-level commands are one of the most dangerous types of operations that an application can hardcode into its backend logic. Multiple vectors for potential attacks are available and must be addressed to secure your application. User input should be reviewed and all non-alphanumeric characters removed. Additionally, the directory structure should be limited to include only the directory or directories where the desired executables reside. As an example, you would restrict users to running commands or executables in /user/local/bin or c:/documents and settings/userX/programs/. Lastly, all output for the application should be captured within the subprocess that has launched the executable. Fork,

CreateProcess, or CreateThread are examples of additional functions that can be used to contain output.

Note: At time of publication, this function was designed for Windows compatibility.

Additional Resources:
http://msdn.microsoft.com/library/default.asp?url=/library/en-us/vccore98/html/_crt_system.2c_._wsystem.asp

Impact: High

Cross References: `_exec`, `exit`, `_flushall`, `_spawn`, `system`

access

Prototype: `int access (const char *filename, int type)`

Summary: This function tests the permissions of a file.

Description: The function attempts to access the file contained in `"filename"` with the requested privileges in `"type"`. The input argument `"type"` can be used to test the read, write, and executable privileges of the file, as well as if the file exists. The function returns a `0` if the file exists and can be accessed by the requested `"type"`. Otherwise, the function returns a `-1`, setting the variable `"errno"` to the appropriate error.

Risk: Testing the permissions of a file could potentially glean sensitive information about that file or the underlying operating system. Ensure that the output of this function is restricted to internal program use only and that humans are disallowed from pointing this function to specific system-level files.

Note: This function has a Windows-compatible version called `"_access"`.

Additional Resources: www.gnu.org/software/libc/manual/html_node/Testing-File-Access.html#Testing%20File%20Access

Impact: Medium

Cross References: `chmod`, `fopen`, `fwrite`, `getuid`, `setuid`

AfxLoadLibrary

Prototype: `HINSTANCE AFXAPI AfxLoadLibrary( LPCTSTR lpszModuleName )`

Summary: This function maps to a module (either DLL or EXE).

Description: This function takes a string containing the path to a module, and links to it (if it exists). The function will return the handle of the loaded library if successful. However, the function will return NULL if it fails for any reason. This function should be used for DLL's explicitly (and not LoadLibrary). You can later unmap this DLL by using the complementary function `AfxFreeLibrary`.

Risk: By default, the `AfxLoadLibrary` function will search multiple locations for both DLL and EXE modules. When you utilize this function, it is imperative that you include the complete path to the desired module that you are implementing within your application. If the complete path is not specified and a default multipath search is conducted then the potential for a malicious program to be executed is increased. For instance, if a Trojanized Microsoft DLL resides on a target system with the name included in the executed application then it may be possible for a remote user to launch that DLL through a vulnerable application.

Note: At time of publication, this function was written for Windows compatibility.

Additional Resources:

http://msdn.microsoft.com/library/default.asp?url=/library/en-us/vccore98/html/_core_loadlibrary_and_afxloadlibrary.asp;

Impact: Medium

Cross References: `AfxFreeLibrary`, `LoadLibrary`

basename

Prototype: `char * basename (const char *filename)`

Summary: This function returns the last part of the path indicated in the input argument.

Description: The function takes in a constant string "filename" stripping it to its last component and returning that as another string. The function has been overloaded (see the Additional Notes). This function can have differing effects on differing systems. This must be taken into account for the sake of portability. In the event of an error, the function returns a null string.

Risk: The basename function is commonly utilized as a target point for attackers looking to compromise applications via a race condition vulnerability. Race conditions have multiple potential outcomes but in this scenario an attacker with access to the application may be able to gain the ability to taken control of a process executing a specific application. Additionally, this function takes in the name of a system filename and as such the proper input and directory restrictions should be included in the code to parse the passed data.

Note: This function is overloaded between two header files, <string.h> and <libgen.h>. Whereas the function definition here is of the "basename" in <string.h>, precedence is taken for the header <libgen.h> and its "basename" will be used. The defining difference between the two is that the function in <libgen.h> can modify the path (like removing trailing /'s). The function in <string.h> prevents that from happening.

Additional Resources: www.gnu.org/software/libc/manual/html_node/Finding-Tokens-in-a-String.html#Finding%20Tokens%20in%20a%20String

Impact: High

bcopy

Prototype: `void bcopy (const void *source, void *destination, size_t size)`

Summary: This function copies the data from one piece of memory to another.

Description: The function takes three inputs to define the copying procedure. The pointer "`source`" defines the donor band of memory, while the variable "`size`" tells the function the amount of memory to be copied. The function then copies the band of memory to the new location at the pointer "`destination`". The function does not return any values. It is for this reason that this function has become fairly obsolete.

Risk: Even though this function is somewhat out-of-date, it is imperative that you ensure the buffer size of the destination memory allocation address is larger or equal to the space required by the source buffer. bcopy is a function that can be utilized as a target for buffer overflow attacks. Memmove is the more commonly utilized function for this purpose.

Note: This function has been updated and is more commonly replaced by the function "memmove".

Additional Resources: www.gnu.org/software/libc/manual/html_node/Copying-and-Concatenation.html#Copying%20and%20Concatenation

Impact: Low

Cross References: memmove, strcpy

Funtion: bind

Prototype: bind SOCKET, NAME

Summary: This function attaches a handle to an open socket.

Description: The function attempts to label an open socket with a name or address. The function has two input arguments: the open socket to be labeled and the name to label it with. The function returns a Boolean TRUE or FALSE based on the result of the function call. Note that the name should be properly assigned for the socket used.

Risk: Raw network data received from a socket has the potential to be malicious in nature due to the great number of attacks that are designed to be executed remotely. Packet fragmentations can cause serious disruptions to the application and underlying operating system. If at all possible, packet reassembly should be conducted at the OS-layer.

Additional Resources:
http://secu.zzu.edu.cn/book/Perl/Perl%20Bookshelf%20%5B3rd%20Ed%5D/prog/ch29_02.htm, www.unix.org.ua/orelly/perl/perlnut/ch05_02.htm

Impact: Low

chmod

Prototype: `int chmod (const char *filename, mode_t mode)`

Summary: This function attempts to change the permissions of a file.

Description: The function takes two inputs, the file name and the requested permissions. The function takes in the constant string "`filename`" and attempts to change its permissions to the values defined by "`mode`". If the function is successful, then it will return 0. However, if the function fails, it returns a -1 and sets the variable "`errno`" to the appropriate value.

Risk: In addition to the potential race condition vulnerability that is associated with this function it also handles potentially sensitive information. The function is inherently flawed if two processes try to access and modify the permissions of a single file simultaneously, one function could receive the overriding permissions from the other. If the application is transmitting this information over the wire, it should utilize strong point-to-point encryption to ensure that an attacker could not ascertain the filename, path, old permissions, or new permissions.

Note: This function has Windows compatible version called "`_chmod`".

Impact: High

Cross References: `access`, `chown`, `chroot`, `fchmod`, `getumask`, `fopen`, `umask`

chown

Prototype: `int chown (const char *filename, uid_t owner, gid_t group)`

Summary: This function is used to change the ownership of a file.

Description: The function takes three inputs: the name of the file to be changed, the user to be made owner, and the group to be made owner. The function requires that the user have the proper permissions to change the owner and group of the file. It also requires that the file not be Read-Only. Each of latter are conditions that "`errno`" will be set to in the event of a failure to change the file's owner/group.

The function returns a 0 if successful or a -1 if not. If the conversion is unsuccessful, then the variable "errno" will be set appropriately.

Risk: The chown function is susceptible to multiple race condition attacks whereas an attacker could attempt to modify the permissions of a file multiple times simultaneously. In addition to the race condition attacks, the chown function should only be executed on files from a local perspective due to the sensitive nature of the information required. If the application is designed to be run in a distributed matter, it is pertinent that you encrypt all session data between the systems communicating, since filenames and permissions are both included.

Additional Resources: www.gnu.org/software/libc/manual/html_node/File-Owner.html#File%20Owner

Impact: High

Cross References: chmod, chroot, fopen, fclose

chroot

Prototype: int chroot (const char *Path)

Summary: This function causes a user-given directory to be treated as root.

Description: The function attempts to "reassign" the root directory to a different path. The function only takes in the path to the new "root" directory. If successful, the function will have made the string passed to it the "effective" root directory. The function returns a zero upon successful completion. In the event of an error, the function returns a -1 and sets the variable "errno" to the appropriate value.

Risk: The chroot function is susceptible to race condition attacks thereby you must ensure that only one instance of this function can be called at any given point in time. Additionally, the chroot function is commonly targeted by attackers to see if they can change the root directory of a target server to that of an Internet-accessible directory. Internet accessible directories would include /public, /incoming, /ftp/public, etc. It is critical that you verify that users do not have direct access to the parameters taken by this function.

Additional Resources:
http://nscp.upenn.edu/aix4.3html/libs/basetrf1/chroot.htm

Impact: High

Cross References: `chdir`

CoImpersonateClient

Prototype: `HRESULT CoImpersonateClient(void)`

Summary: This function allows a server to impersonate a client for a time.

Description: The function attempts to let the server impersonate a client for the time of function call. The function does not require any input values. The return values, on the other hand, are simple, preset values to indicate success and failure.

Risk: The following impersonate function can be utilized by an attacker if they have direct access to the application and wish to simulate an attack on a third party application. Verify that the function is called by an internal system routine and that the output is contained within the application and not easily accessible by the end user.

Note: At time of publication, this function was designed for Windows compatibility.

Additional Resources:
http://msdn.microsoft.com/library/default.asp?url=/library/en-us/com/htm/cmf_a2c_6mwk.asp

Impact: Low

Cross References: `ImpersonateDdeClientWindow`, `ImpersonateLoggedOnUser`, `ImpersonateNamedPipeClient`, `ImpersonateSecurityContext`

CopyMemory

Prototype: `void CopyMemory( void* destination, const void* source, size_t size )`

Summary: This function copies one patch of memory to another.

Description: The purpose of the function's is to copy a band of memory to another. It takes three inputs: the pointer for the source of the copying, the pointer to the destination, and the size of the band to copy. The function starts at the beginning of the source, traversing and copying the memory to the destination for the given size. The function does not return any values.

Risk: The `CopyMemory` function can facilitate a buffer overflow attack where an attacker would attempt to send more data to the destination buffer than was allocated. Buffer overflow attacks are some of the more dangerous and popular attacks against static C and C++ applications. For this function, ensure that users can not directly input data into the source or destination buffer while also ensuring that the proper space is allocated for each memory slot.

Note: At time of publication, this function was designed for Windows compatibility.

Additional Resources:
http://msdn.microsoft.com/library/default.asp?url=/library/en-us/memory/base/copymemory.asp

Impact: Medium

Cross References: `FillMemory`, `MoveMemory`, `SecureZeroMemory`, `ZeroMemory`

CreateProcess

Prototype: `BOOL CreateProcess(LPCTSTR lpApplicationName, LPTSTR lpCommandLine, LPSECURITY_ATTRIBUTES lpProcessAttributes, LPSECURITY_ATTRIBUTES lpThreadAttributes, BOOL bInheritHandles, DWORD dwCreationFlags, LPVOID lpEnvironment, LPCTSTR lpCurrentDirectory, LPSTARTUPINFO lpStartupInfo, LPPROCESS_INFORMATION lpProcessInformation)`

Summary: This function creates a new process and its primary thread.

Description: The function creates a new process and primary thread. The function has ten input variables: the application name, the command line, process and thread attributes, a few checks and balances, a pointer to the environmental block, the current directory, a structure containing the startup info, and a structure for keeping process information. The function only returns a Boolean variable indicating success or failure.

Risk: `CreateProcess` can be leveraged in an attack in multiple ways and is especially common in launching Denial-of-Service attacks against the underlying operating system. Thus, you should deny human users from accessing or launching this function or from controlling any type of execution for this function. Additionally, you should close all processes as soon as their execution logic is complete while being aware that it is extremely risky to ever launch a subprocess within an overarching process.

Note: At time of publication, this function was written for Windows compatibility.

Additional Resources:
http://msdn.microsoft.com/library/default.asp?url=/library/en-us/dllproc/base/createprocess.asp

Impact: Low

Cross References: `CreateProcessAsUser`, `CreateProcessWithLogin`

CreateProcessAsUser

Prototype: `BOOL CreateProcessAsUser(HANDLE hToken, LPCTSTR lpApplicationName, LPTSTR lpCommandLine, LPSECURITY_ATTRIBUTES lpProcessAttributes, LPSECURITY_ATTRIBUTES lpThreadAttributes, BOOL bInheritHandles, DWORD dwCreationFlags, LPVOID lpEnvironment, LPCTSTR lpCurrentDirectory, LPSTARTUPINFO lpStartupInfo, LPPROCESS_INFORMATION lpProcessInformation`

Summary: This function creates a new process and its primary thread.

Description: The function creates a new process and primary thread, though under the ownership of a given user. The function has 11 input variables: the handle the indicates the primary user, the application name, the command line, process and thread attributes, a few checks and balances, a pointer to the environmental block, the current directory, a structure containing the startup info, and a structure for keeping process information. The function only returns a Boolean variable indicating success or failure.

Risk: CreateProcessAsUser can be leveraged in an attack in multiple ways and is especially common in launching Denial-of-Service attacks against the underlying operating system. Deny human users from accessing or launching this function or from controlling any type of execution for this function. Additionally, you should close all processes as soon as their execution logic is complete while being aware that it is extremely risky to ever launch a subprocess within an over-arching process.

Note: At time of publication, this function was written for Windows compatibility.

Additional Resources:

http://msdn.microsoft.com/library/default.asp?url=/library/en-us/dllproc/base/createprocessasuser.asp

Impact: Low

Cross References: CreateProcess, CreateProcessWithLogin

CreateProcessWithLogonW

Prototype: BOOL CreateProcessWithLogonW(LPCWSTR lpUsername, LPCWSTR lpDomain, LPCWSTR lpPassword, DWORD dwLogonFlags, LPCWSTR lpApplicationName, LPWSTR lpCommandLine, DWORD dwCreationFlags, LPVOID lpEnvironment, LPCWSTR lpCurrentDirectory, LPSTARTUPINFOW lpStartupInfo, LPPROCESS_INFORMATION lpProcessInfo)

Summary: This function creates a new process and its primary thread.

Description: The function creates a new process and primary thread. The function has eleven input variables: strings containing the username, domain and password for login, a flag for the login, the application name, the command line, a few checks and balances, a pointer to the environmental block, the current directory, a structure containing the startup info, and a structure for keeping process information. The function only returns a Boolean variable indicating success or failure.

Risk: `CreateProcessWithLogonW` can be leveraged in an attack in multiple ways and is especially common in launching Denial-of-Service attacks against the underlying operating system. Thus, you should deny human users from accessing or launching this function or from controlling any type of execution for this function. Additionally, you should close all processes as soon as their execution logic is complete while being aware that it is extremely risky to ever launch a subprocess within an over-arching process.

Note: At time of publication, this function was written for Windows compatibility.

Additional Resources:
http://msdn.microsoft.com/library/default.asp?url=/library/en-us/dllproc/base/createprocesswithlogonw.asp

Impact: Low

Cross References: `CreateProcess, CreateProcessAsUser`

cuserid

Prototype: `char * cuserid (char *string)`

Summary: This function is used to retrieve the user ID of the owner of a process.

Description: The function is used to get the user ID of the owner of a process. It takes in only one input, the pointer (possibly NULL) to where the string containing the user ID is to be stored. It returns the same pointer after having put the user ID there.

Risk: The `cuserid` function ascertains the ID owner of a process without verifying the validity of that process. It is possible for an attacker to easily forge this process ID with that of another owner which may lead to a further compromise of the application later down the line. It is recommended that this function not be utilized at all.

Note: This function is becoming obsolete and being phased out of several environments.

Additional Resources: www.gnu.org/software/libc/manual/html_node/Who-Logged-In.html#Who%20Logged%20In

Impact: Medium

Cross References: `getlogin`

dirname

Prototype: `char * dirname (char *path)`

Summary: This function is used to retrieve the parent directory of a file.

Description: The function is used to acquire the parent directory of a file. It takes in only one input, the string containing the path of a file. The function returns another string, this one containing the name of the parent directory to the file in question. If the path name is NULL, empty, or does not contain any slashes, then the function returns a single period ("").

Risk: As with any function that is utilized to ascertain system-level information, `dirname` is susceptible to a race condition attack. The race condition attack could occur if two instances of this function are launched simultaneously. In addition to this type of attack, it is recommended that you control the data that is passed to this function as it may be susceptible to directory traversal attacks such as the ../../../ attack. Ensure that only the parent directory is viewable and that wildcards are stripped from all input datastreams.

Additional Resources: www.gnu.org/software/libc/manual/html_node/Finding-Tokens-in-a-String.html#Finding%20Tokens%20in%20a%20String

Impact: Low

Cross References: `basename`

drand48

Prototype: `double drand48 (void)`

Summary: This function produces a random number.

Description: The function produces a random number between 0 and 1. It produces a double-precision number. However, since a 64-bit, double precision number is a 1-11-52 bit breakdown, this function only uses 48 of the 52 possible bits for the non-exponential part of the number. The remaining four bits are taken to be 0 and are the last bits of memory (i.e., the least significant).

Risk: As with most standard random functions implemented within the C and C++ libraries, this function is susceptible to bruteforce or easily guessed number generating attacks due to a poor seed algorithm within the backend code. Amongst numerous other secure random number generating functions, Microsoft .Net has secure methods for implementing properly seeded numbers. ISAAC, designed by Bob Jenkins, is a fast cryptographic random number generator is as strong as they come. Available in multiple languages, ISAAC is a standard for many freeware and commercial solutions and should be considered the next time a random number is required within an application.

Additional Resources: www.gnu.org/software/libc/manual/html_node/SVID-Random.html#SVID%20Random, www.burtleburtle.net/bob/rand/isaacafa.html

Impact: Medium

Cross References: `erand48`, `jrand48`, `lrand48`, `mrand48`, `nrand48`, `seed48`, `srand48`

EnterCriticalSection

Prototype: `void EnterCriticalSection( LPCRITICAL_SECTION lpCriticalSection )`

Summary: This function awaits the ownership of a critical section object.

Description: The function waits for ownership of a critical section object. It has only single input argument: a pointer to the critical section object. The function call ends when the ownership is transferred. The function does not return a value.

Risk: In most cases, direct human user input is passed to this function when it is called. Restrict the input to that of the expected character base and disallow all unauthorized users from potentially ascertaining ownership of the object.

Note: At time of publication, this function was designed for Windows compatibility.

Cross References: InititalizeCriticalSection

Additional Resources:

http://msdn.microsoft.com/library/default.asp?url=/library/en-us/dllproc/base/entercriticalsection.asp

Impact: Low

Cross References: InititalizeCriticalSection

erand48

Prototype: double erand48 (unsigned short int xsubi[3])

Summary: This function produces a random number.

Description: This function also returns a random number between 0 and 1. It follows much of the same ideas of the "standard" function "drand48". However, this function can be passed an array with the description of the random number generator (RNG) state. This ability is useful when wishing to seed the RNG or use it to reproduce results.

Risk: As with most standard random functions implemented within the C and C++ libraries, this function is susceptible to bruteforce or easily guessed number generating attacks due to a poor seed algorithm within the backend code. Amongst numerous other secure random number generating functions, Microsoft .Net has secure methods for implementing properly seeded numbers. ISAAC, designed by Bob Jenkins, is a fast cryptographic random number generator is as strong as they come. Available in multiple languages, ISAAC is a standard for many freeware and commercial solutions and should be considered the next time a random number is required within an application.

Additional Resources: www.burtleburtle.net/bob/rand/isaacafa.html, www.gnu.org/software/libc/manual/html_node/SVID-Random.html#SVID%20Random

Impact: Medium

Cross References: drand48, jrand48, lrand48, mrand48, nrand48, seed48, srand48

execl

Prototype: `int execl (const char *filename, const char *arg0, )`

Summary: This function is used to execute a command.

Description: The function will execute a file pointed to by the argument "filename" which contains the path to file to be executed. The other input arguments (`arg0, arg1, …, argN`) are command line parameters to be used in the execution of the file. Ideally, the function does not return a value, as it does not return to the calling process.

Risk: This function has the ability to execute a file on the local system. Attackers commonly target functions similar to this since they have the ability to launch potentially dangerous or malicious executables with differing privileges. It is imperative that you filter all input and never allow a user direct access to passing variables as the parameters for this function. Ensure that all special characters are stripped before the data is parsed and passed in addition to limiting access to only the desired executables. Lastly, require that all executable output is controlled within a forked or spawned process within the local application to ensure the integrity of the outputted data. If possible, avoid calling dynamic programs from within applications. Static program execution is more secure.

Additional Resources:
www.gnu.org/software/libc/manual/html_node/Executing-a-File.html#Executing%20a%20File

Impact: High

Cross References: `execle, execlp, execv, execve, execvp`

execle

Prototype: `int execle ( const char *cmdname, const char *arg0, const char *argn, NULL, const char *const *envp )`

Summary: This function executes a file with control given over the environmental parameters.

Description: The function will execute a file pointed to by the argument "cmd-name" which contains the path to file to be executed. The second set of input arguments (arg0, arg1, ..., argN) are command line parameters to be used in the execution of the file. The final input argument is the array of pointers to environmental parameters needed for file execution. Like _execl, the function does not return a value unless an error occurs, as it does not return to the calling process. However, upon an error, a value of –1 is returned and the global variable ERRNO is set.

Risk: This function has the ability to execute a file on the local system. Attackers commonly target functions similar to this since they have the ability to launch potentially dangerous or malicious executables with differing privileges. It is imperative that you filter all input and never allow a user direct access to passing variables as the parameters for this function. Ensure that all special characters are stripped before the data is parsed and passed in addition to limiting access to only the desired executables. Lastly, require that all executable output is controlled within a forked or spawned process within the local application to ensure the integrity of the outputted data. If possible, avoid calling dynamic programs from within applications. Static program execution is more secure.

Additional Resources:

www.gnu.org/software/libc/manual/html_node/Executing-a-File.html#Executing%20a%20File

Impact: High

Cross References: execl, execlp, execv, execve, execvp

execlp

Prototype: `int execlp( const char *cmdname, const char *arg0, const char *argn, NULL )`

Summary: This function executes a file from within the current shell, searching for it from the PATH environment variable.

Description: The function will execute a file pointed to by the argument "cmd-name" searching in the system's PATH for the file. The other input arguments (arg0, arg1, ..., argN) are command line parameters to be used in the execution of the file. Ideally, the function does not return a value, as it does not return to the calling process. However, upon an error, a value of -1 is returned and the global variable ERRNO is set.

Risk: This function has the ability to execute a file on the local system. Attackers commonly target functions similar to this since they have the ability to launch potentially dangerous or malicious executables with differing privileges. It is imperative that you filter all input and never allow a user direct access to passing variables as the parameters for this function. Ensure that all special characters are stripped before the data is parsed and passed in addition to limiting access to only the desired executables. Lastly, require that all executable output is controlled within a forked or spawned process within the local application to ensure the integrity of the outputted data. If possible, avoid calling dynamic programs from within applications. Static program execution is more secure.

Additional Resources:
www.gnu.org/software/libc/manual/html_node/Executing-a-File.html#Executing%20a%20File

Impact: High

Cross References: execl, execle, execv, execve, execvp

execv

Prototype: int execv(const char *cmdname, const char *const *argv)

Summary: This function executes a file with an array of pointers to be passed to the command line.

Description: The function will execute a file pointed to by the argument "cmdname" which contains the path to file to be executed. The other input argument, "argv" is an array command line parameters to be used in the execution of the file. Ideally, the function does not return a value, as it does not return to the calling process. However, upon an error, a value of -1 is returned and the global variable ERRNO is set.

Risk: This function has the ability to execute a file on the local system. Attackers commonly target functions similar to this since they have the ability to launch potentially dangerous or malicious executables with differing privileges. It is imperative that you filter all input and never allow a user direct access to passing variables as the parameters for this function. Ensure that all special characters are stripped before the data is parsed and passed in addition to limiting access to only the desired executables. Lastly, require that all executable output is controlled within a forked or spawned process within the local application to ensure the integrity of the outputted data. If possible, avoid calling dynamic programs from within applications. Static program execution is more secure.

Additional Resources:

www.gnu.org/software/libc/manual/html_node/Executing-a-File.html#Executing%20a%20File

Impact: Medium

Cross References: `exec1`, `execle`, `execlp`, `execve`, `execvp`

execve

Prototype: `int execve( const char *cmdname, const char *const *argv, const char *const *envp )`

Summary: This function executes a file with an array of pointers to be passed to the command line, keeping control over the environmental parameters.

Description: The function will execute a file pointed to by the argument "`cmd-name`" which contains the path to file to be executed. The next input argument, "`argv`", is an array command line parameters to be used in the execution of the file. The final input argument is an array of environmental parameters for file execution. Ideally, the function does not return a value, as it does not return to the calling process. However, upon an error, a value of `-1` is returned and the global variable ERRNO is set.

Risk: This function has the ability to execute a file on the local system. Attackers commonly target functions similar to this since they have the ability to launch potentially dangerous or malicious executables with differing privileges. It is imperative that you filter all input and never allow a user direct access to passing variables as the parameters for this function. Ensure that all special characters are stripped before the data is parsed and passed in addition to limiting access to only the desired executables. Lastly, require that all executable output is controlled within a forked or spawned process within the local application to ensure the integrity of the outputted data. If possible, avoid calling dynamic programs from within applications. Static program execution is more secure.

Additional Resources:
www.gnu.org/software/libc/manual/html_node/Executing-a-File.html#Executing%20a%20File

Impact: Medium

Cross References: execl, execle, execlp, execv, execvp

execvp

Prototype: int execvp(const char *cmdname, const char *const *argv)

Summary: This function executes a file with an array of pointers to be passed to the command line using the environment variable PATH to find the file.

Description: The function will execute a file pointed to by the argument "cmdname" searching for it using the environmental variable PATH. The other input argument, "argv", is an array command line parameters to be used in the execution of the file. Ideally, the function does not return a value, as it does not return to the calling process. However, upon an error, a value of -1 is returned and the global variable ERRNO is set.

Risk: This function has the ability to execute a file on the local system. Attackers commonly target functions similar to this since they have the ability to launch potentially dangerous or malicious executables with differing privileges. It is imperative that you filter all input and never allow a user direct access to passing variables as the parameters for this function. Ensure that all special characters are stripped before the data is parsed and passed in addition to limiting access to only the desired executables. Lastly, require that all executable output is controlled within a forked or spawned process within the local application to ensure the integrity of the outputted

data. If possible, avoid calling dynamic programs from within applications. Static program execution is more secure.

Additional Resources:

www.gnu.org/software/libc/manual/html_node/Executing-a-File.html#Executing%20a%20File

Impact: Medium

Cross References: `exec1, execle, execlp, execv, execve`

fgetc

Prototype: `int fgetc (FILE *stream)`

Summary: This function retrieves a character from a filestream.

Description: This function reads the next character in a filestream, returning it as an integer. The only input variable is the pointer to the filestream. The only output is the integer version of the character read. The function will increment the filestream during the read, and if it attempts to read the end of file, it will return EOF.

Risk: The `fgetc` function is susceptible to buffer overflow attacks where the filestream has malicious characters that could overwrite the allocated memory. Developers should validate all user input and ensure that malicious data is controlled within the internal `fgetc` buffer.

Additional Resources:

www.gnu.org/software/libc/manual/html_node/Character-Input.html#Character%20Input;
http://msdn.microsoft.com/library/default.asp?url=/library/en-us/vccore98/html/_crt_fgetc.2c_.fgetwc.2c_._fgetchar.2c_._fgetwchar.asp

Impact: Low

Cross References: `fputc, getc`

fgets

Prototype: `char * fgets (char *string, int count, FILE *stream)`

Summary: This function reads a string from a filestream.

Description: The function attempts to retrieve a string from a given filestream. It has three inputs, the string to the hold the incoming data, the size of our string, and the filestream to read our data from. The size of the string should be set according to the fact that a null character will be added to the end. The function will read new line characters, but not null characters. It will append a null character at the end. The function returns the string read from the filestream.

Risk: The `fgets` function is susceptible to buffer overflow attacks where the filestream has malicious characters that could overwrite the allocated memory. Developers should validate all user input and ensure that malicious data is controlled within the internal `fgets` buffer. Because the function reads in streams of strings (a.k.a., arrays of characters) it is mandatory to ensure that the strings are of expected length.

Additional Resources: www.gnu.org/software/libc/manual/html_node/Line-Input.html#Line%20Input;
http://msdn.microsoft.com/library/default.asp?url=/library/en-us/vccore98/html/_crt_fgets.2c_.fgetws.asp

Impact: Low

Cross References: `fputs`, `gets`, `puts`

fopen

Prototype: `FILE *fopen( const char *filename, const char *mode )`

Summary: This function opens a file for processing.

Description: This function attempts to open a file for processing by the program. It has two input arguments (both constant). They are the filename (and/or path to the file) and the mode in which to open it. The function will return a pointer (or handle) to the file if successful. However, in the event of an error, the function will return a NULL pointer.

Risk: All special and wildcard characters should be removed before the filename is computed on the local filesystem. Malicious filenames are interpreted differently on varying systems and as such, directory control is critical to limiting the ability of an attacker to potentially compromise files at varying levels within the application or underlying subsystem.

Additional Resources: www.gnu.org/software/libc/manual/html_node/Opening-Streams.html#Opening%20Streams;
http://msdn.microsoft.com/library/default.asp?url=/library/en-us/vccore98/HTML/_crt_fopen.2c_._wfopen.asp

Impact: Medium

Cross References: `fclose, freopen, open`

fork

Prototype: `pid_t fork (void)`

Summary: This function creates a new process.

Description: This attempts to open a new process for the program to manipulate. The function does not take in any input variables. The only return variable for the function is the process ID. If successful, the function returns a `0` to the child process and the aforementioned process ID to the parent. However, if unsuccessful, the function returns a `-1` to the parent process.

Risk: `Fork` can be leveraged in an attack in multiple ways and is especially common in launching Denial-of-Service attacks against the underlying operating system. Thus, you should deny human users from accessing or launching this function or from controlling any type of execution for this function. Additionally, you should close all processes as soon as their execution logic is complete while being aware that it is extremely risky to ever launch a subprocess within an over-arching process.

Additional Resources: www.gnu.org/software/libc/manual/html_node/Creating-a-Process.html#Creating%20a%20Process

Impact: Low

Cross References: vfork

fprintf

Prototype: int fprintf(FILE *stream, const char *format [, argument]...)

Summary: This function prints a string to a file stream.

Description: This function attempts to print a string to a filestream. It has two format input arguments. The first is the filestream to be written to, while the second is the actual string to write. Informally, the function may have more arguments, as the string could have its own arguments due to formatting. The function returns the number of characters written to the stream. In the event of an error, the function returns a negative value.

Risk: This function is potentially vulnerable to a format string attack where an attacker could cause the application to crash unexpected or execute arbitrary code. Format string bugs were discovered in 2000 and the problem is typically spawned from user input that is not properly filtered. Both Microsoft .Net and SPI Dynamics to name two have secure objects that can be implemented to check strings and user input gained from human sources within applications to protect against input-directed vulnerabilities. It is critical that you verify the inputted data have only proper and expected characters in addition to ensuring that your function is properly called. For example, the functions should always utilize their parameters such as printf(""%s"", malicious_string) instead of printf(malicious_string).

Additional Resources:
www.gnu.org/software/libc/manual/html_node/Formatted-Output-Functions.html#Formatted%20Output%20Functions;
http://msdn.microsoft.com/library/default.asp?url=/library/en-us/vccore98/html/_crt_fprintf.2c_.fwprintf.asp

Impact: Low

Cross References: _cprintf, fscanf, sprintf

fread

Prototype: `size_t fread( void *buffer, size_t size, size_t count, FILE *stream )`

Summary: This function reads from a filestream into an array.

Description: This function attempts to read in data from a filestream into a general patch of memory. The incremental data size is given by the input variable "`size`". The function will read "`count`" number objects from the filestream into the array "`buffer`". The function will return the total number of bytes written to the stream upon completion.

Risk: All special and wildcard characters should be removed before the filename is computed on the local filesystem. Malicious filenames are interpreted differently on varying systems and as such, directory control is critical to limiting the ability of an attacker to potentially compromise files at varying levels within the application or underlying subsystem.

Additional Resources: www.gnu.org/software/libc/manual/html_node/Block-Input-Output.html#Block%20Input%2fOutput; http://msdn.microsoft.com/library/default.asp?url=/library/en-us/vccore98/html/_crt_fread.asp

Impact: Low

freopen

Prototype: `FILE *freopen( const char *filename, const char *mode, FILE *stream )`

Summary: This function reassigns an open filestream to a different file.

Description: The function attempts to reassign an open/active filestream to a different file. There are three input arguments: the path to the new file, the processing mode (read, write, etc...), and the filestream to reassign. The function returns only one value, the new reassigned filestream. In the event of an error, the original filestream is closed and the function returns a NULL pointer.

Risk: The following function can be redirected to target an additional file where potentially sensitive information could be stored. Restrict human data from being passed to this function in addition to restricting (or static coding if possible) the destination filename and location.

Additional Resources: www.gnu.org/software/libc/manual/html_node/Opening-Streams.html#Opening%20Streams; http://msdn.microsoft.com/library/default.asp?url=/library/en-us/vccore98/html/_crt_freopen.2c_._wfreopen.asp

Impact: Low

Cross References: `fclose`, `fopen`, `open`

fscanf

Prototype: `int fscanf( FILE *stream, const char *format [, argument ]... )`

Summary: This function reads preformatted data from a filestream.

Description: This function attempts to read formatted data from given filestream. The function has two formal arguments: the filestream and the string, which will house the new data read into it. The function may have informal arguments due to the formatting of the data, and the requisite arguments needed for compiler clarification in the string. The function will return the number of characters read. However, in the event of an error, it will return a negative number.

Risk: This function is potentially vulnerable to a format string attack where an attacker could cause the application to crash unexpected or execute arbitrary code. Format string bugs were discovered in 2000 and the problem is typically spawned from user input that is not properly filtered. Both Microsoft .Net and SPI Dynamics to name two have secure objects that can be implemented to check strings and user input gained from human sources within applications to protect against input-directed vulnerabilities. It is critical that you verify the inputted data have only proper and expected characters in addition to ensuring that your function is properly called. For example, the functions should always utilize their parameters such as `printf("%s", malicious_string)` instead of `printf(malicious_string)`.

Additional Resources:

www.gnu.org/software/libc/manual/html_node/Formatted-Input-Functions.html#Formatted%20Input%20Functions;
http://msdn.microsoft.com/library/default.asp?url=/library/en-us/vccore98/html/_crt_fscanf.2c_.fwscanf.asp

Impact: Medium

Cross References: `_cscanf`, `fprintf`, `scanf`, `sscanf`

fwprintf

Prototype: `int fwprintf (FILE *stream, const wchar_t *format, ...)`

Summary: This function prints a wide-character string to a filestream.

Description: This function attempts to print a string to a filestream. It has two format input arguments. The first is the filestream to be written to, while the second is the actual wide-character string to write. Informally, the function may have more arguments, as the string could have its own arguments due to formatting. The function returns the number of characters written to the stream. In the event of an error, the function returns a negative value.

Risk: This function is potentially vulnerable to a format string attack where an attacker could cause the application to crash unexpected or execute arbitrary code. Format string bugs were discovered in 2000 and the problem is typically spawned from user input that is not properly filtered. Both Microsoft .Net and SPI Dynamics to name two have secure objects that can be implemented to check strings and user input gained from human sources within applications to protect against input-directed vulnerabilities. It is critical that you verify the inputted data have only proper and expected characters in addition to ensuring that your function is properly called. For example, the functions should always utilize their parameters such as `printf("%s", malicious_string)` instead of `printf(malicious_string)`.

Note: This function is practically identical to "`fprintf`" with the exception of using wide-character strings.

Additional Resources:
www.gnu.org/software/libc/manual/html_node/Formatted-Output-
Functions.html#Formatted%20Output%20Functions;
http://msdn.microsoft.com/library/default.asp?url=/library/en-
us/vccore98/html/_crt_fprintf.2c_.fwprintf.asp

Impact: Medium

Cross References: `_cprintf, fscanf, sprintf`

fwscanf

Prototype: `int fwscanf( FILE *stream, const wchar_t *format [, argument ]... )`

Summary: This function reads formatted data from a filestream into a wide-character string.

Description: This function attempts to read formatted data from given filestream. The function has two formal arguments: the filestream and the wide-character string which will house the new data read into it. The function may have informal arguments due to the formatting of the data, and the requisite arguments needed for compiler clarification in the string. The function will return the number of characters read. However, in the event of an error, it will return a negative number.

Risk: This function is potentially vulnerable to a format string attack where an attacker could cause the application to crash unexpected or execute arbitrary code. Format string bugs were discovered in 2000 and the problem is typically spawned from user input that is not properly filtered. Both Microsoft .Net and SPI Dynamics to name two have secure objects that can be implemented to check strings and user input gained from human sources within applications to protect against input-directed vulnerabilities. It is critical that you verify the inputted data have only proper and expected characters in addition to ensuring that your function is properly called. For example, the functions should always utilize their parameters such as `printf("%s", malicious_string)` instead of `printf(malicious_string)`.

Note: This function is practically identical to "`fscanf`" with the exception of using wide-character strings.

Additional Resources:

www.gnu.org/software/libc/manual/html_node/Formatted-Input-Functions.html#Formatted%20Input%20Functions;
http://msdn.microsoft.com/library/default.asp?url=/library/en-us/vccore98/html/_crt_fscanf.2c_.fwscanf.asp

Impact: Medium

Cross References: `_cscanf`, `fprintf`, `scanf`, `sscanf`

getc

Prototype: `int getc( FILE *stream )`

Summary: This function reads a character from a filestream.

Description: The function attempts to read a character from an open filestream. The function has only one input: the open filestream. Upon reading the next character in the stream, it prompts the stream to read the next character. The function returns only one value, the integer representation of the character read. However, in the event of a failure or the end of the stream, the function will return the EOF indicator.

Risk: The `getc` function is susceptible to buffer overflow attacks where the filestream has malicious characters that could overwrite the allocated memory. Developers should validate all user input and ensure that malicious data is controlled within the internal `getc` buffer.

Additional Resources:

www.gnu.org/software/libc/manual/html_node/Character-Input.html#Character%20Input;
http://msdn.microsoft.com/library/default.asp?url=/library/en-us/vccore98/html/_crt_getc.2c_.getwc.2c_.getchar.2c_.getwchar.asp

Impact: Low

Cross References: `fgetc`, `_getch`, `putc`, `ungetc`

getchar

Prototype: `int getchar (void)`

Summary: This function retrieves a character from the "stdin" filestream.

Description: The function attempts to retrieve a character from the "stdin" filestream. The function is identical to "getc" with the exception that it uses "stdin" as the filestream. Accordingly, the function does not have any input variables. The function does return a value, the integer representation of the character retrieved. To check for an error, however, the functions "ferror" or "feof" must be used.

Risk: The `getc` function is susceptible to buffer overflow attacks where the filestream has malicious characters that could overwrite the allocated memory. Developers should validate all user input and ensure that malicious data is controlled within the internal getc buffer.

Additional Resources:
www.gnu.org/software/libc/manual/html_node/Character-Input.html#Character%20Input;
http://msdn.microsoft.com/library/default.asp?url=/library/en-us/vccore98/html/_crt_getc.2c_.getwc.2c_.getchar.2c_.getwchar.asp

Impact: Low

Cross References: `fgetc`, `_getch`, `putc`, `ungetc`

getenv

Prototype: `char *getenv( const char *varname )`

Summary: This function gets a value for an environment variable.

Description: The function attempts to retrieve the value for an environment variable. The function has only one input, the name of the variable. The function will return the value of the variable as a string. If the function cannot find the environment variable, it will return NULL.

Risk: This function handles system-specific sensitive information that an attacker could leverage during a period of target reconnaissance. This function should only

be utilized if it is absolutely necessary for proper execution of the application. All analysis for the output of this function should be conducted securely within the application and never sent across the wire in cleartext.

Additional Resources:

www.gnu.org/software/libc/manual/html_node/Environment-Access.html#Environment%20Access;

http://msdn.microsoft.com/library/default.asp?url=/library/en-us/vccore98/html/_crt_getenv.2c_._wgetenv.asp

Impact: Medium

Cross References: `clearenv`, `putenv`, `setenv`, `unsetenv`

GetExtensionVersion

Prototype: `virtual BOOL GetExtensionVersion( HSE_VERSION_INFO *pVer )`

Summary: This function gets the version information for a server.

Description: This function attempts to get the server's version information. It takes in a pointer to a HSE_VERSION_INFO structure, allowing the user to modify the contents. The function will return a non-zero value if it is successful, and zero if it fails. The information retrieved will be available in the structure upon successful completion.

Risk: This function handles system-specific sensitive information that an attacker could leverage during a period of target reconnaissance. This function should only be utilized if it is absolutely necessary for proper execution of the application. All analysis for the output of this function should be conducted securely within the application and never sent across the wire in cleartext.

Additional Resources:

http://msdn.microsoft.com/library/default.asp?url=/library/en-us/vcmfc98/html/_mfc_chttpserver.3a3a.getextensionversion.asp

Impact: Medium

gethostbyaddr

Prototype: `struct hostent * gethostbyaddr (const char *addr, size_t length, int format`

Summary: This function gets an Internet host's information by the address.

Description: The function attempts to get the host information at a given address. The function takes three inputs: the host address, the size of the address, and the format of the address. The function will return a "hostent" structure, containing the desired information. However, in the event of an error, the function will return a null pointer. It will also appropriately set the value "h_errno".

Risk: This function handles system-specific sensitive information that an attacker could leverage during a period of target reconnaissance. This function should only be utilized if it is absolutely necessary for proper execution of the application. All analysis for the output of this function should be conducted securely within the application and never sent across the wire in cleartext.

Additional Resources: www.gnu.org/software/libc/manual/html_node/Host-Names.html#Host%20Names

Impact: Low

Cross References: `gethostbyname`

getlogin

Prototype: `char * getlogin (void)`

Summary: This function retrieves the username of the person logged into the process's terminal.

Description: The function will attempt to get the username of the person logged into the terminal where the current process is running. It does not require any input arguments. The function will return a string containing the requested username if successful. If the username is unavailable or there is another error, the function will return a null pointer. Subsequent calls to this function will overwrite the previous call's string.

Risk: This function handles system-specific sensitive information that an attacker could leverage during a period of target reconnaissance. This function should only be utilized if it is absolutely necessary for proper execution of the application. All analysis for the output of this function should be conducted securely within the application and never sent across the wire in cleartext.

Additional Resources: www.gnu.org/software/libc/manual/html_node/Who-Logged-In.html#Who%20Logged%20In

Impact: High

Cross References: `cuserid`

getopt

Prototype: `int getopt (int argc, char **argv, const char *options)`

Summary: This function gets the next option argument from the "`argv`" and "`argc`" lists.

Description: The function attempts to retrieve the next option argument from the argument list "`argv`". The function has three input variables: the input count "`argc`" the argument list "`argv`" and the constant string "`options`". The input "`options`" is a string containing the characters that can be used for the program. The function returns only one value, the integer representation of the option character. The function will return `-1` if an error occurs or there are no more option arguments to read.

Risk: While in general command line attacks are much more seldom and have considerable less risk when compared to their remote code execution counterparts, it is common to see attackers attempt to pass atypically large strings into a program's logic via the command line options. Ensure that all command line options are restricted to alphanumeric characters and that the source data length is restricted to a number less than that of the destination buffer.

Additional Resources: www.gnu.org/software/libc/manual/html_node/Using-Getopt.html#Using%20Getopt

Impact: Low

Cross References: `getopt_long`

getopt_long

Prototype: `int getopt_long (int argc, char *const *argv, const char *shortopts, const struct option *longopts, int *ind-exptr)`

Summary: This function retrieves the option arguments from the argument list "`argv`".

Description: The function works similarly to "`getopt`". However, this function replaces the string of all option arguments with two separate strings: one for "`short`" arguments and one for "`long`" arguments. It also requires an index pointer to keep track of its position. The function will return value of the next option argument in "`argv`" unless it is at the end, when it will return a `-1`.

Risk: While in general command line attacks are much more seldom and have considerable less risk when compared to their remote code execution counterparts, it is common to see attackers attempt to pass atypically large strings into a program's logic via the command line options. Ensure that all command line options are restricted to alphanumeric characters and that the source data length is restricted to a number less than that of the destination buffer.

Additional Resources: www.gnu.org/software/libc/manual/html_node/Getopt-Long-Options.html#Getopt%20Long%20Options

Impact: Low

Cross References: `getopt`

getpass

Prototype: `char * getpass (const char *prompt)`

Summary: This function reads a password in from a terminal.

Description: The function attempts to read a password from the terminal. The input variable "`prompt`" is output to the screen, signaling the user to enter the password. The function reads the password and returns a string containing. There are several precautions made to protect the password during the read stage (no echoing of the terminal, flushed I/O, etc…). The function, if unsuccessful, will return a null pointer.

Risk: This function handles system-specific sensitive information that an attacker could leverage during a period of target reconnaissance. This function should only be utilized if it is absolutely necessary for proper execution of the application. All analysis for the output of this function should be conducted securely within the application and never sent across the wire in cleartext.

Note: This function may have different attributes depending on the system used. One possibility is that it will have a limit on the size of the password to read (and thus not retrieve all of it).

Additional Resources:

www.gnu.org/software/libc/manual/html_node/getpass.html#getpass

Impact: High

gets

Prototype: `char * gets (char *buffer)`

Summary: This function gets a string from the I/O stream.

Description: The function will attempt to read a string in from the I/O stream. The function has only one input argument, the location of where the new string will be held. The function will read the I/O stream up to the next new line argument. The function returns the string, as read from the stream.

Risk: The gets function is susceptible to buffer overflow attacks where the filestream has malicious characters that could overwrite the allocated memory. Developers should validate all user input and ensure that malicious data is controlled within the internal gets buffer. Because the function reads in streams of strings (a.k.a., arrays of characters) it is mandatory to ensure that the strings are of expected length.

Additional Resources: www.gnu.org/software/libc/manual/html_node/Line-Input.html#Line%20Input;

http://msdn.microsoft.com/library/default.asp?url=/library/en-us/vccore98/html/_crt_gets.2c_.getws.asp

Impact: Low

Cross References: `fgets`, `fputs`, `puts`

GetTempFileName

Prototype: `UINT GetTempFileName( LPCTSTR lpPathName, LPCTSTR lpPrefixString, UINT uUnique, LPTSTR lpTempFileName )`

Summary: This function creates a name for a temporary file.

Description: The function will attempt to create a temporary file to be use by the program. It takes in four input arguments: the path to where the file will be, the prefix for the file, a unique number to be used in file creation (after the prefix), and the handle for the file. The function returns only one value, the unique number to assigned after the prefix that was input. The function will return 0 in the event of an error.

Risk: Temporary filenames are often created with static and easily guessable algorithms such as the system time or application name appended with the day, month, and year. If at all possible, do not use this function and instead store temporary information in a secure memory space. If a temporary file is necessary, ensure that it is removed upon exiting the program or in the case where a program exits unexpectedly is removed upon program relaunch. Consider utilizing a random number generator such as ISAAC for creating secure random filenames.

Note: At the time of publication, this function was designed for Windows compatibility.

Additional Resources:
http://msdn.microsoft.com/library/default.asp?url=/library/en-us/fileio/base/gettempfilename.asp

Impact: Low

Cross References: `GetTempFileNameA`, `GetTempFileNameW`, `GetTempPath`

GetTempFileNameW

Prototype: `UINT GetTempFileNameW( LPCTSTR lpPathName, LPCTSTR lpPrefixString, UINT uUnique, LPTSTR lpTempFileName )`

Summary: This function creates a name for a temporary file.

Description: The function will attempt to create a temporary file to be use by the program. It takes in four input arguments: the path to where the file will be, the prefix for the file, a unique number to be used in file creation (after the prefix), and the handle for the file. The function returns only one value, the unique number to assigned after the prefix that was input. The function will return 0 in the event of an error.

Risk: Temporary filenames are often created with static and easily guessable algorithms such as the system time or application name appended with the day, month, and year. If at all possible, do not use this function and instead store temporary information in a secure memory space. If a temporary file is necessary, ensure that it is removed upon exiting the program or in the case where a program exits unexpectedly is removed upon program relaunch. Consider utilizing a random number generator such as ISAAC for creating secure random filenames.

Note: At the time of publication, this function was designed for Windows compatibility. This particular function is from the Windows Layer for Unicode and requires additional files to be used in Win 95/98/Me.

Additional Resources:

http://msdn.microsoft.com/library/default.asp?url=/library/en-us/fileio/base/get-tempfilename.asp

Impact: Low

Cross References: `GetTempFileName, GetTempFileNameA, GetTempPath`

GetTempPath

Prototype: `DWORD GetTempPath( DWORD nBufferLength, LPTSTR lpBuffer )`

Summary: This function gets the path for the directory where temporary files are stored.

Description: The function attempts to retrieve the path to where temporary files are stored. It has two input variables: the length of the t-char string used to store the path and the actual pointer to the string. The function returns the number of t-char's copied to the buffer. The path will also include a trailing slash (for easy concatenation of the file name). In the event of an error, the function will return a 0.

Risk: This function handles system-specific sensitive information that an attacker could leverage during a period of target reconnaissance. This function should only be utilized if it is absolutely necessary for proper execution of the application. All analysis for the output of this function should be conducted securely within the application and never sent across the wire in cleartext.

Note: At the time of publication, this function was designed for Windows compatibility.

Additional Resources:
http://msdn.microsoft.com/library/default.asp?url=/library/en-us/fileio/base/get-temppath.asp

Impact: Medium

Cross References: `GetTempFileName, GetTempPathA, GetTempPathW`

GetTempPathW

Prototype: `DWORD GetTempPathW( DWORD nBufferLength, LPTSTR lpBuffer ) C`

Summary: This function gets the path for the directory where temporary files are stored.

Description: The function attempts to retrieve the path to where temporary files are stored. It has two input variables: the length of the t-char string used to store the path and the actual pointer to the string. The function returns the number of t-char's copied to the buffer. The path will also include a trailing slash (for easy concatenation of the file name). In the event of an error, the function will return a 0.

Risk: This function handles system-specific sensitive information that an attacker could leverage during a period of target reconnaissance. This function should only be utilized if it is absolutely necessary for proper execution of the application. All analysis for the output of this function should be conducted securely within the application and never sent across the wire in cleartext.

Note: At the time of publication, this function was designed for Windows compatibility. This particular function is from the Windows Layer for Unicode and requires additional files to be used in Win 95/98/Me.

Additional Resources:

http://msdn.microsoft.com/library/default.asp?url=/library/en-us/fileio/base/get-temppath.asp

Impact: Medium

Cross References: `GetTempFileName, GetTempPath, GetTempPathA`

ImpersonateLoggedOnUser

Prototype: `BOOL ImpersonateLoggedOnUser(HANDLE hToken )C`

Summary: This function attempts to impersonate a logged-on user.

Description: This function attempts to impersonate the security context of a logged-on user. The function has only one input argument: the handle of the user to impersonate. The function will return a non-zero value if successful, a zero if not. The impersonation will last until the end of the current thread or the impersonation is overtly stopped.

Risk: Applications that have the ability to impersonate local systems, users, or security information are extremely dangerous; furthermore, functions that leverage this type of functionality should be controlled and only used as a last resort! All impersonation functions should be controlled by internal application-specific routines in addition to the controlled use of their output.

Note: At time of publication, this function was designed for Windows compatibility.

Additional Resources:

hhttp://msdn.microsoft.com/library/default.asp?url=/library/en-us/security/security/impersonateloggedonuser.asp

Impact: Medium

Cross References: `CoImpersonateClient`, `ImpersonateDdeClientWindow`, `ImpersonateNamedPipeClient`, `ImpersonateSecurityContext`

initstate

Prototype: `void * initstate (unsigned int seed, void *state, size_t size)`

Summary: This function initializes the random number generator state.

Description: The function attempts to initialize the random number generator (RNG) state. It has three input variables: the seed for the RNG, an empty pointer, and the size of the array that the pointer is associated with. The function will store the state of the RNG in the array, and thus should large enough to suffice. The function will return the pointer to the array upon completion.

Risk: The initialization for this weak random generator should be substituted with a more secure algorithm. As with most standard random functions implemented within the C and C++ libraries, this function is susceptible to bruteforce or easily guessed number generating attacks due to a poor seed algorithm within the backend code. Amongst numerous other secure random number generating functions, Microsoft .Net has secure methods for implementing properly seeded numbers. ISAAC, designed by Bob Jenkins, is a fast cryptographic random number generator is as strong as they come. Available in multiple languages, ISAAC is a standard for many freeware and commercial solutions and should be considered the next time a random number is required within an application.

Additional Resources: www.gnu.org/software/libc/manual/html_node/BSD-Random.html#BSD%20Random

Impact: Medium

Cross References: `random`, `setstate`, `srandom`

C

jrand48

Prototype: `long int jrand48 (unsigned short int xsubi[3])`

Summary: This function produces a random number.

Description: The function produces a random number between -2^31 and 2^31. It produces a long integer. The function takes in as an input variable the array containing the state of the random number generator.

Risk: As with most standard random functions implemented within the C and C++ libraries, this function is susceptible to bruteforce or easily guessed number generating attacks due to a poor seed algorithm within the backend code. Amongst numerous other secure random number generating functions, Microsoft .Net has secure methods for implementing properly seeded numbers. ISAAC, designed by Bob Jenkins, is a fast cryptographic random number generator is as strong as they come. Available in multiple languages, ISAAC is a standard for many freeware and commercial solutions and should be considered the next time a random number is required within an application.

Additional Resources: www.burtleburtle.net/bob/rand/isaacafa.html, www.gnu.org/software/libc/manual/html_node/SVID-Random.html#SVID%20Random

Impact: Medium

Cross References: `drand48`, `erand48`, `lrand48`, `mrand48`, `nrand48`, `seed48`, `srand48`

lchown

Prototype: `int lchown(const char *path, uid_t owner, gid_t group)`

Summary: This function changes the owner/group of a file or symbolic link.

Description: The function attempts to change the owner and or group associated with a file. If, in the event, the file is a symbolic link, it will change the ownership of the link. The function takes in three input arguments: the path to the file, the new owner, and the new group. The function will return a 0 if successful or a -1 if not. If the function is unsuccessful, then the variable "errno" will be set appropriately.

Risk: The ownership of a file or symbolic link should be restricted to that of pre-defined application logic or fully vetted human input. If human input is an option then it should be mandatory to ensure that only the appropriate users are options for switching ownership. For example, you would not want a malicious user to have the ability to change the ownership of a file to bad_user_joe.

Additional Resources: www.scit.wlv.ac.uk/cgi-bin/mansec?2+lchown

Impact: High

Cross References: chown

lcong48

Prototype: void lcong48 (unsigned short int param[7])

Summary: This function is used to change the complete state of the random number generator.

Description: The function changes the complete state of the random number generator. There is only one input argument for this function, and that is the array of parameters to be sent to the random number generator. The function does not return any values, and successful completion may be unknown.

Risk: As with most standard random functions implemented within the C and C++ libraries, this function is susceptible to bruteforce or easily guessed number generating attacks due to a poor seed algorithm within the backend code. Amongst numerous other secure random number generating functions, Microsoft .Net has secure methods for implementing properly seeded numbers. ISAAC, designed by Bob Jenkins, is a fast cryptographic random number generator is as strong as they come. Available in multiple languages, ISAAC is a standard for many freeware and commercial solutions and should be considered the next time a random number is required within an application.

Additional Resources: www.gnu.org/software/libc/manual/html_node/SVID-Random.html#SVID%20Random

Impact: High

Cross References: `seed48`

link

Prototype: `int link (const char *oldname, const char *newname)`

Summary: This function creates a symbolic link between an old and new file.

Description: The function attempts to create a symbolic link between an old file and a new name. The function takes two inputs: the string containing the path to the old file and a string for which the "new" file will be known. The function returns only a Boolean integer. If successful, the function returns 0. If not, the function will return a -1 and appropriately set "errno".

Risk: Characters used in the filenames should be restricted to the alphanumeric base or less depending on the underlying operating platform. Ensure that all links are removed before the program executes or are cleaned up before program execution, in the case where a program crashes or exits unexpectedly. The link function is commonly targeted in Denial-of-Service attacks attempting to consume all of the local CPU or memory resources.

Additional Resources: www.gnu.org/software/libc/manual/html_node/Hard-Links.html#Hard%20Links

Impact: Low

LoadLibrary

Prototype: `HMODULE LoadLibrary( LPCTSTR lpFileName )`

Summary: This function maps an executable module.

Description: The function attempts to map the calling process to an executable module. The function has only one input argument: a string containing the path to the executable file. The function will return a pointer to the address of the file. In the event of an error, the function will return a NULL pointer.

Risk: By default, the `LoadLibrary` function will search multiple locations for both DLL and EXE modules. When you utilize this function, it is imperative that you include the complete path to the desired module that you are implementing within your application. If the complete path is not specified and a default multi-path search is conducted then the potential for a malicious program to be executed is increased. For instance, if a Trojanized Microsoft DLL resides on a target system with the name included in the executed application then it may be possible for a remote user to launch that DLL through a vulnerable application.

Note: At time of publication, this function was written for Windows compatibility.

Additional Resources:
http://msdn.microsoft.com/library/default.asp?url=/library/en-us/dllproc/base/loadlibrary.asp

Impact: Medium

Cross References: `AfxLoadLibrary`, `FreeLibrary`

lstat

Prototype: `int lstat ( const char *filename, struct stat *buffer )`

Summary: This function reads the attributes of a file.

Description: The function attempts to read the attributes of a file. It has two input arguments: the path to a file and a pointer to a structure to house the file attributes. The function can not follow symbolic links, so if the file pointed to in the path is a symbolic link, the function will only return information on that particular file (not the one linked to). The function, if successful, will return 0. If unsuccessful, it will return a -1 and set "`errno`" appropriately.

Risk: As with most standard random functions implemented within the C and C++ libraries, this function is susceptible to bruteforce or easily guessed number generating attacks due to a poor seed algorithm within the backend code. Amongst numerous other secure random number generating functions, Microsoft .Net has secure methods for implementing properly seeded numbers. ISAAC, designed by Bob Jenkins, is a fast cryptographic random number generator is as strong as they come. Available in multiple languages, ISAAC is a standard for many freeware and

commercial solutions and should be considered the next time a random number is required within an application.

Additional Resources: www.gnu.org/software/libc/manual/html_node/Reading-Attributes.html#Reading%20Attributes

Impact: Low

Cross References: stat

lstrcat

Prototype: `LPTSTR lstrcat( LPTSTR destination, LPTSTR source )`

Summary: This function appends a string onto the end of another.

Description: The function attempts to copy one string onto the end of another. The function has two input arguments: the source and destination strings. When completed, the function will return the destination string. However, in the event of an error, the function will return NULL. One must be careful in using this function, as the destination string must be long enough hold all of the source string and the null character.

Risk: Functions that are utilized to copy or concatenate strings are commonly misused and fall victim to buffer overflow attacks. It is critical that you ensure before execution of this function that the destination source is large enough to house the source data. Additionally, limiting the source data memory space will not only make your application more efficient, it will also add another layer of security by relying less on the destination buffer. For example, if X should be copied to Y, then ensure that Y's space is less than X-1's total space allocation. It is similar for concatenation functions where as the strings are limited to a total length.

Note: At time of publication, this function was designed for Windows compatibility.

Additional Resources:

http://msdn.microsoft.com/library/default.asp?url=/library/en-us/winui/WinUI/WindowsUserInterface/Resources/Strings/StringReference/StringFunctions/lstrcat.asp

Impact: Low

Cross References: lstrcpy

lstrcpy

Prototype: LPTSTR lstrcpy(LPTSTR destination, LPTSTR source)

Summary: This function copies one string to another.

Description: The function attempts to copy one string to another. The function two input variables: the source and destination strings. The function will copy the source string to the destination, and return the destination string. The destination string must be long enough to hold the source string and the null character. In the event of failure, the function will return NULL.

Risk: Functions that are utilized to copy or concatenate strings are commonly misused and fall victim to buffer overflow attacks. It is critical that you ensure before execution of this function that the destination source is large enough to house the source data. Additionally, limiting the source data memory space will not only make your application more efficient, it will also add another layer of security by relying less on the destination buffer. For example, if X should be copied to Y, then ensure that Y's space is less than X-1's total space allocation. It is similar for concatenation functions where as the strings are limited to a total length.

Note: At time of publication, this function was designed for Windows compatibility.

Additional Resources:
http://msdn.microsoft.com/library/default.asp?url=/library/en-us/winui/WinUI/WindowsUserInterface/Resources/Strings/StringReference/StringFunctions/lstrcpy.asp

Impact: Medium

Cross References: lstrcat, lstrcpyn

lstrcpyA

Prototype: `static extern int lstrcpyA ( string destination, string source )`

Summary: This function copies one string to another.

Description: The function attempts to copy one string to another. The function two input variables: the source and destination strings. The function will copy the source string to the destination, and return the number of characters copied. The destination string must be long enough to hold the source string and the null character. In the event of failure, the function will return NULL.

Risk: Functions that are utilized to copy or concatenate strings are commonly misused and fall victim to buffer overflow attacks. It is critical that you ensure before execution of this function that the destination source is large enough to house the source data. Additionally, limiting the source data memory space will not only make your application more efficient, it will also add another layer of security by relying less on the destination buffer. For example, if X should be copied to Y, then ensure that Y's space is less than X-1's total space allocation. It is similar for concatenation functions where as the strings are limited to a total length.

Note: At time of publication, this function was designed for Windows compatibility.

Additional Resources: http://custom.programming-in.net/articles/art9-1.asp?f=lstrcpy

Impact: Medium

Cross References: `lstrcpy`

lstrcpynW

Prototype: `LPTSTR lstrcpynW( LPWSTR destination, LPCWSTR source, int count )`

Summary: This function copies one string to another.

Description: The function attempts to copy one wide-character string to another. The function three input variables: the source and destination wide-character strings and a maximum number of characters to copy. The function will copy the source string to the destination (stopping at "count"), and return the destination string. The destination string must be long enough to hold the source string and the null character. In the event of failure, the function will return NULL.

Risk: Functions that are utilized to copy or concatenate strings are commonly misused and fall victim to buffer overflow attacks. It is critical that you ensure before execution of this function that the destination source is large enough to house the source data. Additionally, limiting the source data memory space will not only make your application more efficient, it will also add another layer of security by relying less on the destination buffer. For example, if X should be copied to Y, then ensure that Y's space is less than X–1's total space allocation. It is similar for concatenation functions where as the strings are limited to a total length.

Note: At time of publication, this function was designed for Windows compatibility.

Additional Resources:
http://msdn.microsoft.com/archive/default.asp?url=/archive/en-us/dx81_c/directx_cpp/htm/lstrcpynw.asp

Impact: Medium

Cross References: `lstrcpy, lstrcpyn`

lstrcpyW

Prototype: `LPTSTR lstrcpyW( LPWSTR destination, LPCWSTR source )`

Summary: This function copies one string to another.

Description: The function attempts to copy one wide-character string to another. The function two input variables: the source and destination wide-character strings. The function will copy the source string to the destination), and return the destination string. The destination string must be long enough to hold the source string and the null character. In the event of failure, the function will return NULL.

Risk: Functions that are utilized to copy or concatenate strings are commonly misused and fall victim to buffer overflow attacks. It is critical that you ensure before execution of this function that the destination source is large enough to house the source data. Additionally, limiting the source data memory space will not only make your application more efficient, it will also add another layer of security by relying less on the destination buffer. For example, if X should be copied to Y, then ensure that Y's space is less than X-1's total space allocation. It is similar for concatenation functions where as the strings are limited to a total length.

Note: At time of publication, this function was designed for Windows compatibility.

Additional Resources:

http://msdn.microsoft.com/archive/default.asp?url=/archive/en-us/dx81_c/directx_cpp/htm/lstrcpyw.asp

Impact: Medium

Cross References: `lstrcpy, lstrcpy`

mkdir

Prototype: `int mkdir (const char *filename, mode_t mode)`

Summary: This function creates a directory.

Description: The function attempts to create a new, empty directory. It has two input arguments: the string containing the new directory name and the mode in which to create it. The function will return a `0` if it completes the task successfully. In the event of failure, the function returns `-1` and sets "errno" appropriately.

Risk: Users should not be given free reign with this function and should be restricted to only create directories from a desired list provided by the development team. Also limit the parent directory of the new directory to a predefined or static source thereby minimizing your risk of enabling an attacker to control your underlying operating system.

Additional Resources: www.gnu.org/software/libc/manual/html_node/Creating-Directories.html#Creating%20Directories

Impact: High

Cross References: `mkdirp`

mkdirp

Prototype: `int mkdirp(const char *path, mode_t mode)`

Summary: This function creates the missing directories in a given path.

Description: The function attempts to create all the necessary directories in a given path. This means that function will attempt to create all the directories that do not exist in the given path. The function has two input variables: the path and the creation mode. The function will return a `0` if it completes successfully. If it fails, however, it will return -1 and set "`errno`" appropriately.

Risk: Users should not be given free reign with this function and should be restricted to only create directories from a desired list provided by the development team. Also limit the parent directory of the new directory to a predefined or static source thereby minimizing your risk of enabling an attacker to control your underlying operating system.

Impact: High

Cross References: `mkdir`

mkfifo

Prototype: `int mkfifo (const char *filename, mode_t mode)`

Summary: This function creates a special FIFO-type file.

Description: The function attempts to create a special FIFO-type file. This type of file functions by having both ends opened for reading, acting similarly to a pipe. The function has two input variables: the string containing the FIFO filename and the mode in which to create it. If the function is successful, the function returns a `0`. Otherwise, the function returns a -1 and sets "`errno`" appropriately.

Risk: In 2002, a myriad of vulnerabilities were identified in Microsoft pipes; however, the implementation and exploitation of these vulnerabilities is not strictly limited to Microsoft Windows operating systems. Similar to socket-level vulnerabilities, the pipe vulnerabilities exploit trusts between the clients and server on the ends of the connection. Ensure that your compiler is up-to-date and that all parameters passed to this function are derived from internal system information and not human data. Human data should be scrubbed and presented with options for selections if this function must be utilized.

Additional Resources: www.gnu.org/software/libc/manual/html_node/FIFO-Special-Files.html#FIFO%20Special%20Files

Impact: High

Cross References: mknod

mknod

Prototype: int mknod (const char *filename, mode_t mode, int dev)

Summary: This function is the basic function that was made to create special files.

Description: The function attempts to create a special file attached to or associated with a device. The function has three input arguments. They are the filename, the mode in which to create it, and the device to which the file will be associated. The function will return a 0 if the file is successfully created. However, in the event of a failure, the function will return a -1 and set "errno" appropriately.

Risk: This function must be controlled at the user level to ensure that only the appropriate users or internal systems can have the ability to execute it. It poses minimal risk to your application; however, as with any function that can create a file on the underlying subsystem, it's important to protect the directory destination.

Additional Resources: www.gnu.org/software/libc/manual/html_node/Making-Special-Files.html#Making%20Special%20Files

Impact: High

Cross References: mkfifo

mrand48

Prototype: long int mrand48 (void)

Summary: This function produces a random integer.

Description: The function produces a random integer between –2^31 and 2^31. It produces the number based on the state of the random number generator. The function does not take in any input arguments. The return value, however, is a long integer.

Risk: As with most standard random functions implemented within the C and C++ libraries, this function is susceptible to bruteforce or easily guessed number generating attacks due to a poor seed algorithm within the backend code. Amongst numerous other secure random number generating functions, Microsoft .Net has secure methods for implementing properly seeded numbers. ISAAC, designed by Bob Jenkins, is a fast cryptographic random number generator is as strong as they come. Available in multiple languages, ISAAC is a standard for many freeware and commercial solutions and should be considered the next time a random number is required within an application.

Additional Resources: www.burtleburtle.net/bob/rand/isaacafa.html, www.gnu.org/software/libc/manual/html_node/SVID-Random.html#SVID%20Random

Impact: Medium

Cross References: `drand48`, `erand48`, `jrand48`, `lrand48`, `nrand48`, `seed48`, `srand48`

nrand48

Prototype: `long int nrand48 (unsigned short int xsubi[3])`

Summary: This function produces a random number.

Description: This function produces a random number between 0 and 2^31. It follows much of the same ideas of the "`standard`" function "`lrand48`". However, this function can be passed an array with the description of the random number generator (RNG) state. This ability is useful when wishing to seed the RNG or use it to reproduce results.

Risk: As with most standard random functions implemented within the C and C++ libraries, this function is susceptible to bruteforce or easily guessed number generating attacks due to a poor seed algorithm within the backend code. Amongst numerous other secure random number generating functions, Microsoft .Net has secure methods for implementing properly seeded numbers. ISAAC, designed by Bob Jenkins, is a fast cryptographic random number generator is as strong as they come. Available in multiple languages, ISAAC is a standard for many freeware and commercial solutions and should be considered the next time a random number is required within an application.

Additional Resources: www.burtleburtle.net/bob/rand/isaacafa.html, www.gnu.org/software/libc/manual/html_node/SVID-Random.html#SVID%20Random

Impact: Medium

Cross References: `drand48`, `erand48`, `jrand48`, `lrand48`, `mrand48`, `seed48`, `srand48`

OemToAnsi (Class Member)

Prototype: `void CStringT::OemToAnsi()`

Summary: This class member converts the string of characters from the OEM character set to the ANSI character set.

Description: This is a member of the class type CStringT. The member will convert the character of the class object "`String`" from the OEM character set to the ANSI character set. It does not return anything, as it modifies the class object itself.

Risk: Certain string manipulation functions to include OEM transition functions are commonly leveraged in buffer overflow attacks. At the most basic level, these functions read in data, perform analysis and execution logic, then output the data to another type of string. It is imperative that the destination string be calculated accordingly and that enough memory space is allocated. Special characters should also be stricken from the conversion.

Note: At time of publication, this function was designed for Windows compatibility.

Additional Resources:

http://msdn.microsoft.com/library/default.asp?url=/library/en-us/vclib/html/vclr-fcstringtoemtoansi.asp

Impact: Low

open

Prototype: `int open (const char *filename, int flags[, mode_t mode])`

Summary: This function opens a file.

Description: This function attempts to create a new file handle. The function opens a file with the given mode/flags, and returns the handle for the file. The function returns a 0 if it is opened correctly. However, if it fails, the function returns a – 1 and appropriately sets "errno".

Risk: All special and wildcard characters should be removed before the filename is computed on the local filesystem. Malicious filenames are interpreted differently on varying systems and as such, directory control is critical to limiting the ability of an attacker to potentially compromise files at varying levels within the application or underlying subsystem.

Additional Resources: www.gnu.org/software/libc/manual/html_node/Opening-and-Closing-Files.html#Opening%20and%20Closing%20Files

Impact: Low

opendir

Prototype: `DIR * opendir (const char *dirname)`

Summary: This function opens a directory.

Description: The function attempts to open a given directory. The function has only one input variable: a string containing the name of the directory to open. The function returns a pointer to the directory. However, if something went wrong, the function returns a NULL pointer and sets "errno" appropriately.

Risk: All special and wildcard characters should be removed before the filename is computed on the local filesystem. Malicious filenames are interpreted differently on varying systems and as such, directory control is critical to limiting the ability of an attacker to potentially compromise files at varying levels within the application or underlying subsystem.

Additional Resources: www.gnu.org/software/libc/manual/html_node/Opening-a-Directory.html#Opening%20a%20Directory

Impact: Low

pathconf

Prototype: `long int pathconf (const char *filename, int parameter)`

Summary: This function retrieves the values of the file system parameters for a given file.

Description: The function attempts to retrieve the file system parameters of a given file. The function has two input arguments: a string containing the filename and a parameter to check. The function will return that parameter value if it is successful and the parameter value applies to the file. However, if the function either fails or the value is not applicable, the function returns a -1. In the case that the function fails, "`errno`" is set appropriately.

Risk: System path information is constantly sought after by attackers or malicious users profiling a target application or system. Path information alone can potentially identify the underlying operating system, installed applications, configurations, and in some cases user and security information. Ensure that non-alphanumeric characters are removed from the string before it is processed and that the information is only processed internally by the application. Limit the end user's ability to ascertain or traverse path information.

Additional Resources:
www.gnu.org/software/libc/manual/html_node/Pathconf.html#Pathconf

Impact: Medium

popen

Prototype: `FILE * popen (const char *command, const char *mode)`

Summary: This function opens a process and keeps it open, leaving a pipe to the process.

Description: The function attempts to open and execute a process. The function, however, does not wait until completion, but rather leaves open the process and creates a pipe to it. The function has two input arguments: a string containing the system command to use and execution mode. The function will return the pipe if it successful or a NULL pointer if not.

Risk: In 2002, myriad vulnerabilities were identified in Microsoft pipes; however, the implementation and exploitation of these vulnerabilities is not strictly limited to Microsoft Windows operating systems. Similar to socket-level vulnerabilities, the pipe vulnerabilities exploit trusts between the clients and server on the ends of the connection. Ensure that your compiler is up-to-date and that all parameters passed to this function are derived from internal system information and not human data. Human data should be scrubbed and presented with options for selections if this function must be utilized.

Additional Resources: www.blakewatts.com, www.gnu.org/software/libc/manual/html_node/Pipe-to-a-Subprocess.html#Pipe%20to%20a%20Subprocess

Impact: Low

printf

Prototype: `int printf( const char *format [, argument]... )`

Summary: This function prints a formatted array of characters to the I/O stream.

Description: The function attempts to print a formatted array of characters to the stream. It has only one formal argument: the array to be printed. However, as it can be formatted data, there can be subsequent, informal arguments. The function will return the number of characters printed. However, in the event of an error, the function returns a negative value.

Risk: This function is potentially vulnerable to a format string attack where an attacker could cause the application to crash unexpected or execute arbitrary code. Format string bugs were discovered in 2000 and the problem is typically spawned from user input that is not properly filtered. Both Microsoft .Net and SPI Dynamics to name two have secure objects that can be implemented to check strings and user input gained from human sources within applications to protect against input-

directed vulnerabilities. It is critical that you verify the inputted data have only proper and expected characters in addition to ensuring that your function is properly called. For example, the functions should always utilize their parameters such as `printf("%s", malicious_string)` instead of `printf(malicious_string)`.

Additional Resources:

www.gnu.org/software/libc/manual/html_node/Formatted-Output-Functions.html#Formatted%20Output%20Functions;
http://msdn.microsoft.com/library/default.asp?url=/library/en-us/vccore98/html/_crt_printf.2c_.wprintf.asp

Impact: Medium

Cross References: `fprintf`, `scanf`, `sprintf`

random

Prototype: `long int random (void)`

Summary: This function generates a random number.

Description: The function generates a random number based on the sequence. It will be between 0 and RAND_MAX. The function has no input variables. It returns a long integer.

Risk: As with most standard random functions implemented within the C and C++ libraries, this function is susceptible to bruteforce or easily guessed number generating attacks due to a poor seed algorithm within the backend code. Amongst numerous other secure random number generating functions, Microsoft .Net has secure methods for implementing properly seeded numbers. ISAAC, designed by Bob Jenkins, is a fast cryptographic random number generator is as strong as they come. Available in multiple languages, ISAAC is a standard for many freeware and commercial solutions and should be considered the next time a random number is required within an application.

Additional Resources: www.burtleburtle.net/bob/rand/isaacafa.html,
www.gnu.org/software/libc/manual/html_node/BSD-Random.html#BSD%20Random

Impact: Medium

Cross References: srandom

read

Prototype: `ssize_t read (int filedes, void *buffer, size_t size)`

Summary: This function reads data from a file.

Description: The function attempts to read the information stored in a file. It has three input arguments: the handle of the file to read, an array to store the information read, and the size of the array. The function will read the file "`blindly`" paying little attention to that which it is reading. It will also not append and special characters (i.e., the null character). The function will return the number of bytes read. The function will return a `0` if the function was already at the end-of-file marker. If there is an error, the function returns `-1` and sets "`errno`" appropriately.

Risk: This function parses input blindly. Additionally, logic should be incorporated into the application to ensure that human supplied input does not contain potentially malicious content. Data streams that are attached to external sources must first verify the integrity of those sources before interpreting and implementing the data. The destination buffer should be verified before any data is copied into memory or another data stream as to minimize the risk for an attack against a buffer overflow.

Additional Resources: www.gnu.org/software/libc/manual/html_node/I-O-Primitives.html#I%2fO%20Primitives

Impact: Low

readdir

Prototype: `struct dirent * readdir (DIR *dirstream)`

Summary: This function reads the next object from the directory stream.

Description: The function attempts to read the next object form the directory stream. It has only one input argument, and that is the directory stream. The function will return a pointer to a structure that contains the necessary data about the next object in the directory stream. It also increments the stream. If there is an error, the function returns a null pointer and sets "errno" appropriately.

Risk: All special and wildcard characters should be removed before the filename is computed on the local filesystem. Malicious filenames are interpreted differently on varying systems and as such, directory control is critical to limiting the ability of an attacker to potentially compromise files at varying levels within the application or underlying subsystem.

Additional Resources: www.gnu.org/software/libc/manual/html_node/Reading-Closing-Directory.html#Reading%2fClosing%20Directory

Impact: Low

readlink

Prototype: `int readlink (const char *filename, char *buffer, size_t size)`

Summary: This function retrieves the file pointed to by a symbolic link.

Description: The function attempts to retrieve the name of a file pointed to by a symbolic link. The function has three input variables: the symbolic link's name, an empty string to house the link's target name, and the maximum number of characters. Note that this function does not append a null character at the end of the target name's string. The function will return the number of characters copied. In the event of failure, however, the function will return -1 and set "errno" appropriately.

Risk: All special and wildcard characters should be removed before the filename is computed on the local filesystem. Malicious filenames are interpreted differently on varying systems and as such, directory control is critical to limiting the ability of an attacker to potentially compromise files at varying levels within the application or underlying subsystem.

Additional Resources:
www.gnu.org/software/libc/manual/html_node/Symbolic-Links.html#Symbolic%20Links

Impact: Low

readv

Prototype: `ssize_t readv (int filedes, const struct iovec *vector, int count)`

Summary: This function reads and scatters data from a file into a vector of buffers.

Description: The function attempts to read and scatter data from a given file into a vector of buffers. The function has three input variables: the file, a pointer to a vector buffer structure, and the number of structures in the vector. The function will return the number of bytes read and scattered. In the event of an end-of-file notification or an error, the function will return a 0 or -1, respectively. If there is an error, "errno" will be set appropriately.

Risk: This function parses input blindly. Additionally, logic should be incorporated into the application to ensure that human supplied input does not contain potentially malicious content. Data streams that are attached to external sources must first verify the integrity of those sources before interpreting and implementing the data. The destination buffer should be verified before any data is copied into memory or another data stream as to minimize the risk for an attack against a buffer overflow.

Additional Resources: www.gnu.org/software/libc/manual/html_node/Scatter-Gather.html#Scatter-Gather

Impact: Low

realloc

Prototype: `void * realloc (void *ptr, size_t newsize)`

Summary: This function reassigns the size of an allocated piece of memory.

Description: The function attempts to resize a piece of allocated memory. The function has two input variables: the pointer to the existing piece of memory and the new size for it. The function will return a pointer to the reallocated piece of memory. If a null pointer is passed into realloc, it acts identically to "malloc". If there is not enough memory to fulfill the request, then a null pointer is returned.

Risk: The `realloc` function does not erase data that was previously stored in a memory address and thereby should not be considered a secure method for removing information.

Additional Resources:

www.gnu.org/software/libc/manual/html_node/Changing-Block-Size.html#Changing%20Block%20Size

Impact: Low

realpath

Prototype: `char * realpath (const char *name, char *resolved)`

Summary: This function canonicalizes a path.

Description: The function attempts to canonicalize a path. The function will act exactly like "`canonicalize_file_name`" if "`resolved`" is null. If it is not, then the function copies the canonicalized path, resolved from "`name`" to the memory pointed to by it. The function returns the pointer to where the string contains the resolved path name.

Risk: System path information is constantly sought after by attackers or malicious users profiling a target application or system. Path information alone can potentially identify the underlying operating system, installed applications, configurations, and in some cases user and security information. Ensure that non-alphanumeric characters are removed from the string before it is processed and that the information is only processed internally by the application. Limit the end user's ability to ascertain or traverse path information.

Additional Resources:

www.gnu.org/software/libc/manual/html_node/Symbolic-Links.html#Symbolic%20Links

Impact: Medium

recv

Prototype: `int recv (int socket, void *buffer, size_t size, int flags)`

Summary: This function receives data from an open socket.

Description: The function attempts to resolve data from a socket and store it. The function has four input variables: the socket to read from, the empty array for the data, the size of the array, and a set of flags. If successful, the function returns the number of bytes read. However, in the event of an error, the function returns a -1 and sets "errno" appropriately.

Risk: Raw network data received from a socket has the potential to be malicious in nature due to the great number of attacks designed to be executed remotely. Packet fragmentations can cause serious disruptions to the application and underlying operating system. If at all possible, packet reassembly should be conducted at the OS-layer.

Additional Resources:
www.gnu.org/software/libc/manual/html_node/Receiving-Data.html#Receiving%20Data

Impact: Low

Cross References: recvfrom

recvfrom

Prototype: int recvfrom (int socket, void *buffer, size_t size, int flags, struct sockaddr *addr, socklen_t *length-ptr)

Summary: This function reads the data from a socket.

Description: The function attempts to resolve the data packets from a socket. The function has six input arguments: the socket, the empty array, the size of the array, the flags to be set, a structure pointer to hold information about the socket, and the size of the aforementioned pointer (array). The function returns the number of bytes read, unless an error occurs. In the event of failure, the function returns a -1 and sets "erno" appropriately.

Risk: Raw network data received from a socket has the potential to be malicious in nature due to the numerous amount of attacks that are designed to be executed remotely. Packet fragmentations can cause serious disruptions to the application and underlying operating system. If at all possible, packet reassembly should be conducted at the OS-layer.

Additional Resources:
www.gnu.org/software/libc/manual/html_node/Receiving-Datagrams.html#Receiving%20Datagrams

Impact: Low

Cross References: recv

recvmsg

Prototype: `int recvmsg(int socket, struct msghdr *message, int flags)`

Summary: This function receives information and/or a message from a socket.

Description: The function attempts to resolve the information, messages, and addresses of a socket. The function has three input arguments: the socket, a structure to hold the necessary information, and a set of flags. The benefit of this function is that the sockets do not have to be connected to read the information from them. The function will return the number of bytes received. However, in the event of failure, the function will return a `-1` and set "`errno`" appropriately.

Risk: Raw network data received from a socket has the potential to be malicious in nature due to the great number of attacks that are designed to be executed remotely. Packet fragmentations can cause serious disruptions to the application and underlying operating system. If at all possible, packet reassembly should be conducted at the OS-layer.

Additional Resources: http://mkssoftware.com/docs/man3/recvmsg.3.asp

Impact: Low

Cross References: recv

remove

Prototype: `int remove (const char *filename)`

Summary: This function removes a file.

Description: The function attempts to delete a file. The function has one input variable: the file to be removed. The function will return a 0 if successful. Otherwise, the function returns a -1 and sets "errno" appropriately.

Risk: In addition to the potential race condition bugs that are associated with this function, a user could also attempt to execute a Denial-of-Service attack. Ensure that only one instance of this function can be called at any given moment. All input passed to this function should be analyzed closely to ensure that only desired resources can be removed from the system. It is not uncommon for worms and viruses to exploit application-layer vulnerabilities to cause damage to files they since would not have had access to.

Impact: Low

Cross References: `rmdir, unlink`

rename

Prototype: `int rename (const char *oldname, const char *new-name)`

Summary: This function renames a file.

Description: The function attempts to rename a file. The function has two input variables: the old file name and the new file name. The function will return a 0 if successful. If the function fails, however, it will return a -1 and set "errno" appropriately.

Risk: In addition to the potential race condition bugs that are associated with this function, a user could also attempt to execute a Denial-of-Service attack. Ensure that only one instance of this function can be called at any given moment. All input passed to this function should be analyzed closely to ensure that only desired resources can be removed from the system. It is not uncommon for worms and viruses to exploit application-layer vulnerabilities to cause damage to files they since would not have had access to by renaming all files within an operating system or renaming files and directories to those that are commonly executed upon system boot.

Additional Resources:

www.gnu.org/software/libc/manual/html_node/Renaming-Files.html#Renaming%20Files

Impact: Low

rmdir

Prototype: `int rmdir (const char *filename)`

Summary: This function removes a directory.

Description: The function attempts to remove a given directory. The directory must be empty before removal. The function has only one input argument: the directory name. The function will return a 0 if it succeeds. However, the function will return a -1 and set "`errno`" if it fails.

Risk: In addition to the potential race condition bugs that are associated with this function, a user could also attempt to execute a Denial-of-Service attack. Ensure that only one instance of this function can be called at any given moment. All input passed to this function should be analyzed closely to ensure that only desired resources can be removed from the system. It is not uncommon for worms and viruses to exploit application-layer vulnerabilities to cause damage to files they since would not have had access to.

Additional Resources: www.gnu.org/software/libc/manual/html_node/Deleting-Files.html#Deleting%20Files

Impact: Low

Cross References: `remove, unlink`

rmdirp

Prototype: `int rmdirp (char *path, char *path1)`

Summary: This function removes a directory.

Description: The function attempts to remove a directory. This function, however, will remove all directories in a path to get to the perceived root directory given in the path. The directories must be empty except for the other directories being removed. The function has two input arguments: the path of directories to remove, and another string to hold a resultant path in case of error. The function returns a `0` if successful, and a `-1` if not. In the case of failure, the function sets `"errno"` appropriately.

Risk: In addition to the potential race condition bugs that are associated with this function, a user could also attempt to execute a Denial-of-Service attack. Ensure that only one instance of this function can be called at any given moment. All input passed to this function should be analyzed closely to ensure that only desired resources can be removed from the system. It is not uncommon for worms and viruses to exploit application-layer vulnerabilities to cause damage to files they since would not have had access to.

Additional Resources: www.mcsr.olemiss.edu/cgi-bin/man-cgi?mkdirp+3

Impact: Low

scandir

Prototype: `int scandir (const char *dir, struct dirent ***namelist, int (*selector) (const struct dirent *), int (*cmp) (const void *, const void *))`

Summary: This function scans a directory.

Description: The function attempts to scan a directory and store the information that it acquires. The function has four input arguments: the directory name to scan, an array of structures to hold the file information, and two sets of flags. The function will return a `0` if it is successful, and a `-1` if it is not. The function will also set the variable `"errno"` if the case is necessary.

Risk: This function poses minimal risk, but the output of a file's existence should be limited to that of the desired resource. In other words, application users should not be able to point this function at any directory or file on the underlying subsystem to determine if the resource exists.

Additional Resources: www.gnu.org/software/libc/manual/html_node/Scanning-Directory-Content.html#Scanning%20Directory%20Content

Impact: Low

scanf

Prototype: `int scanf( const char *format [,argument])`

Summary: The function reads a formatted array of characters from the I/O stream.

Description: The function attempts to scan a formatted array of characters from the stream. It has only one formal argument: the array to be read in to. However, as it can be formatted data, there can be subsequent, informal arguments. The function will return the number of characters read. However, in the event of an error, the function returns a negative value.

Risk: This function is potentially vulnerable to a format string attack where an attacker could cause the application to crash unexpected or execute arbitrary code. Format string bugs were discovered in 2000 and the problem is typically spawned from user input that is not properly filtered. Both Microsoft .Net and SPI Dynamics to name two have secure objects that can be implemented to check strings and user input gained from human sources within applications to protect against input-directed vulnerabilities. It is critical that you verify the inputted data have only proper and expected characters in addition to ensuring that your function is properly called. For example, the functions should always utilize their parameters such as `printf("%s", malicious_string)` instead of `printf(malicious_string)`.

Additional Resources:

www.gnu.org/software/libc/manual/html_node/Formatted-Input-Functions.html#Formatted%20Input%20Functions;
http://msdn.microsoft.com/library/default.asp?url=/library/en-us/vccore98/html/_crt_scanf.2c_.wscanf.asp

Impact: Medium

Cross References: `fscanf`, `printf`, `sprintf`

seed48

Prototype: `unsigned short int * seed48 (unsigned short int seed16v[3])`

Summary: This function sets the seed for the random number generator.

Description: The function attempts to initialize the random number generator. It will give the ability to store the state of a random number generator so one can keep track of the results. The function has only one input value and that is the array that will hold the state of the random number generator upon completion. In the event of a failure, the function returns a null pointer.

Risk: As with most standard random functions implemented within the C and C++ libraries, this function is susceptible to bruteforce or easily guessed number generating attacks due to a poor seed algorithm within the backend code. Amongst numerous other secure random number generating functions, Microsoft .Net has secure methods for implementing properly seeded numbers. ISAAC, designed by Bob Jenkins, is a fast cryptographic random number generator is as strong as they come. Available in multiple languages, ISAAC is a standard for many freeware and commercial solutions and should be considered the next time a random number is required within an application.

Additional Resources: www.burtleburtle.net/bob/rand/isaacafa.html, www.gnu.org/software/libc/manual/html_node/SVID-Random.html#SVID%20Random

Impact: Medium

setstate

Prototype: `void * setstate (void *state)`

Summary: This function sets the state for a random number generator.

Description: This function is used to reset the state of the random number generator to a previous value. The function receives and returns the same values: the random number generator state. The function will return a null pointer, however, in the event of failure.

Risk: As with most standard random functions implemented within the C and C++ libraries, this function is susceptible to bruteforce or easily guessed number generating attacks due to a poor seed algorithm within the backend code. Amongst numerous other secure random number generating functions, Microsoft .Net has secure methods for implementing properly seeded numbers. ISAAC, designed by Bob Jenkins, is a fast cryptographic random number generator is as strong as they come. Available in multiple languages, ISAAC is a standard for many freeware and commercial solutions and should be considered the next time a random number is required within an application.

Additional Resources: www.gnu.org/software/libc/manual/html_node/BSD-Random.html#BSD%20Random

Impact: Low

signal

Prototype: `sighandler_t signal (int signum, sighandler_t action)`

Summary: This function sets an action for a signal.

Description: The function attempts to set the action for a signal. The function has two input arguments: the signal and the action for the signal. The function, if successful, will return the previous action associated with the given signal. If not, the function returns `SIG_ERR` and sets `errno` appropriately.

Risk: Functions that handle or pass data to signals could be open for attacks to race condition bugs found within your logic. Ensure that only one instance of the signal function can be called at any given period of time and that if utilized in multiple locations within an application, a time delay routine be implemented to monitor the function usage.

Additional Resources: www.gnu.org/software/libc/manual/html_node/Basic-Signal-Handling.html#Basic%20Signal%20Handling

Impact: Low

snprintf

Prototype: `int snprintf (char *string, size_t count, const char *template)`

Summary: This function prints a formatted output string to another string.

Description: The function attempts to print a formatted string to another. The function also specifies the maximum number of characters to write. It has three formal arguments: the destination string, the max number of characters to write, and the formatted string. The function may have other, informal arguments deriving from the string formatting. The function will return the number of characters that would have been generated (meaning that if your return value is greater than "count", there was information lost).

Risk: This function is potentially vulnerable to a format string attack where an attacker could cause the application to crash unexpected or execute arbitrary code. Format string bugs were discovered in 2000 and the problem is typically spawned from user input that is not properly filtered. Both Microsoft .Net and SPI Dynamics to name two have secure objects that can be implemented to check strings and user input gained from human sources within applications to protect against input-directed vulnerabilities. It is critical that you verify the inputted data have only proper and expected characters in addition to ensuring that your function is properly called. For example, the functions should always utilize their parameters such as `printf("%s", malicious_string)` instead of `printf(malicious_string)`.

Additional Resources:
www.gnu.org/software/libc/manual/html_node/Formatted-Output-Functions.html#Formatted%20Output%20Functions

Impact: Medium

sprintf

Prototype: `int sprintf (char *buffer, const char *template, ...)`

Summary: This function prints a formatted array of characters to a string.

Description: The function attempts to print a formatted array of characters to a string. It has two formal arguments: the new string and the array to be printed. However, as it can be formatted data, there can be subsequent, informal arguments. The function will return the number of characters printed. However, in the event of an error, the function returns a negative value.

Risk: This function is potentially vulnerable to a format string attack where an attacker could cause the application to crash unexpected or execute arbitrary code. Format string bugs were discovered in 2000 and the problem is typically spawned from user input that is not properly filtered. Both Microsoft .Net and SPI Dynamics to name two have secure objects that can be implemented to check strings and user input gained from human sources within applications to protect against input-directed vulnerabilities. It is critical that you verify the inputted data have only proper and expected characters in addition to ensuring that your function is properly called. For example, the functions should always utilize their parameters such as `printf("%s", malicious_string)` instead of `printf(malicious_string)`.

Additional Resources:
www.gnu.org/software/libc/manual/html_node/Formatted-Output-Functions.html#Formatted%20Output%20Functions;
http://msdn.microsoft.com/library/default.asp?url=/library/en-us/vccore98/html/_crt_sprintf.2c_.swprintf.asp

Impact: Medium

Cross References: `fprintf, scanf, sprintf`

srand

Prototype: `void srand (unsigned int seed)`

Summary: This function seeds the random number generator.

Description: The function attempts to seed the random number generator. The function utilizes a seed passed in to set the random number generator state. The function has only one input value: the seed for the random number generator. The function will not return any values.

Risk: As with most standard random functions implemented within the C and C++ libraries, this function is susceptible to bruteforce or easily guessed number generating attacks due to a poor seed algorithm within the backend code. Amongst numerous other secure random number generating functions, Microsoft .Net has secure methods for implementing properly seeded numbers. ISAAC, designed by Bob Jenkins, is a fast cryptographic random number generator is as strong as they come. Available in multiple languages, ISAAC is a standard for many freeware and commercial solutions and should be considered the next time a random number is required within an application.

Additional Resources: www.burtleburtle.net/bob/rand/isaacafa.html, www.gnu.org/software/libc/manual/html_node/ISO-Random. html#ISO%20Random

Impact: Medium

srand48

Prototype: `void srand48 (long int seedval)`

Summary: This function seeds the random number generator.

Description: The function attempts to seed the random number generator. The function utilizes a seed passed in to set the random number generator state. The function has only one input value: the seed for the random number generator. The function will not return any values.

Risk: As with most standard random functions implemented within the C and C++ libraries, this function is susceptible to bruteforce or easily guessed number generating attacks due to a poor seed algorithm within the backend code. Amongst numerous other secure random number generating functions, Microsoft .Net has secure methods for implementing properly seeded numbers. ISAAC, designed by Bob Jenkins, is a fast cryptographic random number generator is as strong as they come. Available in multiple languages, ISAAC is a standard for many freeware and commercial solutions and should be considered the next time a random number is required within an application.

Additional Resources: www.burtleburtle.net/bob/rand/isaacafa.html, www.gnu.org/software/libc/manual/html_node/SVID-Random.html#SVID%20Random

Impact: Medium

Cross References: drand48, erand48, jrand48, lrand48, mrand48, nrand48, seed48

srandom

Prototype: void srandom (unsigned int seed)

Summary: This function seeds the random number generator.

Description: The function attempts to seed the random number generator. The function utilizes a seed passed in to set the random number generator state. The function has only one input value: the seed for the random number generator. The function will not return any values.

Risk: As with most standard random functions implemented within the C and C++ libraries, this function is susceptible to bruteforce or easily guessed number generating attacks due to a poor seed algorithm within the backend code. Amongst numerous other secure random number generating functions, Microsoft .Net has secure methods for implementing properly seeded numbers. ISAAC, designed by Bob Jenkins, is a fast cryptographic random number generator is as strong as they come. Available in multiple languages, ISAAC is a standard for many freeware and commercial solutions and should be considered the next time a random number is required within an application.

Additional Resources: www.burtleburtle.net/bob/rand/isaacafa.html, www.gnu.org/software/libc/manual/html_node/BSD-Random.html#BSD%20Random

Impact: Medium

Cross References: random

sscanf

Prototype: `int sscanf( const char *buffer, const char *format [, argument ])`

Summary: The function reads a formatted array of characters from a string.

Description: The function attempts to scan a formatted array of characters from a string. It has two formal arguments: the string (which the function will read) and the array to be read in to. However, as it can be formatted data, there can be subsequent, informal arguments. The function will return the number of characters read. However, in the event of an error, the function returns a negative value.

Risk: This function is potentially vulnerable to a format string attack where an attacker could cause the application to crash unexpected or execute arbitrary code. Format string bugs were discovered in 2000 and the problem is typically spawned from user input that is not properly filtered. Both Microsoft .Net and SPI Dynamics to name two have secure objects that can be implemented to check strings and user input gained from human sources within applications to protect against input-directed vulnerabilities. It is critical that you verify the inputted data have only proper and expected characters in addition to ensuring that your function is properly called. For example, the functions should always utilize their parameters such as `printf("%s", malicious_string)` instead of `printf(malicious_string)`.

Additional Resources:
www.gnu.org/software/libc/manual/html_node/Formatted-Input-Functions.html#Formatted%20Input%20Functions;
http://msdn.microsoft.com/library/default.asp?url=/library/en-us/vccore98/html/_crt_sscanf.2c_.swscanf.asp

Impact: Medium

Cross References: `fscanf`, `scanf`, `sprintf`

stat

Prototype: `int stat (const char *filename, struct stat *buffer)`

Summary: This function retrieves the attributes of a given file.

Description: The function attempts to acquire the attributes of a given file. The function has two input variables: the string containing the file name and structure to hold the requested information. The function will return a 0 if it is successful. The resultant information will be in the structure. If the function is unsuccessful, it returns a −1 and sets "errno" appropriately.

Risk: The stat function output should be restricted to trusted administrative-level users or the internal workings of the application. stat output contains sensitive information that an attacker could leverage to advance an attack scenario.

Additional Resources: www.gnu.org/software/libc/manual/html_node/Reading-Attributes.html#Reading%20Attributes

Impact: Low

strcadd

Prototype: `char *strcadd (char *destination, const char *source)`

Summary: This function copies a string onto another.

Description: The function attempts to copy one string onto another. The function has two input arguments: the source and destination strings. It also compresses the C escape sequences to their respective characters. The function returns the pointer to the destination string. This function is identical to "strccpy" except that the pointer returned is to the null character at the end of the destination. The function will return a null pointer in the event of an error.

Risk: Functions that are utilized to copy or concatenate strings are commonly misused and fall victim to buffer overflow attacks. It is critical that you ensure before execution of this function that the destination source is large enough to house the source data. Additionally, limiting the source data memory space will not only make your application more efficient, it will also add another layer of security by relying

less on the destination buffer. For example, if X should be copied to Y then ensure that Y's space is less than X-1's total space allocation. It is similar for concatenation functions where as the strings are limited to a total length.

Additional Resources: http://docsrv.sco.com/cgi-bin/man/man?strccpy+3G

Impact: Low

Cross References: `strccpy`, `streadd`, `strecpy`

strcat

Prototype: char *strcat(char *destination, const char *source)

Summary: This function concatenates a string onto the end of another.

Description: The function attempts to append one string onto the end of another. It has two input arguments: the source and destination strings. The function will return a pointer to the destination string when finished. In the event of an error, the function can return a NULL pointer.

Risk: Functions that are utilized to copy or concatenate strings are commonly misused and fall victim to buffer overflow attacks. It is critical that you ensure before execution of this function that the destination source is large enough to house the source data. Additionally, limiting the source data memory space will not only make your application more efficient, it will also add another layer of security by relying less on the destination buffer. For example, if X should be copied to Y then ensure that Y's space is less than X-1's total space allocation. It is similar for concatenation functions, where the strings are limited to a total length.

Additional Resources: www.gnu.org/software/libc/manual/html_node/Copying-and-Concatenation.html#Copying%20and%20Concatenation; http://msdn.microsoft.com/library/default.asp?url=/library/en-us/vccore98/html/_crt_strcat.2c_.wcscat.2c_._mbscat.asp

Impact: High

Cross References: `strcpy`, `strlen`, `strncat`, `strncpy`

strccpy

Prototype: `char *strccpy (char *destination, const char *source)`

Summary: This function copies a string onto another.

Description: The function attempts to copy one string onto another. The function has two input arguments: the source and destination strings. It also compresses the C escape sequences to their respective characters. The function returns the pointer to the destination string. This function is identical to "strcadd" except that the pointer returned is to the first character of the destination string. The function will return a null pointer in the event of an error.

Risk: Functions that are utilized to copy or concatenate strings are commonly misused and fall victim to buffer overflow attacks. It is critical that you ensure before execution of this function that the destination source is large enough to house the source data. Additionally, limiting the source data memory space will not only make your application more efficient, it will also add another layer of security by relying less on the destination buffer. For example, if X should be copied to Y, then ensure that Y's space is less than X-1's total space allocation. It is similar for concatenation functions where as the strings are limited to a total length.

Impact: Low

Cross References: `strcadd`, `streadd`, `strecpy`

strcpy

Prototype: `char *strcpy( char *destination, const char *source )`

Summary: This function copies a string onto another.

Description: The function attempts to copy one string onto another. It has two input arguments: the source and destination strings. The function will return a pointer to the destination string when finished. In the event of an error, the function can return a NULL pointer.

Risk: Functions that are utilized to copy or concatenate strings are commonly mis-used and fall victim to buffer overflow attacks. It is critical that you ensure before execution of this function that the destination source is large enough to house the source data. Additionally, limiting the source data memory space will not only make your application more efficient, it will also add another layer of security by relying less on the destination buffer. For example, if X should be copied to Y, then ensure that Y's space is less than X-1's total space allocation. It is similar for concatenation functions where as the strings are limited to a total length.

Impact: High

Cross References: `strcat, strlen, strncat, strncpy`

streadd

Prototype: `char *streadd (char *destination, const char *source, const char *exceptions)`

Summary: This function copies a string onto another.

Description: The function attempts to copy one string onto another. The function has three input arguments: the source and destination strings and a string for exception handling. It also expands the C escape sequences from their respective characters. The function returns the pointer to the destination string. This function is identical to "`strecpy`" except that the pointer returned is to the null character at the end of the destination. The function will return a null pointer in the event of an error.

Risk: Functions that are utilized to copy or concatenate strings are commonly mis-used and fall victim to buffer overflow attacks. It is critical that you ensure before execution of this function that the destination source is large enough to house the source data. Additionally, limiting the source data memory space will not only make your application more efficient, it will also add another layer of security by relying less on the destination buffer. For example, if X should be copied to Y then ensure

C

that Y's space is less than X-1's total space allocation. It is similar for concatenation functions where as the strings are limited to a total length.

Impact: Low

Cross References: `strcadd, strccpy, strecpy`

strecpy

Prototype: `char *strecpy (char *destination, const char *source, const char *exceptions)`

Summary: This function copies a string onto another.

Description: The function attempts to copy one string onto another. The function has three input arguments: the source and destination strings and a string for exception handling. It also expands the C escape sequences from their respective characters. The function returns the pointer to the destination string. This function is identical to "`streadd`" except that the pointer returned is to the first character of the destination string. The function will return a null pointer in the event of an error.

Risk: Functions that are utilized to copy or concatenate strings are commonly misused and fall victim to buffer overflow attacks. It is critical that you ensure before execution of this function that the destination source is large enough to house the source data. Additionally, limiting the source data memory space will not only make your application more efficient, it will also add another layer of security by relying less on the destination buffer. For example, if X should be copied to Y then ensure that Y's space is less than X-1's total space allocation. It is similar for concatenation functions where as the strings are limited to a total length.

Impact: Low

Cross References: `strcadd, strccpy, streadd`

strfry

Prototype: `char *strfry (char *string)`

Summary: This function shuffles the order of characters in a string.

Description: The function attempts to shuffle a string's contents. The function has only one input variable: the string in question. The function, with uniform distribution, perturbs the characters in the string to create an anagram of the original string. The function returns the pointer to the string.

Risk: This function should never be utilized to obfuscate data with the goal of protecting it from prying eyes. Only industry-standard cryptography algorithms should be implemented to secure data. This function is out-of-date and should not be used!

Note: At time of publication, this function was designed for compatibility in the GNU Library.

Additional Resources:
www.gnu.org/software/libc/manual/html_node/strfry.html#strfry

Impact: High

strlen

Prototype: `size_t strlen( const char *string )`

Summary: This function finds the length of a string.

Description: The function attempts to find the length of the string. It has only one input argument: the string to get the length of. The function will return an integer indicating the length of the string. In the event that the string does not exist or an error occurs, the function can return 0.

Risk: The length of a string is commonly ascertained before it is passed to a function that utilizes it to calculate the space required for a destination buffer. Ensure that human users do not have the ability to modify this number thereby potentially making it smaller than the destination. Calculate the length of the source then add one byte so to avoid off-by-one application buffer overflow attacks.

Additional Resources: www.gnu.org/software/libc/manual/html_node/String-Length.html#String%20Length;
http://msdn.microsoft.com/library/default.asp?url=/library/en-us/vccore98/html/_crt_strlen.2c_.wcslen.2c_._mbslen.2c_._mbstrlen.asp

Impact: Low

Cross References: strcat, strcpy, strncat, strncpy

strncat

Prototype: `char *strncat( char *destination, const char *source, size_t count )`

Summary: This function concatenates a string onto the end of another.

Description: The function attempts to append one string onto the end of another. It has three input arguments: the source and destination strings and the max number of characters to concatenate. The function will return a pointer to the destination string when finished. In the event of an error, the function can return a NULL pointer.

Risk: Functions that are utilized to copy or concatenate strings are commonly misused and fall victim to buffer overflow attacks. It is critical that you ensure before execution of this function that the destination source is large enough to house the source data. Additionally, limiting the source data memory space will not only make your application more efficient, it will also add another layer of security by relying less on the destination buffer. For example, if X should be copied to Y then ensure that Y's space is less than X-1's total space allocation. It is similar for concatenation functions where as the strings are limited to a total length.

Additional Resources: www.gnu.org/software/libc/manual/html_node/Copying-and-Concatenation.html#Copying%20and%20Concatenation;
http://msdn.microsoft.com/library/default.asp?url=/library/en-us/vccore98/html/_crt_strncat.2c_.wcsncat.2c_._mbsncat.asp

Impact: High

Cross References: strcat, strcpy, strlen, strncpy

strncpy

Prototype: `char *strncpy( char *destination, const char *source, size_t count )`

Summary: This function copies a string onto another.

Description: The function attempts to copy one string onto another with control over the number of characters to copy. It has three input arguments: the source and destination strings and the maximum number of characters to copy. The function will return a pointer to the destination string when finished. In the event of an error, the function can return a NULL pointer.

Risk: Functions that are utilized to copy or concatenate strings are commonly misused and fall victim to buffer overflow attacks. It is critical that you ensure before execution of this function that the destination source is large enough to house the source data. Additionally, limiting the source data memory space will not only make your application more efficient, it will also add another layer of security by relying less on the destination buffer. For example, if X should be copied to Y, then ensure that Y's space is less than X-1's total space allocation. It is similar for concatenation functions where as the strings are limited to a total length.

Additional Resources: www.gnu.org/software/libc/manual/html_node/Copying-and-Concatenation.html#Copying%20and%20Concatenation; http://msdn.microsoft.com/library/default.asp?url=/library/en-us/vccore98/html/_crt_strncpy.2c_.wcsncpy.2c_._mbsncpy.asp

Impact: High

Cross References: `strcat, strcpy, strlen, strncat`

strtrns

Prototype: `char *strtrns (const char *source, const char *old, const char *new, char *destination)`

Summary: This function transforms a string and copies it to a new string.

Description: The function attempts to transform a source string under a given set of parameters and copy the result to a new string. The function takes in four input arguments: the source and destination strings, and the transformation parameter strings. The function requires that the strings "old" and "new" be the same length. It takes the letters in "old" searches for them in the source string, replaces them with the corresponding character in "new" (i.e., in the same position), and copies the resultant string to "destination". The function then returns a pointer to the destination string.

Risk: This function should never be utilized to obfuscate data with the goal of protecting it from prying eyes. Only industry-standard cryptography algorithms should be implemented to secure data. This function is out-of-date and should not be used!

Impact: High

Cross References: strxfrm

strxfrm

Prototype: size_t strxfrm(char *destination, const char *source, size_t count)

Summary: This function transforms a string based off of the locale.

Description: The function attempts to transform a string based on the locale information of the system. It takes in three input arguments: the source and destination strings and the maximum number of characters to put in the destination string. The function will return the length of the string written. In the event of an error, the function returns -1.

Risk: Functions that are utilized to copy or concatenate strings are commonly misused and fall victim to buffer overflow attacks. It is critical that you ensure before execution of this function that the destination source is large enough to house the source data. Additionally, limiting the source data memory space will not only make your application more efficient, it will also add another layer of security by relying less on the destination buffer. For example, if X should be copied to Y, then ensure that Y's space is less than X-1's total space allocation. It is similar for concatenation functions where as the strings are limited to a total length.

Additional Resources:
www.gnu.org/software/libc/manual/html_node/Collation-
Functions.html#Collation%20Functions;
http://msdn.microsoft.com/library/default.asp?url=/library/en-
us/vccore98/html/_crt_strxfrm.2c_.wcsxfrm.asp

Impact: Medium

Cross References: wcsxfrm

swprintf

Prototype: `int swprintf (wchar_t *string, size_t size, const wchar_t *format)`

Summary: This function prints a formatted, wide-character string to another string.

Description: This function attempts to print a formatted string to another string. It has three format input arguments. The first is the string to be written to, while the second is the length of that string. The final input argument is the formatted string to write. Informally, the function may have more arguments, as the string could have its own arguments due to the formatting. The function returns the number of characters written to the string. In the event of an error, the function returns a negative value.

Risk: This function is potentially vulnerable to a format string attack where an attacker could cause the application to crash unexpected or execute arbitrary code. Format string bugs were discovered in 2000 and the problem is typically spawned from user input that is not properly filtered. Both Microsoft .Net and SPI Dynamics to name two have secure objects that can be implemented to check strings and user input gained from human sources within applications to protect against input-directed vulnerabilities. It is critical that you verify the inputted data have only proper and expected characters in addition to ensuring that your function is properly called. For example, the functions should always utilize their parameters such as `printf("%s", malicious_string)` instead of `printf(malicious_string)`.

Note: This function is practically identical to "`sprintf`" with the exception of using wide-character strings.

Additional Resources:

www.gnu.org/software/libc/manual/html_node/Formatted-Output-Functions.html#Formatted%20Output%20Functions

Impact: Medium

Cross References: `sprintf, swscanf`

swscanf

Prototype: `int swscanf (const wchar_t *string, const char *format)`

Summary: This function reads a wide-character string into a formatted string.

Description: This function attempts to read a formatted, wide-character string according to a given format. It has two formal input arguments: the string and the format of it. The function may have additional arguments from the formatting. The function returns the number of characters read or negative value in the event of failure.

Risk: This function is potentially vulnerable to a format string attack where an attacker could cause the application to crash unexpected or execute arbitrary code. Format string bugs were discovered in 2000 and the problem is typically spawned from user input that is not properly filtered. Both Microsoft .Net and SPI Dynamics to name two have secure objects that can be implemented to check strings and user input gained from human sources within applications to protect against input-directed vulnerabilities. It is critical that you verify the inputted data have only proper and expected characters in addition to ensuring that your function is properly called. For example, the functions should always utilize their parameters such as `printf("%s", malicious_string)` instead of `printf(malicious_string)`.

Additional Resources:

www.gnu.org/software/libc/manual/html_node/Formatted-Input-Functions.html#Formatted%20Input%20Functions

Impact: Medium

Cross References: `sscanf`, `swprintf`

syslog

Prototype: `void syslog (int facility_priority, char *message)`

Summary: The function sends a message to the Syslog facility.

Description: The function attempts to send a message to the Syslog facility through a Unix domain socket. The function has only two input variables: the message and the priority of it. The function does not return any values. However, in the event of failure, the function closes the socket.

Risk: The syslog facility is commonly utilized on Unix and Linux systems; however, versions are available on Windows systems. Applications that leverage this type of functionality are easily susceptible to attacks that could potentially leak confidential information outside of the application and operating system. In general the UDP cleartext nature of syslog allows attackers to quickly sniff sensitive information. This function should never transmit critical or sensitive information.

Additional Resources: www.gnu.org/software/libc/manual/html_node/ syslog—vsyslog.html#syslog%3b%20vsyslog

Impact: High

system

Prototype: `int system (const char *command)`

Summary: This function executes a system shell command.

Description: The function attempts to execute a given command in the shell. The function has only one input variable: the command to execute (held as a string). The function has several exit scenarios. If the function succeeds, it returns the status of the new process. If the function fails, it returns -1 and sets "`errno`" appropriately. However, if the command is just a null string, it will return a 0.

Risk: This function has the ability to execute a file on the local system. Attackers commonly target functions similar to this since they have the ability to launch potentially dangerous or malicious executables with differing privileges. It is imperative that you filter all input and never allow a user direct access to passing variables as the parameters for this function. Ensure that all special characters are stripped before the data is parsed and passed in addition to limiting access to only the desired executables. Lastly, require that all executable output is controlled within a forked or spawned process within the local application to ensure the integrity of the outputted data. If possible, avoid calling dynamic programs from within applications. Static program execution is more secure.

Additional Resources: www.gnu.org/software/libc/manual/html_node/ Running-a-Command.html#Running%20a%20Command

Impact: High

tempnam

Prototype: `char * tempnam (const char *path, const char *prefix)`

Summary: This function creates a temporary file name.

Description: The function attempts to create a temporary file name. The function has two input arguments: the path to where the file will be created and a prefix to use. If the prefix is not null, up to five characters of the prefix string will be used in the file name. The function returns a pointer to the string that has the new file name.

Risk: Temporary filenames are often created with static and easily guessable algorithms such as the system time or application name appended with the day, month, and year. If at all possible, do not use this function and instead store temporary information in a secure memory space. If a temporary file is necessary, ensure that it is removed upon exiting the program or in the case where a program exits unexpectedly is removed upon program relaunch. Consider utilizing a random number generator such as ISAAC for creating secure random filenames.

Additional Resources:
www.gnu.org/software/libc/manual/html_node/Temporary-Files.html#Temporary%20Files

Impact: High

Cross References: `tmpnam`

tmpfile

Prototype: `FILE * tmpfile (void)`

Summary: This function creates a temporary file for modification.

Description: The function attempts to create a temporary file to use. The function does not take any input arguments, and only returns a pointer to the new filestream. The temporary file is automatically deleted when closed or when the program closes.

Risk: Temporary filenames are often created with static and easily guessable algorithms such as the system time or application name appended with the day, month, and year. If at all possible, do not use this function and instead store temporary information in a secure memory space. If a temporary file is necessary, ensure that it is removed upon exiting the program or in the case where a program exits unexpectedly is removed upon program relaunch. Consider utilizing a random number generator such as ISAAC for creating secure random filenames.

Additional Resources:

www.gnu.org/software/libc/manual/html_node/Temporary-Files.html#Temporary%20Files

Impact: High

tmpnam

Prototype: `char * tmpnam (char *destination)`

Summary: This function creates a temporary file name.

Description: The function creates a temporary file name. The function has only one input argument: the string to house the new file name. It returns the same string (once modified). The function will return a null pointer if it fails. The function may also overwrite another temporary file if called too many times due to finite number of temporary file names available.

Risk: Temporary filenames are often created with static and easily guessable algorithms such as the system time or application name appended with the day, month, and year. If at all possible, do not use this function and instead store temporary information in a secure memory space. If a temporary file is necessary, ensure that it is removed upon exiting the program or in the case where a program exits unexpectedly is removed upon program relaunch. Consider utilizing a random number generator such as ISAAC for creating secure random filenames.

Additional Resources:

www.gnu.org/software/libc/manual/html_node/Temporary-Files.html#Temporary%20Files

Impact: High

Cross References: tempnam

ttyname

Prototype: char * ttyname (int file)

Summary: This function determines if a file is associated with a device.

Description: This function attempts to resolve if a file is associated with a terminal device. The function takes only the file handle in as the input argument. It will check if the file is associated with a device. If it is, the function returns the associated terminal file. Otherwise, the function returns a null pointer.

Risk: This function handles system-specific sensitive information that an attacker could leverage during a period of target reconnaissance. This function should only be utilized if it is absolutely necessary for proper execution of the application. All analysis for the output of this function should be conducted securely within the application and never sent across the wire in cleartext.

Additional Resources: www.gnu.org/software/libc/manual/html_node/Is-It-a-Terminal.html#Is%20It%20a%20Terminal

Impact: Low

unlink

Prototype: `int unlink (const char *filename)`

Summary: The function deletes a file and/or string containing the filename.

Description: The function attempts to delete the string containing a filename, and if applicable, the associated file. The function takes in only the string containing the filename in question. It checks if the filename has an associated file. If so, both are deleted, and if not, only the filename string is. The function returns a `0` if successful, or `-1` if not and sets "`errno`" appropriately.

Risk: The `unlink` function can be leveraged to cause a denial of service on the target application. If improperly secured, an attacker could unlink multiple files required by the application to function thereby disrupting normal execution. Ensure that human input is passed as a parameter for this function.

Additional Resources: www.gnu.org/software/libc/manual/html_node/Deleting-Files.html#Deleting%20Files

Impact: Low

Cross References: `remove, rmdir`

vfork

Prototype: `pid_t vfork (void)`

Summary: This function creates a new process.

Description: This attempts to open a new process for the program to manipulate. The function does not take in any input variables. The only return variable for the function is the process ID. If successful, the function returns a `0` to the child process and the aforementioned process ID to the parent. However, if unsuccessful, the function returns a `-1` to the parent process. On many systems, this function is more efficient than the similar function "`fork`".

Risk: `vfork` can be leveraged in an attack in multiple ways and is especially common in launching Denial-of-Service attacks against the underlying operating system. Thus, you should deny human users from accessing or launching this function or from controlling any type of execution for this function. Additionally, you should close all processes as soon as their execution logic is complete while being aware that it is extremely risky to ever launch a subprocess within an over-arching process.

Additional Resources: www.gnu.org/software/libc/manual/html_node/Creating-a-Process.html#Creating%20a%20Process

Impact: Low

Cross References: fork

vfprintf

Prototype: `int vfprintf (FILE *stream, const char *format, va_list varg)`

Summary: This function prints a string to a file stream.

Description: The function attempts to print a formatted array of characters to the stream. It has only three arguments: the file stream to print to, the array to be printed and the list of arguments for the formatted data. The function will return the number of characters printed. However, in the event of an error, the function returns a negative value.

Risk: This function is potentially vulnerable to a format string attack where an attacker could cause the application to crash unexpected or execute arbitrary code. Format string bugs were discovered in 2000 and the problem is typically spawned from user input that is not properly filtered. Both Microsoft .Net and SPI Dynamics to name two have secure objects that can be implemented to check strings and user input gained from human sources within applications to protect against input-directed vulnerabilities. It is critical that you verify the inputted data have only proper and expected characters in addition to ensuring that your function is properly called. For example, the functions should always utilize their parameters such as `printf("%s", malicious_string)` instead of `printf(malicious_string)`.

Additional Resources: www.gnu.org/software/libc/manual/html_node/Variable-Arguments-Output.html#Variable%20Arguments%20Output

Impact: Medium

Cross References: `vprintf, vfwprintf, vsprintf, vswprintf, vwprintf, vscanf`

vfscanf

Prototype: `int vscanf (FILE *stream, const char *format, va_list varg)`

Summary: This function reads a string of formatted data from a filestream.

Description: The function attempts to scan a formatted array of characters from a filestream. It has three arguments: the file stream to read, the array to be read in to and the argument list for the formatted data. The function will return the number of characters read. However, in the event of an error, the function returns a negative value.

Risk: This function is potentially vulnerable to a format string attack where an attacker could cause the application to crash unexpected or execute arbitrary code. Format string bugs were discovered in 2000 and the problem is typically spawned from user input that is not properly filtered. Both Microsoft .Net and SPI Dynamics to name two have secure objects that can be implemented to check strings and user input gained from human sources within applications to protect against input-directed vulnerabilities. It is critical that you verify the inputted data have only proper and expected characters in addition to ensuring that your function is properly called. For example, the functions should always utilize their parameters such as `printf("%s", malicious_string)` instead of `printf(malicious_string)`.

Additional Resources: www.gnu.org/software/libc/manual/html_node/Variable-Arguments-Input.html#Variable%20Arguments%20Input

Impact: Medium

Cross References: `vprintf, vscanf, vsscanf`

vfwprintf

Prototype: `int vfwprintf (FILE *stream, const wchar_t *format, va_list varg)`

Summary: This function prints a wide-character string to a filestream.

Description: This function attempts to print a string to a filestream. It has three input arguments. The first is the filestream to be written to, while the second is the actual wide-character string to write, the final argument is the formatting argument list. The function returns the number of characters written to the stream. In the event of an error, the function returns a negative value.

Risk: This function is potentially vulnerable to a format string attack where an attacker could cause the application to crash unexpected or execute arbitrary code. Format string bugs were discovered in 2000 and the problem is typically spawned from user input that is not properly filtered. Both Microsoft .Net and SPI Dynamics to name two have secure objects that can be implemented to check strings and user input gained from human sources within applications to protect against input-directed vulnerabilities. It is critical that you verify the inputted data have only proper and expected characters in addition to ensuring that your function is properly called. For example, the functions should always utilize their parameters such as `printf("%s", malicious_string)` instead of `printf(malicious_string)`.

Additional Resources: www.gnu.org/software/libc/manual/html_node/Variable-Arguments-Output.html#Variable%20Arguments%20Output

Impact: Medium

Cross References: `vprintf`, `vfprintf`, `vsprintf`, `vswprintf`, `vwprintf`, `vscanf`

vprintf

Prototype: `int vprintf (const char *format, va_list varg)`

Summary: This function prints a string to the I/O stream.

Description: The function attempts to print a formatted array of characters to the stream. It has only two arguments: the array to be printed and the list of arguments for the formatted data. The function will return the number of characters printed. However, in the event of an error, the function returns a negative value.

Risk: This function is potentially vulnerable to a format string attack where an attacker could cause the application to crash unexpected or execute arbitrary code. Format string bugs were discovered in 2000 and the problem is typically spawned from user input that is not properly filtered. Both Microsoft .Net and SPI Dynamics to name two have secure objects that can be implemented to check strings and user input gained from human sources within applications to protect against input-directed vulnerabilities. It is critical that you verify the inputted data have only proper and expected characters in addition to ensuring that your function is properly called. For example, the functions should always utilize their parameters such as `printf("%s", malicious_string)` instead of `printf(malicious_string)`.

Additional Resources: www.gnu.org/software/libc/manual/html_node/Variable-Arguments-Output.html#Variable%20Arguments%20Output

Impact: Medium

Cross References: `vfprintf, vfwprintf, vsprintf, vswprintf, vwprintf, vscanf`

vscanf

Prototype: `int vscanf (const char *format, va_list varg)`

Summary: This function reads a string of formatted data from the I/O stream.

Description: The function attempts to scan a formatted array of characters from the stream. It has two arguments: the array to be read in to and the argument list for the formatted data. The function will return the number of characters read. However, in the event of an error, the function returns a negative value.

Risk: This function is potentially vulnerable to a format string attack where an attacker could cause the application to crash unexpected or execute arbitrary code. Format string bugs were discovered in 2000 and the problem is typically spawned from user input that is not properly filtered. Both Microsoft .Net and SPI Dynamics to name two have secure objects that can be implemented to check strings and user input gained from human sources within applications to protect against input-directed vulnerabilities. It is critical that you verify the inputted data have only proper and expected characters in addition to ensuring that your function is properly called. For example, the functions should always utilize their parameters such as `printf("%s", malicious_string)` instead of `printf(malicious_string)`.

Additional Resources: www.gnu.org/software/libc/manual/html_node/Variable-Arguments-Input.html#Variable%20Arguments%20Input

Impact: Medium

Cross References: `vprintf, vsfprintf, vsscanf`

vsprintf

Prototype: `int vsprintf (char *string, const char *format, va_list varg)`

Summary: This function prints a string to another string.

Description: The function attempts to print a formatted array of characters to a string. It has only three arguments: the string to print to, the array to be printed and the list of arguments for the formatted data. The function will return the number of characters printed. However, in the event of an error, the function returns a negative value.

Risk: This function is potentially vulnerable to a format string attack where an attacker could cause the application to crash unexpected or execute arbitrary code. Format string bugs were discovered in 2000 and the problem is typically spawned from user input that is not properly filtered. Both Microsoft .Net and SPI Dynamics to name two have secure objects that can be implemented to check strings and user input gained from human sources within applications to protect against input-directed vulnerabilities. It is critical that you verify the inputted data have only proper and expected characters in addition to ensuring that your function is properly called. For example, the functions should always utilize their parameters such as

```
printf("%s", malicious_string) instead of
printf(malicious_string).
```

Additional Resources: www.gnu.org/software/libc/manual/html_node/
Variable-Arguments-Output.html#Variable%20Arguments%20Output

Impact: Medium

Cross References: vprintf, vfprintf, vfwprintf, vswprintf, vwprintf, vscanf

vsscanf

Prototype: `int vsscanf (const char *string, const char *format, va_list varg)`

Summary: This function reads a string of formatted data from a string.

Description: The function attempts to scan a formatted array of characters from a string. It has three arguments: the string to read, the array to be read in to and the argument list for the formatted data. The function will return the number of characters read. However, in the event of an error, the function returns a negative value.

Risk: This function is potentially vulnerable to a format string attack where an attacker could cause the application to crash unexpected or execute arbitrary code. Format string bugs were discovered in 2000 and the problem is typically spawned from user input that is not properly filtered. Both Microsoft .Net and SPI Dynamics to name two have secure objects that can be implemented to check strings and user input gained from human sources within applications to protect against input-directed vulnerabilities. It is critical that you verify the inputted data have only proper and expected characters in addition to ensuring that your function is properly called. For example, the functions should always utilize their parameters such as `printf("%s", malicious_string)` instead of `printf(malicious_string)`.

Additional Resources: www.gnu.org/software/libc/manual/html_node/
Variable-Arguments-Input.html#Variable%20Arguments%20Input

Impact: Medium

Cross References: vprintf, vscanf, vfscanf

vswprintf

Prototype: `int vswprintf (wchar_t *string, size_t count, const wchar_t *format, va_list varg)`

Summary: This function prints a string to another string.

Description: The function attempts to print a formatted array of wide-characters to a wide-character string. It has four arguments: the string to print to, the size of that string (i.e., the maximum size), the wide-character array to be printed and the list of arguments for the formatted data. The function will return the number of characters printed. However, in the event of an error, the function returns a negative value.

Risk: This function is potentially vulnerable to a format string attack where an attacker could cause the application to crash unexpected or execute arbitrary code. Format string bugs were discovered in 2000 and the problem is typically spawned from user input that is not properly filtered. Both Microsoft .Net and SPI Dynamics to name two have secure objects that can be implemented to check strings and user input gained from human sources within applications to protect against input-directed vulnerabilities. It is critical that you verify the inputted data have only proper and expected characters in addition to ensuring that your function is properly called. For example, the functions should always utilize their parameters such as `printf("%s", malicious_string)` instead of `printf(malicious_string)`.

Additional Resources: www.gnu.org/software/libc/manual/html_node/Variable-Arguments-Output.html#Variable%20Arguments%20Output

Impact: Medium

Cross References: vprintf, vfprintf, vfwprintf, vsprintf, vwprintf, vscanf

vwprintf

Prototype: `int vwprintf (const wchar_t *format, va_list varg)`

Summary: This function prints a string to the I/O stream.

Description: The function attempts to print a formatted array of wide-characters to the stream. It has only two arguments: the wide-character array to be printed and the list of arguments for the formatted data. The function will return the number of wide-characters printed. However, in the event of an error, the function returns a negative value.

Risk: This function is potentially vulnerable to a format string attack where an attacker could cause the application to crash unexpected or execute arbitrary code. Format string bugs were discovered in 2000 and the problem is typically spawned from user input that is not properly filtered. Both Microsoft .Net and SPI Dynamics to name two have secure objects that can be implemented to check strings and user input gained from human sources within applications to protect against input-directed vulnerabilities. It is critical that you verify the inputted data have only proper and expected characters in addition to ensuring that your function is properly called. For example, the functions should always utilize their parameters such as `printf("%s", malicious_string)` instead of `printf(malicious_string)`.

Additional Resources: www.gnu.org/software/libc/manual/html_node/Variable-Arguments-Output.html#Variable%20Arguments%20Output

Impact: Medium

Cross References: `vprintf, vfprintf, vfwprintf, vsprintf, vswprintf, vscanf`

wcscat

Prototype: `wchar_t * wcscat (wchar_t *destination, const wchar_t *source)`

Summary: The function appends a string onto the end of another.

Description: This function attempts to concatenate one string onto the end of another. It has two input arguments: the source and destination wide-character strings. The function will copy the source string onto the end of the destination string, overwriting the null character (if it exists). The function will return the destination string when completed.

Risk: Functions that are utilized to copy or concatenate strings are commonly misused and fall victim to buffer overflow attacks. It is critical that you ensure before execution of this function that the destination source is large enough to house the source data. Additionally, limiting the source data memory space will not only make your application more efficient, it will also add another layer of security by relying less on the destination buffer. For example, if X should be copied to Y then ensure that Y's space is less than X-1's total space allocation. It is similar for concatenation functions where as the strings are limited to a total length.

Additional Resources: www.gnu.org/software/libc/manual/html_node/Copying-and-Concatenation.html#Copying%20and%20Concatenation

Impact: Low

Cross References: wcscpy, wcslen, wcsncat, wcsncpy

wcscpy

Prototype: wchar_t * wcscpy (wchar_t *destination, const wchar_t *source)

Summary: The function copies a string onto another.

Description: This function attempts to copy one string onto another. It has two input arguments: the source and destination wide-character strings. The function will copy the source string onto destination string, writing the null character (if it exists). The function will return the destination string when completed.

Risk: Functions that are utilized to copy or concatenate strings are commonly misused and fall victim to buffer overflow attacks. It is critical that you ensure before execution of this function that the destination source is large enough to house the source data. Additionally, limiting the source data memory space will not only make your application more efficient, it will also add another layer of security by relying less on the destination buffer. For example, if X should be copied to Y then ensure that Y's space is less than X-1's total space allocation. It is similar for concatenation functions where as the strings are limited to a total length.

Additional Resources: www.gnu.org/software/libc/manual/html_node/Copying-and-Concatenation.html#Copying%20and%20Concatenation

Impact: Low

Cross References: wcscat, wcslen, wcsncat, wcsncpy

wcslen

Prototype: size_t wcslen (const wchar_t *string)

Summary: This function finds the length of a string.

Description: The function attempts to find the length of the wide-character string. It has only one input argument: the string to get the length of. The function will return an integer indicating the length of the wide-character string. In the event that the string does not exist or an error occurs, the function can return 0.

Risk: The length of a string is commonly ascertained before it is passed to a function that utilizes it to calculate the space required for a destination buffer. Ensure that human users do not have the ability to modify this number thereby potentially making it smaller than the destination. Calculate the length of the source then add one byte so to avoid off-by-one application buffer overflow attacks.

Additional Resources: www.gnu.org/software/libc/manual/html_node/ String-Length.html#String%20Length

Impact: Low

Cross References: strlen

wcsncat

Prototype: wchar_t * wcsncat (wchar_t *destination, const wchar_t *source, size_t count)

Summary: The function appends a string onto the end of another.

Description: This function attempts to concatenate one string onto the end of another. It has three input arguments: the source and destination wide-character strings, and the maximum number of characters to append. The function will copy the source string onto the end of the destination string (up to the max count), overwriting the null character (if it exists). The function will return the destination string when completed.

Risk: Functions that are utilized to copy or concatenate strings are commonly misused and fall victim to buffer overflow attacks. It is critical that you ensure before execution of this function that the destination source is large enough to house the source data. Additionally, limiting the source data memory space will not only make your application more efficient, it will also add another layer of security by relying less on the destination buffer. For example, if X should be copied to Y, then ensure that Y's space is less than X-1's total space allocation. It is similar for concatenation functions where as the strings are limited to a total length.

Additional Resources: www.gnu.org/software/libc/manual/html_node/Copying-and-Concatenation.html#Copying%20and%20Concatenation

Impact: Low

Cross References: wcscat, wcscpy, wcslen, wcsncpy

wcsncpy

Prototype: wchar_t * wcsncpy (wchar_t *destination, const wchar_t *source, size_t count)

Summary: The function copies a string onto another.

Description: This function attempts to copy one string onto another. It has three input arguments: the source and destination wide-character strings, and the maximum number of characters to copy. The function will copy the source string onto destination string (up to the maximum count), writing the null character (if it exists). The function will return the destination string when completed.

Risk: Functions that are utilized to copy or concatenate strings are commonly misused and fall victim to buffer overflow attacks. It is critical that you ensure before execution of this function that the destination source is large enough to house the source data. Additionally, limiting the source data memory space will not only make your application more efficient, it will also add another layer of security by relying less on the destination buffer. For example, if X should be copied to Y, then ensure that Y's space is less than X-1's total space allocation. It is similar for concatenation functions where as the strings are limited to a total length.

Additional Resources: www.gnu.org/software/libc/manual/html_node/ Copying-and-Concatenation.html#Copying%20and%20Concatenation

Impact: Low

Cross References: `wcscat`, `wcscpy`, `wcslen`, `wcsncat`

wcsxfrm

Prototype: `size_t strxfrm (wchar_t *destination, const wchar_t *source, size_t count )`

Summary: This function transforms a string based off of the locale.

Description: The function attempts to transform a wide-character string based on the locale information of the system. It takes in three input arguments: the source and destination wide-character strings and the maximum number of characters to put in the destination string. The function will return the length of the string written. In the event of an error, the function returns `-1`.

Risk: Functions that are utilized to copy or concatenate strings are commonly misused and fall victim to buffer overflow attacks. It is critical that you ensure before execution of this function that the destination source is large enough to house the source data. Additionally, limiting the source data memory space will not only make your application more efficient, it will also add another layer of security by relying less on the destination buffer. For example, if X should be copied to Y, then ensure that Y's space is less than X-1's total space allocation. It is similar for concatenation functions where as the strings are limited to a total length.

Additional Resources:

www.gnu.org/software/libc/manual/html_node/Collation-Functions.html# Collation%20Functions

Impact: High

Cross References: `strxfrm`

wscanf

Prototype: `int wscanf( const wchar_t *format)`

Summary: The function reads a formatted array of characters from the I/O stream.

Description: The function attempts to scan a formatted array of wide-characters from the stream. It has only one formal argument: the array to be read in to. However, as it can be formatted data, there can be subsequent, informal arguments. The function will return the number of wide-characters read. However, in the event of an error, the function returns a negative value.

Risk: This function is potentially vulnerable to a format string attack where an attacker could cause the application to crash unexpected or execute arbitrary code. Format string bugs were discovered in 2000 and the problem is typically spawned from user input that is not properly filtered. Both Microsoft .Net and SPI Dynamics to name two have secure objects that can be implemented to check strings and user input gained from human sources within applications to protect against input-directed vulnerabilities. It is critical that you verify the inputted data have only proper and expected characters in addition to ensuring that your function is properly called. For example, the functions should always utilize their parameters such as `printf("%s", malicious_string)` instead of `printf(malicious_string)`.

Additional Resources:
www.gnu.org/software/libc/manual/html_node/Formatted-Input-Functions.html#Formatted%20Input%20Functions;
http://msdn.microsoft.com/library/default.asp?url=/library/en-us/vccore98/html/_crt_scanf.2c_.wscanf.asp

Impact: Medium

Cross References: `scanf`, `wprintf`

wsprintf

Prototype: `int wsprintf( LPTSTR string, LPCTSTR format)`

Summary: This function prints a formatted string to another string.

Description: The function attempts to print a formatted, wide-character string to another string. It has two formal input arguments: the wide-character string and the format for the string. The informal arguments may be necessary for the formatting. The function returns the number of characters in the output string (not including the null character). If the function fails, however, it will return an unexpected value.

Risk: This function is potentially vulnerable to a format string attack where an attacker could cause the application to crash unexpected or execute arbitrary code. Format string bugs were discovered in 2000 and the problem is typically spawned from user input that is not properly filtered. Both Microsoft .Net and SPI Dynamics to name two have secure objects that can be implemented to check strings and user input gained from human sources within applications to protect against input-directed vulnerabilities. It is critical that you verify the inputted data have only proper and expected characters in addition to ensuring that your function is properly called. For example, the functions should always utilize their parameters such as `printf("%s", malicious_string)` instead of `printf(malicious_string)`.

Additional Resources:
http://msdn.microsoft.com/library/default.asp?url=/library/en-us/winui/WinUI/WindowsUserInterface/Resources/Strings/StringReference/StringFunctions/wsprintf.asp

Impact: Medium

Cross References: `wsprintfA`, `wsprintfW`

Programmer's Ultimate Security DeskRef: C++

chdir

Prototype: `int chdir (const char *Path)`

Summary: This function changes the current directory.

Description: The function changes the directory to which the current path points. The function only takes in the path to the new directory. The function returns a zero upon successful completion. In the event of an error, the function returns a -1 and sets the variable `errno` to the appropriate value.

Risk: Directory information is sought after by attackers to ascertain underlying operating system, configuration, and application-layer information. Human options should be limited to only include the desired directories via the appropriate access controls.

Additional Resources:
http://nscp.upenn.edu/aix4.3html/libs/basetrf1/chdir.htm

Impact: High

Cross References: `chroot`

creat

Prototype: `int creat (const char *filename, mode_t mode)`

Summary: This function is used to open a file.

Description: This function is used to open a file for processing, whether that be reading and/or writing. The function takes two inputs: the first being the filename and the second being the mode in which to open the file. The function returns a 0 if it is successful, and a -1 if not. In the event of an unsuccessful attempt to open the file, the variable `errno` will be set appropriately.

Risk: The `creat` function is susceptible to race condition attacks thereby it is mandatory that you undertake the proper precautions when implementing this function. Ensure that only a single instance of this function can execute at any given time. Additionally, ensure the data for the filename is properly parsed and controlled. Input should be verified to be without special characters and controls denying access to unauthorized should be enabled within the application.

Note: There exists a Windows-compatible version of this function called `_create`, as well as a Windows-compatible, wide-character-capable `_wcreate`. This function is obsolete, and has been replaced by `open`.

Additional Resources: www.gnu.org/software/libc/manual/html_node/Opening-and-Closing-Files.html#Opening%20and%20Closing%20Files; http://msdn.microsoft.com/library/default.asp?url=/library/en-us/vccore98/html/_crt__creat.2c_._wcreat.asp

Impact: Low

Cross References: `open`

gethostbyname

Prototype: `struct hostent * gethostbyname (const char *name)`

Summary: This function gets an Internet host's information by the name.

Description: The function attempts to retrieve an Internet host's information using its name. The function takes only one input value, the name of the host. The function will return a `hostent` structure containing the requested information. In the event of a failure, the function will return a null pointer. It will also appropriately set the variable h_errno.

Risk: This function handles system-specific sensitive information that an attacker could leverage during a period of target reconnaissance. This function should only be utilized if it is absolutely necessary for proper execution of the application. All analysis for the output of this function should be conducted securely within the application and never sent across the wire in cleartext.

Additional Resources: www.gnu.org/software/libc/manual/html_node/Host-Names.html#Host%20Names

Impact: Low

Cross References: gethostbyaddr

GetTempFileNameA

Summary: This function creates a name for a temporary file.

Description: This function attempts to create a temporary file name. It has four input arguments: the path of the file, the prefix for the file, a unique number, and the file handle. The function returns the unique number for the file name if successful. However, if an error occurs, it will return 0.

Risk: Temporary filenames are often created with static and easily guessable algorithms such as the system time or application name appended with the day, month, and year. If at all possible, do not use this function and instead store temporary information in a secure memory space. If a temporary file is necessary, ensure that it is removed upon exiting the program or in the case where a program exits unexpectedly is removed upon program relaunch. Consider utilizing a random number generator such as ISAAC for creating secure random filenames.

Note: At time of publication, this function was designed for Windows compatibility.

Additional Resources: www.webtropy.com/articles/art9-1.asp?f=GetTempFileName

Impact: Low

Cross References: GetTempFileName, GetTempFileNameW, GetTempPath

C++

ImpersonateNamedPipeClient

Prototype: `BOOL ImpersonateNamedPipeClient( HANDLE hNamedPipe )`

Summary: This function attempts to impersonate a named-pipe client application.

Description: This function attempts to impersonate the security context of a named-pipe client application. The function has only one input argument: the handle of the pipe to impersonate. The function will return a non-zero value if successful, a zero if not. The impersonation will last until the end of the current thread or the impersonation is overtly stopped.

Risk: Applications that have the ability to impersonate local systems, users, or security information are extremely dangerous; furthermore, functions that leverage this type of functionality should be controlled and only used as a last resort! All impersonation functions should be controlled by internal application-specific routines in addition to the controlled use of their output.

Note: At time of publication, this function was designed for Windows compatibility.

Additional Resources:

http://msdn.microsoft.com/library/default.asp?url=/library/en-us/security/security/impersonatenamedpipeclient.asp

Impact: Medium

Cross References: `CoImpersonateClient, ImpersonateDdeClientWindow, ImpersonateLoggedOnUser, ImpersonateSecurityContext`

ImpersonateSecurityContext

Prototype: `SECURITY_STATUS SEC_Entry ImpersonateSecurityContext( PCtxtHandle phContext )`

Summary: This function attempts to impersonate a security context of a client application.

Description: This function attempts to impersonate the security context of a client application. The function has only one input argument: the handle of the application to impersonate. The function will return `SEC_E_OK` if successful. If not, the function returns `SEC_E_INVALID_HANDLE`.

Risk: Applications that have the ability to impersonate local systems, users, or security information are extremely dangerous; furthermore, functions that leverage this type of functionality should be controlled and only used as a last resort! All impersonation functions should be controlled by internal application-specific routines in addition to the controlled use of their output.

Note: At time of publication, this function was designed for Windows compatibility.

Additional Resources:
http://msdn.microsoft.com/library/default.asp?url=/library/en-us/security/security/impersonatesecuritycontext.asp

Impact: Medium

Cross References: `CoImpersonateClient`, `ImpersonateDdeClientWindow`, `ImpersonateLoggedOnUser`, `ImpersonateNamedPipeClient`

InitializeCriticalSection

Prototype: `void InitializeCriticalSection( LPCRITICAL_SECTION lpCriticalSection )`

Summary: This function initializes a critical section object.

Description: The function will attempt to initialize a critical section object. The function only has one input argument: the pointer to the critical section object. The function does not return any values. However, if memory consumption causes an error, the `STATUS_NO_MEMORY` flag will be activated.

Risk: This function should be analyzed to ensure that the critical section object that is initialized is restricted to the appropriate processes and users. All critical section objects should be closed when their application execution logic is complete.

Note: At time of publication, this function was designed for Windows compatibility.

Additional Resources:
http://msdn.microsoft.com/library/default.asp?url=/library/en-us/dllproc/base/initializecriticalsection.asp

Impact: Low

Cross References: `EnterCriticalSection`

C++

memcpy

Prototype: `void * memcpy (void *destination, const void *source, size_t size)`

Summary: This function copies one band of memory to another.

Description: The function's purpose is to copy a band of memory to another. It takes three inputs: the pointer for the source of the copying, the pointer to the destination, and the size of the band to copy. The function starts at the beginning of the source, traversing and copying the memory to the destination for the given size. The function does not return a pointer to the destination memory.

Risk: At the most basic level, these functions read in data, perform analysis, then output the data to another location in memory. It is imperative that the destination string be calculated accordingly and that enough memory space is allocated. This function should not be utilized in any case and more secure functions for securely copying memory allocations should be implemented.

Additional Resources: www.gnu.org/software/libc/manual/html_node/Copying-and-Concatenation.html#Copying%20and%20Concatenation

Impact: Medium

MultiByteToWideChar

Prototype: `int MultiByteToWideChar( UINT CodePage, DWORD dwFlags, LPCSTR destination, int countD, LPWSTR source, int countS )`

Summary: This function translates a multibyte-character string to a wide-character string.

Description: The function attempts to translate a source multibyte-character string into a wide-character string. The function has six input arguments: the code page to give the conversion data, a flag set, the source string and its size, and the destination string and its size. The function will return an integer which can have several meanings. Depending on the size of strings, the flag setting, and whether the function was successful, it can return many different values. See the reference for more information.

Risk: Multi-byte strings have the potential to be very large strings that can be potentially leveraged in a buffer overflow attack scenario. These strings should restrict characters to include only those that are required by the application to function. Additionally, standard string manipulation functions should be utilized instead of large multi-byte strings in all cases possible. Ensure that the destination buffer is of appropriate size and that the source buffer is limited to that size −1.

Note: At time of publication, this function was designed for Windows compatibility.

Additional Resources:
http://msdn.microsoft.com/library/default.asp?url=/library/en-us/intl/unicode_17si.asp

Impact: Low

Cross References: `WideCharToMultiByte`

OemToAnsiA(ClassMember)

Prototype: `void CStringT::OemToAnsiA()`

Summary: This class member converts the string of characters from the OEM character set to the ANSI character set.

Description: This is a member of the class type CStringT. The member will convert the character of the class object `String` from the OEM character set to the ANSI character set. It does not return anything, as it modifies the class object itself.

Risk: Certain string manipulation functions to include OEM transition functions are commonly leveraged in buffer overflow attacks. At the most basic level, these functions read in data, perform analysis and execution logic, then output the data to another type of string. It is imperative that the destination string be calculated accordingly and that enough memory space is allocated. Special characters should also be stricken from the conversion.

Note: At time of publication, this function was designed for Windows compatibility.

Additional Resources:
http://msdn.microsoft.com/library/default.asp?url=/library/en-us/vclib/html/vclr-fcstringtoemtoansi.asp

Impact: Low

OemToAnsiBuffA(ClassMember)

Prototype: `void CStringT::OemToAnsiBuffA()`

Summary: This class member converts the string of characters from the OEM character set to the ANSI character set.

Description: This is a member of the class type CStringT. The member will convert the character of the class object `String` from the OEM character set to the ANSI character set. It does not return anything, as it modifies the class object itself. This member, however, is careful with the use of 16-bit applications.

Risk: Certain string manipulation functions to include OEM transition functions are commonly leveraged in buffer overflow attacks. At the most basic level, these functions read in data, perform analysis and execution logic, then output the data to another type of string. It is imperative that the destination string be calculated accordingly and that enough memory space is allocated. Special characters should also be stricken from the conversion.

Note: At time of publication, this function was designed for Windows compatibility.

Additional Resources:

http://msdn.microsoft.com/library/default.asp?url=/library/en-us/vclib/html/vclr-fcstringtoemtoansi.asp

Impact: Low

OemToAnsiBuffW(ClassMember)

Prototype: `void CStringT::OemToAnsiBuffW()`

Summary: This class member converts the string of characters from the OEM character set to the ANSI character set.

Description: This is a member of the class type CStringT. The member will convert the character of the class object `String` from the OEM character set to the ANSI character set. It does not return anything, as it modifies the class object itself. This member, however, is careful with the use of 16-bit applications.

Risk: Certain string manipulation functions to include OEM transition functions are commonly leveraged in buffer overflow attacks. At the most basic level, these functions read in data, perform analysis and execution logic, then output the data to another type of string. It is imperative that the destination string be calculated accordingly and that enough memory space is allocated. Special characters should also be stricken from the conversion.

Note: At time of publication, this function was designed for Windows compatibility.

Additional Resources:
http://msdn.microsoft.com/library/default.asp?url=/library/en-us/vclib/html/vclr-fcstringtoemtoansi.asp

Impact: Low

OemToAnsiW(ClassMember)

Prototype: `void CStringT::OemToAnsiW()`

Summary: This class member converts the string of characters from the OEM character set to the ANSI character set.

Description: This is a member of the class type CStringT. The member will convert the character of the class object `String` from the OEM character set to the ANSI character set. It does not return anything, as it modifies the class object itself.

Risk: Certain string manipulation functions to include OEM transition functions are commonly leveraged in buffer overflow attacks. At the most basic level, these functions read in data, perform analysis and execution logic, then output the data to another type of string. It is imperative that the destination string be calculated accordingly and that enough memory space is allocated. Special characters should also be stricken from the conversion.

Note: At time of publication, this function was designed for Windows compatibility.

Additional Resources:
http://msdn.microsoft.com/library/default.asp?url=/library/en-us/vclib/html/vclr-fcstringtoemtoansi.asp

Impact: Low

C++

OemToChar

Prototype: `BOOL OemToChar( LPCSTR source, LPTSTR destination )`

Summary: This function converts string from the OEM character set to the ANSI character set.

Description: The function attempts to translate a string in the OEM character to the ANSI character set. The function has two input variables: the source OEM-character string and the destination ANSI-character string. The function will return either 0 if unsuccessful or 1 if it succeeds.

Risk: Certain string manipulation functions to include OEM transition functions are commonly leveraged in buffer overflow attacks. At the most basic level, these functions read in data, perform analysis and execution logic, then output the data to another type of string. It is imperative that the destination string be calculated accordingly and that enough memory space is allocated. Special characters should also be stricken from the conversion.

Note: At time of publication, this function was designed for Windows compatibility. This function replaces `OemToAnsi` member of a CStringT type object.

Additional Resources:
http://msdn.microsoft.com/library/default.asp?url=/library/en-us/winui/winui/windowsuserinterface/resources/strings/stringreference/stringfunctions/oemtochar.asp

Impact: Low

Cross References: `OemToCharBuff`

OemToCharA

Prototype: `BOOL OemToCharA( LPCSTR source, LPTSTR destination)`

Summary: This function converts string from the OEM character set to the ANSI character set.

Description: The function attempts to translate a string in the OEM character to the ANSI character set. The function has two input variables: the source OEM-character string and the destination ANSI-character string. The function will return either 0 if unsuccessful or 1 if it succeeds.

Risk: Certain string manipulation functions to include OEM transition functions are commonly leveraged in buffer overflow attacks. At the most basic level, these functions read in data, perform analysis and execution logic, then output the data to another type of string. It is imperative that the destination string be calculated accordingly and that enough memory space is allocated. Special characters should also be stricken from the conversion.

Note: At time of publication, this function was designed for Windows compatibility. This function replaces OemToAnsiA member of a CStringT type object.

Additional Resources:
http://msdn.microsoft.com/library/default.asp?url=/library/en-us/winui/winui/windowsuserinterface/resources/strings/stringreference/stringfunctions/oemtochar.asp

Impact: Low

Cross References: OemToChar

OemToCharBuff

Prototype: BOOL OemToCharBuff(LPCTSTR source, LPTSTR destination, DWORD count)

Summary: This function translates a defined number of characters in a string from the OEM character set to the ANSI character set.

Description: The function attempts to translate a string in the OEM character to the ANSI character set. The function has three input variables: the source OEM-character string, the destination ANSI-character string, and the maximum number of characters to translate. The function will return either 0 if unsuccessful or 1 if it succeeds.

Risk: Certain string manipulation functions to include OEM transition functions are commonly leveraged in buffer overflow attacks. At the most basic level, these functions read in data, perform analysis and execution logic, then output the data to another type of string. It is imperative that the destination string be calculated

C++

accordingly and that enough memory space is allocated. Special characters should also be stricken from the conversion.

Note: At time of publication, this function was designed for Windows compatibility. This function replaces `OemToAnsiBuff` member of a CStringT type object.

Additional Resources:

http://msdn.microsoft.com/library/default.asp?url=/library/en-us/winui/WinUI/WindowsUserInterface/Resources/Strings/StringReference/StringFunctions/OemToCharBuff.asp

Impact: Low

Cross References: `OemToChar`

OemToCharBuffA

Prototype: `static extern int OemToCharBuffA( string source, string destination, int count )`

Summary: This function translates a defined number of characters in a string from the OEM character set to the ANSI character set.

Description: The function attempts to translate a string in the OEM character to the ANSI character set. The function has three input variables: the source OEM-character string, the destination ANSI-character string, and the maximum number of characters to translate. The function will return either 0 if unsuccessful or 1 if it succeeds.

Risk: Certain string manipulation functions to include OEM transition functions are commonly leveraged in buffer overflow attacks. At the most basic level, these functions read in data, perform analysis and execution logic, then output the data to another type of string. It is imperative that the destination string be calculated accordingly and that enough memory space is allocated. Special characters should also be stricken from the conversion.

Note: At time of publication, this function was designed for Windows compatibility. This function replaces `OemToAnsiBuffA` member of a CStringT type object.

Additional Resources: http://custom.programming-in.net/articles/art9-1.asp?f=OemToCharBuff

Impact: Low

Cross References: `OemToCharBuff`

OemToCharW

Prototype: `BOOL OemToCharW( LPCSTR source, LPTSTR destination )`

Summary: This function converts string from the OEM character set to the ANSI character set.

Description: The function attempts to translate a string in the OEM character to the ANSI character set. The function has two input variables: the source OEM-character string and the destination ANSI-character string. The function will return either 0 if unsuccessful or 1 if it succeeds.

Risk: Certain string manipulation functions to include OEM transition functions are commonly leveraged in buffer overflow attacks. At the most basic level, these functions read in data, perform analysis and execution logic, then output the data to another type of string. It is imperative that the destination string be calculated accordingly and that enough memory space is allocated. Special characters should also be stricken from the conversion.

Note: At time of publication, this function was designed for Windows compatibility. This function replaces `OemToAnsiW` member of a CStringT type object. This particular function is from the Windows Layer for Unicode and requires additional files to be used in Win 95/98/Me.

Additional Resources:
http://msdn.microsoft.com/library/default.asp?url=/library/en-us/winui/winui/windowsuserinterface/resources/strings/stringreference/stringfunctions/oemtochar.asp

Impact: Low

Cross References: `OemToChar`

PathAddBackslash

Prototype: `LPTSTR PathAddBackslash( LPTSTR path )`

Summary: This function adds a backslash to the end of path string.

Description: The function attempts to add a backslash to the end of a path given in a string. The function has one input argument: the string containing the path. The function will add the backslash (as long as one is not already present) and return the string.

Risk: System path information is constantly sought after by attackers or malicious users profiling a target application or system. Path information alone can potentially identify the underlying operating system, installed applications, configurations, and in some cases user and security information. Ensure that non-alphanumeric characters are removed from the string before it is processed and that the information is only processed internally by the application. Limit the end user's ability to ascertain or traverse path information.

Note: At time of publication, this function was designed for Windows compatibility.

Additional Resources:

http://msdn.microsoft.com/library/default.asp?url=/library/en-us/shellcc/platform/shell/reference/shlwapi/path/pathaddbackslash.asp

Impact: Medium

Cross References: `PathAddBackslashA, PathAddBackslashW`

PathAddBackslashA

Prototype: `LPTSTR PathAddBackslashA( LPTSTR path )`

Summary: This function adds a backslash to the end of path string.

Description: The function attempts to add a backslash to the end of a path given in a string. The function has one input argument: the string containing the path. The function will add the backslash (as long as one is not already present) and return the string.

Risk: System path information is constantly sought after by attackers or malicious users profiling a target application or system. Path information alone can potentially identify the underlying operating system, installed applications, configurations, and in some cases user and security information. Ensure that non-alphanumeric characters are removed from the string before it is processed and that the information is only processed internally by the application. Limit the end user's ability to ascertain or traverse path information.

Note: At time of publication, this function was designed for Windows compatibility.

Additional Resources:
http://msdn.microsoft.com/library/default.asp?url=/library/en-us/shellcc/plat-form/shell/reference/shlwapi/path/pathaddbackslash.asp

Impact: Medium

Cross References: `PathAddBackslash, PathAddBackslashW`

PathAddBackslashW

Prototype: `LPTSTR PathAddBackslashW( LPCWSTR path )`

Summary: This function adds a backslash to the end of path string.

Description: The function attempts to add a backslash to the end of a path given in a wide-character string. The function has one input argument: the string containing the path. The function will add the backslash (as long as one is not already present) and return the resulting wide-character string.

Risk: System path information is constantly sought after by attackers or malicious users profiling a target application or system. Path information alone can potentially identify the underlying operating system, installed applications, configurations, and in some cases user and security information. Ensure that non-alphanumeric characters are removed from the string before it is processed and that the information is only processed internally by the application. Limit the end user's ability to ascertain or traverse path information.

C++

Note: At time of publication, this function was designed for Windows compatibility.

Additional Resources:

http://msdn.microsoft.com/library/default.asp?url=/library/en-us/shellcc/plat-form/shell/reference/shlwapi/path/pathaddbackslash.asp

Impact: Medium

Cross References: `PathAddBackslash`, `PathAddBackslashA`

PathAddExtension

Prototype: `BOOL PathAddExtension( LPTSTR path, LPCTSTR extension )`

Summary: This function adds an extension (given as a string) to a path.

Description: This function attempts to add an extension to a given path. The function has two input values: the string containing the path and the string containing the extension. The function will append the extension to the end of the path. It will return `1` if the extension is added correctly, or a `0` if it fails.

Risk: System path information is constantly sought after by attackers or malicious users profiling a target application or system. Path information alone can potentially identify the underlying operating system, installed applications, configurations, and in some cases user and security information. Ensure that non-alphanumeric characters are removed from the string before it is processed and that the information is only processed internally by the application. Limit the end user's ability to ascertain or traverse path information.

Note: At time of publication, this function was designed for Windows compatibility.

Additional Resources:

http://msdn.microsoft.com/library/default.asp?url=/library/en-us/shellcc/plat-form/shell/reference/shlwapi/path/pathaddextension.asp

Impact: Medium

Cross References: `PathAddExtensionA`, `PathAddExtensionW`

C++

PathAddExtensionA

Prototype: `BOOL PathAddExtensionA( LPTSTR path, LPCTSTR extension )`

Summary: This function adds an extension (given as a string) to a path.

Description: This function attempts to add an extension to a given path. The function has two input values: the string containing the path and the string containing the extension. The function will append the extension to the end of the path. It will return 1 if the extension is added correctly, or a 0 if it fails.

Risk: System path information is constantly sought after by attackers or malicious users profiling a target application or system. Path information alone can potentially identify the underlying operating system, installed applications, configurations, and in some cases user and security information. Ensure that non-alphanumeric characters are removed from the string before it is processed and that the information is only processed internally by the application. Limit the end user's ability to ascertain or traverse path information.

Note: At time of publication, this function was designed for Windows compatibility.

Additional Resources:

http://msdn.microsoft.com/library/default.asp?url=/library/en-us/shellcc/platform/shell/reference/shlwapi/path/pathaddextension.asp

Impact: Medium

Cross References: `PathAddExtension, PathAddExtensionW`

PathAddExtensionW

Prototype: `BOOL PathAddExtensionW( LPWSTR path, LPCWSTR extension )`

Summary: This function adds an extension (given as a string) to a path.

Description: This function attempts to add an extension to a given path. The function has two input values: the wide-character string containing the path and the wide-character string containing the extension. The function will append the extension to the end of the path. It will return 1 if the extension is added correctly, or a 0 if it fails.

Risk: System path information is constantly sought after by attackers or malicious users profiling a target application or system. Path information alone can potentially identify the underlying operating system, installed applications, configurations, and in some cases user and security information. Ensure that non-alphanumeric characters are removed from the string before it is processed and that the information is only processed internally by the application. Limit the end user's ability to ascertain or traverse path information.

Note: At time of publication, this function was designed for Windows compatibility.

Additional Resources:

http://msdn.microsoft.com/library/default.asp?url=/library/en-us/shellcc/plat-form/shell/reference/shlwapi/path/pathaddextension.asp

Impact: Medium

Cross References: PathAddExtension, PathAddExtensionA

PathAppend

Prototype: BOOL PathAppend(LPTSTR destination, LPCTSTR source)

Summary: This function appends a path onto the end of another.

Description: This function attempts to add an extension to a given path. The function has two input values: the string containing the destination path and the string containing the source path to be appended. The function will append the source path to the end of the destination path. It will return 1 if the extension is added correctly, or a 0 if it fails.

Risk: System path information is constantly sought after by attackers or malicious users profiling a target application or system. Path information alone can potentially identify the underlying operating system, installed applications, configurations, and in some cases user and security information. Ensure that non-alphanumeric characters are removed from the string before it is processed and that the information is only

C++

processed internally by the application. Limit the end user's ability to ascertain or traverse path information.

Note: At time of publication, this function was designed for Windows compatibility.

Additional Resources:

http://msdn.microsoft.com/library/default.asp?url=/library/en-us/shellcc/plat-form/shell/reference/shlwapi/path/pathappend.asp

Impact: Medium

Cross References: PathAppendA, PathAppendW

PathAppendA

Prototype: BOOL PathAppendA(LPTSTR destination, LPCTSTR source)

Summary: This function appends a path onto the end of another.

Description: This function attempts to add an extension to a given path. The function has two input values: the string containing the destination path and the string containing the source path to be appended. The function will append the source path to the end of the destination path. It will return 1 if the extension is added correctly, or a 0 if it fails.

Risk: System path information is constantly sought after by attackers or malicious users profiling a target application or system. Path information alone can potentially identify the underlying operating system, installed applications, configurations, and in some cases user and security information. Ensure that non-alphanumeric characters are removed from the string before it is processed and that the information is only processed internally by the application. Limit the end user's ability to ascertain or traverse path information.

Note: At time of publication, this function was designed for Windows compatibility.

Additional Resources:

http://msdn.microsoft.com/library/default.asp?url=/library/en-us/shellcc/plat-form/shell/reference/shlwapi/path/pathappend.asp

C++

Impact: Medium

Cross References: PathAppend, PathAppendW

PathAppendW

Prototype: BOOL PathAppendW(LPWSTR destination, LPCWSTR source)

Summary: This function appends a path onto the end of another.

Description: This function attempts to add an extension to a given path. The function has two input values: the wide-character string containing the destination path and the wide-character string containing the source path to be appended. The function will append the source path to the end of the destination path. It will return 1 if the extension is added correctly, or a 0 if it fails.

Risk: System path information is constantly sought after by attackers or malicious users profiling a target application or system. Path information alone can potentially identify the underlying operating system, installed applications, configurations, and in some cases user and security information. Ensure that non-alphanumeric characters are removed from the string before it is processed and that the information is only processed internally by the application. Limit the end user's ability to ascertain or traverse path information.

Note: At time of publication, this function was designed for Windows compatibility.

Additional Resources:

http://msdn.microsoft.com/library/default.asp?url=/library/en-us/shellcc/platform/shell/reference/shlwapi/path/pathappend.asp

Impact: Medium

Cross References: PathAppend, PathAppendA

PathCanonicalize

Prototype: BOOL PathCanonicalize(LPTSTR destination, LPCTSTR source)

Summary: This function canonicalizes a path.

Description: The function attempts to canonicalize a path. The function has two input arguments: the source string for the path and a destination string for the canonicalized path. The function will canonicalize the path by removing appropriate directories from the path when objects like " . " and " . . " are used in it. The function will return a 1 if it is successful and a 0 when not.

Risk: System path information is constantly sought after by attackers or malicious users profiling a target application or system. Path information alone can potentially identify the underlying operating system, installed applications, configurations, and in some cases user and security information. Ensure that non-alphanumeric characters are removed from the string before it is processed and that the information is only processed internally by the application. Limit the end user's ability to ascertain or traverse path information.

Note: At time of publication, this function was designed for Windows compatibility.

Additional Resources:

http://msdn.microsoft.com/library/default.asp?url=/library/en-us/shellcc/plat-form/shell/reference/shlwapi/path/pathcanonicalize.asp

Impact: Medium

Cross References: `PathCanonicalizeA, PathCanonicalizeW`

PathCanonicalizeA

Prototype: `BOOL PathCanonicalizeA( LPTSTR destination, LPCTSTR source )`

Summary: This function canonicalizes a path.

Description: The function attempts to canonicalize a path. The function has two input arguments: the source string for the path and a destination string for the canonicalized path. The function will canonicalize the path by removing appropriate directories from the path when objects like " . " and " . . " are used in it. The function will return a 1 if it is successful and a 0 when not.

Risk: System path information is constantly sought after by attackers or malicious users profiling a target application or system. Path information alone can potentially identify the underlying operating system, installed applications, configurations, and in some cases user and security information. Ensure that non-alphanumeric characters are removed from the string before it is processed and that the information is only processed internally by the application. Limit the end user's ability to ascertain or traverse path information.

Note: At time of publication, this function was designed for Windows compatibility.

Additional Resources:
http://msdn.microsoft.com/library/default.asp?url=/library/en-us/shellcc/platform/shell/reference/shlwapi/path/pathcanonicalize.asp

Impact: Medium

Cross References: PathCanonicalize, PathCanonicalizeW

PathCanonicalizeW

Prototype: BOOL PathCanonicalizeW(LPWSTR destination, LPCWSTR source)

Summary: This function canonicalizes a path.

Description: The function attempts to canonicalize a path. The function has two input arguments: the source wide-character string for the path and a destination wide-character string for the canonicalized path. The function will canonicalize the path by removing appropriate directories from the path when objects like " . " and " . . " are used in it. The function will return a 1 if it is successful and a 0 when not.

Risk: System path information is constantly sought after by attackers or malicious users profiling a target application or system. Path information alone can potentially identify the underlying operating system, installed applications, configurations, and in some cases user and security information. Ensure that non-alphanumeric characters are removed from the string before it is processed and that the information is only

processed internally by the application. Limit the end user's ability to ascertain or traverse path information.

Note: At time of publication, this function was designed for Windows compatibility.

Additional Resources:

http://msdn.microsoft.com/library/default.asp?url=/library/en-us/shellcc/plat-form/shell/reference/shlwapi/path/pathcanonicalize.asp

Impact: Medium

Cross References: `PathCanonicalize, PathCanonicalizeA`

PathCombine

Prototype: `BOOL PathCombine( LPTSTR destination, LPCTSTR sourceD, LPCTSTR sourceF )`

Summary: This function combines a directory path and a file path.

Description: The function attempts to combine a directory path and a file path. The function has three input arguments: the source string for the directory path, the source string for the file path, and a destination string for the combined path. The function will combine the paths by appending the file path onto the end of the directory path and store it in the destination string. The function will return a `1` if it is successful and a `0` when not.

Risk: System path information is constantly sought after by attackers or malicious users profiling a target application or system. Path information alone can potentially identify the underlying operating system, installed applications, configurations, and in some cases user and security information. Ensure that non-alphanumeric characters are removed from the string before it is processed and that the information is only processed internally by the application. Limit the end user's ability to ascertain or traverse path information.

Note: At time of publication, this function was designed for Windows compatibility.

Additional Resources:

http://msdn.microsoft.com/library/default.asp?url=/library/en-us/shellcc/plat-form/shell/reference/shlwapi/path/pathcombine.asp

C++

Impact: Medium

Cross References: PathCombineA, PathCombineW

PathCombineA

Prototype: BOOL PathCombineA(LPTSTR destination, LPCTSTR sourceD, LPCTSTR sourceF)

Summary: This function combines a directory path and a file path.

Description: The function attempts to combine a directory path and a file path. The function has three input arguments: the source string for the directory path, the source string for the file path, and a destination string for the combined path. The function will combine the paths by appending the file path onto the end of the directory path and store it in the destination string. The function will return a 1 if it is successful and a 0 when not.

Risk: System path information is constantly sought after by attackers or malicious users profiling a target application or system. Path information alone can potentially identify the underlying operating system, installed applications, configurations, and in some cases user and security information. Ensure that non-alphanumeric characters are removed from the string before it is processed and that the information is only processed internally by the application. Limit the end user's ability to ascertain or traverse path information.

Note: At time of publication, this function was designed for Windows compatibility.

Additional Resources:

http://msdn.microsoft.com/library/default.asp?url=/library/en-us/shellcc/plat-form/shell/reference/shlwapi/path/pathcombine.asp

Impact: Medium

Cross References: PathCombine, PathCombineW

C++

PathCombineW

Prototype: `BOOL PathCombineW( LPWSTR destination, LPCWSTR sourceD, LPCWSTR sourceF )`

Summary: This function combines a directory path and a file path.

Description: The function attempts to combine a directory path and a file path. The function has three input arguments: the source wide-character string for the directory path, the source wide-character string for the file path, and a destination wide-character string for the combined path. The function will combine the paths by appending the file path onto the end of the directory path and store it in the destination string. The function will return a 1 if it is successful and a 0 when not.

Risk: System path information is constantly sought after by attackers or malicious users profiling a target application or system. Path information alone can potentially identify the underlying operating system, installed applications, configurations, and in some cases user and security information. Ensure that non-alphanumeric characters are removed from the string before it is processed and that the information is only processed internally by the application. Limit the end user's ability to ascertain or traverse path information.

Note: At time of publication, this function was designed for Windows compatibility.

Additional Resources:

http://msdn.microsoft.com/library/default.asp?url=/library/en-us/shellcc/platform/shell/reference/shlwapi/path/pathcombine.asp

Impact: Medium

Cross References: `PathCombine, PathCombineA`

C++

QuerySecurityContextToken

Prototype: `SECURITY_STATUS SEC_Entry QuerySecurityContextToken( PCtxtHandle context, HANDLE* token )`

Summary: This function acquires a token for client security context.

Description: The function attempts to retrieve a token for some client security context. The function has two input arguments: the security context handle and the token handle. If the function succeeds, it will return `SEC_E_OK`. If not, it will return one of a variety of error codes.

Risk: Ensure that only administrative-level users have the ability to ascertain security tokens from within the application. Also all security token information should be transmitted securely through an encrypted tunnel and when stored utilize a strong encryption algorithm. Ensure that security-sensitive information is removed from memory upon application execution.

Note: At time of publication, this function was designed for Windows compatibility.

Additional Resources:

http://msdn.microsoft.com/library/default.asp?url=/library/en-us/security/security/querysecuritycontexttoken.asp

Impact: Low

RpcImpersonateClient

Prototype: `RPC_STATUS RPC_ENTRY RpcImpersonateClient( RPC_BINDING_HANDLE BindingHandle )`

Summary: This function allows a server to impersonate a client when running remote procedure calls.

Description: The function attempts for a server to impersonate an active client when running remote procedure calls. The function has one input variable: the handle of the active client. If the function is successful, it will return `RPC_S_OK`. However, it is unsuccessful, it will return one of a varied list of error handles.

Risk: Applications that have the ability to impersonate local systems, users, or security information are extremely dangerous; furthermore, functions that leverage this type of functionality should be controlled and only used as a last resort! All impersonation functions should be controlled by internal application-specific routines in addition to the controlled use of their output.

Note: At time of publication, this function was designed for Windows compatibility.

Additional Resources:

http://msdn.microsoft.com/library/default.asp?url=/library/en-us/rpc/rpc/rpcim-personateclient.asp

Impact: Low

SetSecurityDescriptorDacl

Prototype: BOOL SetSecurityDescriptorDacl(PSECURITY_DESCRIPTOR pSecurityDescriptor, BOOL bDaclPresent, PACL pDacl, BOOL bDaclDefaulted)

Summary: This function sets the information in a DACL of a security descriptor.

Description: The function attempts to set the information of a DACL in a security descriptor. If a DACL already exists, it is overwritten. The function has four input arguments: the handle for the security descriptor, two different Boolean flags, and the DACL to be used. The function will return a non-zero value if it is successful, and zero if not. In the event of an error, the function GetLastError can be called to retrieve more information.

Risk: The access control list for a security descriptor contains highly targeted and sensitive information. Ensure that only administrative-level users can access this data and that if it must be stored externally to the application it is done so in a securely encrypted manner.

Note: At time of publication, this function was designed for Windows compatibility.

Additional Resources:

http://msdn.microsoft.com/library/default.asp?url=/library/en-us/security/security/setsecuritydescriptordacl.asp

Impact: High

C++

SetThreadToken

Prototype: `BOOL SetThreadToken( PHANDLE Thread, HANDLE Token )`

Summary: This function either allows or restricts a thread from using an impersonation token.

Description: The function attempts to either set an impersonation token for a thread, or it can stop a thread from using one. It has two input variables: the thread handle and the token handle. If the token handle is set to `NULL`, then the function stops the thread from using a token. If the function succeeds, it will return a `1`. If not, it returns a `0`.

Risk: Applications that have the ability to impersonate local systems, users, or security information are extremely dangerous; furthermore, functions that leverage this type of functionality should be controlled and only used as a last resort! All impersonation functions should be controlled by internal application-specific routines in addition to the controlled use of their output.

Note: At time of publication, this function was designed for Windows compatibility.

Additional Resources:
http://msdn.microsoft.com/library/default.asp?url=/library/en-us/security/security/setthreadtoken.asp

Impact: Low

ShellExecute

Prototype: `HINSTANCE ShellExecute( HWND hwnd, LPCTSTR operation, LPCTSTR file, LPCTSTR parameters, LPCTSTR directory, INT showCmd )`

Summary: This function performs an operation on a file.

Description: The function attempts to perform a given operation on a file. The function has six input arguments: the handle for process window, the string containing the operation to be performed, the string containing the path to the file, the string containing parameters for file execution (if the file is executable, otherwise it is `NULL`), the string containing the default directory, and a flag defining how the file should be opened. If the function is successful, it will return a number greater than 32. However, in the event of an error, it will return a value less than 32 that will correspond to a particular error that can be found in the reference.

Risk: This function is utilized to execute system-level commands from within an application. Executing system-level commands are one of the most dangerous types of operations that an application can hardcode into its backend logic. Multiple vectors for potential attacks are available and must be addressed to secure your application. User input should be reviewed and all non-alphanumeric characters removed. Additionally, the directory structure should be limited to include only the directory or directories where the desired executables reside. As an example, you would restrict users to running commands or executables in /user/local/bin or c:/documents and settings/userX/programs/. Lastly, all output for the application should be captured within the subprocess that has launched the executable. `Fork`, `CreateProcess`, or `CreateThread` are examples of additional functions that can be used to contain output.

Note: At time of publication, this function was designed for Windows compatibility.

Additional Resources:
http://msdn.microsoft.com/library/default.asp?url=/library/en-us/shellcc/platform/shell/reference/functions/shellexecute.asp

Impact: High

Cross References: `ShellExecuteA, ShellExecuteW`

ShellExecuteA

Prototype: `HINSTANCE ShellExecuteA( HWND hwnd, LPCTSTR operation, LPCTSTR file, LPCTSTR parameters, LPCTSTR directory, INT showCmd )`

Summary: This function performs an operation on a file.

Description: The function attempts to perform a given operation on a file. The function has six input arguments: the handle for process window, the string containing the operation to be performed, the string containing the path to the file, the string containing parameters for file execution (if the file is executable, otherwise it is NULL), the string containing the default directory, and a flag defining how the file should be opened. If the function is successful, it will return a number greater than 32. However, in the event of an error, it will return a value less than 32 that will correspond to a particular error that can be found in the reference.

Risk: This function is utilized to execute system-level commands from within an application. Executing system-level commands are one of the most dangerous types of operations that an application can hardcode into its backend logic. Multiple vectors for potential attacks are available and must be addressed to secure your application. User input should be reviewed and all non-alphanumeric characters removed. Additionally, the directory structure should be limited to include only the directory or directories where the desired executables reside. As an example, you would restrict users to running commands or executables in /user/local/bin or c:/documents and settings/userX/programs/. Lastly, all output for the application should be captured within the subprocess that has launched the executable. `Fork`, `CreateProcess`, or `CreateThread` are examples of additional functions that can be used to contain output.

Note: At time of publication, this function was designed for Windows compatibility.

Additional Resources:

http://msdn.microsoft.com/library/default.asp?url=/library/en-us/shellcc/platform/shell/reference/functions/shellexecute.asp

Impact: High

Cross References: `ShellExecute`, `ShellExecuteW`

ShellExecuteEx

Prototype: `BOOL ShellExecuteEx( LPSHELLEXECUTEINFO information )`

Summary: This function performs a requested action on a file.

Description: The function attempts to perform a given action on a file. The function has only one input argument: a pointer to a structure that contains all of the necessary data for the action to be performed on a file. This function keeps track of the information produced by the file action. The function returns a standard Boolean depending on success or failure.

Risk: This function is utilized to execute system-level commands from within an application. Executing system-level commands are one of the most dangerous types of operations that an application can hardcode into its backend logic. Multiple vectors for potential attacks are available and must be addressed to secure your application. User input should be reviewed and all non-alphanumeric characters removed. Additionally, the directory structure should be limited to include only the directory or directories where the desired executables reside. As an example, you would restrict users to running commands or executables in /user/local/bin or c:/documents and settings/userX/programs/. Lastly, all output for the application should be captured within the subprocess that has launched the executable. `Fork`, `CreateProcess`, or `CreateThread` are examples of additional functions that can be used to contain output.

Note: At time of publication, this function was designed for Windows compatibility.

Additional Resources:
http://msdn.microsoft.com/library/default.asp?url=/library/en-us/shellcc/platform/shell/reference/functions/shellexecuteex.asp

Impact: High

Cross References: `ShellExecuteExA, ShellExecuteExW`

ShellExecuteExA

Prototype: `BOOL ShellExecuteExA( LPSHELLEXECUTEINFO information )`

Summary: This function performs a requested action on a file.

Description: The function attempts to perform a given action on a file. The function has only one input argument: a pointer to a structure that contains all of the necessary data for the action to be performed on a file. This function keeps track of the information produced by the file action. The function returns a standard Boolean depending on success or failure.

Risk: This function is utilized to execute system-level commands from within an application. Executing system-level commands are one of the most dangerous types of operations that an application can hardcode into its backend logic. Multiple vec-

C++

tors for potential attacks are available and must be addressed to secure your application. User input should be reviewed and all non-alphanumeric characters removed. Additionally, the directory structure should be limited to include only the directory or directories where the desired executables reside. As an example, you would restrict users to running commands or executables in /user/local/bin or c:/documents and settings/userX/programs/. Lastly, all output for the application should be captured within the subprocess that has launched the executable. `Fork`, `CreateProcess`, or `CreateThread` are examples of additional functions that can be used to contain output.

Note: At time of publication, this function was designed for Windows compatibility.

Additional Resources:
http://msdn.microsoft.com/library/default.asp?url=/library/en-us/shellcc/platform/shell/reference/functions/shellexecuteex.asp

Impact: High

Cross References: `ShellExecuteEx, ShellExecuteExW`

ShellExecuteExW

Prototype: `BOOL ShellExecuteExW( LPSHELLEXECUTEINFO information )`

Summary: This function performs a requested action on a file.

Description: The function attempts to perform a given action on a file. The function has only one input argument: a pointer to a structure that contains all of the necessary data for the action to be performed on a file. This function keeps track of the information produced by the file action. The information stored in the structure will be kept in wide-character strings when necessary. The function returns a standard Boolean depending on success or failure.

Risk: This function is utilized to execute system-level commands from within an application. Executing system-level commands are one of the most dangerous types of operations that an application can hardcode into its backend logic. Multiple vectors for potential attacks are available and must be addressed to secure your application. User input should be reviewed and all non-alphanumeric characters removed.

Additionally, the directory structure should be limited to include only the directory or directories where the desired executables reside. As an example, you would restrict users to running commands or executables in /user/local/bin or c:/documents and settings/userX/programs/. Lastly, all output for the application should be captured within the subprocess that has launched the executable. `Fork`, `CreateProcess`, or `CreateThread` are examples of additional functions that can be used to contain output.

Note: At time of publication, this function was designed for Windows compatibility.

Additional Resources:
http://msdn.microsoft.com/library/default.asp?url=/library/en-us/shellcc/platform/shell/reference/functions/shellexecuteex.asp

Impact: High

Cross References: `ShellExecuteEx, ShellExecuteExA`

ShellExecuteW

Prototype: `HINSTANCE ShellExecuteW( HWND hwnd, LPCWSTR operation, LPCWSTR file, LPCWSTR parameters, LPCWSTR directory, INT showCmd )`

Summary: This function performs an operation on a file.

Description: The function attempts to perform a given operation on a file. The function has six input arguments: the handle for process window, the wide-character string containing the operation to be performed, the wide-character string containing the path to the file, the wide-character string containing parameters for file execution (if the file is executable, otherwise it is `NULL`), the wide-character string containing the default directory, and a flag defining how the file should be opened. If the function is successful, it will return a number greater than 32. However, in the event of an error, it will return a value less than 32 that will correspond to a particular error that can be found in the reference.

Risk: This function is utilized to execute system-level commands from within an application. Executing system-level commands are one of the most dangerous types of operations that an application can hardcode into its backend logic. Multiple vec-

C++

tors for potential attacks are available and must be addressed to secure your application. User input should be reviewed and all non-alphanumeric characters removed. Additionally, the directory structure should be limited to include only the directory or directories where the desired executables reside. As an example, you would restrict users to running commands or executables in /user/local/bin or c:/documents and settings/userX/programs/. Lastly, all output for the application should be captured within the subprocess that has launched the executable. `Fork`, `CreateProcess`, or `CreateThread` are examples of additional functions that can be used to contain output.

Note: At time of publication, this function was designed for Windows compatibility.

Additional Resources:

http://msdn.microsoft.com/library/default.asp?url=/library/en-us/shellcc/platform/shell/reference/functions/shellexecute.asp

Impact: High

Cross References: `ShellExecute, ShellExecuteA`

StrCat

Prototype: `LPTSTR StrCat( LPTSTR destination, LPCTSTR source )`

Summary: The function appends a string onto the end of another.

Description: This function attempts to concatenate one string onto the end of another. It has two input arguments: the source and destination strings. The function will copy the source string onto the end of the destination string, overwriting the null character (if it exists). The function will return the destination string when completed.

Risk: Functions that are utilized to copy or concatenate strings are commonly misused and fall victim to buffer overflow attacks. It is critical that you ensure before execution of this function that the destination source is large enough to house the source data. Additionally, limiting the source data memory space will not only make your application more efficient, it will also add another layer of security by relying less on the destination buffer. For example, if X should be copied to Y then ensure that Y's space is less than X-1's total space allocation. It is similar for concatenation functions where as the strings are limited to a total length.

Note: At time of publication, this function was designed for Windows compatibility.

Additional Resources:

http://msdn.microsoft.com/library/default.asp?url=/library/en-us/shellcc/platform/shell/reference/shlwapi/string/strcat.asp

Impact: Medium

Cross References: StrCatA, StrCatW, StrCpy

StrCatA

Prototype: LPTSTR StrCatA(LPTSTR destination, LPCTSTR source)

Summary: The function appends a string onto the end of another.

Description: This function attempts to concatenate one string onto the end of another. It has two input arguments: the source and destination strings. The function will copy the source string onto the end of the destination string, overwriting the null character (if it exists). The function will return the destination string when completed.

Risk: Functions that are utilized to copy or concatenate strings are commonly misused and fall victim to buffer overflow attacks. It is critical that you ensure before execution of this function that the destination source is large enough to house the source data. Additionally, limiting the source data memory space will not only make your application more efficient, it will also add another layer of security by relying less on the destination buffer. For example, if X should be copied to Y then ensure that Y's space is less than X-1's total space allocation. It is similar for concatenation functions where as the strings are limited to a total length.

Note: At time of publication, this function was designed for Windows compatibility.

Additional Resources:

http://msdn.microsoft.com/library/default.asp?url=/library/en-us/shellcc/platform/shell/reference/shlwapi/string/strcat.asp

Impact: Medium

Cross References: `StrCat, StrCatW`

StrCatBuff

Prototype: `LPTSTR StrCatBuff( LPTSTR destination, LPCTSTR source, int count)`

Summary: The function appends a string onto the end of another.

Description: This function attempts to concatenate one string onto the end of another. It has three input arguments: the source and destination strings and the size of the buffer. The function will copy the source string onto the end of the destination string, overwriting the null character (if it exists). The function will return the destination string when completed.

Risk: Functions that are utilized to copy or concatenate strings are commonly misused and fall victim to buffer overflow attacks. It is critical that you ensure before execution of this function that the destination source is large enough to house the source data. Additionally, limiting the source data memory space will not only make your application more efficient, it will also add another layer of security by relying less on the destination buffer. For example, if X should be copied to Y then ensure that Y's space is less than X-1's total space allocation. It is similar for concatenation functions where as the strings are limited to a total length.

Note: At time of publication, this function was designed for Windows compatibility.

Additional Resources:

http://msdn.microsoft.com/library/default.asp?url=/library/en-us/shellcc/platform/shell/reference/shlwapi/string/strcatbuff.asp

Impact: Medium

Cross References: `StrCatBuffA, StrCatBuffW, StrCpy`

C++

StrCatBuffA

Prototype: `LPTSTR StrCatBuffA( LPTSTR destination, LPCTSTR source, int count)`

Summary: The function appends a string onto the end of another.

Description: This function attempts to concatenate one string onto the end of another. It has three input arguments: the source and destination strings and the size of the buffer. The function will copy the source string onto the end of the destination string, overwriting the null character (if it exists). The function will return the destination string when completed.

Risk: Functions that are utilized to copy or concatenate strings are commonly misused and fall victim to buffer overflow attacks. It is critical that you ensure before execution of this function that the destination source is large enough to house the source data. Additionally, limiting the source data memory space will not only make your application more efficient, it will also add another layer of security by relying less on the destination buffer. For example, if X should be copied to Y then ensure that Y's space is less than X-1's total space allocation. It is similar for concatenation functions where as the strings are limited to a total length.

Note: At time of publication, this function was designed for Windows compatibility.

Additional Resources:
http://msdn.microsoft.com/library/default.asp?url=/library/en-us/shellcc/platform/shell/reference/shlwapi/string/strcatbuff.asp

Impact: Medium

Cross References: `StrCatBuff, StrCatBuffW`

StrCatBuffW

Prototype: `LPTSTR StrCatBuffW( LPWSTR destination, LPCWSTR source, int count)`

Summary: The function appends a string onto the end of another.

Description: This function attempts to concatenate one string onto the end of another. It has three input arguments: the source and destination wide-character

C++

strings and the size of the buffer. The function will copy the source string onto the end of the destination string, overwriting the null character (if it exists). The function will return the destination wide-character string when completed.

Risk: Functions that are utilized to copy or concatenate strings are commonly misused and fall victim to buffer overflow attacks. It is critical that you ensure before execution of this function that the destination source is large enough to house the source data. Additionally, limiting the source data memory space will not only make your application more efficient, it will also add another layer of security by relying less on the destination buffer. For example, if X should be copied to Y then ensure that Y's space is less than X-1's total space allocation. It is similar for concatenation functions where as the strings are limited to a total length.

Note: At time of publication, this function was designed for Windows compatibility.

Additional Resources:

http://msdn.microsoft.com/library/default.asp?url=/library/en-us/shellcc/platform/shell/reference/shlwapi/string/strcatbuff.asp

Impact: Medium

Cross References: StrCatBuff, StrCatBuffA

StrCatN

Prototype: LPTSTR StrCatN(LPTSTR destination, LPCTSTR source, int count)

Summary: The function appends a string onto the end of another.

Description: This function attempts to concatenate one string onto the end of another. It has three input arguments: the source and destination strings and the max number of characters to append. The function will copy the source string onto the end of the destination string, overwriting the null character (if it exists). The function will return the destination string when completed.

Risk: Functions that are utilized to copy or concatenate strings are commonly misused and fall victim to buffer overflow attacks. It is critical that you ensure before execution of this function that the destination source is large enough to house the source data. Additionally, limiting the source data memory space will not only make your application more efficient, it will also add another layer of security by relying less on the destination buffer. For example, if X should be copied to Y then ensure that Y's space is less than X-1's total space allocation. It is similar for concatenation functions where as the strings are limited to a total length.

Note: At time of publication, this function was designed for Windows compatibility.

Additional Resources:

http://msdn.microsoft.com/library/default.asp?url=/library/en-us/shellcc/platform/shell/reference/shlwapi/string/strncat.asp

Impact: Medium

Cross References: StrCatNA, StrCatNW, StrCpy

StrCatNA

Prototype: LPTSTR StrCatNA(LPTSTR destination, LPCTSTR source, int count)

Summary: The function appends a string onto the end of another.

Description: This function attempts to concatenate one string onto the end of another. It has three input arguments: the source and destination strings and the max number of characters to append. The function will copy the source string onto the end of the destination string, overwriting the null character (if it exists). The function will return the destination string when completed.

Risk: Functions that are utilized to copy or concatenate strings are commonly misused and fall victim to buffer overflow attacks. It is critical that you ensure before execution of this function that the destination source is large enough to house the source data. Additionally, limiting the source data memory space will not only make your application more efficient, it will also add another layer of security by relying less on the destination buffer. For example, if X should be copied to Y then ensure that Y's space is less than X-1's total space allocation. It is similar for concatenation functions where as the strings are limited to a total length.

Note: At time of publication, this function was designed for Windows compatibility.

C++

Additional Resources:

http://msdn.microsoft.com/library/default.asp?url=/library/en-us/shellcc/plat-form/shell/reference/shlwapi/string/strncat.asp

Impact: Medium

Cross References: `StrCatN`, `StrCatNW`

StrCatNW

Prototype: `LPTSTR StrCatNW( LPWSTR destination, LPCWSTR source, int count )`

Summary: The function appends a string onto the end of another.

Description: This function attempts to concatenate one string onto the end of another. It has three input arguments: the source and destination wide-character strings and the max number of characters to append. The function will copy the source string onto the end of the destination string, overwriting the null character (if it exists). The function will return the destination wide-character string when completed.

Risk: Functions that are utilized to copy or concatenate strings are commonly misused and fall victim to buffer overflow attacks. It is critical that you ensure before execution of this function that the destination source is large enough to house the source data. Additionally, limiting the source data memory space will not only make your application more efficient, it will also add another layer of security by relying less on the destination buffer. For example, if X should be copied to Y then ensure that Y's space is less than X-1's total space allocation. It is similar for concatenation functions where as the strings are limited to a total length.

Note: At time of publication, this function was designed for Windows compatibility.

Additional Resources:

http://msdn.microsoft.com/library/default.asp?url=/library/en-us/shellcc/plat-form/shell/reference/shlwapi/string/strncat.asp

Impact: Medium

Cross References: `StrCatN`, `StrCatNA`

StrCatW

Prototype: `LPTSTR StrCatW( LPWSTR destination, LPCWSTR source )`

Summary: The function appends a string onto the end of another.

Description: This function attempts to concatenate one string onto the end of another. It has two input arguments: the source and destination wide-character strings. The function will copy the source string onto the end of the destination string, overwriting the null character (if it exists). The function will return the destination string when completed.

Risk: Functions that are utilized to copy or concatenate strings are commonly misused and fall victim to buffer overflow attacks. It is critical that you ensure before execution of this function that the destination source is large enough to house the source data. Additionally, limiting the source data memory space will not only make your application more efficient, it will also add another layer of security by relying less on the destination buffer. For example, if X should be copied to Y then ensure that Y's space is less than X-1's total space allocation. It is similar for concatenation functions where as the strings are limited to a total length.

Note: At time of publication, this function was designed for Windows compatibility.

Additional Resources:

http://msdn.microsoft.com/library/default.asp?url=/library/en-us/shellcc/plat-form/shell/reference/shlwapi/string/strcat.asp

Impact: Medium

Cross References: `StrCat, StrCatA`

StrCpy

Prototype: `LPTSTR StrCpy( LPTSTR destination, LPCTSTR source )`

Summary: The function copies a string into another.

Description: This function attempts to copy one string into another. It has two input arguments: the source and destination strings. The function will copy the source string into the destination string, as well as the null character (if it exists). The function will return the destination string when completed.

Risk: Functions that are utilized to copy or concatenate strings are commonly misused and fall victim to buffer overflow attacks. It is critical that you ensure before execution of this function that the destination source is large enough to house the source data. Additionally, limiting the source data memory space will not only make your application more efficient, it will also add another layer of security by relying less on the destination buffer. For example, if X should be copied to Y then ensure that Y's space is less than X-1's total space allocation. It is similar for concatenation functions where as the strings are limited to a total length.

Note: At time of publication, this function was designed for Windows compatibility.

Additional Resources:

http://msdn.microsoft.com/library/default.asp?url=/library/en-us/shellcc/platform/shell/reference/shlwapi/string/strcpy.asp

Impact: High

Cross References: `StrCat, StrCpyA, StrCpyW`

StrCpyA

Prototype: `LPTSTR StrCpyA( LPTSTR destination, LPCTSTR source )`

Summary: The function copies a string into another.

Description: This function attempts to copy one string into another. It has two input arguments: the source and destination strings. The function will copy the source string into the destination string, as well as the null character (if it exists). The function will return the destination string when completed.

Risk: Functions that are utilized to copy or concatenate strings are commonly misused and fall victim to buffer overflow attacks. It is critical that you ensure before execution of this function that the destination source is large enough to house the source data. Additionally, limiting the source data memory space will not only make your application more efficient, it will also add another layer of security by relying less on the destination buffer. For example, if X should be copied to Y then ensure that Y's space is less than X-1's total space allocation. It is similar for concatenation functions where as the strings are limited to a total length.

Note: At time of publication, this function was designed for Windows compatibility.

Additional Resources:

http://msdn.microsoft.com/library/default.asp?url=/library/en-us/shellcc/plat-form/shell/reference/shlwapi/string/strcpy.asp

Impact: High

Cross References: StrCpy, StrCpyW

StrCpyN

Prototype: LPTSTR StrCpyN(LPTSTR destination, LPCTSTR source, int count)

Summary: The function copies a string into another.

Description: This function attempts to copy one string into another. It has three input arguments: the source and destination strings and the max number of charac-ters to copy. The function will copy the source string into the destination string, as well as the null character (if it exists). The function will return the destination string when completed.

Risk: Functions that are utilized to copy or concatenate strings are commonly mis-used and fall victim to buffer overflow attacks. It is critical that you ensure before execution of this function that the destination source is large enough to house the source data. Additionally, limiting the source data memory space will not only make your application more efficient, it will also add another layer of security by relying less on the destination buffer. For example, if X should be copied to Y then ensure that Y's space is less than X-1's total space allocation. It is similar for concatenation functions where as the strings are limited to a total length.

Note: At time of publication, this function was designed for Windows compatibility.

Additional Resources:

http://msdn.microsoft.com/library/default.asp?url=/library/en-us/shellcc/plat-form/shell/reference/shlwapi/string/strcpyn.asp

Impact: High

Cross References: StrCatN, StrCpyNA, StrCpyNW

C++

StrCpyNA

Prototype: `LPTSTR StrCpyNA( LPTSTR destination, LPCTSTR source, int count )`

Summary: The function copies a string into another.

Description: This function attempts to copy one string into another. It has three input arguments: the source and destination strings and the max number of characters to copy. The function will copy the source string into the destination string, as well as the null character (if it exists). The function will return the destination string when completed.

Risk: Functions that are utilized to copy or concatenate strings are commonly misused and fall victim to buffer overflow attacks. It is critical that you ensure before execution of this function that the destination source is large enough to house the source data. Additionally, limiting the source data memory space will not only make your application more efficient, it will also add another layer of security by relying less on the destination buffer. For example, if X should be copied to Y then ensure that Y's space is less than X-1's total space allocation. It is similar for concatenation functions where as the strings are limited to a total length.

Note: At time of publication, this function was designed for Windows compatibility.

Additional Resources:

http://msdn.microsoft.com/library/default.asp?url=/library/en-us/shellcc/platform/shell/reference/shlwapi/string/strcpyn.asp

Impact: High

Cross References: `StrCpyN, StrCpyNW`

StrCpyNW

Prototype: `LPTSTR StrCpyN( LPWSTR destination, LPWTSTR source, int count )`

Summary: The function copies a string into another.

Description: This function attempts to copy one string into another. It has three input arguments: the source and destination wide-character strings and the max number of characters to copy. The function will copy the source string into the destination string, as well as the null character (if it exists). The function will return the destination wide-character string when completed.

Risk: Functions that are utilized to copy or concatenate strings are commonly misused and fall victim to buffer overflow attacks. It is critical that you ensure before execution of this function that the destination source is large enough to house the source data. Additionally, limiting the source data memory space will not only make your application more efficient, it will also add another layer of security by relying less on the destination buffer. For example, if X should be copied to Y then ensure that Y's space is less than X-1's total space allocation. It is similar for concatenation functions where as the strings are limited to a total length.

Note: At time of publication, this function was designed for Windows compatibility.

Additional Resources:

http://msdn.microsoft.com/library/default.asp?url=/library/en-us/shellcc/platform/shell/reference/shlwapi/string/strcpyn.asp

Impact: High

Cross References: StrCpyN, StrCpyNA

StrCpyW

Prototype: LPTSTR StrCpyW(LPWSTR destination, LPCWSTR source)

Summary: The function copies a string into another.

Description: This function attempts to copy one wide-character string into another. It has two input arguments: the source and destination strings. The function will copy the source string into the destination string, as well as the null character (if it exists). The function will return the destination wide-character string when completed.

Risk: Functions that are utilized to copy or concatenate strings are commonly misused and fall victim to buffer overflow attacks. It is critical that you ensure before execution of this function that the destination source is large enough to house the source data. Additionally, limiting the source data memory space will not only make your application more efficient, it will also add another layer of security by relying

C++

less on the destination buffer. For example, if X should be copied to Y then ensure that Y's space is less than X-1's total space allocation. It is similar for concatenation functions where as the strings are limited to a total length.

Note: At time of publication, this function was designed for Windows compatibility.

Additional Resources:

http://msdn.microsoft.com/library/default.asp?url=/library/en-us/shellcc/plat-form/shell/reference/shlwapi/string/strcpy.asp

Impact: High

Cross References: StrCpy, StrCpyA

StrFormatByteSize

Prototype: LPTSTR StrFormatByteSize(DWORD value, LPSTR buffer, UINT size)

Summary: This function converts a numeric value into a string.

Description: The function attempts to convert a numeric value into a string that is a representation in bytes. This means that a numeric value of 750 becomes 750 bytes, 1500 becomes 1.5 KB, and so on. The function has three input values: the number to convert, the string, and the size of the string. If the function is successful, it will return the string. However, if unsuccessful, it will return NULL.

Risk: Certain string manipulation functions to include numeric to string transition functions are commonly leveraged in buffer overflow attacks. At the most basic level, these functions read in data, perform analysis and execution logic, then output the data to another type of string. It is imperative that the destination string be calculated accordingly and that enough memory space is allocated. Special characters should also be stricken from the conversion. Lastly, it is critical to ensure that the number is restricted to a size desirable by the application.

Note: At time of publication, this function was designed for Windows compatibility.

Additional Resources:

http://msdn.microsoft.com/library/default.asp?url=/library/en-us/shellcc/plat-form/shell/reference/shlwapi/string/strformatbytesizea.asp

Impact: Low

Cross References: `StrFormatByteSizeA`, `StrFormatByteSizeW`

StrFormatByteSize64

Prototype: `LPTSTR StrFormatByteSize64( LONGLONG value, LPTSTR buffer, UINT size )`

Summary: This function converts a numeric value into a string.

Description: The function attempts to convert a numeric value into a string that is a representation in bytes. This means that a numeric value of 750 becomes 750 bytes, 1500 becomes `1.5 KB`, ans os on. The function has three input values: the number to convert, the string, and the size of the string. If the function is successful, it will return the string. However, if unsuccessful, it will return `NULL`.

Risk: Certain string manipulation functions to include numeric to string transition functions are commonly leveraged in buffer overflow attacks. At the most basic level, these functions read in data, perform analysis and execution logic, then output the data to another type of string. It is imperative that the destination string be calculated accordingly and that enough memory space is allocated. Special characters should also be stricken from the conversion. Lastly, it is critical to ensure that the number is restricted to a size desirable by the application.

Note: At time of publication, this function was designed for Windows compatibility.

Additional Resources:

http://msdn.microsoft.com/library/default.asp?url=/library/en-us/shellcc/plat-form/shell/reference/shlwapi/string/strformatbytesize64.asp

Impact: Low

Cross References: `StrFormatByteSize64A`, `StrFormatByteSize64W`

C++

StrFormatByteSize64A

Prototype: `LPTSTR StrFormatByteSize64A( LONGLONG value, LPTSTR buffer, UINT size )`

Summary: This function converts a numeric value into a string.

Description: The function attempts to convert a numeric value into a string that is a representation in bytes. This means that a numeric value of 750 becomes `750 bytes`, 1500 becomes `1.5 KB`, and so on. The function has three input values: the number to convert, the string, and the size of the string. If the function is successful, it will return the string. However, if unsuccessful, it will return `NULL`.

Risk: Certain string manipulation functions to include numeric to string transition functions are commonly leveraged in buffer overflow attacks. At the most basic level, these functions read in data, perform analysis and execution logic, then output the data to another type of string. It is imperative that the destination string be calculated accordingly and that enough memory space is allocated. Special characters should also be stricken from the conversion. Lastly, it is critical to ensure that the number is restricted to a size desirable by the application.

Note: At time of publication, this function was designed for Windows compatibility.

Additional Resources:

http://msdn.microsoft.com/library/default.asp?url=/library/en-us/shellcc/platform/shell/reference/shlwapi/string/strformatbytesize64.asp

Impact: Low

Cross References: `StrFormatByteSize64, StrFormatByteSize64W`

StrFormatByteSize64W

Prototype: `LPTSTR StrFormatByteSize64W( LONGLONG value, LPWSTR buffer, UINT size )`

Summary: This function converts a numeric value into a string.

Description: The function attempts to convert a numeric value into a wide-character string that is a representation in bytes. This means that a numeric value of 750 becomes `750 bytes`, 1500 becomes `1.5 KB`, and so on. The function has three input values: the number to convert, the string, and the size of the string. If the function is successful, it will return the string. However, if unsuccessful, it will return NULL.

Risk: Certain string manipulation functions to include numeric to string transition functions are commonly leveraged in buffer overflow attacks. At the most basic level, these functions read in data, perform analysis and execution logic, then output the data to another type of string. It is imperative that the destination string be calculated accordingly and that enough memory space is allocated. Special characters should also be stricken from the conversion. Lastly, it is critical to ensure that the number is restricted to a size desirable by the application.

Note: At time of publication, this function was designed for Windows compatibility.

Additional Resources:

http://msdn.microsoft.com/library/default.asp?url=/library/en-us/shellcc/platform/shell/reference/shlwapi/string/strformatbytesize64.asp

Impact: Low

Cross References: StrFormatByteSize64, StrFormatByteSize64A

StrFormatByteSizeW

Prototype: LPTSTR StrFormatByteSizeW(LONGLONG value, LPWSTR buffer, UINT size)

Summary: This function converts a numeric value into a string.

Description: The function attempts to convert a numeric value into a wide-character string that is a representation in bytes. This means that a numeric value of 750 becomes 750 bytes, 1500 becomes 1.5 KB, etc... The function has three input values: the number to convert, the string, and the size of the string. If the function is successful, it will return the string. However, if unsuccessful, it will return NULL.

Risk: Certain string manipulation functions to include numeric to string transition functions are commonly leveraged in buffer overflow attacks. At the most basic level, these functions read in data, perform analysis and execution logic, then output the

C++

data to another type of string. It is imperative that the destination string be calculated accordingly and that enough memory space is allocated. Special characters should also be stricken from the conversion. Lastly, it is critical to ensure that the number is restricted to a size desirable by the application.

Note: At time of publication, this function was designed for Windows compatibility.

Additional Resources:

http://msdn.microsoft.com/library/default.asp?url=/library/en-us/shellcc/platform/shell/reference/shlwapi/string/strformatbytesizea.asp

Impact: Low

Cross References: StrFormatByteSize, StrFormatByteSizeA

StrFormatKBSize

Prototype: LPTSTR StrFormatKBSize(LONGLONG value, LPTSTR buffer, UINT size)

Summary: This function converts a numeric value into a string.

Description: The function attempts to convert a numeric value into a string that is a representation in bytes. This means that a numeric value of 750 becomes 0.75 KB, 1500 becomes 1.5 KB, etc... The function has three input values: the number to convert, the string, and the size of the string. If the function is successful, it will return the string. However, if unsuccessful, it will return NULL.

Risk: Certain string manipulation functions to include numeric to string transition functions are commonly leveraged in buffer overflow attacks. At the most basic level, these functions read in data, perform analysis and execution logic, then output the data to another type of string. It is imperative that the destination string be calculated accordingly and that enough memory space is allocated. Special characters should also be stricken from the conversion. Lastly, it is critical to ensure that the number is restricted to a size desirable by the application.

Note: At time of publication, this function was designed for Windows compatibility.

Additional Resources:

http://msdn.microsoft.com/library/default.asp?url=/library/en-us/shellcc/platform/shell/reference/shlwapi/string/strformatkbsize.asp

Impact: Low

Cross References: StrFormatKBSizeA, StrFormatKBSizeW

StrFormatKBSizeA

Prototype: LPTSTR StrFormatKBSizeA(LONGLONG value, LPTSTR buffer, UINT size)

Summary: This function converts a numeric value into a string.

Description: The function attempts to convert a numeric value into a string that is a representation in bytes. This means that a numeric value of 750 becomes 0.75 KB, 1500 becomes 1.5 KB, etc... The function has three input values: the number to convert, the string, and the size of the string. If the function is successful, it will return the string. However, if unsuccessful, it will return NULL.

Risk: Certain string manipulation functions to include numeric to string transition functions are commonly leveraged in buffer overflow attacks. At the most basic level, these functions read in data, perform analysis and execution logic, then output the data to another type of string. It is imperative that the destination string be calculated accordingly and that enough memory space is allocated. Special characters should also be stricken from the conversion. Lastly, it is critical to ensure that the number is restricted to a size desirable by the application.

Note: At time of publication, this function was designed for Windows compatibility.

Additional Resources:
http://msdn.microsoft.com/library/default.asp?url=/library/en-us/shellcc/platform/shell/reference/shlwapi/string/strformatkbsize.asp

Impact: Low

Cross References: StrFormatKBSize, StrFormatKBSizeW

C++

StrFormatKBSizeW

Prototype: `LPTSTR StrFormatKBSizeW( LONGLONG value, LPWSTR buffer, UINT size )`

Summary: This function converts a numeric value into a string.

Description: The function attempts to convert a numeric value into a wide-character string that is a representation in bytes. This means that a numeric value of 750 becomes `0.75 KB`, 1500 becomes `1.5 KB`, etc... The function has three input values: the number to convert, the string, and the size of the string. If the function is successful, it will return the string. However, if unsuccessful, it will return `NULL`.

Risk: Certain string manipulation functions to include numeric to string transition functions are commonly leveraged in buffer overflow attacks. At the most basic level, these functions read in data, perform analysis and execution logic, then output the data to another type of string. It is imperative that the destination string be calculated accordingly and that enough memory space is allocated. Special characters should also be stricken from the conversion. Lastly, it is critical to ensure that the number is restricted to a size desirable by the application.

Note: At time of publication, this function was designed for Windows compatibility.

Additional Resources:

http://msdn.microsoft.com/library/default.asp?url=/library/en-us/shellcc/platform/shell/reference/shlwapi/string/strformatkbsize.asp

Impact: Low

Cross References: `StrFormatKBSize, StrFormatKBSizeA`

StrFromTimeInterval

Prototype: `int StrFromTimeInterval( LPTSTR buffer, UINT count, DWORD time, int digits )`

Summary: This function creates a string from a time interval.

Description: The function attempts to convert a given time interval into a string. This means that a time interval of 73000 becomes `73 sec` with two or more digits of accuracy or `70 sec` with one. The function has four input arguments: the destination string and its size, the time interval in milliseconds, and the number of digits of precision to use. If the function is successful, it returns the number or characters in the string `buffer`.

Risk: This function handles system-specific sensitive information that an attacker could leverage during a period of target reconnaissance. This function should only be utilized if it is absolutely necessary for proper execution of the application. All analysis for the output of this function should be conducted securely within the application and never sent across the wire in cleartext.

Note: At time of publication, this function was designed for Windows compatibility.

Additional Resources:
http://msdn.microsoft.com/library/default.asp?url=/library/en-us/shellcc/platform/shell/reference/shlwapi/string/strfromtimeinterval.asp

Impact: Low

Cross References: `StrFromTimeIntervalA, StrFromTimeIntervalW`

StrFromTimeIntervalA

Prototype: `int StrFromTimeIntervalA( LPTSTR buffer, UINT count, DWORD time, int digits )`

Summary: This function creates a string from a time interval.

Description: The function attempts to convert a given time interval into a string. This means that a time interval of 73000 becomes `73 sec` with two or more digits of accuracy or `70 sec` with one. The function has four input arguments: the destination string and its size, the time interval in milliseconds, and the number of digits of precision to use. If the function is successful, it returns the number or characters in the string `buffer`.

Risk: This function handles system-specific sensitive information that an attacker could leverage during a period of target reconnaissance. This function should only be utilized if it is absolutely necessary for proper execution of the application. All analysis for the output of this function should be conducted securely within the application and never sent across the wire in cleartext.

Note: At time of publication, this function was designed for Windows compatibility.

C++

Additional Resources:

http://msdn.microsoft.com/library/default.asp?url=/library/en-us/shellcc/plat-form/shell/reference/shlwapi/string/strfromtimeinterval.asp

Impact: Low

Cross References: StrFromTimeInterval, StrFromTimeIntervalW

StrFromTimeIntervalW

Prototype: int StrFromTimeInterval(LPWSTR buffer, UINT count, DWORD time, int digits)

Summary: This function creates a string from a time interval.

Description: The function attempts to convert a given time interval into a wide-character string. This means that a time interval of 73000 becomes 73 sec with two or more digits of accuracy or 70 sec with one. The function has four input arguments: the destination string and its size, the time interval in milliseconds, and the number of digits of precision to use. If the function is successful, it returns the number or characters in the string buffer.

Risk: This function handles system-specific sensitive information that an attacker could leverage during a period of target reconnaissance. This function should only be utilized if it is absolutely necessary for proper execution of the application. All analysis for the output of this function should be conducted securely within the application and never sent across the wire in cleartext.

Note: At time of publication, this function was designed for Windows compatibility.

Additional Resources:

http://msdn.microsoft.com/library/default.asp?url=/library/en-us/shellcc/plat-form/shell/reference/shlwapi/string/strfromtimeinterval.asp

Impact: Low

Cross References: StrFromTimeInterval, StrFromTimeIntervalW

StrNCat

Prototype: `LPTSTR StrNCat( LPTSTR destination, LPCTSTR source, int count )`

Summary: The function appends a string onto the end of another.

Description: This function attempts to concatenate one string onto the end of another. It has three input arguments: the source and destination strings and the max number of characters to append. The function will copy the source string onto the end of the destination string, overwriting the null character (if it exists). The function will return the destination string when completed.

Risk: Functions that are utilized to copy or concatenate strings are commonly misused and fall victim to buffer overflow attacks. It is critical that you ensure before execution of this function that the destination source is large enough to house the source data. Additionally, limiting the source data memory space will not only make your application more efficient, it will also add another layer of security by relying less on the destination buffer. For example, if X should be copied to Y then ensure that Y's space is less than X-1's total space allocation. It is similar for concatenation functions where as the strings are limited to a total length.

Note: At time of publication, this function was designed for Windows compatibility.

Additional Resources:
http://msdn.microsoft.com/library/default.asp?url=/library/en-us/shellcc/plat-form/shell/reference/shlwapi/string/strncat.asp

Impact: Low

WideCharToMultiByte

Prototype: `int WideCharToMultiByte( UINT CodePage, DWORD dwFlags, LPCWSTR source, int countS, LPSTR destination, int countD, LPCSTR unmappable, LPBOOL unmappableFlag )`

Summary: This function translates a wide-character string to a multibyte-character string.

C++

Description: The function attempts to translate a source wide-character string into a multibyte-character string. The function has eight input arguments: the code page to give the conversion data, a flag set, the source string and its size, the destination string and its size, a string for unmappable characters, and a flag for the unmappable set. The function will return an integer that can have several meanings. Depending on the size of strings, the flag setting, and whether the function was successful, it can return many different values. See the reference for more information.

Risk: Multi-byte strings have the potential to be very large strings that can be potentially leveraged in a buffer overflow attack scenario. These strings should restrict characters to include only those that are required by the application to function. Additionally, standard string manipulation functions should be utilized instead of large multi-byte strings in all cases possible. Ensure that the destination buffer is of appropriate size and that the source buffer is limited to that size -1.

Note: At time of publication, this function was designed for Windows compatibility.

Additional Resources:

http://msdn.microsoft.com/library/default.asp?url=/library/en-us/intl/unicode_2bj9.asp

Impact: Low

Cross References: `MultiByteToWideChar`

WinExec

Prototype: `UINT WinExec( LPCSTR lpCmdLine, UINT uCmdShow )`

Summary: This function runs a given application.

Description: The function attempts to execute a given application. It has only two input variables: the path to the application and a flag for determining the application call. The function is compatible only with 16-bit Windows. It will return an integer greater than 31 if it successfully completes the task. However, in the event of a failure, the function will return an integer less than 31 that corresponds to an error.

C++

Risk: This function has the ability to execute a file on the local system. Attackers commonly target functions similar to this since they have the ability to launch potentially dangerous or malicious executables with differing privileges. It is imperative that you filter all input and never allow a user direct access to passing variables as the parameters for this function. Ensure that all special characters are stripped before the data is parsed and passed in addition to limiting access to only the desired executables. Lastly, require that all executable output is controlled within a forked or spawned process within the local application to ensure the integrity of the outputted data. If possible, avoid calling dynamic programs from within applications. Static program execution is more secure.

Note: At time of publication, this function was designed for Windows compatibility.

Additional Resources:
http://msdn.microsoft.com/library/default.asp?url=/library/en-us/dllproc/base/winexec.asp

Impact: High

wnsprintf

Prototype: `int wnsprintf( LPTSTR string, int count, LPCTSTR format, ...)`

Summary: This function prints a formatted string to another string.

Description: The function attempts to print a formatted, wide-character string to another string. It has three formal input arguments: the wide-character string, its length (i.e., max length) and the format for the string. The informal arguments may be necessary for the formatting. The function returns the number of characters in the output string (not including the null character). If the function fails, however, it will return an unexpected value.

Risk: This function is potentially vulnerable to a format string attack where an attacker could cause the application to crash unexpected or execute arbitrary code. Format string bugs were discovered in 2000 and the problem is typically spawned from user input that is not properly filtered. Both Microsoft .Net and SPI Dynamics to name two have secure objects that can be implemented to check strings and user input gained from human sources within applications to protect against input-

C++

directed vulnerabilities. It is critical that you verify the inputted data have only proper and expected characters in addition to ensuring that your function is properly called. For example, the functions should always utilize their parameters such as `printf("%s", malicious_string)` instead of `printf(malicious_string)`.

Additional Resources:

http://msdn.microsoft.com/library/default.asp?url=/library/en-us/shellcc/ platform/shell/reference/shlwapi/string/wnsprintf.asp

Impact: Medium

Cross References: `wnsprintfA`, `wnsprintfW`

wnsprintfA

Prototype: `int wnsprintfA( LPTSTR string, int count, LPCTSTR format, …)`

Summary: This function prints a formatted string to another string.

Description: The function attempts to print a formatted, wide-character string to another string. It has three formal input arguments: the wide-character string, its length (i.e., max length) and the format for the string. The informal arguments may be necessary for the formatting. The function returns the number of characters in the output string (not including the null character). If the function fails, however, it will return an unexpected value.

Risk: This function is potentially vulnerable to a format string attack where an attacker could cause the application to crash unexpected or execute arbitrary code. Format string bugs were discovered in 2000 and the problem is typically spawned from user input that is not properly filtered. Both Microsoft .Net and SPI Dynamics to name two have secure objects that can be implemented to check strings and user input gained from human sources within applications to protect against input-directed vulnerabilities. It is critical that you verify the inputted data have only proper and expected characters in addition to ensuring that your function is properly called. For example, the functions should always utilize their parameters such as `printf("%s", malicious_string)` instead of `printf(malicious_string)`.

Additional Resources:

http://msdn.microsoft.com/library/default.asp?url=/library/en-us/shellcc/plat-form/shell/reference/shlwapi/string/wnsprintf.asp

Impact: Medium

Cross References: `wnsprintf`, `wnsprintfW`

wnsprintfW

Prototype: `int wnsprintfW( LPTSTR string, int count, LPCTSTR format, ...)`

Summary: This function prints a formatted string to another string.

Description: The function attempts to print a formatted, wide-character string to another string. It has three formal input arguments: the wide-character string, its length (i.e., max length) and the format for the string. The informal arguments may be necessary for the formatting. The function returns the number of characters in the output string (not including the null character). If the function fails, however, it will return an unexpected value.

Risk: This function is potentially vulnerable to a format string attack where an attacker could cause the application to crash unexpected or execute arbitrary code. Format string bugs were discovered in 2000 and the problem is typically spawned from user input that is not properly filtered. Both Microsoft .Net and SPI Dynamics to name two have secure objects that can be implemented to check strings and user input gained from human sources within applications to protect against input-directed vulnerabilities. It is critical that you verify the inputted data have only proper and expected characters in addition to ensuring that your function is properly called. For example, the functions should always utilize their parameters such as `printf("%s", malicious_string)` instead of `printf(malicious_string)`.

Additional Resources:

http://msdn.microsoft.com/library/default.asp?url=/library/en-us/shellcc/plat-form/shell/reference/shlwapi/string/wnsprintf.asp

Impact: Medium

C++

Cross References: `wnsprintf, wnsprintfA`

wprintf

Prototype: `int wprintf( const wchar_t *format, ... )`

Summary: This function prints a formatted array of characters to the I/O stream.

Description: The function attempts to print a formatted array of wide-characters to the stream. It has only one formal argument: the array to be printed. However, as it can be formatted data, there can be subsequent, informal arguments. The function will return the number of characters printed. However, in the event of an error, the function returns a negative value.

Risk: This function is potentially vulnerable to a format string attack where an attacker could cause the application to crash unexpected or execute arbitrary code. Format string bugs were discovered in 2000 and the problem is typically spawned from user input that is not properly filtered. Both Microsoft .Net and SPI Dynamics to name two have secure objects that can be implemented to check strings and user input gained from human sources within applications to protect against input-directed vulnerabilities. It is critical that you verify the inputted data have only proper and expected characters in addition to ensuring that your function is properly called. For example, the functions should always utilize their parameters such as `printf("%s", malicious_string)` instead of `printf(malicious_string)`.

Additional Resources:
www.gnu.org/software/libc/manual/html_node/Formatted-Output-Functions.html#Formatted%20Output%20Functions;
http://msdn.microsoft.com/library/default.asp?url=/library/en-us/vccore98/html/_crt_printf.2c_.wprintf.asp

Impact: Medium

Cross References: `printf, wscanf`

wsprintfA

Prototype: `int wsprintfA( LPTSTR string, LPCTSTR format, …)`

Summary: This function prints a formatted string to another string.

Description: The function attempts to print a formatted, wide-character string to another string. It has two formal input arguments: the wide-character string and the format for the string. The informal arguments may be necessary for the formatting. The function returns the number of characters in the output string (not including the null character). If the function fails, however, it will return an unexpected value.

Risk: This function is potentially vulnerable to a format string attack where an attacker could cause the application to crash unexpected or execute arbitrary code. Format string bugs were discovered in 2000 and the problem is typically spawned from user input that is not properly filtered. Both Microsoft .Net and SPI Dynamics to name two have secure objects that can be implemented to check strings and user input gained from human sources within applications to protect against input-directed vulnerabilities. It is critical that you verify the inputted data have only proper and expected characters in addition to ensuring that your function is properly called. For example, the functions should always utilize their parameters such as `printf("%s", malicious_string)` instead of `printf(malicious_string)`.

Additional Resources:
http://msdn.microsoft.com/library/default.asp?url=/library/en-us/winui/WinUI/WindowsUserInterface/Resources/Strings/StringReference/StringFunctions/wsprintf.asp

Impact: None

Cross References: `wsprintf, wsprintfW`

wsprintfW

Prototype: `int wsprintfW( LPTSTR string, LPCTSTR format, …)`

Summary: This function prints a formatted string to another string.

Description: The function attempts to print a formatted, wide-character string to another string. It has two formal input arguments: the wide-character string and the format for the string. The informal arguments may be necessary for the formatting.

C++

The function returns the number of characters in the output string (not including the null character). If the function fails, however, it will return an unexpected value.

Risk: This function is potentially vulnerable to a format string attack where an attacker could cause the application to crash unexpected or execute arbitrary code. Format string bugs were discovered in 2000 and the problem is typically spawned from user input that is not properly filtered. Both Microsoft .Net and SPI Dynamics to name two have secure objects that can be implemented to check strings and user input gained from human sources within applications to protect against input-directed vulnerabilities. It is critical that you verify the inputted data have only proper and expected characters in addition to ensuring that your function is properly called. For example, the functions should always utilize their parameters such as `printf("%s", malicious_string)` instead of `printf(malicious_string)`.

Additional Resources:
http://msdn.microsoft.com/library/default.asp?url=/library/en-us/winui/WinUI/WindowsUserInterface/Resources/Strings/StringReference/StringFunctions/wsprintf.asp

Impact: Medium

Cross References: `wsprintf, wsprintfA`

wvnsprintf

Prototype: `int wvnsprintf( LPTSTR string, int count, LPCTSTR format, va_list arglist )`

Summary: This function prints a formatted string to another string.

Description: The function attempts to print a formatted, wide-character string to another string. It has four input arguments: the wide-character string, its length (i.e., max length), the format for the string, and a list of arguments for the formatting. The function returns the number of characters in the output string (not including the null character). If the function fails, however, it will return an unexpected value.

Risk: This function is potentially vulnerable to a format string attack where an attacker could cause the application to crash unexpected or execute arbitrary code. Format string bugs were discovered in 2000 and the problem is typically spawned from user input that is not properly filtered. Both Microsoft .Net and SPI Dynamics to name two have secure objects that can be implemented to check strings and user input gained from human sources within applications to protect against input-directed vulnerabilities. It is critical that you verify the inputted data have only proper and expected characters in addition to ensuring that your function is properly called. For example, the functions should always utilize their parameters such as `printf("%s", malicious_string)` instead of `printf(malicious_string)`.

Additional Resources:

http://msdn.microsoft.com/library/default.asp?url=/library/en-us/shellcc/platform/shell/reference/shlwapi/string/wvnsprintf.asp

Impact: Medium

Cross References: `wvnsprintfA`, `wvnsprintfW`

wvnsprintfA

Prototype: `int wvnsprintfA( LPTSTR string, int count, LPCTSTR format, va_list arglist )`

Summary: This function prints a formatted string to another string.

Description: The function attempts to print a formatted, wide-character string to another string. It has four input arguments: the wide-character string, its length (i.e., max length), the format for the string, and a list of arguments for the formatting. The function returns the number of characters in the output string (not including the null character). If the function fails, however, it will return an unexpected value.

Risk: This function is potentially vulnerable to a format string attack where an attacker could cause the application to crash unexpected or execute arbitrary code. Format string bugs were discovered in 2000 and the problem is typically spawned from user input that is not properly filtered. Both Microsoft .Net and SPI Dynamics to name two have secure objects that can be implemented to check strings and user input gained from human sources within applications to protect against input-

C++

directed vulnerabilities. It is critical that you verify the inputted data have only proper and expected characters in addition to ensuring that your function is properly called. For example, the functions should always utilize their parameters such as `printf("%s", malicious_string)` instead of `printf(malicious_string)`.

Additional Resources:

http://msdn.microsoft.com/library/default.asp?url=/library/en-us/shellcc/platform/shell/reference/shlwapi/string/wvnsprintf.asp

Impact: Medium

Cross References: `wvnsprintf`, `wvnsprintfW`

wvnsprintfW

Prototype: `int wvnsprintfW( LPTSTR string, int count, LPCTSTR format, va_list arglist )`

Summary: This function prints a formatted string to another string.

Description: The function attempts to print a formatted, wide-character string to another string. It has four input arguments: the wide-character string, its length (i.e., max length), the format for the string, and a list of arguments for the formatting. The function returns the number of characters in the output string (not including the null character). If the function fails, however, it will return an unexpected value.

Risk: This function is potentially vulnerable to a format string attack where an attacker could cause the application to crash unexpected or execute arbitrary code. Format string bugs were discovered in 2000 and the problem is typically spawned from user input that is not properly filtered. Both Microsoft .Net and SPI Dynamics to name two have secure objects that can be implemented to check strings and user input gained from human sources within applications to protect against input-directed vulnerabilities. It is critical that you verify the inputted data have only proper and expected characters in addition to ensuring that your function is properly called. For example, the functions should always utilize their parameters such as `printf("%s", malicious_string)` instead of `printf(malicious_string)`.

Additional Resources:

http://msdn.microsoft.com/library/default.asp?url=/library/en–us/shellcc/plat–form/shell/reference/shlwapi/string/wvnsprintf.asp

Impact: Medium

Cross References: `wvnsprintf, wvnsprintfA`

Programmer's Ultimate Security Desk Ref: C#

GetTempPathA

Prototype: `static extern int GetTempPathA ( int nBufferLength, string lpBuffer)`

Summary: This function gets the path for the directory where temporary files are stored.

Description: The function attempts to retrieve the path to where temporary files are stored. It has two input variables: the length of the t-char string used to store the path and the actual pointer to the string. The function returns the number of characters copied to the buffer. The path will also include a trailing slash (for easy concatenation of the file name). In the event of an error, the function will return a 0.

Risk: System path information is constantly sought after by attackers or malicious users profiling a target application or system. Path information alone can potentially identify the underlying operating system, installed applications, configurations, and in some cases user and security information. Ensure that non–alphanumeric characters are removed from the string before it is processed and that the infor-

263

mation is only processed internally by the application. Limit the end user's ability to ascertain or traverse path information.

Note: At time of publication, this function was designed for Windows compatibility.

Additional Resources: www.webtropy.com/articles/art9-1.asp?f=GetTempPath

Impact: Low

Cross References: `GetTempFileName, GetTempPath, GetTempPathW`

ImpersonateDdeClientWindow

Prototype: `BOOL ImpersonateDdeClientWindow( HWND hWndClient, HWND hWndServer )`

Summary: This function allows a DDE server application to impersonate a DDE client's context.

Description: The function attempts to impersonate a DDE client application's context. The function has two input arguments. The first is the handle of the client to impersonate. The second is the handle of the server window. The function will return a non-zero number if successful, zero if not.

Risk: Applications that have the ability to impersonate local systems, users, or security information are extremely dangerous; furthermore, functions that leverage this type of functionality should be controlled and only used as a last resort! All impersonation functions should be controlled by internal application-specific routines in addition to the controlled use of their output.

Note: At time of publication, this function was designed for Windows compatibility.

Additional Resources:

http://msdn.microsoft.com/library/default.asp?url=/library/en-us/winui/winui/windowsuserinterface/dataexchange/dynamicdataexchange/dynamicdataexchangereference/dynamicdataexchangefunctions/impersonateddeclientwindow.asp

Impact: Low

Cross References: `CoImpersonateClient, ImpersonateLoggedOnUser, ImpersonateNamedPipeClient, ImpersonateSecurityContext`

lstrcpyn

Prototype: `LPTSTR lstrcpyn( LPTSTR destination, LPTSTR source, int count )`

Summary: This function copies one string to another.

Description: The function attempts to copy one string to another. The function three input variables: the source and destination strings and a maximum number of characters to copy. The function will copy the source string to the destination (stopping at `count`), and return the destination string. The destination string must be long enough to hold the source string and the null character. In the event of failure, the function will return `NULL`.

Risk: Functions that are utilized to copy or concatenate strings are commonly misused and fall victim to buffer overflow attacks. It is critical that you ensure before execution of this function that the destination source is large enough to house the source data. Additionally, limiting the source data memory space will not only make your application more efficient, it will also add another layer of security by relying less on the destination buffer. For example, if X should be copied to Y then ensure that Y's space is less than X-1's total space allocation. It is similar for concatenation functions where as the strings are limited to a total length.

Note: At time of publication, this function was designed for Windows compatibility.

Additional Resources:
http://msdn.microsoft.com/library/default.asp?url=/library/en-us/winui/WinUI/WindowsUserInterface/Resources/Strings/StringReference/StringFunctions/lstrcpyn.asp

Impact: Medium

Cross References: `lstrcat, lstrcpy`

OemToAnsiBuff (Class Member)

Prototype: `void CStringT::OemToAnsiBuff()`

Summary: This class member converts the string of characters from the OEM character set to the ANSI character set.

Description: This is a member of the class type CStringT. The member will convert the character of the class object `String` from the OEM character set to the ANSI character set. It does not return anything, as it modifies the class object itself. This member, however, is careful with the use of 16-bit applications.

Risk: Certain string manipulation functions to include OEM transition functions are commonly leveraged in buffer overflow attacks. At the most basic level, these functions read in data, perform analysis and execution logic, then output the data to another type of string. It is imperative that the destination string be calculated accordingly and that enough memory space is allocated. Special characters should also be stricken from the conversion.

Note: At time of publication, this function was designed for Windows compatibility.

Additional Resources:

http://msdn.microsoft.com/library/default.asp?url=/library/en-us/vclib/html/vclr-fcstringtoemtoansi.asp

Impact: Low

OemToCharBuffW

Prototype: BOOL OemToCharBuffW(LPCTSTR source, LPTSTR destination, DWORD count)

Summary: This function translates a defined number of characters in a string from the OEM character set to the ANSI character set.

Description: The function attempts to translate a string in the OEM character to the ANSI character set. The function has three input variables: the source OEM-character string, the destination ANSI-character string, and the maximum number of characters to translate. The function will return either 0 if unsuccessful or 1 if it succeeds.

Risk: Certain string manipulation functions to include OEM transition functions are commonly leveraged in buffer overflow attacks. At the most basic level, these functions read in data, perform analysis and execution logic, then output the data to another type of string. It is imperative that the destination string be calculated accordingly and that enough memory space is allocated. Special characters should also be stricken from the conversion.

Note: At time of publication, this function was designed for Windows compatibility. This function replaces the `OemToAnsiBuff` member of a CStringT type object. This particular function is from the Windows Layer for Unicode and requires additional files to be used in Win 95/98/Me.

Additional Resources:

http://msdn.microsoft.com/library/default.asp?url=/library/en-us/winui/WinUI/WindowsUserInterface/Resources/Strings/StringReference/StringFunctions/OemToCharBuff.asp

Impact: Low

Cross References: `OemToCharBuff`

Programmer's Ultimate Security Desk Ref: ColdFusion

Access

Prototype: `Access(path, mode)`

Summary: This function is used to test the accessibility of a file.

Description: This function is used to test for the availability of a file. The function requires two input arguments: the path to the file and the mode in which to access it. The function tests the permissions of the file compared to the requested mode. The function returns a 0 if access is not allowed, it returns a 1 if the file is accessible.

Risk: Ensure that either the application logic or human users are limited to the files that require analysis. Attackers could potentially leverage this type of functionality while attempting to compromise a specific file.

Impact: Low

ArrayInsertAt

Prototype: `ArrayInsertAt(array, position, value)`

Summary: This function inserts an element into an array.

Description: The function attempts to insert an element into an array at a given position. The function has three input variables: the array, the position, and the new element. The function will return TRUE if successful, and FALSE if not. The function will recalculate the indexing, as well. Inserting an element at an interior position will increase the position for all remaining elements in the array.

Risk: Elements in an array are common targets of SQL injection and manipulation attacks in addition to cross-site scripting (CSS/XSS) attacks. These data elements are commonly stored and allowed to pass through weakly vetted input streams and during analysis within the program are executed thereby potentially putting additional data at risk. Restrict all input data for arrays that is human generated.

Additional Resources: http://livedocs.macromedia.com/coldfusion/6.1/htmldocs/function.htm#wp3082862

Impact: Medium

Cross References: ArrayDeleteAt, ArrayNew, ArrayToList

ArrayNew

Prototype: ArrayNew(dimension)

Summary: This function creates a new array.

Description: The function is used to declare a new array. The function has one input variable: the number of dimensions in the new array (1,2, or 3). The array will expand as needed, and no length needs to be declared. However, for some functions to work properly, the function ArraySet must be used in conjunction with this function.

Risk: Elements in an array are common targets of SQL injection and manipulation attacks in addition to cross-site scripting (CSS/XSS) attacks. These data elements are commonly stored and allowed to pass through weakly vetted input streams and during analysis within the program are executed thereby potentially putting additional data at risk. Restrict all input data for arrays that is human generated.

Additional Resources: http://livedocs.macromedia.com/coldfusion/6.1/htmldocs/function.htm#wp3082862

Impact: Low

Cross References: `ArrayDeleteAt, ArrayInsertAt, ArrayToList`

ArrayToList

Prototype: `ArrayToList(array [, delimiter ])`

Summary: This function converts an array to a list.

Description: The function creates a list from an array. The array must be one-dimensional. There is one required and one optional input argument: the former being the array to convert, and the latter being a delimiter to use to separate the elements of the list. The default option for the delimiter is a comma. The list created will be in the format of a string.

Risk: Elements in an array are common targets of SQL injection and manipulation attacks in addition to cross-site scripting (CSS/XSS) attacks. These data elements are commonly stored and allowed to pass through weakly vetted input streams and during analysis within the program are executed thereby potentially putting additional data at risk. Restrict all input data for arrays that is human generated.

Additional Resources: http://livedocs.macromedia.com/coldfusion/6.1/htmldocs/function.htm#wp3082862

Impact: Low

Cross References: `ArrayDeleteAt, ArrayInsertAt, ArrayNew`

Asc

Prototype: `Asc(string)`

Summary: This function determines the value of the first element of a string.

Description: The function attempts to ascertain the value of the first element of a string. The function takes only one input argument: the string to analyze. The function returns the value in question. However, in the event that the string is empty, the function returns zero.

Risk: Certain string manipulation functions to include string and character transition functions are commonly leveraged in buffer overflow attacks. At the most basic level, these functions read in data, perform analysis and execution logic, then output the data to another type of string. It is imperative that the destination string be calculated accordingly and that enough memory space is allocated. Special characters should also be stricken from the conversion where possible.

Additional Resources: http://livedocs.macromedia.com/coldfusion/6.1/ htmldocs/function.htm#wp3082862

Impact: Low

BitAnd

Prototype: `BitAnd(number1, number2)`

Summary: This function performs the logical and operator on two long integers.

Description: The function performs the logical "and" operator on two integers. The function looks at the integers in binary form and performs the operation bitwise along the length of the integer. The function returns the result of the operation.

Risk: Ensure that the destination buffer is large enough for the source data stream. First determining if the memory space available is sufficient will allow you to bypass multiple buffer overflow attacks.

Additional Resources: http://livedocs.macromedia.com/coldfusion/6.1/ htmldocs/function.htm#wp3082862

Impact: Low

Cross References: `BitSHLN, BitSHRN, BitXor`

BitSHLN

Prototype: `BitSHLN(number, count)`

Summary: This function shifts an integer by a number of digits to the left.

Description: The function shifts an integer by a given number of digits. The function has two input variables: the number in question and the number of bits to shift. The function takes the number in question (in binary form) and shifts it by the given amount to the left. The function returns this shifted value. This function does

ColdFusion

not rotate the bits either, meaning that if a bit "falls off" the left side of the 32-bit barrier, it does not reappear on the right.

Risk: This function should never be utilized to obfuscate data with the goal of protecting it from prying eyes. Only industry-standard cryptography algorithms should be implemented to secure data. This function is out-of-date and should not be used!

Additional Resources: http://livedocs.macromedia.com/coldfusion/6.1/htmldocs/function.htm#wp3082862

Impact: Low

Cross References: BitAnd, BitSHRN, BitXor

BitSHRN

Prototype: BitSHRN(number, count)

Summary: This function shifts an integer by a number of digits to the right.

Description: The function shifts an integer by a given number of digits. The function has two input variables: the number in question and the number of bits to shift. The function takes the number in question (in binary form) and shifts it by the given amount to the right. The function returns this shifted value. This function does not rotate the bits either, meaning that if a bit "falls off" the right side of the 32-bit barrier, it does not reappear on the left.

Risk: This function should never be utilized to obfuscate data with the goal of protecting it from prying eyes. Only industry-standard cryptography algorithms should be implemented to secure data. This function is out-of-date and should not be used!

Additional Resources: http://livedocs.macromedia.com/coldfusion/6.1/htmldocs/function.htm#wp3082862

Impact: Low

Cross References: BitAnd, BitSHLN, BitXor

BitXor

Prototype: BitXor(number1, number2)

ColdFusion

Summary: This function performs the logical `exclusive or` operator on two long integers.

Description: The function performs the logical `xor` operator on two integers. The function looks at the integers in binary form and performs the operation bitwise along the length of the integer. The function returns the result of the operation.

Risk: This function should never be utilized to obfuscate data with the goal of protecting it from prying eyes. Only industry-standard cryptography algorithms should be implemented to secure data. This function is out-of-date and should not be used!

Additional Resources: http://livedocs.macromedia.com/coldfusion/6.1/htmldocs/function.htm#wp3082862

Impact: High

Cross References: `BitAnd`, `BitSHLN`, `BitSHRN`

CreateObject

Prototype: `CreateObject(type [, options ])`

Summary: This function creates a new Coldfusion object.

Description: The function attempts to create a new Coldfusion object. The function is overloaded to include several different objects. The first input argument is the type of object to create. The remaining objects are dependent on the type being created. For more information on the required arguments, see the Coldfusion documentation noted later.

Risk: This function does not have a significant security risk but is useful to determine where objects are created. All created objects should be released or deleted at the end of execution.

Additional Resources: http://livedocs.macromedia.com/coldfusion/6.1/htmldocs/function.htm#wp3082862

Impact: Low

CreateODBCDate

Prototype: `CreateODBCDate(date)`

Summary: This function creates a date object, normalized in the ODBC format.

Description: The function attempts to create an ODBC-normalized date object from a date. The function takes the date in as an input variable. It returns the normalized date object. This function is not the same as `CreateDate`.

Risk: ODBC-enabled functions are utilized to aid in the connection and data transmission to backend databases. It is imperative that all SQL injection and manipulation characters are removed from strings that are stored or utilized to connect to those databases. Such characters include all special characters and even words like DELETE, ADD, and INSERT.

Additional Resources: http://livedocs.macromedia.com/coldfusion/6.1/htmldocs/function.htm#wp3082862

Impact: Low

Cross References: `CreateODBCDateTime, CreateODBCTime`

CreateODBCDateTime

Prototype: `CreateODBCDateTime(date)`

Summary: This function creates an ODBC-normalized format Date-Time object.

Description: The function attempts to create an ODBC-normalized date-time object from a date. The function takes the date in as an input variable. It returns the normalized date-time object. This function is not the same as `CreateDateTime`.

Risk: ODBC-enabled functions are utilized to aid in the connection and data transmission to backend databases. It is imperative that all SQL injection and manipulation characters are removed from strings that are stored or utilized to connect to those databases. Such characters include all special characters and even words like DELETE, ADD, and INSERT.

Additional Resources: http://livedocs.macromedia.com/coldfusion/6.1/htmldocs/function.htm#wp3082862

ColdFusion

Impact: Low

Cross References: `CreateODBCDate, CreateODBCTime`

CreateODBCTime

Prototype: `CreateODBCTime(date)`

Summary: This function creates an ODBC-normalized format Time object.

Description: The function attempts to create an ODBC-normalized time object from a date. The function takes the date in as an input variable. It returns the normalized time object. This function is not the same as `CreateTime`.

Risk: ODBC-enabled functions are utilized to aid in the connection and data transmission to backend databases. It is imperative that all SQL injection and manipulation characters are removed from strings that are stored or utilized to connect to those databases. Such characters include all special characters and even words like DELETE, ADD, and INSERT.

Additional Resources: http://livedocs.macromedia.com/coldfusion/6.1/htmldocs/function.htm#wp3082862

Impact: Low

Cross References: `CreateODBCDate, CreateODBCDateTime`

CreateTime

Prototype: `CreateTime(hour, minute, second)`

Summary: This function creates a time object from a given time.

Description: The function creates an object of type `time` from a given time. The function has three input arguments: the hour, the minute, and second. The function returns the time object with the given values. This function is distinct from `CreateODEBCTime`.

Risk: This function poses minimal risk, which is only realized if the local system time is utilized to create the time object. If the local time is utilized then realize that attackers could potentially ascertain geographical information about the target server based on time receipts.

Additional Resources: http://livedocs.macromedia.com/coldfusion/6.1/ htmldocs/function.htm#wp3082862

Impact: Low

CreateUUID

Prototype: `CreateUUID()`

Summary: This function creates a Universally Unique Identifier.

Description: The function attempts to create a UUID, which is a 35-character representation of a 128-bit integer. The function creates a UUID of the format: 8-4-4-16, where each non-dash character is a hexadecimal number (32 characters + 3 dashes = 35 total characters). The function returns this UUID. It is statistically improbable to create the same UUID twice.

Risk: The internal UUID function creates easily guessable numbers that were not generated with a secure random number generator. Number generators such as ISAAC in combination with a time seed could be a suitable option instead of utilizing the CreateUUID function.

Additional Resources: http://livedocs.macromedia.com/coldfusion/6.1/ htmldocs/function.htm#wp3082862

Impact: Medium

DE

Prototype: `DE(string)`

Summary: This function postpones evaluation of a string.

Description: The function postpones the evaluation of a string. The function has one input argument: the string. This function is best used in coordination with other functions.

Risk: This function does not pose a significant security risk when utilized alone but ensure that the time of postponement is not driven from human user input.

Additional Resources: http://livedocs.macromedia.com/coldfusion/6.1/ htmldocs/function.htm#wp3082862

Impact: Low

Cross References: Evaluate

Decrypt

Prototype: Decrypt(encrypted_string, seed)

Summary: This function decrypts an encrypted string.

Description: The function attempts to decrypt an encrypted string. The function has two input arguments: the encrypted string and the 32-bit key that was used to encrypt the string. The function works in coordination with the Encrypt function in Coldfusion. The function returns the decrypted string.

Risk: The use of this function indicates the use of the corresponding Encrypt() function. Both of these functions are large security risks and as such neither should be utilized. Only use strong commercial-grade cryptography implementations, including AES, DES, Blowfisk, or RSA to name a few.

Additional Resources: http://livedocs.macromedia.com/coldfusion/6.1/ htmldocs/function.htm#wp3082862

Impact: High

Cross References: Encrypt

DirectoryExists

Prototype: DirectoryExists(absolute_path)

Summary: This function checks whether a target directory exists.

Description: The function ascertains whether a directory exists. The function has only one input variable: the path to the target directory. If the target exists, then the function returns TRUE. If not, then the function returns FALSE.

Risk: This function poses minimal risk but the output of a directory's existence should be limited to that of the desired resource. In other words, application users should not be able to point this function at any directory on the underlying subsystem to determine if a directory exists.

Additional Resources: http://livedocs.macromedia.com/coldfusion/6.1/ htmldocs/function.htm#wp3082862

Impact: Medium

Cross References: ExpandPath, FileExists

Encrypt

Prototype: Encrypt(string, seed)

Summary: This function encrypts a string.

Description: The function attempts to encrypt a string. The function has two input arguments: the string and the 32-bit key that will be used to encrypt the string. The function works in coordination with the Decrypt function in Coldfusion. The function returns the encrypted string.

Risk: This function should never be utilized to obfuscate data with the goal of protecting it from prying eyes. Only industry-standard cryptography algorithms should be implemented to secure data. This function is out-of-date and should not be used! It is recommended that a commercially accepted encryption algorithm be utilized for any type of encryption. These types of implementations include DES, AES, Blowfish, or RSA to mention a few.

Additional Resources: http://livedocs.macromedia.com/coldfusion/6.1/ htmldocs/function.htm#wp3082862

Impact: High

Cross References: Decrypt

Evaluate

Prototype: Evaluate(string_expression1 [, string_expression2 [, ...]])

ColdFusion

Summary: This function evaluates an expression.

Description: The function attempts to evaluate an expression in string format (possibly many). The function takes as input variables the expressions to evaluate. The function can handle multiple expressions, evaluating them left-to-right (i.e., the first one entered is the first one evaluated). The function returns an object containing the results of the last expression.

Risk: All special and wildcard characters should be removed before the filename is computed on the local filesystem. Malicious filenames are interpreted differently on varying systems and as such, directory control is critical to limiting the ability of an attacker to potentially compromise files at varying levels within the application or underlying subsystem.

Additional Resources: http://livedocs.macromedia.com/coldfusion/6.1/htmldocs/function.htm#wp3082862

Impact: Medium

Cross References: DE

ExpandPath

Prototype: `ExpandPath(relative_path)`

Summary: This function expands an abbreviated (or relative) path to its full counterpart.

Description: The function expands a relative path to its full, platform-dependent form. The function takes the relative path in as its input variable (though it can handle a full path, as well). The function returns the full path.

Risk: System path information is constantly sought after by attackers or malicious users profiling a target application or system. Path information alone can potentially identify the underlying operating system, installed applications, configurations, and in some cases user and security information. Ensure that non-alphanumeric characters are removed from the string before it is processed and that the information is only processed internally by the application. Limits the end-user's ability to ascertain or traverse path information.

Additional Resources: http://livedocs.macromedia.com/coldfusion/6.1/htmldocs/function.htm#wp3082862

Impact: High

Cross References: DirectoryExists, FileExists

FileExists

Prototype: FileExists(absolute_path)

Summary: This function checks whether a file exists.

Description: The function attempts to ascertain the existence of a given file. The function takes in the absolute path of the file in question as the only input argument. If the file exists, the function returns TRUE. Otherwise, the function returns FALSE.

Risk: This function poses minimal risk but the output of a file's existence should be limited to that of the desired resource. In other words, application users should not be able to point this function at any directory or file on the underlying subsystem to determine if the resource exists.

Additional Resources: http://livedocs.macromedia.com/coldfusion/6.1/htmldocs/function.htm#wp3082862

Impact: Medium

Cross References: DirectoryExists, ExpandPath

Find

Prototype: Find(substring, string [, start])

Summary: This function finds the first occurrence of a substring in a string.

Description: The function attempts to locate the first instance of a substring in a given string. The function can start looking at a designated beginning position. The function thus has three input variables: the substring to look for, the string, and the place to start looking (if desired). The function returns the location of the beginning of the substring (if it exists). Otherwise, the function returns zero.

ColdFusion

Risk: Functions that search for patterns open files and input their datastreams into allocated memory spaces. Outside of the race condition bugs that could occur if you attempted to open a file more than once simultaneously, a buffer overflow attack may also open up memory space for a root-level attack. Ensure that the files or datastreams that are passed for analysis to these functions are properly controlled and vetted by application logic. Users should not have the ability to identify if strings are within operating system resources such as configuration or log files.

Additional Resources: http://livedocs.macromedia.com/coldfusion/6.1/htmldocs/function.htm#wp3082862

Impact: Low

Cross References: FindOneOf

FindOneOf

Prototype: FindOneOf(set, string [, start])

Summary: This function looks for the first instance of set of characters in a string.

Description: The function looks for the first instance of a set of characters in a string. The function can start the search at a designated position. The function can have three input arguments: the set of characters, the string to search, and the start position (if desired). The function returns the position of the first instance of one of the characters. If none exist, then the function returns zero.

Risk: Functions that search for patterns open files and input their datastreams into allocated memory spaces. Outside of the race condition bugs that could occur if you attempted to open a file more than once simultaneously, a buffer overflow attack may also open up memory space for a root-level attack. Ensure that the files or datastreams that are passed for analysis to these functions are properly controlled and vetted by application logic. Users should not have the ability to identify if strings are within operating system resources such as configuration or log files.

Additional Resources: http://livedocs.macromedia.com/coldfusion/6.1/htmldocs/function.htm#wp3082862

Impact: Low

Cross References: Find

FormatBaseN

Prototype: `FormatBaseN(number, radix)`

Summary: This function converts a number (in a given base) to a string.

Description: The function converts a number in a given base to a string. The function has two input variables: the number to convert, and the base in which it is. The function returns a string that contains the value.

Risk: Functions that search for patterns open files and input their datastreams into allocated memory spaces. Outside of the race condition bugs that could occur if you attempted to open a file more than once simultaneously, a buffer overflow attack may also open up memory space for a root-level attack. Ensure that the files or datastreams that are passed for analysis to these functions are properly controlled and vetted by application logic. Users should not have the ability to identify if strings are within operating system resources such as configuration or log files.

Additional Resources: http://livedocs.macromedia.com/coldfusion/6.1/htmldocs/function.htm#wp3082862

Impact: Low

Cross References: `InputBaseN`

GetAuthUser

Prototype: `GetAuthUser()`

Summary: This function gets the name of an authorized user.

Description: The function attempts to get the name of an authorized user. The function does not have any input arguments. It returns the name of a user.

Risk: This function handles system-specific sensitive information that an attacker could leverage during a period of target reconnaissance. This function should only be utilized if it is absolutely necessary for proper execution of the application. All analysis for the output of this function should be conducted securely within the application and never sent across the wire in cleartext.

ColdFusion

Additional Resources: http://livedocs.macromedia.com/coldfusion/6.1/htmldocs/function.htm#wp3082862

Impact: Low

GetBaseTagData

Prototype: `GetBaseTagData(tagname [, instancenumber ] )`

Summary: This function attempts to get the data from its ancestor's tag.

Description: The function tries to retrieve the data from one of its ancestors form the tag. The function has optional arguments as well. It takes the tag name (of the ancestor) and can handle the number of generations to skip when looking for this ancestor. The function returns the data of the ancestor. However, an error can occur if the data is unavailable or the ancestor does not exist.

Risk: This function handles system-specific sensitive information that an attacker could leverage during a period of target reconnaissance. This function should only be utilized if it is absolutely necessary for proper execution of the application. All analysis for the output of this function should be conducted securely within the application and never sent across the wire in cleartext.

Additional Resources: http://livedocs.macromedia.com/coldfusion/6.1/htmldocs/function.htm#wp3082862

Impact: Low

Cross References: `GetBaseTagList`

GetBaseTagList

Prototype: `GetBaseTagList()`

Summary: This function attempts to make a list of its ancestors.

Description: The function attempts to create a list of its ancestors. Starting with itself, then its parent, etc... the function creates a list of all its ancestors. The function does not require any input variables. It returns a comma-delimited list of the ancestor's tag names.

ColdFusion

Risk: System-specific information should be treated as sensitive data and should not be open for users to ascertain data that could lead to an educated attack from a remote perspective. Do not use this function unless it is absolutely necessary!

Additional Resources: http://livedocs.macromedia.com/coldfusion/6.1/htmldocs/function.htm#wp3082862

Impact: Low

Cross References: GetBaseTagData

GetBaseTemplatePath

Prototype: GetBaseTemplatePath()

Summary: This function gets the full path name of an application's base page.

Description: The function attempts to ascertain the full path of an application's base page. The function does not require any input parameters. The function returns a string containing the absolute path of the base page.

Risk: This function handles system-specific sensitive information that an attacker could leverage during a period of target reconnaissance. This function should only be utilized if it is absolutely necessary for proper execution of the application. All analysis for the output of this function should be conducted securely within the application and never sent across the wire in cleartext.

Additional Resources: http://livedocs.macromedia.com/coldfusion/6.1/htmldocs/function.htm#wp3082862

Impact: Low

Cross References: GetCurrentTemplatePath

GetClientVariablesList

Prototype: GetClientVariablesList()

Summary: This function creates a list of variables to which a page has write permission.

ColdFusion

Description: The function creates a list of variables that a page can modify. The function does not require any input variables. The function then returns a comma-delimited list of write-permission-enabled variables. The list returned can then be used in any of the other ColdFusion list-enabled functions.

Risk: This function handles system-specific sensitive information that an attacker could leverage during a period of target reconnaissance. This function should only be utilized if it is absolutely necessary for proper execution of the application. All analysis for the output of this function should be conducted securely within the application and never sent across the wire in cleartext.

Additional Resources: http://livedocs.macromedia.com/coldfusion/6.1/htmldocs/function.htm#wp3082862

Impact: Medium

GetCurrentTemplatePath

Prototype: GetCurrentTemplatePath()

Summary: This function gets the path of the page that called it.

Description: The function gets the full path of the page that called this function. The function does not need an input variable. The function returns the full path of the calling page in string form.

Risk: System path information is constantly sought after by attackers or malicious users profiling a target application or system. Path information alone can potentially identify the underlying operating system, installed applications, configurations, and in some cases user and security information. Ensure that non-alphanumeric characters are removed from the string before it is processed and that the information is only processed internally by the application. Limits the end-user's ability to ascertain or traverse path information.

Additional Resources: http://livedocs.macromedia.com/coldfusion/6.1/htmldocs/function.htm#wp3082862

Impact: Medium

Cross References: GetBaseTemplatePath

GetDirectoryFromPath

Prototype: `GetDirectoryFromPath(path)`

Summary: This function returns the top-most directory from a path.

Description: The function gets the top-layer directory from a given path. The function has only one input argument. It is the full path of the directory (including the trailing slash or back-slash) as a string. The function returns a string containing the requested directory.

Risk: System path information is constantly sought after by attackers or malicious users profiling a target application or system. Path information alone can potentially identify the underlying operating system, installed applications, configurations, and in some cases user and security information. Ensure that non-alphanumeric characters are removed from the string before it is processed and that the information is only processed internally by the application. Limits the end-user's ability to ascertain or traverse path information.

Additional Resources: http://livedocs.macromedia.com/coldfusion/6.1/htmldocs/function.htm#wp3082862

Impact: High

GetEncoding

Prototype: `GetEncoding(scope_name)`

Summary: This function gets the character encoding of an object.

Description: The function attempts to ascertain the character encoding of a particular object. The function has one input parameter: the object to look at (whether that be a URL, database form, or any other user provided input). The function returns a string containing the encoding scheme for the character set.

Risk: This function handles system-specific sensitive information that an attacker could leverage during a period of target reconnaissance. This function should only be utilized if it is absolutely necessary for proper execution of the application. All analysis for the output of this function should be conducted securely within the application and never sent across the wire in cleartext.

ColdFusion

Additional Resources: http://livedocs.macromedia.com/coldfusion/6.1/html-docs/function.htm#wp3082862

Impact: Medium

GetException

Prototype: GetException(object)

Summary: This function retrieves a Java exception object from a Java object.

Description: The function attempts to get a Java exception object from a given Java object. The function will take one input argument: the Java object. The function examines the object for an exception object. If it exists, then the function returns it as an object. The function will overwrite previous calls of itself.

Risk: System path information is constantly sought after by attackers or malicious users profiling a target application or system. Path information alone can potentially identify the underlying operating system, installed applications, configurations, and in some cases user and security information. Ensure that non-alphanumeric characters are removed from the string before it is processed and that the information is only processed internally by the application. Limits the end-user's ability to ascertain or traverse path information.

Additional Resources: http://livedocs.macromedia.com/coldfusion/6.1/htmldocs/function.htm#wp3082862

Impact: Low

GetFileFromPath

Prototype: GetFileFromPath(path)

Summary: This function retrieves the file name from a full path.

Description: The function takes the full path name and extracts the file name from it. The function has only one input argument. It is the full path name. The function returns, as a string, the file name.

Risk: This function handles system-specific sensitive information that an attacker could leverage during a period of target reconnaissance. This function should only

be utilized if it is absolutely necessary for proper execution of the application. All analysis for the output of this function should be conducted securely within the application and never sent across the wire in cleartext.

Additional Resources: http://livedocs.macromedia.com/coldfusion/6.1/html-docs/function.htm#wp3082862

Impact: Low

GetFunctionList

Prototype: `GetFuncionList()`

Summary: This function retrieves a list of the available ColdFusion functions.

Description: This function creates a list of the available ColdFusion functions. The function does not require any input arguments. The function returns a structure containing the list of functions.

Risk: This function handles system-specific sensitive information that an attacker could leverage during a period of target reconnaissance. This function should only be utilized if it is absolutely necessary for proper execution of the application. All analysis for the output of this function should be conducted securely within the application and never sent across the wire in cleartext.

Additional Resources: http://livedocs.macromedia.com/coldfusion/6.1/htmldocs/function.htm#wp3082862

Impact: Low

GetHttpRequestData

Prototype: `GetHttpRequestData()`

Summary: This function retrieves a structure of data about an HTTP page.

Description: The function is used to pull information about an HTTP page for use in ColdFusion pages. The function does not require an input parameter. The function returns a ColdFusion structure. The structure contains assorted information about the calling HTTP page, including the headers, content, etc…

ColdFusion

Risk: This function handles system-specific sensitive information that an attacker could leverage during a period of target reconnaissance. This function should only be utilized if it is absolutely necessary for proper execution of the application. All analysis for the output of this function should be conducted securely within the application and never sent across the wire in cleartext.

Additional Resources: http://livedocs.macromedia.com/coldfusion/6.1/ htmldocs/function.htm#wp3082862

Impact: High

GetHttpTimeString

Prototype: `GetHttpTimeString(date_time_object)`

Summary: This function gets the current time.

Description: This function gets the current time in the Universal Time Code format. The function takes an input variable: a date-time object. The function reads the time, and outputs it in a string format. The returned time is consistent with HTTP time standard.

Risk: This function handles system-specific sensitive information that an attacker could leverage during a period of target reconnaissance. This function should only be utilized if it is absolutely necessary for proper execution of the application. All analysis for the output of this function should be conducted securely within the application and never sent across the wire in cleartext.

Additional Resources: http://livedocs.macromedia.com/coldfusion/6.1/ htmldocs/function.htm#wp3082862

Impact: Low

GetK2ServerDocCount

Prototype: `GetK2ServerDocCount()`

Summary: This function finds the number of documents that a K2 server can search.

Description: The function attempts to determine the total number of documents that can be searched on a ColdFusion-registered K2 server. The function does not take any input arguments. The return value is the number of metadata items collected. This function is currently being phased out, and its expensive computational time should be considered when using it.

Risk: This function handles system-specific sensitive information that an attacker could leverage during a period of target reconnaissance. This function should only be utilized if it is absolutely necessary for proper execution of the application. All analysis for the output of this function should be conducted securely within the application and never sent across the wire in cleartext.

Additional Resources: http://livedocs.macromedia.com/coldfusion/6.1/htmldocs/function.htm#wp3082862

Impact: Medium

Cross References: `GetK2ServerDocCountLimit`

GetK2ServerDocCountLimit

Prototype: `GetK2ServerDocCountLimit()`

Summary: This function finds the total number of documents that a K2 server is allowed to search.

Description: The function attempts to determine the total number of documents that can be searched on a ColdFusion-registered K2 server. The function does not take any input arguments. The return value is the allowable number of documents that can be searched. This limit is imposed by the particular version of ColdFusion used. This function is currently being phased out.

Risk: This function handles system-specific sensitive information that an attacker could leverage during a period of target reconnaissance. This function should only be utilized if it is absolutely necessary for proper execution of the application. All analysis for the output of this function should be conducted securely within the application and never sent across the wire in cleartext.

Additional Resources: http://livedocs.macromedia.com/coldfusion/6.1/htmldocs/function.htm#wp3082862

ColdFusion

Impact: Medium

Cross References: GetK2ServerDocCount

GetLocale

Prototype: GetLocale()

Summary: This function gets the current value for the geographic and/or language locale.

Description: This function retrieves the current locale information. The function does not require any input arguments. The function returns a string containing the desired information. This function is primarily used in conjunction with the SetLocale function.

Risk: This function handles system-specific sensitive information that an attacker could leverage during a period of target reconnaissance. This function should only be utilized if it is absolutely necessary for proper execution of the application. All analysis for the output of this function should be conducted securely within the application and never sent across the wire in cleartext.

Additional Resources: http://livedocs.macromedia.com/coldfusion/6.1/htmldocs/function.htm#wp3082862

Impact: Medium

Cross References: SetLocale

GetMetaData

Prototype: GetMetaData(object)

Summary: This function gets the metadata associated with an object from a server.

Description: The function retrieves the metadata linked to an object on a ColdFusion server. The function has one input argument: the object. The function returns the metadata. This can include the name, parameters, methods, etc... of an object.

Risk: This function handles system-specific sensitive information that an attacker could leverage during a period of target reconnaissance. This function should only be utilized if it is absolutely necessary for proper execution of the application. All analysis for the output of this function should be conducted securely within the application and never sent across the wire in cleartext.

Additional Resources: http://livedocs.macromedia.com/coldfusion/6.1/htmldocs/function.htm#wp3082862

Impact: Low

GetMetricData

Prototype: `GetMetricData(mode)`

Summary: This function retrieves the metrics for server performance.

Description: The function attempts to retrieve the measurements of server performance. The function has one input variable: a string that tells the function what kind of data to get. The function returns different types of values depending on the mode requested. The most common return value is a ColdFusion object containing all possible metrics.

Risk: This function handles system-specific sensitive information that an attacker could leverage during a period of target reconnaissance. This function should only be utilized if it is absolutely necessary for proper execution of the application. All analysis for the output of this function should be conducted securely within the application and never sent across the wire in cleartext.

Additional Resources: http://livedocs.macromedia.com/coldfusion/6.1/htmldocs/function.htm#wp3082862

Impact: Low

GetProfileSections

Prototype: `GetProfileSections(iniFile)`

Summary: This function reads an initialization file into a ColdFusion structure.

ColdFusion

Description: This function reads an .ini file into a ColdFusion structure. The function takes one input parameter: the full path of the .ini file to be read. The function reads the entire file, and parses it appropriately. It then returns a ColdFusion structure containing the data from the file.

Risk: This function parses input blindly. Additionally, logic should be incorporated into the application to ensure that human supplied input does not contain potentially malicious content. Data streams that are attached to external sources must first verify the integrity of those sources before interpreting and implementing the data. The destination buffer should be verified before any data is copied into memory or another data stream as to minimize the risk for an attack against a buffer overflow.

Additional Resources: http://livedocs.macromedia.com/coldfusion/6.1/htmldocs/function.htm#wp3082862

Impact: Low

Cross References: GetProfileString, SetProfileString

GetProfileString

Prototype: GetProfileString(iniFile, section, entry)

Summary: This function gets a value of a configuration variable in an initialization file.

Description: The function attempts to retrieve the value of a configuration variable. The function requires three input parameters: the full path of the initialization file, the section in which the variable resides, and the variable name. The function then returns, as a string, the value of the variable. The function returns an empty string if the variable does not exist.

Risk: This function parses input blindly. Additionally, logic should be incorporated into the application to ensure that human supplied input does not contain potentially malicious content. Data streams that are attached to external sources must first verify the integrity of those sources before interpreting and implementing the data. The destination buffer should be verified before any data is copied into memory or another data stream as to minimize the risk for an attack against a buffer overflow.

ColdFusion

Additional Resources: http://livedocs.macromedia.com/coldfusion/6.1/htmldocs/function.htm#wp3082862

Impact: Medium

Cross References: `GetProfileSections, SetProfileString`

GetTempDirectory

Prototype: `GetTempDirectory()`

Summary: This function gets the full path of a ColdFusion-administered temporary directory.

Description: The function attempts to retrieve the path of a ColdFusion-used temporary directory. This directory will depend on the account used and other assorted reasons. The function does not require an input parameter. The function returns the full path of the directory if successful.

Risk: System path information is constantly sought after by attackers or malicious users profiling a target application or system. Path information alone can potentially identify the underlying operating system, installed applications, configurations, and in some cases user and security information. Ensure that non-alphanumeric characters are removed from the string before it is processed and that the information is only processed internally by the application. Limits the end-user's ability to ascertain or traverse path information.

Additional Resources: http://livedocs.macromedia.com/coldfusion/6.1/htmldocs/function.htm#wp3082862

Impact: Low

Cross References: `GetTempFile`

GetTempFile

Prototype: `GetTempFile(dir, prefix)`

Summary: This function creates a temporary ColdFusion file.

Description: The function attempts to create a temporary file. The function takes two input parameters: the full path of the directory in which to place the temporary directory and up to a three-digit prefix to use for the file. The function returns, as a string, the name of the temporary file created.

Risk: Temporary filenames are often created with static and easily guessable algorithms such as the system time or application name appended with the day, month, and year. If at all possible, do not use this function and instead store temporary information in a secure memory space. If a temporary file is necessary, ensure that it is removed upon exiting the program or in the case where a program exits unexpectedly is removed upon program relaunch. Consider utilizing a random number generator such as ISAAC for creating secure random filenames.

Additional Resources: http://livedocs.macromedia.com/coldfusion/6.1/htmldocs/function.htm#wp3082862

Impact: Low

Cross References: `GetTempDirectory`

GetTickCount

Prototype: `GetTickCount`

Summary: This function gets the value of the system clock.

Description: This function attempts to retrieve the value of the internal system clock (in milliseconds). The function does not require any input parameters. The function returns, in milliseconds, the system time. The time is represented as a string.

Risk: This function handles system-specific sensitive information that an attacker could leverage during a period of target reconnaissance. This function should only be utilized if it is absolutely necessary for proper execution of the application. All analysis for the output of this function should be conducted securely within the application and never sent across the wire in cleartext.

Additional Resources: http://livedocs.macromedia.com/coldfusion/6.1/htmldocs/function.htm#wp3082862

Impact: Low

GetTimeZoneInfo

Prototype: `GetTimeZoneInfo()`

Summary: This function retrieves the information for the time zone on the computer called.

Description: The function attempts to ascertain the time zone information of the calling computer. The function does not take any input parameters. The function returns a structure. The structure contains the time offset in seconds, minutes, and hours, as well as whether Daylight Savings Time was on.

Risk: This function handles system-specific sensitive information that an attacker could leverage during a period of target reconnaissance. This function should only be utilized if it is absolutely necessary for proper execution of the application. All analysis for the output of this function should be conducted securely within the application and never sent across the wire in cleartext.

Additional Resources: http://livedocs.macromedia.com/coldfusion/6.1/htmldocs/function.htm#wp3082862

Impact: Low

Hash

Prototype: `Hash(string)`

Summary: This function converts a string to a 32-byte, hexadecimal string.

Description: The function attempts to transform a string into a special 32-byte, hexadecimal string using the MD5 algorithm. The function takes only one input value: the string to convert. The function returns the 32-byte converted string. The original string cannot be retrieved once converted, i.e. this is irreversible.

Risk: This function should never be utilized to obfuscate data with the goal of protecting it from prying eyes. Only industry-standard cryptography algorithms should be implemented to secure data. Do not use this function!

Additional Resources: http://livedocs.macromedia.com/coldfusion/6.1/htmldocs/function.htm#wp3082862

ColdFusion

Impact: High

HTMLCodeFormat

Prototype: HTMLCodeFormat(string [, version])

Summary: This function converts a string into its HTML equivalent.

Description: The function attempts to convert a string into its HTML equivalent. The takes one required input parameter: the string in question. However, an optional argument can be added: the HTML version number. The function replaces any special characters in the string with the HTML version and adds the header and footer for the string. The function then returns the converted string.

Risk: Certain string manipulation functions to include string and character transition functions are commonly leveraged in buffer overflow attacks. At the most basic level, these functions read in data, perform analysis and execution logic, then output the data to another type of string. It is imperative that the destination string be calculated accordingly and that enough memory space is allocated. Special characters should also be stricken from the conversion where possible.

Additional Resources: http://livedocs.macromedia.com/coldfusion/6.1/htmldocs/function.htm#wp3082862

Impact: High

Cross References: HTMLEditFormat

HTMLEditFormat

Prototype: HTMLEditFormat(string [, version])

Summary: This function converts a string into its HTML equivalent (without special header/footer).

Description: The function attempts to convert a string into its HTML equivalent. The takes one required input parameter: the string in question. However, an optional argument can be added: the HTML version number. The function replaces any special characters in the string with the HTML version. The function then returns the converted string.

Risk: Certain string manipulation functions to include string and character transition functions are commonly leveraged in buffer overflow attacks. At the most basic level, these functions read in data, perform analysis and execution logic, then output the data to another type of string. It is imperative that the destination string be calculated accordingly and that enough memory space is allocated. Special characters should also be stricken from the conversion where possible.

Additional Resources: http://livedocs.macromedia.com/coldfusion/6.1/htmldocs/function.htm#wp3082862

Impact: High

Cross References: HTMLCodeFormat

Insert

Prototype: Insert(substring, string, position)

Summary: This function inserts a substring into a string at a given position.

Description: The function attempts to insert a string into another string at some given position. The function has three input arguments: the substring to insert, the string to be inserted into, and the position in which to insert it. The function returns the complete string. The string is also dynamically allocated, i.e. if a substring is inserted into a 4-character string at position 6, there will be an empty placeholder in between.

Risk: Certain string manipulation functions to include string and character transition functions are commonly leveraged in buffer overflow attacks. At the most basic level, these functions read in data, perform analysis and execution logic, then output the data to another type of string. It is imperative that the destination string be calculated accordingly and that enough memory space is allocated. Special characters should also be stricken from the conversion where possible.

Additional Resources: http://livedocs.macromedia.com/coldfusion/6.1/htmldocs/function.htm#wp3082862

Impact: Low

Cross References: RemoveChars

ColdFusion

IsBinary

Prototype: `IsBinary(value)`

Summary: This function determines whether a data-value is binary.

Description: The function attempts to ascertain whether a value is stored in binary format. The function takes only one input variable: the value in question. The function returns TRUE if it is binary. It returns FALSE otherwise.

Risk: This function poses little risk; however, believe it or not, some developers have been obfuscating data in binary payloads, which is not a secure way to store or transmit sensitive data. Ensure that sensitive data is not simply being converted to binary out of convenience.

Additional Resources: http://livedocs.macromedia.com/coldfusion/6.1/htmldocs/function.htm#wp3082862

Impact: Low

Cross References: `ToBinary, ToBase64`

IsK2ServerABroker

Prototype: `IsK2ServerABroker()`

Summary: This function checks if a given ColdFusion server is a broker.

Description: The function attempts to ascertain whether a K2 server is a broker. The function does not take any input arguments. The function returns TRUE if it is a broker, FALSE if not. This function is currently being phased out.

Risk: Connecting to your K2 server from within your application poses minimal risk to your embedded application; however, data received from your server should be taken with a grain of salt. Multiple vulnerabilities have been identified in the K2 server and as such only data that is required should be collected from the server. The greatest risk of connecting to your K2 server resides in the link. If sensitive data is going to be transferred over the web then SSL should be utilized.

Additional Resources: http://livedocs.macromedia.com/coldfusion/6.1/htmldocs/function.htm#wp3082862

Impact: Low

Cross References: GetK2ServerDocCountLimit, IsK2ServerDocCountExceeded, IsK2ServerOnline

IsK2ServerDocCountExceeded

Prototype: IsK2ServerDocCountExceeded()

Summary: This function checks if the maximum document count is surpassed on a server.

Description: The function determines if the maximum count is violated for documents on a K2 server. The function does not require any input arguments. The function returns TRUE if the count is exceeded, FALSE if not. This function is being phased out.

Risk: Connecting to your K2 server from within your application poses minimal risk to your embedded application; however, data received from your server should be taken with a grain of salt. Multiple vulnerabilities have been identified in the K2 server and as such only data that is required should be collected from the server. The greatest risk of connecting to your K2 server resides in the link. If sensitive data is going to be transferred over the web then SSL should be utilized.

Additional Resources: http://livedocs.macromedia.com/coldfusion/6.1/ htmldocs/function.htm#wp3082862

Impact: Low

Cross References: GetK2ServerDocCountLimit, IsK2ServerABroker, IsK2ServerOnline

IsK2ServerOnline

Prototype: IsK2ServerOnline()

Summary: This function checks if the K2 server is running and available for searches.

ColdFusion

Description: The function determines if the K2 server is online and available. The function does not require any input arguments. The function returns TRUE if the server is online, FALSE if not. This function is being phased out.

Risk: Connecting to your K2 server from within your application poses minimal risk to your embedded application; however, data received from your server should be taken with a grain of salt. Multiple vulnerabilities have been identified in the K2 server and as such only data that is required should be collected from the server. The greatest risk of connecting to your K2 server resides in the link. If sensitive data is going to be transferred over the web then SSL should be utilized.

Additional Resources: http://livedocs.macromedia.com/coldfusion/6.1/htmldocs/function.htm#wp3082862

Impact: Low

Cross References: GetK2ServerDocCountLimit, IsK2ServerABroker, IsK2ServerDocCountExceeded

IsQuery

Prototype: IsQuery(value)

Summary: This function checks whether a given value is a query.

Description: The function attempts to ascertain whether a given value is a query. The function takes only one input argument: the value to check. The function checks whether it is a query or not, and returns an appropriate Boolean.

Risk: Queries commonly hide attacks in payloads that closely resemble legitimate application requests. Either hard code all queries then execute them solely on application logic or thoroughly vet all human user input. This will indeed be a medium exploited by attackers.

Additional Resources: http://livedocs.macromedia.com/coldfusion/6.1/htmldocs/function.htm#wp3082862

Impact: Low

Cross References: QueryAddRow

IsWDDX

Prototype: `IsWDDX(value)`

Summary: This function checks if a value is a well-defined WDDX packet.

Description: The function attempts to ascertain if the given value is a well-defined WDDX packet. The function takes one input parameter: the value to check. The function returns a Boolean value based on the status of the value.

Risk: Raw network data received from a socket has the potential to be malicious in nature due to the numerous amounts of attacks designed to be executed remotely. Packet fragmentations can cause serious disruptions to the application and underlying operating system. If at all possible, packet reassembly should be conducted at the OS-layer.

Additional Resources: http://livedocs.macromedia.com/coldfusion/6.1/htmldocs/function.htm#wp3082862

Impact: Low

IsXmlDoc

Prototype: `IsXmlDoc(value)`

Summary: This function checks if a given value is an XML document object.

Description: The function attempts to determine if a given value is an XML document object. The function takes only one input parameter: the value in question. The function returns a Boolean value based on the status of the object.

Risk: Functions that evaluate XML data must first open files or data streams for processing. During this period, its critical to ensure that the destination buffer is large enough for the processed data in addition to limiting the resources that can be analyzed for XML compatibility. This function poses minimal risk; but as "a rule of thumb" do not trust your XML data source and prepare for the worst.

Additional Resources: http://livedocs.macromedia.com/coldfusion/6.1/htmldocs/function.htm#wp3082862

Impact: Low

ColdFusion

Cross References: IsXmlElem, IsXmlRoot

IsXmlElem

Prototype: IsXmlElem(value)

Summary: This function checks if a given value is an XML document object element.

Description: The function attempts to determine if a given value is an XML document object element. The function takes only one input parameter: the value in question. The function returns a Boolean value based on the status of the value.

Risk: Functions that evaluate XML data must first open files or data streams for processing. During this period, its critical to ensure that the destination buffer is large enough for the processed data in addition to limiting the resources that can be analyzed for XML compatibility. This function poses minimal risk; but as "a rule of thumb" do not trust your XML data source and prepare for the worst.

Additional Resources: http://livedocs.macromedia.com/coldfusion/6.1/htmldocs/function.htm#wp3082862

Impact: Low

Cross References: IsXmlDoc, IsXmlRoot

IsXmlRoot

Prototype: IsXmlRoot(value)

Summary: This function checks if a given value is the root element of an XML document object.

Description: The function attempts to determine if a given value is the root element of an XML document object. The function takes only one input parameter: the value in question. The function returns a Boolean value based on the status of the value.

Risk: Functions that evaluate XML data must first open files or data streams for processing. During this period, its critical to ensure that the destination buffer is large enough for the processed data in addition to limiting the resources that can be analyzed for XML compatibility. This function poses minimal risk; but as "a rule of thumb" do not trust your XML data source and prepare for the worst.

Additional Resources: http://livedocs.macromedia.com/coldfusion/6.1/ htmldocs/function.htm#wp3082862

Impact: Medium

Cross References: IsXmlDoc, IsXmlElem

JavaCast

Prototype: JavaCast(type, variable)

Summary: This function converts a Coldfusion variable to a Java object.

Description: This function attempts to convert a Coldfusion variable to a Java object. The function takes two input arguments: the type of object to convert variable to and the variable itself. It should only be used for numerical or string objects. The function returns the variable in the new type of object.

Risk: The JavaCast function has little inherent risk associated with the general use of the function; however, the data should not be implicitly trusted by either the Java application. Attackers could potentially compromise any Java object that is created and stored in cleartext outside the object. Ensure that the files are stored in a secure manner and are not executable for lesser-privileged user accounts.

Additional Resources: http://livedocs.macromedia.com/coldfusion/6.1/ htmldocs/function.htm#wp3082862

Impact: Low

Lcase

Prototype: LCase(string)

Summary: This function converts the letters of a string to lower case.

Description: The function attempts to convert the letters of a string to the lower case. The function takes only one input argument: the string. The function will return the resultant string, once the letters have been converted.

Risk: Certain string manipulation functions to include string and character transition functions are commonly leveraged in buffer overflow attacks. At the most basic level, these functions read in data, perform analysis and execution logic, then output the data to another type of string. It is imperative that the destination string be calculated accordingly and that enough memory space is allocated. Special characters should also be stricken from the conversion where possible.

Additional Resources: http://livedocs.macromedia.com/coldfusion/6.1/htmldocs/function.htm#wp3082862

Impact: Low

Cross References: Ucase

ListChangeDelims

Prototype: ListChangeDelims(list, new_delimiter [, delimiters])

Summary: This function changes the parsing delimiter of a list.

Description: This function attempts to change the delimiter of a list. The function has two required input arguments: the list and the new delimiter. In the event that the list is not comma delimited to start with, then the function requires a third argument giving the list's current delimiter. The function then returns the list with the new delimiter.

Risk: Functions that modify lists commonly go unnoticed when verifying human user input or validating the security Access Control Lists (ACLs). It is highly recommended that you verify that the list input cannot have malicious data and that only the proper users and processes have access to the appropriate lists.

Additional Resources: http://livedocs.macromedia.com/coldfusion/6.1/htmldocs/function.htm#wp3082862

Impact: Low

ListDeleteAt

Prototype: ListDeleteAt(list, position [, delimiters])

Summary: This function deletes a member of a list.

Description: The function attempts to remove an element of a list at a given position. The function requires two input arguments: the list and the position. However, in the event that the list is not comma-delimited, then the function requires the special delimiter. The function returns the new list (missing the deleted member).

Risk: Functions that modify lists commonly go unnoticed when verifying human user input or validating the security Access Control Lists (ACLs). It is highly recommended that you verify that the list input cannot have malicious data and that only the proper users and processes have access to the appropriate lists.

Additional Resources: http://livedocs.macromedia.com/coldfusion/6.1/htmldocs/function.htm#wp3082862

Impact: Low

Cross References: `ListInsertAt`

ListFind

Prototype: `ListFind(list, value [, delimiters ])`

Summary: This function finds the first instance of a given value in a list.

Description: The function attempts to determine the position of the first occurrence of given value in a list. The function has two required input variables: the list and the value to find. If the list is not comma-delimited, then the function requires the special delimiter, as well. The function returns the position of the value. If it is not in the list, the function returns zero.

Risk: Functions that search for patterns open files and input their datastreams into allocated memory spaces. Outside of the race condition bugs that could occur if you attempted to open a file more than once simultaneously, a buffer overflow attack may also open up memory space for a root-level attack. Ensure that the files or datastreams that are passed for analysis to these functions are properly controlled and vetted by application logic. Users should not have the ability to identify if strings are within operating system resources such as configuration or log files.

ColdFusion

Additional Resources: http://livedocs.macromedia.com/coldfusion/6.1/htmldocs/function.htm#wp3082862

Impact: Low

ListInsertAt

Prototype: `ListInsertAt(list, position, value [, delimiters ])`

Summary: This function inserts a value into a list at a given position.

Description: The function attempts to insert a value into a list at some position. The function requires three input arguments: the list, the position, and the value to insert. The function also requires the special delimiter if the list is not comma-separated. The function returns the new list.

Risk: Functions that modify lists commonly go unnoticed when verifying human user input or validating the security Access Control Lists (ACLs). It is highly recommended that you verify that the list input cannot have malicious data and that only the proper users and processes have access to the appropriate lists.

Additional Resources: http://livedocs.macromedia.com/coldfusion/6.1/htmldocs/function.htm#wp3082862

Impact: Low

Cross References: `ListDeleteAt`

ListPrepend

Prototype: `ListPrepend(list, value [, delimiters ])`

Summary: This function inserts a value at the beginning of a list.

Description: The function attempts to insert a value into a list in the first position. The function requires only two input values: the list and the value to insert. The function also requires the special delimiter if the function is not comma-separated.

Risk: Functions that modify lists commonly go unnoticed when verifying human user input or validating the security Access Control Lists (ACLs). It is highly recommended that you verify that the list input cannot have malicious data and that only the proper users and processes have access to the appropriate lists.

Additional Resources: http://livedocs.macromedia.com/coldfusion/6.1/ htmldocs/function.htm#wp3082862

Impact: Low

Cross References: `ListInsertAt, ListSetAt`

ListSetAt

Prototype: `ListSetAt(list, position, value [, delimiters ])`

Summary: This function replaces an element of the list with a new one.

Description: The function attempts to replace a member of the list with a new a given position. The function requires three input values: the list, the position, and the value to use. The function will also require the list delimiter if it is not comma-separated. The function will return the new list.

Risk: Functions that modify lists commonly go unnoticed when verifying human user input or validating the security Access Control Lists (ACLs). It is highly recommended that you verify that the list input cannot have malicious data and that only the proper users and processes have access to the appropriate lists.

Additional Resources: http://livedocs.macromedia.com/coldfusion/6.1/ htmldocs/function.htm#wp3082862

Impact: Low

Cross References: `ListInsertAt`

LSIsDate

Prototype: `LSIsDate(string)`

Summary: This function checks whether a string is in proper date format.

Description: The function attempts to determine if a given string is in date format. The function takes only one input argument: the string in question. The function then checks if the string is in valid date/time format for the current locale. The function returns TRUE if it is valid, and FALSE if not.

ColdFusion

Risk: Certain string manipulation functions to include string and character transition functions are commonly leveraged in buffer overflow attacks. At the most basic level, these functions read in data, perform analysis and execution logic, then output the data to another type of string. It is imperative that the destination string be calculated accordingly and that enough memory space is allocated. Special characters should also be stricken from the conversion where possible.

Additional Resources: http://livedocs.macromedia.com/coldfusion/6.1/htmldocs/function.htm#wp3082862

Impact: Low

LSTimeFormat

Prototype: `LSTimeFormat(time [, mask ])`

Summary: This function formats the time part of a date-time object into a string.

Description: The function attempts to extract the time from a date-time object and put it into a string. The function requires only the time object to proceed. However, in the event that there is a special masking associated with the time, it must be specified. The function returns the string form of the time.

Risk: Certain string manipulation functions to include string and character transition functions are commonly leveraged in buffer overflow attacks. At the most basic level, these functions read in data, perform analysis and execution logic, then output the data to another type of string. It is imperative that the destination string be calculated accordingly and that enough memory space is allocated. Special characters should also be stricken from the conversion where possible.

Additional Resources: http://livedocs.macromedia.com/coldfusion/6.1/htmldocs/function.htm#wp3082862

Impact: Low

Now

Prototype: `Now()`

Summary: This function gets the current date and time.

Description: The function attempts to retrieve the date and time from the ColdFusion server. The function does not require any input arguments. The function returns a date-time object. This object is suitable to use similar time and date object functions.

Risk: This function handles system-specific sensitive information that an attacker could leverage during a period of target reconnaissance. This function should only be utilized if it is absolutely necessary for proper execution of the application. All analysis for the output of this function should be conducted securely within the application and never sent across the wire in cleartext.

Additional Resources: http://livedocs.macromedia.com/coldfusion/6.1/ htmldocs/function.htm#wp3082862

Impact: Low

PreserveSingleQuotes

Prototype: `PreserveSingleQuotes(variable)`

Summary: This function prevents ColdFusion from escaping a string containing single quotation marks.

Description: The function tries to keep ColdFusion from escaping out of a string containing single quotation marks. The function has one input argument: the string (possibly containing single quotation marks). The function does return anything, per se. ColdFusion does not evaluate the string when using this function.

Risk: Certain string manipulation functions to include string and character transition functions are commonly leveraged in buffer overflow attacks. At the most basic level, these functions read in data, perform analysis and execution logic, then output the data to another type of string. It is imperative that the destination string be calculated accordingly and that enough memory space is allocated. Special characters should also be stricken from the conversion where possible.

Additional Resources: http://livedocs.macromedia.com/coldfusion/6.1/ htmldocs/function.htm#wp3082862

Impact: High

ColdFusion

QueryAddColumn

Prototype: `QueryAddColumn(query, column-name, array-name)`

Summary: This function adds a new column to a query.

Description: This function attempts to add a column to an existing query. The function inserts a column into the query, filling its rows with the members of an array. It takes three input arguments: the query, the new column's name, and the array to fill the column's elements. The function will return the column number that was added when completed successful.

Risk: In most scenarios, query functions are utilized to execute launched attacks on backend databases. These query functions should be analyzed and stripped of any potentially malicious characters commonly utilized in database attacks. Such characters include **<, >, /, %, *,** and **&**. Additionally, ensure that human input is strictly monitored and controlled within the application so that raw queries cannot be created and injected into the application.

Additional Resources: http://livedocs.macromedia.com/coldfusion/6.1/htmldocs/function.htm#wp3082862

Impact: High

Cross References: `QueryNew, QueryAddRow, QuerySetCell`

QueryAddRow

Prototype: `QueryAddRow(query [, number ])`

Summary: This function adds a row (or several) to an existing query.

Description: The function attempts to append one/many rows to an existing query. The function requires only the query name to add the default number of rows: one. However, an optional argument exists that allows the user to specify the number of rows to add. The function will return the total number rows in the query upon completion.

Risk: In most scenarios, query functions are utilized to execute launched attacks on backend databases. These query functions should be analyzed and stripped of any potentially malicious characters commonly utilized in database attacks. Such characters include **<, >, /, %, *,** and **&;.** Additionally, ensure that human input is strictly monitored and controlled within the application so that raw queries cannot be created and injected into the application.

Additional Resources: http://livedocs.macromedia.com/coldfusion/6.1/ htmldocs/function.htm#wp3082862

Impact: High

Cross References: IsQuery, QueryAddColumn, QuerySetCell, QueryNew

QueryNew

Prototype: QueryNew(columnlist)

Summary: This function creates an empty query.

Description: The function attempts to create a new, empty query. The function has only one input argument: the list of column names for the query. A user is allowed to send an empty string for the column list and add columns later. The function will return the query object when completed.

Risk: In most scenarios, query functions are utilized to execute launched attacks on backend databases. These query functions should be analyzed and stripped of any potentially malicious characters commonly utilized in database attacks. Such characters include **<, >, /, %, *,** and **&;.** Additionally, ensure that human input is strictly monitored and controlled within the application so that raw queries cannot be created and injected into the application.

Additional Resources: http://livedocs.macromedia.com/coldfusion/6.1/ htmldocs/function.htm#wp3082862

Impact: High

Cross References: QueryAddColumn, QueryAddRow, QuerySetCell

QuerySetCell

Prototype: QuerySetCell(query, column_name, value [, row_number])

Summary: This function changes the value of a single cell in a query.

ColdFusion

Description: The function attempts to alter the value of a cell in an existing query. The function requires three input values: the query's name, the name of the column in which the cell exists, and the value to change it to. The function will default to the last row of the query if the function is not given the optional input argument: the row number. The function will return TRUE if completed successfully, FALSE if not.

Risk: In most scenarios, query functions are utilized to execute launched attacks on backend databases. These query functions should be analyzed and stripped of any potentially malicious characters commonly utilized in database attacks. Such characters include **<, >, /, %, ***, and **&;**. Additionally, ensure that human input is strictly monitored and controlled within the application so that raw queries cannot be created and injected into the application.

Additional Resources: http://livedocs.macromedia.com/coldfusion/6.1/htmldocs/function.htm#wp3082862

Impact: High

Cross References: QueryAddColumn, QueryAddRow, QueryNew

QuotedValueList

Prototype: QuotedValueList(query.column [, delimiter])

Summary: This function creates a list from the members of a column in a query.

Description: This function makes a list and fills it with the members of a column of an existing query. The function requires only one input argument: query/column in a period separated form (i.e., query.column). However, if a user wishes to have a delimiter other than commas, that can be specified in an optional input argument. The function returns the complete list when finished. Each list member is surrounded with single quotes.

Risk: Functions that modify lists commonly go unnoticed when verifying human user input or validating the security Access Control Lists (ACLs). It is highly recommended that you verify that the list input cannot have malicious data and that only the proper users and processes have access to the appropriate lists.

Additional Resources: http://livedocs.macromedia.com/coldfusion/6.1/htmldocs/function.htm#wp3082862

Impact: Medium

Cross References: ValueList

Rand

Prototype: Rand()

Summary: This function generates a random number.

Description: The function creates a random number. The function does not require any input arguments. The function returns the random number (between 0 and 1). This function works best when called after the "Randomize" function.

Risk: As with most standard random functions implemented within the C and C++ libraries, this function is susceptible to brute-force or easily guessed number generating attacks due to a poor seed algorithm within the backend code. Amongst numerous other secure random number generating functions, Microsoft .Net has secure methods for implementing properly seeded numbers. ISAAC, designed by Bob Jenkins, is a fast cryptographic random number generator is as strong as they come. Available in multiple languages, ISAAC is a standard for many freeware and commercial solutions and should be considered the next time a random number is required within an application.

Additional Resources: www.burtleburtle.net/bob/rand/isaacafa.html, http://livedocs.macromedia.com/coldfusion/6.1/htmldocs/function.htm#wp3082862

Impact: Medium

Cross References: Randomize, RandRange

Randomize

Prototype: Randomize(number)

Summary: This function seeds the random number generator.

Description: The function uses a given number to seed ColdFusion's random number generator. The function takes only one input variable: the number to use when seeding the generator. The function returns a non-random number between 0 and 1 when completed. This function is best used before the "Rand" function.

Risk: As with most standard random functions implemented within the C and C++ libraries, this function is susceptible to brute-force or easily guessed number generating attacks due to a poor seed algorithm within the backend code. Amongst numerous other secure random number generating functions, Microsoft .Net has secure methods for implementing properly seeded numbers. ISAAC, designed by Bob Jenkins, is a fast cryptographic random number generator is as strong as they come. Available in multiple languages, ISAAC is a standard for many freeware and commercial solutions and should be considered the next time a random number is required within an application.

Additional Resources: www.burtleburtle.net/bob/rand/isaacafa.html, http://livedocs.macromedia.com/coldfusion/6.1/htmldocs/function.htm#wp3082862

Impact: Medium

Cross References: Rand, RandRange

RandRange

Prototype: RandRange(number1, number2)

Summary: This function generates a random number within a desired range.

Description: The function attempts to create a random number within a given range. The function takes two input arguments: the two integers that serve as bounds for the random number generator. The function returns the random number. There is a functional-imposed limit for the bounds. The function will not take any numbers over 100,000,000 for the bounds to prevent overflow.

Risk: As with most standard random functions implemented within the C and C++ libraries, this function is susceptible to brute-force or easily guessed number generating attacks due to a poor seed algorithm within the backend code. Amongst numerous other secure random number generating functions, Microsoft .Net has secure methods for implementing properly seeded numbers. ISAAC, designed by

Bob Jenkins, is a fast cryptographic random number generator is as strong as they come. Available in multiple languages, ISAAC is a standard for many freeware and commercial solutions and should be considered the next time a random number is required within an application.

Additional Resources: http://livedocs.macromedia.com/coldfusion/6.1/htmldocs/function.htm#wp3082862

Impact: Medium

Cross References: Rand, Randomize

REFind

Prototype: REFind(reg_expression, string [, start]   [, returnsubexpressions])

Summary: This function searches for a pattern in strings.

Description: The function uses regular expressions to search a string for case-sensitive patterns. The function requires two input arguments: the expression and the string to search. It has two optional arguments: a start position to search the string and whether the substrings containing the regular expressions should be returned. The function normally returns the position at which the regular expression begins. However, if the Boolean option argument for the return of the subexpressions is TRUE, then it will return two arrays—"len" and "pos"—giving the details on the existence of the subexpressions.

Risk: Functions that search for patterns open files and input their datastreams into allocated memory spaces. Outside of the race condition bugs that could occur if you attempted to open a file more than once simultaneously, a buffer overflow attack may also open up memory space for a root-level attack. Ensure that the files or datastreams that are passed for analysis to these functions are properly controlled and vetted by application logic. Users should not have the ability to identify if strings are within operating system resources such as configuration or log files.

Note: This function is identical to REFindNoCase, except that this function is case-sensitive.

ColdFusion

Additional Resources: www.burtleburtle.net/bob/rand/isaacafa.html, http://livedocs.macromedia.com/coldfusion/6.1/htmldocs/function.htm#wp3082862

Impact: Low

Cross References: Find, REFindNoCase

REFindNoCase

Prototype: REFindNoCase(reg_expression, string [, start] [, returnsubexpressions])

Summary: This function searches for a string for a given pattern.

Description: The function uses regular expressions to search a string for case-insensitive patterns. The function requires two input arguments: the expression and the string to search. It has two optional arguments: a start position to search the string and whether the substrings containing the regular expressions should be returned. The function normally returns the position at which the regular expression begins. However, if the Boolean option argument for the return of the subexpressions is TRUE, then it will return two arrays—"len" and "pos"—giving the details on the existence of the subexpressions.

Risk: Functions that search for patterns open files and input their datastreams into allocated memory spaces. Outside of the race condition bugs that could occur if you attempted to open a file more than once simultaneously, a buffer overflow attack may also open up memory space for a root-level attack. Ensure that the files or datastreams that are passed for analysis to these functions are properly controlled and vetted by application logic. Users should not have the ability to identify if strings are within operating system resources such as configuration or log files.

Note: This function is identical to REFind, except that this function is case-insensitive.

Additional Resources: http://livedocs.macromedia.com/coldfusion/6.1/htmldocs/function.htm#wp3082862

Impact: Low

Cross References: Find, REFind

ReleaseComObject

Prototype: `ReleaseComObject(objectName)`

Summary: This function releases a COM object.

Description: This function releases a COM object and frees its resources. The function takes only input argument: the COM object to release. The function does not return anything. This function also frees the children COM objects of the requested COM object.

Risk: Ensure that only the proper COM objects have been accessed and are released. Human users should not be able to launch or pass data to this function, nor should the use of this function be made aware of to the application user base.

Additional Resources: http://livedocs.macromedia.com/coldfusion/6.1/ htmldocs/function.htm#wp3082862

Impact: Low

RemoveChars

Prototype: `RemoveChars(string, start, count)`

Summary: This function deletes a given number of characters from a string.

Description: The function attempts to remove a series of characters from a string. The function takes three input arguments: the string, the position to start deleting characters, and the number to delete. The function requires that the position be positive. It will return the resultant string, unless no characters are removed. In this case, the function returns zero.

Risk: This function poses minimal threat to an enterprise application; however, ensure that users not intended to see the output are restricted from doing so. Additionally, ensure that only the proper strings can be modified via application logic.

Additional Resources: http://livedocs.macromedia.com/coldfusion/6.1/ htmldocs/function.htm#wp3082862

Impact: Low

Cross References: `Insert`

ReplaceList

Prototype: `ReplaceList(string, list1, list2)`

Summary: This function replaces instances of a string in one list with members of another list.

Description: The function searches a list for a given string and replaces occurrences of this string with members of a different list. The function requires three input parameters: the string to search for, the list to search, and the list housing the replacements. The function returns the resultant list. This search is case-sensitive (like `REFind`).

Risk: In addition to the potential race condition bugs that are associated with this function, a user could also attempt to execute a denial of service attack. Ensure that only one instance of this function can be called at any given moment. All input passed to this function should be analyzed closely to ensure that only desired resources can be removed from the system. It is not uncommon for worms and viruses to exploit application-layer vulnerabilities to cause damage to files they since would not have had access to.

Additional Resources: http://livedocs.macromedia.com/coldfusion/6.1/htmldocs/function.htm#wp3082862

Impact: Low

Cross References: `Find, REFind`

Reverse

Prototype: `Reverse(string)`

Summary: This function reverses the order of a string (or number, array, etc...).

Description: The function attempts to reverse the order of some collection of items. Given a multi-digit number, string, array, etc, the function reverses the order and returns this. The function takes only one input argument: the object to reverse the order. The function returns the reversed object.

Risk: This function should never be utilized to obfuscate data with the goal of protecting it from prying eyes. Only industry-standard cryptography algorithms should be implemented to secure data. This function is out-of-date and should not be used!

Additional Resources: http://livedocs.macromedia.com/coldfusion/6.1/htmldocs/function.htm#wp3082862

Impact: High

SetEncoding

Prototype: `SetEncoding(scope_name,charset)`

Summary: This function sets the character set for a given object.

Description: The function attempts to set the encoding scheme for some object (whether it is a page, form, etc…). The function requires two input arguments: the object to set the scheme and the character set to use. The function does not return anything. For a list of available character sets, see the MacroMedia documentation.

Risk: This function should never be utilized to obfuscate data with the goal of protecting it from prying eyes. Only industry-standard cryptography algorithms should be implemented to secure data. This function is out-of-date and should not be used!

Additional Resources: http://livedocs.macromedia.com/coldfusion/6.1/htmldocs/function.htm#wp3082862

Impact: High

Cross References: `GetEncoding, URLDecode, URLEncodedFormat`

SetLocale

Prototype: `SetLocale(new_locale)`

Summary: This function changes the locale.

Description: The function attempts to alter the current locale for ColdFusion processing purposes. The function takes only one input parameter: the new locale. The function returns the old locale information when completed. The locale information determines how the time, date, etc… values are stored/displayed.

ColdFusion

Risk: This function should only be accessed and launched by administrative-level users or systems that wish to affect the underlying operating system. In nearly all cases, this function is not truly required and should be removed before an application gets released as production.

Additional Resources: http://livedocs.macromedia.com/coldfusion/6.1/ htmldocs/function.htm#wp3082862

Impact: Medium

Cross References: `GetHttpTimeString, GetLocale`

SetProfileString

Prototype: `SetProfileString(iniPath, section, entry, value)`

Summary: This function sets the value of an entry in an initialization file.

Description: The function attempts to set value of a profile entry in an .ini file. The function takes four input parameters: the .ini file, the section to search, the name of the profile entry, and the value to use. The function will return an empty string when complete. However, if the function fails, an error message will be generated.

Risk: All special and wildcard characters should be removed before the filename is computed on the local filesystem. Malicious filenames are interpreted differently on varying systems and as such, directory control is critical to limiting the ability of an attacker to potentially compromise files at varying levels within the application or underlying subsystem.

Additional Resources: http://livedocs.macromedia.com/coldfusion/6.1/ htmldocs/function.htm#wp3082862

Impact: Low

Cross References: `GetProfileSections, GetProfileString`

ColdFusion

StripCR

Prototype: `StripCR(string)`

Summary: This function removes the carriage-return characters from a string.

Description: The function attempts to delete the return characters from a string. The function takes only one input variable: the string to strip. The function returns a copy of the resultant carriage-return-free string.

Risk: Certain string manipulation functions to include string and character transition functions are commonly leveraged in buffer overflow attacks. At the most basic level, these functions read in data, perform analysis and execution logic, then output the data to another type of string. It is imperative that the destination string be calculated accordingly and that enough memory space is allocated. Special characters should also be stricken from the conversion where possible.

Additional Resources: http://livedocs.macromedia.com/coldfusion/6.1/ htmldocs/function.htm#wp3082862

Impact: Low

StructClear

Prototype: `StructClear(structure)`

Summary: This function clears the data from ColdFusion structure.

Description: The function deletes the data from a ColdFusion structure. The function has only one input argument: the structure to clear. The function returns TRUE if successful, and FALSE if not. This function can also handle XML objects.

Risk: Functions that modify structures commonly go unnoticed when verifying human user input or validating the security Access Control Lists (ACLs). It is highly recommended that you verify that the structure input cannot have malicious data and that only the proper users and processes have the appropriate access.

Additional Resources: http://livedocs.macromedia.com/coldfusion/6.1/ htmldocs/function.htm#wp3082862

ColdFusion

Impact: Low

Cross References: StructDelete, StructGet, StructInsert, StructUpdate

StructDelete

Prototype: StructDelete(structure, key [, indicatenotexisting])

Summary: This function removes an element from a structure.

Description: The function attempts to delete an element from an existing structure. The function requires two input arguments: the structure and the element to delete. The function also has a Boolean flag optional argument that changes the return value depending on whether the field to delete exists. The function returns normally TRUE if successful or the field does not exist. However, if the flag is activated, the function returns TRUE if successful and the field existed.

Risk: Functions that modify structures commonly go unnoticed when verifying human user input or validating the security Access Control Lists (ACLs). It is highly recommended that you verify that the structure input cannot have malicious data and that only the proper users and processes have the appropriate access.

Additional Resources: http://livedocs.macromedia.com/coldfusion/6.1/htmldocs/function.htm#wp3082862

Impact: Low

Cross References: StructClear, StructGet, StructInsert, StructUpdate

StructGet

Prototype: StructGet(pathDesired)

Summary: This function retrieves a structure from a given path.

Description: The function attempts to grab a structure from a given path. The function takes only one input argument: the path to the structure. The function returns a variable alias to the struct pointed to in the path. The function is dynamic,

ColdFusion

creating required structures and/or arrays to make the path given valid (i.e., you can create a new structure).

Risk: This function parses input blindly. Additionally, logic should be incorporated into the application to ensure that human supplied input does not contain potentially malicious content. Data streams that are attached to external sources must first verify the integrity of those sources before interpreting and implementing the data. The destination buffer should be verified before any data is copied into memory or another data stream as to minimize the risk for an attack against a buffer overflow.

Additional Resources: http://livedocs.macromedia.com/coldfusion/6.1/htmldocs/function.htm#wp3082862

Impact: Low

Cross References: StructClear, StructDelete, StructInsert, StructUpdate

StructInsert

Prototype: StructInsert(structure, key, value [, allowoverwrite])

Summary: This function inserts a field–value pair into an existing structure.

Description: The function attempts to insert a field and value into a ColdFusion structure. The function requires three input arguments: the structure, the field, and the value. However, an optional flagging argument exists to allow overwriting (the default value is FALSE). The function returns TRUE if successful. However, depending on the state of the flagging input, the existence of the structure, etc, the function may return FALSE.

Risk: Functions that modify structures commonly go unnoticed when verifying human user input or validating the security Access Control Lists (ACLs). It is highly recommended that you verify that the structure input cannot have malicious data and that only the proper users and processes have the appropriate access.

Additional Resources: http://livedocs.macromedia.com/coldfusion/6.1/htmldocs/function.htm#wp3082862

ColdFusion

Impact: Low

Cross References: StructClear, StructDelete, StructGet, StructUpdate

StructUpdate

Prototype: StructUpdate(structure, key, value)

Summary: This function updates the value in a particular field of a ColdFusion structure.

Description: The function attempts to update the value in a field of some ColdFusion structure. The function takes three input parameters: the structure, the field, and the new value to use. It returns TRUE if successful, FALSE if not. This function can be used on XML objects.

Risk: Functions that modify structures commonly go unnoticed when verifying human user input or validating the security Access Control Lists (ACLs). It is highly recommended that you verify that the structure input cannot have malicious data and that only the proper users and processes have the appropriate access.

Additional Resources: http://livedocs.macromedia.com/coldfusion/6.1/htmldocs/function.htm#wp3082862

Impact: Low

Cross References: StructClear, StructDelete, StructGet, StructInsert

ToBase64

Prototype: ToBase64(string or binary_object[, encoding]

Summary: This function computes the base-64 representation of a binary or string object.

Description: The function attempts to convert a binary or string object into its base-64 representation. The function requires one input parameter: the object to convert. The function also takes one optional argument, in the event that an object is a string: the encoding of the string. The function returns the base-64 representation of the object.

Risk: This function should never be utilized to obfuscate data with the goal of protecting it from prying eyes. Only industry-standard cryptography algorithms should be implemented to secure data. Do not use this function!

Additional Resources: http://livedocs.macromedia.com/coldfusion/6.1/htmldocs/function.htm#wp3082862

Impact: High

Cross References: IsBinary, ToBinary, ToString

ToBinary

Prototype: ToBinary(string_in_Base64 or binary_value)

Summary: This function converts an object to binary format.

Description: The function attempts to convert an object to binary format. The function takes only one input argument: the object to convert. The function also acts similar to IsBinary if the function is given a binary object to convert. It checks the validity of the binary object. It returns the binary representation of the input object.

Risk: Certain string manipulation functions to include string and character transition functions are commonly leveraged in buffer overflow attacks. At the most basic level, these functions read in data, perform analysis and execution logic, then output the data to another type of string. It is imperative that the destination string be calculated accordingly and that enough memory space is allocated. Special characters should also be stricken from the conversion where possible.

Additional Resources: http://livedocs.macromedia.com/coldfusion/6.1/htmldocs/function.htm#wp3082862

Impact: High

Cross References: IsBinary, ToBase64, ToString

ColdFusion

ToString

Prototype: `ToString(any_value[, encoding])`

Summary: This function converts any given value to a string.

Description: The function attempts to convert a given value to its string representation. The function requires only one input parameter: the value to convert. However, the function can handle an optional argument stipulating the character set to use for the resultant string. The function defaults to the encoding of the page that calls it. The function returns the string representation of the given value (in the requested encoding scheme, if applicable).

Risk: Certain string manipulation functions to include string and character transition functions are commonly leveraged in buffer overflow attacks. At the most basic level, these functions read in data, perform analysis and execution logic, then output the data to another type of string. It is imperative that the destination string be calculated accordingly and that enough memory space is allocated. Special characters should also be stricken from the conversion where possible.

Additional Resources: http://livedocs.macromedia.com/coldfusion/6.1/htmldocs/function.htm#wp3082862

Impact: Low

Cross References: `ToBase64, ToBinary`

Ucase

Prototype: `UCase(string)`

Summary: This function converts the letters of a string to upper case.

Description: The function attempts to convert the letters of a string to the upper case. The function takes only one input argument: the string. The function will return the resultant string, once the letters have been converted.

Risk: Certain string manipulation functions to include string and character transition functions are commonly leveraged in buffer overflow attacks. At the most basic level, these functions read in data, perform analysis and execution logic, then output the data to another type of string. It is imperative that the destination string be calculated accordingly and that enough memory space is allocated. Special characters should also be stricken from the conversion where possible.

Additional Resources: http://livedocs.macromedia.com/coldfusion/6.1/ htmldocs/function.htm#wp3082862

Impact: Low

Cross References: Lcase

URLDecode

Prototype: URLDecode(urlEncodedString[, charset])

Summary: This function decodes an URL-encoded string.

Description: The function attempts to decode an URL-encoded string. The function requires only one input parameter: the encoded string. The function, though, can handle an optional argument that gives encoding scheme of the string. The function returns, upon completion, the decoded string.

Risk: The fact that this function is utilized may mean that the URLEncodedFormat function was already called. These functions do not pose immediate danger or risk to an application unless they are utilized to obfuscate sensitive information.

Additional Resources: http://livedocs.macromedia.com/coldfusion/6.1/ htmldocs/function.htm#wp3082862

Impact: High

Cross References: URLEncodedFormat

URLEncodedFormat

Prototype: URLEncodedFormat(string [, charset])

Summary: This function URL-encodes a given string.

Description: The function attempts to encode a given string in a URL scheme. The function requires only input argument: the string to encode. However, the function can take an optional argument stipulating the encoding format to use. The function returns the URL-encoded string when completed.

Risk: This function should never be utilized to obfuscate data with the goal of protecting it from prying eyes. Only industry-standard cryptography algorithms should be implemented to secure data. This function is out-of-date and should not be used!

Additional Resources: http://livedocs.macromedia.com/coldfusion/6.1/htmldocs/function.htm#wp3082862

Impact: High

Cross References: URLDecode

URLSessionFormat

Prototype: URLSessionFormat(request_URL)

Summary: This function determines the format of an URL session.

Description: The function attempts to ascertain the format of the URL session. The function works in two ways, depending on whether cookies are being accepted by a client computer. If accepted, the function does not append any client information and sends only the required. However, if cookies are not being accepted by the client computer, the function appends the client information to any data sent. The function returns a URL, and if cookies are not accepted, the client information.

Risk: Functions that modify lists commonly go unnoticed when verifying human user input or validating the security Access Control Lists (ACLs). It is highly recommended that you verify that the list input cannot have malicious data and that only the proper users and processes have access to the appropriate lists.

Additional Resources: http://livedocs.macromedia.com/coldfusion/6.1/htmldocs/function.htm#wp3082862

Impact: High

ValueList

Prototype: `ValueList(query.column [, delimiter ])`

Summary: This function creates a delimited list from a column of a query.

Description: The function attempts to create a list populated with the columns of an existing query. The function requires only one input parameter: the query and column name in period-separated format (i.e., query.column). The function can handle a second, optional argument stipulating the delimiter to use in the list (the default is a comma). It returns the resultant list. However, unlike `QuotedValueList`, the members do not have single quotes around them.

Risk: Functions that modify lists commonly go unnoticed when verifying human user input or validating the security Access Control Lists (ACLs). It is highly recommended that you verify that the list input cannot have malicious data and that only the proper users and processes have access to the appropriate lists.

Additional Resources: http://livedocs.macromedia.com/coldfusion/6.1/htmldocs/function.htm#wp3082862

Impact: Low

Cross References: `QuotedValueList`

XmlFormat

Prototype: `XmlFormat(string)`

Summary: This function converts a string into the XML-appropriate format.

Description: The function attempts to convert a string into an XML-capable format. The function escapes the special characters of string, allowing the string to be interpreted properly in XML. It takes only one input parameter: the string to convert. The function returns the corrected/converted string.

Risk: Functions that evaluate XML data must either open or save the information to a file or data stream for processing. During this period, its critical to ensure that the destination buffer is large enough for the processed data in addition to limiting the resources that can be analyzed for XML compatibility. This function poses min-

ColdFusion

imal risk; but as "a rule of thumb" do not trust your XML data source and prepare for the worst.

Additional Resources: http://livedocs.macromedia.com/coldfusion/6.1/htmldocs/function.htm#wp3082862

Impact: Low

Cross References: IsXmlDoc, XmlNew, XmlTransform

XmlNew

Prototype: XmlNew([caseSensitive])

Summary: This function creates a new XML document object.

Description: The function attempts to create a new XML document. It does not require any input parameters. However, the function can handle one optional argument: a flag to tell ColdFusion to whether to consider case in this object. The function returns the new, empty XML document object when complete.

Risk: Functions that evaluate XML data must either open or save the information to a file or data stream for processing. During this period, its critical to ensure that the destination buffer is large enough for the processed data in addition to limiting the resources that can be analyzed for XML compatibility. This function poses minimal risk; but as "a rule of thumb" do not trust your XML data source and prepare for the worst.

Additional Resources: http://livedocs.macromedia.com/coldfusion/6.1/htmldocs/function.htm#wp3082862

Impact: Low

Cross References: IsXmlDoc, XmlFormat, XmlTransform

XmlTransform

Prototype: XmlTransform(xmlString or xmlObj, xslString)

Summary: This function transforms an XML document or string to another format.

Description: The function attempts to convert an XML document/string to a different format. The function applies the transformation to either a string or the entire XML document. The function thus takes two input arguments: the object to convert (either a string or document) and the conversion format. The function returns the converted string or document.

Risk: Functions that evaluate XML data must either open or save the information to a file or data stream for processing. During this period, its critical to ensure that the destination buffer is large enough for the processed data in addition to limiting the resources that can be analyzed for XML compatibility. This function poses minimal risk; but as "a rule of thumb" do not trust your XML data source and prepare for the worst.

Additional Resources: http://livedocs.macromedia.com/coldfusion/6.1/ htmldocs/function.htm#wp3082862

Impact: Low

Cross References: IsXmlDoc, XmlFormat, XmlNew

Programmer's Ultimate Security Desk Ref: JavaScript

alert

Prototype: `alert(message)`

Summary: Displays a modal dialog window with a message and an OK button.

Description: This method is attached to the `window` object. When called it displays a modal dialog with the specified message, dismissed with the OK button. Use it to inform users of errors, important actions, or results. Since the only user input is dismissing the dialog, no value is returned. Example: alert("You need to enter a valid telephone number.")

Risk: Input boxes are commonly misused for password and other types of sensitive information storage. Sensitive information should never be transmitted from clients to servers via Web page input boxes. In addition, SSL should be implemented when transferring sensitive data. Lastly, ensure that all user input is fully scrutinized whereas non-alphanumeric characters are removed where possible.

Additional Resources:

http://devedge.netscape.com/library/manuals/2000/javascript/1.3/
reference/window.html#1201497

Impact: Medium

Cross Reference: confirm, prompt

apply

Prototype: apply(newThis[, argsArray])

Summary: Changes the this object used in a method call.

Description: When an object calls a method, it is implicitly passed to the method as this. The apply method allows you to explicitly change the object passed. This is useful for chaining object constructors. One can initialize the fields specific to the current object, then pass the unused arguments to the next object's constructor. The only required argument is the new this object. You can also pass an optional Array of method arguments.

Risk: Ensure that only site administrators have access to modify or statically pass parameters to this function. Strip all special characters before passing the parameter(s) to this function.

Notes: Not yet in the ECMA spec, but expected in the next revision.

Proper Usage: otherObj.apply(otherObj, [arg1, arg2, ..])

Additional Resources:

http://devedge.netscape.com/library/manuals/2000/javascript/1.5/reference/
function.html#1194017

Impact: Low

Cross Reference: call

captureEvents

Prototype: `captureEvents(type1[| type2 | ..])`

Summary: Allows a window to capture all events of the specified type that occur within it.

Description: The `captureEvents` method allows a window to capture all events that occur within it. This is useful for capturing events that occur in a frame contained in the window, even frames containing contents from a different server. The method accepts an event mask. Use requires the browser's `UniversalBrowserWrite` privilege and the `enableExternalCapture` method.

Risk: Input boxes are commonly misused for password and other types of sensitive information storage. Sensitive information should never be transmitted from clients to servers via Web page input boxes. In addition, SSL should be implemented when transferring sensitive data. Lastly, ensure that all user input is fully scrutinized whereas non-alphanumeric characters are removed where possible.

Additional Resources:

http://devedge.netscape.com/library/manuals/2000/javascript/1.3/reference/window.html#1201687

Impact: Medium

Cross Reference: `enableExternalCapture`, `releaseEvents`, `routeEvent`, `handleEvent`, `disableExternalCapture`

clearTimeout

Prototype: `clearTimeout(timeoutID)`

Summary: Clears a timeout on the `window` object previously set by `setTimeout`.

Description: When `setTimeout` is called it returns a timeout ID. Call `clearTimeout` with this ID and that timeout is cleared for the window.

Risk: The `clearTimeout` function could be leveraged by an attacker to clear previously set timeouts instantiated by earlier function routines.

Additional Resources:

http://devedge.netscape.com/library/manuals/2000/javascript/1.3/reference/window.html#1201775

Impact: Medium

Cross Reference: `setTimeout`

compile

Prototype: `compile(pattern[, flags])`

Summary: Compiles a regular expression.

Description: The `compile` method compiles a regular expression so that it can be efficiently re-used. It accepts a pattern and optional flags. The flag is one of "g", "i", or "gi", for global match, ignore case, or both.

Risk: This function is used to compile code. Syntax errors in the string being executed can lead to errors in other areas of the code. To ensure code continues to be executed as intended it is important to guard the usage of this function carefully. Otherwise, unpredictable results may occur which can compromise the system.

Notes: Deprecated in JavaScript 1.5.

Proper Usage: `compile("match[0-9]+", "g")`

Additional Resources:

http://devedge.netscape.com/library/manuals/2000/javascript/1.3/reference/regexp.html#1194687

Impact: Low

disableExternalCapture

Prototype: `disableExternalCapture()`

Summary: Disables external event capturing on the window.

Description: The `disableExternalCapture` method disables external event capturing on the window set by `enableExternalCapture`. It has no arguments.

Risk: Capturing windows events may enable a malicious developer to ascertain sensitive pieces of information about a user to include usernames, passwords, personal information, and even financial information. Ensure that all captured data, if data is indeed being captured is stored securely on a backend server.

Additional Resources:
http://devedge.netscape.com/library/manuals/2000/javascript/1.3/reference/window.html#1202117

Impact: Low

Cross Reference: `enableExternalCapture`, `captureEvents`

enableExternalCapture

Prototype: `enableExternalCapture()`

Summary: Allows a window to capture all events that occur within it.

Description: The `enableExternalCapture` method allows a window to capture external events, for example those that originate in a contained frame. This method has no arguments. Requires the `UniversalBrowserWrite` privilege. Used in conjunction with the `captureEvents` method.

Risk: Capturing windows events may enable a malicious developer to ascertain sensitive pieces of information about a user to include usernames, passwords, personal information, and even financial information. Ensure that all captured data, if data is indeed being captured, is stored securely on a backend server.

Additional Resources:
http://devedge.netscape.com/library/manuals/2000/javascript/1.3/reference/window.html#1202163

Impact: Low

Cross Reference: `disableExternalCapture`, `captureEvents`

eval

Prototype: `object eval(string)`

Summary: Evaluates and runs a string containing JavaScript code.

Description: The `eval` method accepts a string containing JavaScript code and evaluates it in the current JavaScript context. The result is returned. Any argument other than a string is returned unchanged. An error may occur if `eval` is called indirectly, for example if `eval` is assigned to a function object of a different name.

Risk: This function is used to compile code. Syntax errors in the string being executed can lead to errors in other areas of the code. To ensure code continues to be executed as intended it is important to guard the usage of this function carefully. Otherwise, unpredictable results may occur which can compromise the system.

Notes: Deprecated as a method of Object in JavaScript 1.5, moved to top level.

Proper Usage: `eval(code)`

Additional Resources:

http://devedge.netscape.com/library/manuals/2000/javascript/1.5/reference/toplev.html#1063795

Impact: Medium

exec

Prototype: `Array exec(string)`

Summary: Executes a regular expression on a string.

Description: The `exec` method executes the `RegExp` object's pattern on a given string. The method accepts a string argument and returns a match Array if a match is found, or `NULL` otherwise. When used with the global flag, exec can be used multiple times to find successive matches. The first element of the match Array is a string containing the characters of the match found. The succeeding elements are matching parenthesized substrings from the regular expression, if any.

Risk: This function is used to compile code. Syntax errors in the string being executed can lead to errors in other areas of the code. To ensure code continues to be executed as intended it is important to guard the usage of this function carefully. Otherwise, unpredictable results may occur which can compromise the system.

Additional Resources:

http://devedge.netscape.com/library/manuals/2000/javascript/1.5/reference/regexp.html#1194735

Impact: Low

Cross Reference: `test`, `search`

fileupload

Summary: The JavaScript object created by an HTML tag with type "file".

Description: A `FileUpload` object is created for each input tag of type "file". A `FileUpload` object is stored in the elements array of the Form containing it. The value property contains the name of the file the user has selected to upload.

Risk: Uploaded files are one of the most commons ways that viruses enter corporate networks today. If you intend to let users upload files to a central server of any kind, it should be required that these files are first scanned by leading virus scanning technologies such as Symantec, McAfee, or TrendMicro. Visit their sites to learn more about their Web-based APIs for scanning for viruses.

Additional Resources:

http://devedge.netscape.com/library/manuals/2000/javascript/1.3/reference/fileup.html

Impact: High

find

Prototype: `Boolean find(string[, caseSensitive[, searchBackwards]])`

Summary: Finds a string in the current window.

Description: The find method performs a search for a given string in the contents of the window. It accepts the string to search for, and optional Booleans indicating whether the search is case sensitive, and whether the search should be performed backwards. Returns TRUE if the specified string is found in the window, FALSE otherwise.

Risk: Functions that search for patterns open files and input their datastreams into allocated memory spaces. Outside of the race condition bugs that could occur if you attempted to open a file more than once simultaneously, a buffer overflow attack may also open up memory space for a root-level attack. Ensure that the files or datastreams that are passed for analysis to these functions are properly controlled and vetted by application logic. Users should not have the ability to identify if strings are within operating system resources such as configuration or log files.

Proper Usage: find("hello", false)

Additional Resources:

http://devedge.netscape.com/library/manuals/2000/javascript/1.3/reference/window.html#1202197

Impact: Low

getDate

Prototype: integer getDate()

Summary: Returns the day of the month in a Date object.

Description: The getDate method returns the day of the month for a Date object, adjusted for local time if necessary. It has no arguments. Returns an integer between 1 and 31.

Risk: This function handles system-specific sensitive information that an attacker could leverage during a period of target reconnaissance. This function should only be utilized if it is absolutely necessary for proper execution of the application. All analysis for the output of this function should be conducted securely within the application and never sent across the wire in cleartext.

Additional Resources:

http://devedge.netscape.com/library/manuals/2000/javascript/1.5/reference/date.html

Impact: Low

Cross Reference: getUTCDate

getDay

Prototype: `integer getDay()`

Summary: Returns the day of the week in a `Date` object.

Description: The `getDay` method returns an integer representation of the day of the week represented by a `Date` object, adjusted for local time if necessary. It has no arguments. Returns 0 for Sunday through 6 for Saturday.

Risk: This function handles system-specific sensitive information that an attacker could leverage during a period of target reconnaissance. This function should only be utilized if it is absolutely necessary for proper execution of the application. All analysis for the output of this function should be conducted securely within the application and never sent across the wire in cleartext.

Additional Resources:

http://devedge.netscape.com/library/manuals/2000/javascript/1.5/reference/date.html

Impact: Low

Cross Reference: `getUTCDay`

getFullYear

Prototype: `integer getFullYear()`

Summary: Returns the year in a `Date` object.

Description: The `getFullYear` method returns the 4-digit (for years between 1000 and 9999) year represented by a `Date` object, adjusted for local time if necessary. It has no arguments. Use this method instead of the `getYear` method for full Y2K compliance.

Risk: This function handles system-specific sensitive information that an attacker could leverage during a period of target reconnaissance. This function should only be utilized if it is absolutely necessary for proper execution of the application. All analysis for the output of this function should be conducted securely within the application and never sent across the wire in cleartext.

Additional Resources:
http://devedge.netscape.com/library/manuals/2000/javascript/1.5/reference/date.html

Impact: Low

Cross Reference: `getUTCFullYear`

getHours

Prototype: `integer getHours()`

Summary: Returns the hour in a `Date` object.

Description: The `getHours` method returns the integer value of the hour contained in a `Date` object, adjusted to local time if necessary. It has no arguments. Returns an integer between 0 and 23.

Risk: This function handles system-specific sensitive information that an attacker could leverage during a period of target reconnaissance. This function should only be utilized if it is absolutely necessary for proper execution of the application. All analysis for the output of this function should be conducted securely within the application and never sent across the wire in cleartext.

Additional Resources:
http://devedge.netscape.com/library/manuals/2000/javascript/1.5/reference/date.html

Impact: Low

Cross Reference: `getUTCHours`

getMilliseconds

Prototype: `integer getMilliseconds()`

Summary: Returns the milliseconds part of a `Date` object.

Description: The `getMilliseconds` method returns the integer value of the milliseconds contained in a `Date` object. It has no arguments. Returns an integer between 0 and 999.

Risk: This function handles system-specific sensitive information that an attacker could leverage during a period of target reconnaissance. This function should only be utilized if it is absolutely necessary for proper execution of the application. All analysis for the output of this function should be conducted securely within the application and never sent across the wire in cleartext.

Additional Resources:

http://devedge.netscape.com/library/manuals/2000/javascript/1.5/reference/date.html

Impact: Low

Cross Reference: `getUTCMilliseconds`

getMinutes

Prototype: `integer getMinutes()`

Summary: Returns the minutes part of a `Date` object.

Description: The `getMinutes` method returns the integer value of the minutes contained in a `Date` object. It has no arguments. Returns an integer between 0 and 59.

Risk: This function handles system-specific sensitive information that an attacker could leverage during a period of target reconnaissance. This function should only be utilized if it is absolutely necessary for proper execution of the application. All analysis for the output of this function should be conducted securely within the application and never sent across the wire in cleartext.

Additional Resources:

http://devedge.netscape.com/library/manuals/2000/javascript/1.5/reference/date.html

Impact: Low

Cross Reference: `getUTCMinutes`

JavaScript

getMonth

Prototype: `integer getMonth()`

Summary: Returns the month part of a `Date` object.

Description: The `getMonth` method returns the integer value of the month contained in a `Date` object, adjusted for local time if necessary. It has no arguments. Returns an integer from 0 (for January) through 11 (for December).

Risk: This function handles system-specific sensitive information that an attacker could leverage during a period of target reconnaissance. This function should only be utilized if it is absolutely necessary for proper execution of the application. All analysis for the output of this function should be conducted securely within the application and never sent across the wire in cleartext.

Additional Resources:

http://devedge.netscape.com/library/manuals/2000/javascript/1.5/reference/date.html

Impact: Low

Cross Reference: `getUTCMonth`

getSeconds

Prototype: `integer getSeconds()`

Summary: Returns the seconds part of a `Date` object.

Description: The `getSeconds` method returns the integer value of the seconds contained in a `Date` object. It has no arguments. Returns an integer between 0 and 59.

Risk: This function handles system-specific sensitive information that an attacker could leverage during a period of target reconnaissance. This function should only be utilized if it is absolutely necessary for proper execution of the application. All analysis for the output of this function should be conducted securely within the application and never sent across the wire in cleartext.

Additional Resources:

http://devedge.netscape.com/library/manuals/2000/javascript/1.5/reference/
date.html

Impact: Low

Cross Reference: `getUTCSeconds`

getSelection

Prototype: `string getSelection()`

Summary: Returns the current selection in the document.

Description: The `getSelection` method returns a string with the text of the current document's selection. This method works only on the currently active document. It has no arguments.

Risk: This function handles system-specific sensitive information that an attacker could leverage during a period of target reconnaissance. This function should only be utilized if it is absolutely necessary for proper execution of the application. All analysis for the output of this function should be conducted securely within the application and never sent across the wire in cleartext.

Additional Resources:

http://devedge.netscape.com/library/manuals/2000/javascript/1.3/reference/
document.html#1195981

Impact: Low

getTime

Prototype: `integer getTime()`

Summary: Returns the numeric value of the time in a `Date` object, adjusted for local time if necessary.

Description: The `getTime` method returns the numeric value of a `Date`, adjusted for local time if necessary. It has no arguments. Returns the number of milliseconds since midnight of January 1, 1970 (1 January 1970 00:00:00).

Risk: This function handles system-specific sensitive information that an attacker could leverage during a period of target reconnaissance. This function should only be utilized if it is absolutely necessary for proper execution of the application. All analysis for the output of this function should be conducted securely within the application and never sent across the wire in cleartext.

Additional Resources:

http://devedge.netscape.com/library/manuals/2000/javascript/1.5/reference/date.html

Impact: Low

getTimezoneOffset

Prototype: `integer getTimezoneOffset()`

Summary: Returns the current locale's time-zone offset from GMT.

Description: The `getTimezoneOffset` method returns the offset of the current locale's time zone from Greenwich Mean Time (GMT). It has no arguments. Returns the number of minutes, so divide the result by 60 for the number of hours. This value can change with daylight savings time.

Risk: This function handles system-specific sensitive information that an attacker could leverage during a period of target reconnaissance. This function should only be utilized if it is absolutely necessary for proper execution of the application. All analysis for the output of this function should be conducted securely within the application and never sent across the wire in cleartext.

Additional Resources:

http://devedge.netscape.com/library/manuals/2000/javascript/1.5/reference/date.html

Impact: Low

getUTCDate

Prototype: `integer getUTCDate()`

Summary: Returns the day of the month in a `Date` object, according to universal time.

Description: The `getUTCDate` method returns the day of the month in universal time for a `Date` object, an integer between 1 and 31. It has no arguments.

Risk: This function handles system-specific sensitive information that an attacker could leverage during a period of target reconnaissance. This function should only be utilized if it is absolutely necessary for proper execution of the application. All analysis for the output of this function should be conducted securely within the application and never sent across the wire in cleartext.

Additional Resources:

http://devedge.netscape.com/library/manuals/2000/javascript/1.5/reference/date.html

Impact: Low

Cross Reference: `getDate`

getUTCDay

Prototype: `integer getUTCDay()`

Summary: Returns the day of the week in a `Date` object, according to universal time.

Description: The `getUTCDay` method returns an integer representation of the day of the week represented by a `Date` object, in universal time. It has no arguments. Returns 0 for Sunday through 6 for Saturday.

Risk: This function handles system-specific sensitive information that an attacker could leverage during a period of target reconnaissance. This function should only be utilized if it is absolutely necessary for proper execution of the application. All analysis for the output of this function should be conducted securely within the application and never sent across the wire in cleartext.

Additional Resources:

http://devedge.netscape.com/library/manuals/2000/javascript/1.5/reference/date.html

Impact: Low

Cross Reference: `getDay`

JavaScript

getUTCFullYear

Prototype: `integer getUTCFullYear()`

Summary: Returns the year in a `Date` object, according to universal time.

Description: The `getUTCFullYear` method returns the 4-digit (for years between 1000 and 9999) year represented by a `Date` object, in universal time. It has no arguments.

Risk: This function handles system-specific sensitive information that an attacker could leverage during a period of target reconnaissance. This function should only be utilized if it is absolutely necessary for proper execution of the application. All analysis for the output of this function should be conducted securely within the application and never sent across the wire in cleartext.

Additional Resources:

http://devedge.netscape.com/library/manuals/2000/javascript/1.5/reference/date.html

Impact: Low

Cross Reference: `getFullYear`

getUTCHours

Prototype: `integer getUTCHours()`

Summary: Returns the hour in a `Date` object, according to universal time.

Description: The `getUTCHours` method returns the integer value of the hour contained in a `Date` object, in universal time. It has no arguments. Returns an integer between 0 and 23.

Risk: This function handles system-specific sensitive information that an attacker could leverage during a period of target reconnaissance. This function should only be utilized if it is absolutely necessary for proper execution of the application. All analysis for the output of this function should be conducted securely within the application and never sent across the wire in cleartext.

Additional Resources:

http://devedge.netscape.com/library/manuals/2000/javascript/1.5/reference/date.html

Impact: Low

Cross Reference: getHours

getUTCMilliseconds

Prototype: integer getUTCMilliseconds()

Summary: Returns the milliseconds in a Date object, according to universal time.

Description: The getUTCMilliseconds method returns the integer value of the milliseconds contained in a Date object. It has no arguments. Returns an integer between 0 and 999. In practice this produces the same result as date.getMilliseconds().

Risk: This function handles system-specific sensitive information that an attacker could leverage during a period of target reconnaissance. This function should only be utilized if it is absolutely necessary for proper execution of the application. All analysis for the output of this function should be conducted securely within the application and never sent across the wire in cleartext.

Additional Resources:

http://devedge.netscape.com/library/manuals/2000/javascript/1.5/reference/date.html

Impact: Low

Cross Reference: getMilliseconds

getUTCMinutes

Prototype: integer getUTCMinutes()

Summary: Returns the minutes in a Date object, according to universal time.

JavaScript

Description: The `getUTCMinutes` method returns the integer value of the minutes contained in a `Date` object. It has no arguments. Returns an integer between 0 and 59. In practice, this produces the same result as `date.getMinutes()`.

Risk: This function handles system-specific sensitive information that an attacker could leverage during a period of target reconnaissance. This function should only be utilized if it is absolutely necessary for proper execution of the application. All analysis for the output of this function should be conducted securely within the application and never sent across the wire in cleartext.

Additional Resources:

http://devedge.netscape.com/library/manuals/2000/javascript/1.5/reference/date.html

Impact: Low

Cross Reference: `getMinutes`

getUTCMonth

Prototype: `integer getUTCMonth()`

Summary: Returns the month of the year in a `Date` object, according to universal time.

Description: The `getMonth` method returns the integer value of the month contained in a `Date` object, in universal time. It has no arguments. Returns an integer between 0 (for January) and 11 (for December).

Risk: This function handles system-specific sensitive information that an attacker could leverage during a period of target reconnaissance. This function should only be utilized if it is absolutely necessary for proper execution of the application. All analysis for the output of this function should be conducted securely within the application and never sent across the wire in cleartext.

Additional Resources:

http://devedge.netscape.com/library/manuals/2000/javascript/1.5/reference/date.html

Impact: Low

Cross Reference: `getMonth`

getUTCSeconds

Prototype: `integer getUTCSeconds()`

Summary: Returns the seconds in a `Date` object, according to universal time.

Description: The `getUTCSeconds` method returns the integer value of the seconds contained in a `Date` object. It has no arguments. Returns an integer between 0 and 59. In practice this produces the same result as `date.getSeconds()`.

Risk: This function handles system-specific sensitive information that an attacker could leverage during a period of target reconnaissance. This function should only be utilized if it is absolutely necessary for proper execution of the application. All analysis for the output of this function should be conducted securely within the application and never sent across the wire in cleartext.

Additional Resources:
http://devedge.netscape.com/library/manuals/2000/javascript/1.5/reference/date.html

Impact: Low

Cross Reference: `getSeconds`

go

Prototype: `go(delta), go(URL)`

Summary: Jumps to a URL in the browser's history.

Description: The `go` method is used to load a URL from the browser's history. It accepts an integer offset from the current location, or a string containing all or part of a URL in the history. If given a string, `go` will attempt a case-insensitive match of the string to a URL in its history, and jump to the closest match. If given a positive integer greater than the number of forward entries, it will attempt to go back that number of entries. For example, to go back one page, use `history.go(-1)`.

Risk: This function is extremely dangerous as it could potentially allow a malicious developer to access target browser history data. Such history data could include visited Web sites, frequency visited, and visitation times. It is critical to ensure that you inform your site users that you will be accessing their historical data, in addition to transmitting and storing all sensitive information in a secure manner—for example, use SSL.

Additional Resources:

http://devedge.netscape.com/library/manuals/2000/javascript/1.3/reference/ history.html#1193970

Impact: High

javaEnabled

Prototype: `Boolean javaEnabled()`

Summary: Returns whether the `navigator` object is Java-enabled.

Description: The `javaEnabled` method is part of the `navigator` object. It has no arguments. Returns `TRUE` if Java is enabled, `FALSE` otherwise. Java can be enabled/disabled by the user.

Risk: A function with minimal risk; however, ensure that the results of this query are transmitted securely as it is local system information that could be utilized by an attacker sniffing the wire. Version information may also be transmitted.

Proper Usage: `navigator.javaEnabled()`

Additional Resources:

http://devedge.netscape.com/library/manuals/2000/javascript/1.3/reference/ nav.html#1193894

Impact: Low

lastIndexOf

Prototype: `integer lastIndexOf(string[, fromIndex])`

Summary: Returns the last position of a substring in a string.

Description: The `lastIndexOf` method returns the last position of a substring in a string object, or −1 if no match is found. It accepts a string containing the text to find, and an optional index argument between 0 and the length of the string.

`lastIndexOf` searches backwards from the given index, which is the length of the string by default.

Risk: Functions that search for patterns open files and input their datastreams into allocated memory spaces. Outside of the race condition bugs that could occur if you attempted to open a file more than once simultaneously, a buffer overflow attack may also open up memory space for a root-level attack. Ensure that the files or datastreams that are passed for analysis to these functions are properly controlled and vetted by application logic. Users should not have the ability to identify if strings are within operating system resources such as configuration or log files.

Additional Resources:
http://devedge.netscape.com/library/manuals/2000/javascript/1.5/reference/string.html#1197005

Impact: Low

link

Prototype: `Link link(URL)`

Summary: Creates an HTML link from a string.

Description: The `link` method accepts a URL and returns a `Link` object. The string's text becomes the contents of the `Link` object. The URL specifies the `Link`'s `href` attribute. Example: `"google".link("www.google.com/")` returns `&lt;a href="www.google.com/"&gt;google&lt;/a&gt;`

Risk: Inputs received after encoding may need to be decoded before being processes, otherwise there is the risk that malicious or otherwise invalid strings can be passed through the application.

Proper Usage: `document.write(someText.link(someURL))`

Additional Resources:
http://devedge.netscape.com/library/manuals/2000/javascript/1.3/reference/string.html#1198070

Impact: Low

JavaScript

load

Prototype: `load(URL, width)`

Summary: Loads content into a layer.

Description: The `load` method accepts a URL string and an integer width and loads the content of the URL into a layer of the specified width. The `width` parameter forces the contents to wrap at the specified width. This is useful for creating dynamically resizable contents of a Web page when combined with mouse drag events.

Risk: Input boxes are commonly misused for password and other types of sensitive information storage. Sensitive information should never be transmitted from clients to servers via Web page input boxes. In addition, SSL should be implemented when transferring sensitive data. Lastly, ensure that all user input is fully scrutinized whereas non-alphanumeric characters are removed where possible.

Additional Resources: http://developer.netscape.com/docs/manuals/communicator/dynhtml/layers38.htm

Impact: Low

open

Prototype: `open(URL, name[, features])`

Summary: Opens a new browser window.

Description: The `open` method creates a new browser window. It accepts a URL argument, a window name, and an optional string containing a comma-separated list of window features. If the URL argument is an empty string, an empty window is created. A comprehensive list of possible new window features can be found at Netscape's DevEdge JavaScript site.

Risk: Opening a new browser window can be extremely dangerous for both the developer and end user of an enterprise application. Initially, it details that you have some level of comfort with a Web-based application. Secondly, the site that is open in the new window may also contain malicious code. Ensure that the site is secure before referring a client to it. Also, ensure that a client cannot directly change or access the parameters for the open function, especially if the main site is considered to be in a trusted zone.

Notes: I found two possibilities: `window.open` and `document.open`. I've included records for both.

Proper Usage: `open(URL, name)`

Additional Resources:
http://devedge.netscape.com/library/manuals/2000/javascript/1.3/reference/window.html#1202731

Impact: Medium

password

Summary: The JavaScript object created by an HTML input tag with type "password".

Description: A `Password` object is created for each input tag of type `password`. A `Password` object is stored in the elements array of the Form containing it. The value field contains the currently entered password in plaintext, so do not store it in a cookie.

Risk: The `password` function is extremely risky and should not be used to store or transmit sensitive information such as an account password. It should only be used to obfuscate letters from viewers at the interface level. It is imperative that you ensure all passwords are transmitted across the wire via strong SSL encryption.

Additional Resources:
http://devedge.netscape.com/library/manuals/2000/javascript/1.3/reference/password.html

Impact: High

preference

Prototype: `value preference(prefName[, newValue])`

Summary: Allows a script to get and set certain browser preferences, if security privileges allow.

Description: The preference method of the navigator object can be used to retrieve or set some browser preferences. Accepts a string containing the preference name to get or set. If a new value is passed in, the specified preference is set to the new value. Returns the value of the specified preference, or the new value if one is set. Requires the UniversalPreferencesRead privilege to read, or the UniversalPreferencesWrite privilege to write.

Risk: A highly controversial feature, it is pertinent that you inform your users that you may be retrieving private browser configuration information from their system before using this function. Additionally, ensure that all configuration information is being transmitted over a SSL-encrypted tunnel to ensure that no prying eyes are viewing potentially sensitive information.

Proper Usage: useJava =
navigator.preference("security.enable_java")

Additional Resources:
http://devedge.netscape.com/library/manuals/2000/javascript/1.3/reference/nav.html#1194000

Impact: High

random

Prototype: float random()

Summary: Returns a pseudo-random number between 0 and 1.

Description: The Math.random method returns a pseudo-random number between 0 and 1, generated using the current time as a seed. It has no arguments.

Risk: As with most standard random functions implemented within the C and C++ libraries, this function is susceptible to bruteforce or easily guessed number-generating attacks due to a poor seed algorithm within the backend code. Amongst numerous other secure random number generating functions, Microsoft .Net has secure methods for implementing properly seeded numbers. ISAAC, designed by Bob Jenkins, is a fast cryptographic random number generator is as strong as they come. Available in multiple languages, ISAAC is a standard for many freeware and

commercial solutions and should be considered the next time a random number is required within an application.

Proper Usage: `luckyNumber = Math.random()`

Additional Resources:
http://devedge.netscape.com/library/manuals/2000/javascript/1.3/reference/math.html#1197697

Impact: High

reload

Prototype: `reload([forceGet])`

Summary: Reloads the current document.

Description: The `reload` method forces the current document to reload, using the `location.href` property. An optional `true` argument can be used to force a new `HTTP GET` from the server, bypassing the user's cache. This can cause an unnecessary load on the server, so use only when the server document is likely to have changed.

Risk: Ensure that all data currently inputted into the main viewing area is wiped from memory before the document is reloaded into the browser's window.

Proper Usage: `location.reload()`

Additional Resources:
http://devedge.netscape.com/library/manuals/2000/javascript/1.3/reference/location.html#1194198

Impact: High

reset

Prototype: `reset()`

Summary: Resets an HTML form.

Description: When called on an HTML form, the `reset` method causes the form's information to reset to its default state. The result is the same as activating the form's reset button. The `reset` method has no arguments.

JavaScript

Risk: Resetting an HTML form has minimal risk associated with the calling function; however, ensure that all data entered into the application is completely wiped from the browser's memory.

Proper Usage: `document.myForm.reset()`

Additional Resources:
http://devedge.netscape.com/library/manuals/2000/javascript/1.3/reference/
form.html#1194089

Impact: Medium

reverse

Prototype: `reverse()`

Summary: Reverses the elements of an Array.

Description: The `reverse` method reverses the ordering of an Array's elements, so that the last element becomes the first. It has no arguments.

Risk: This function should never be utilized to obfuscate data with the goal of protecting it from prying eyes. Only industry-standard cryptography algorithms should be implemented to secure data. This function is out-of-date and should not be used!

Proper Usage: `myArray.reverse()`

Additional Resources:
http://devedge.netscape.com/library/manuals/2000/javascript/1.5/reference/
array.html#1193641

Impact: Medium

scriptEngine

Prototype: `string ScriptEngine()`

Summary: Returns the scripting language currently in use.

Description: The `ScriptEngine` function returns a string containing the name of the scripting language currently in use. Returns one of "JScript", "VBA", or "VBScript". It has no arguments.

Risk: This function handles system-specific sensitive information that an attacker could leverage during a period of target reconnaissance. This function should only be utilized if it is absolutely necessary for proper execution of the application. All analysis for the output of this function should be conducted securely within the application and never sent across the wire in cleartext.

Additional Resources:
http://msdn.microsoft.com/library/default.asp?url=/library/en-us/jscript7/html/jsoriFunctions.asp

Impact: Medium

Cross Reference: `ScriptEngineBuildVersion`, `ScriptEngineMajorVersion`, `ScriptEngineMinorVersion`

setDate

Prototype: `setDate(day)`

Summary: Sets the day of the month for a `Date` object.

Description: The `setDate` method sets the day of the month for a `Date` object, given in local time. Accepts an `integer` argument between 1 and 31.

Risk: This function should only be accessed and launched by administrative-level users or systems that wish to affect the underlying operating system. In nearly all cases this function is not truly required and should be removed before an application gets released as production.

Notes: Integers outside the range 1 to 31 are modded in Mozilla's JavaScript implementation. I could not find support in the specification for this.

Proper Usage: `theIdes.setDate(15)`

Additional Resources:
http://devedge.netscape.com/library/manuals/2000/javascript/1.5/reference/date.html

Impact: Medium

Cross Reference: `setUTCDate`

JavaScript

setFullYear

Prototype: `setFullYear(year)`

Summary: Sets the 4-digit year for a `Date` object.

Description: The `setFullYear` method sets the year for a `Date` object, given in local time. Four-digit years are between 1000 and 9999. Accepts an `integer` argument specifying the full year of the `Date` object.

Risk: This function should only be accessed and launched by administrative-level users or systems that wish to affect the underlying operating system. In nearly all cases this function is not truly required and should be removed before an application gets released as production.

Proper Usage: `moon.setFullYear(1969)`

Additional Resources:

http://devedge.netscape.com/library/manuals/2000/javascript/1.5/reference/date.html

Impact: Medium

Cross Reference: `setUTCFullYear`

setHours

Prototype: `setHours(hour)`

Summary: Sets the hour of the day for a `Date` object.

Description: The `setHours` method sets the hour of the day for a `Date` object, given in local time. Accepts an `integer` argument between 0 and 23.

Risk: This function should only be accessed and launched by administrative-level users or systems that wish to affect the underlying operating system. In nearly all cases this function is not truly required and should be removed before an application gets released as production.

Notes: Integers outside the range 0 to 23 are modded in Mozilla's JavaScript implementation. I could not find support in the specification for this.

Proper Usage: `witches.setHour(0)`

Additional Resources:

http://devedge.netscape.com/library/manuals/2000/javascript/1.5/reference/
date.html

Impact: Medium

Cross Reference: `setUTCHours`

setInterval

Prototype: `intervalID setInterval(expression, time)`,
`intervalID setInterval(function, time[, args])`

Summary: Performs a task every specified number of milliseconds.

Description: The `setInterval` method is used to execute tasks that need to be repeated at a specified interval. The first argument can be a string containing an expression to be evaluated, or a function to be called. The second argument is the interval time in milliseconds. If a function is specified, extra arguments are passed to it. `setInterval` returns an interval ID.

Risk: This function should only be accessed and launched by administrative-level users or systems that wish to affect the underlying operating system. In nearly all cases this function is not truly required and should be removed before an application gets released as production.

Proper Usage: `annoying = setInterval(alert, 10000, "10 seconds have passed!")`

Additional Resources:

http://devedge.netscape.com/library/manuals/2000/javascript/1.3/reference/
window.html#1203669

Impact: Medium

Cross Reference: `setTimeout`

JavaScript

setMilliseconds

Prototype: `setMilliseconds(milliseconds)`

Summary: Sets the milliseconds for a `Date` object.

Description: The `setMilliseconds` method sets the milliseconds for a `Date` object, given in local time. Accepts an integer argument between 0 and 999.

Risk: This function should only be accessed and launched by administrative-level users or systems that wish to affect the underlying operating system. In nearly all cases this function is not truly required and should be removed before an application gets released as production.

Additional Resources:
http://devedge.netscape.com/library/manuals/2000/javascript/1.5/reference/date.html

Impact: Medium

Cross Reference: `setUTCMilliseconds`

setMinutes

Prototype: `setMinutes(minutes)`

Summary: Sets the minutes for a `Date` object.

Description: The `setMinutes` method sets the minutes for a `Date` object, given in local time. Accepts an `integer` argument between 0 and 59.

Risk: This function should only be accessed and launched by administrative-level users or systems that wish to affect the underlying operating system. In nearly all cases this function is not truly required and should be removed before an application gets released as production.

Additional Resources:
http://devedge.netscape.com/library/manuals/2000/javascript/1.5/reference/date.html

Impact: Medium

Cross Reference: `setUTCMinutes`

setMonth

Prototype: `setMonth(month)`

Summary: Sets the month of the year for a `Date` object.

Description: The `setMonth` method sets the month of the year for a `Date` object, given in local time. Accepts an `integer` argument between 0 for January and 11 for December.

Risk: This function should only be accessed and launched by administrative-level users or systems that wish to affect the underlying operating system. In nearly all cases this function is not truly required and should be removed before an application gets released as production.

Additional Resources:
http://devedge.netscape.com/library/manuals/2000/javascript/1.5/reference/date.html

Impact: Medium

Cross Reference: `setUTCMonth`

setSeconds

Prototype: `setSeconds(seconds[, milliseconds])`

Summary: Sets the seconds for a `Date` object.

Description: The `setSeconds` method sets the seconds for a `Date` object, given in local time. Accepts an `integer` argument between 0 and 59. Optionally accepts a millisecond argument between 0 and 999, equivalent to `setMilliseconds`.

Risk: This function should only be accessed and launched by administrative-level users or systems that wish to affect the underlying operating system. In nearly all cases this function is not truly required and should be removed before an application gets released as production.

Additional Resources:
http://devedge.netscape.com/library/manuals/2000/javascript/1.5/reference/date.html

JavaScript

Impact: Medium

Cross Reference: `setUTCSeconds`

setTime

Prototype: `setTime(milliseconds)`

Summary: Sets the exact time of a `Date` object.

Description: The `setTime` method accepts an `integer` parameter representing the number of milliseconds elapsed since January 1, 1970 (1 January 1970 00:00:00), given in local time.

Risk: This function should only be accessed and launched by administrative-level users or systems that wish to affect the underlying operating system. In nearly all cases this function is not truly required and should be removed before an application gets released as production.

Notes: Can be useful for storing and retrieving dates across sessions.

Additional Resources:

http://devedge.netscape.com/library/manuals/2000/javascript/1.5/reference/date.html

Impact: Medium

setTimeout

Prototype: `timeoutID setTimeout(expression, time)`, `timeoutID setTimeout(function, time[, args])`

Summary: Performs a task after a specified number of milliseconds has elapsed.

Description: The `setTimeout` method is used to execute tasks that need to be done once after a specified period of time has elapsed. The first argument can be a string containing an expression to be evaluated, or a function to be called. The second argument is the timeout in milliseconds. If a function is specified, extra arguments are passed to it. `setTimeout` returns a timeout ID.

Risk: This function should only be accessed and launched by administrative-level users or systems that wish to affect the underlying operating system. In nearly all cases this function is not truly required and should be removed before an application gets released as production.

Proper Usage: `errorTimeout = setTimeout(alert, 60000, "Error: task timed out after 1 minute.")`

Additional Resources:
http://devedge.netscape.com/library/manuals/2000/javascript/1.3/reference/window.html#1203758

Impact: Medium

Cross Reference: `setInterval`

setUTCDate

Prototype: `setUTCDate(day)`

Summary: Sets the day of the month for a `Date` object.

Description: The `setUTCDate` method sets the day of the month for a `Date` object, given in universal time. Accepts an `integer` argument between 1 and 31.

Risk: This function should only be accessed and launched by administrative-level users or systems that wish to affect the underlying operating system. In nearly all cases this function is not truly required and should be removed before an application gets released as production.

Notes: Integers outside the range 1 to 31 are modded in Mozilla's JavaScript implementation. I could not find support in the specification for this.

Proper Usage: `valentine.setDate(14)`

Additional Resources:
http://devedge.netscape.com/library/manuals/2000/javascript/1.5/reference/date.html

Impact: Medium

Cross Reference: `setDate`

JavaScript

setUTCFullYear

Prototype: `setUTCFullYear(year)`

Summary: Sets the 4-digit year for a `Date` object.

Description: The `setUTCFullYear` method sets the year for a `Date` object, given in universal time. Four-digit years are between 1000 and 9999. Accepts an `integer` argument specifying the full year of the `Date` object.

Risk: This function should only be accessed and launched by administrative-level users or systems that wish to affect the underlying operating system. In nearly all cases this function is not truly required and should be removed before an application gets released as production.

Proper Usage: `orwell.setUTCFullYear(1984)`

Additional Resources:
http://devedge.netscape.com/library/manuals/2000/javascript/1.5/reference/date.html

Impact: Medium

Cross Reference: `setFullYear`

setUTCHours

Prototype: `setUTCHours(hour)`

Summary: Sets the hour of the day for a `Date` object.

Description: The `setUTCHours` method sets the hour of the day for a `Date` object, given in universal time. Accepts an `integer` argument between 0 and 23.

Risk: This function should only be accessed and launched by administrative-level users or systems that wish to affect the underlying operating system. In nearly all cases this function is not truly required and should be removed before an application gets released as production.

Notes: Integers outside the range 0 to 23 are modded in Mozilla's JavaScript implementation. I could not find support in the specification for this.

Proper Usage: `coffee.setUTCHours(5)`

Additional Resources:

http://devedge.netscape.com/library/manuals/2000/javascript/1.5/reference/date.html

Impact: Medium

Cross Reference: setHours

setUTCMilliseconds

Prototype: setUTCMilliseconds(milliseconds)

Summary: Sets the milliseconds for a Date object.

Description: The setUTCMilliseconds method sets the milliseconds for a Date object, given in local time. Accepts an integer argument between 0 and 999. In practice, this method is the same as setMilliseconds.

Risk: This function should only be accessed and launched by administrative-level users or systems that wish to affect the underlying operating system. In nearly all cases this function is not truly required and should be removed before an application gets released as production.

Additional Resources:

http://devedge.netscape.com/library/manuals/2000/javascript/1.5/reference/date.html

Impact: Medium

Cross Reference: setMilliseconds

setUTCMinutes

Prototype: setUTCMinutes(minutes)

Summary: Sets the minutes for a Date object.

Description: The setUTCMinutes method sets the minutes for a Date object, given in local time. Accepts an integer argument between 0 and 59. In practice, this method is the same as setMinutes.

Risk: This function should only be accessed and launched by administrative-level users or systems that wish to affect the underlying operating system. In nearly all cases this function is not truly required and should be removed before an application gets released as production.

Additional Resources:

http://devedge.netscape.com/library/manuals/2000/javascript/1.5/reference/date.html

Impact: Medium

Cross Reference: setMinutes

setUTCMonth

Prototype: setUTCMonth(month)

Summary: Sets the month of the year for a Date object.

Description: The setUTCMonth method sets the month of the year for a Date object, given in universal time. Accepts an integer argument between 0 for January and 11 for December.

Risk: This function should only be accessed and launched by administrative-level users or systems that wish to affect the underlying operating system. In nearly all cases this function is not truly required and should be removed before an application gets released as production.

Additional Resources:

http://devedge.netscape.com/library/manuals/2000/javascript/1.5/reference/date.html

Impact: Medium

Cross Reference: setMonth

setUTCSeconds

Prototype: setUTCSeconds(seconds[, milliseconds])

Summary: Sets the seconds for a Date object.

Description: The setUTCSeconds method sets the seconds for a Date object, given in universal time. Accepts an integer argument between 0 and 59. In practice, this method is the same as setSeconds. Optionally accepts a millisecond argument between 0 and 999, equivalent to setUTCMilliseconds.

Risk: This function should only be accessed and launched by administrative-level users or systems that wish to affect the underlying operating system. In nearly all cases this function is not truly required and should be removed before an application gets released as production.

Additional Resources:
http://devedge.netscape.com/library/manuals/2000/javascript/1.5/reference/date.html

Impact: Medium

Cross Reference: setSeconds

submit

Prototype: submit()

Summary: Submits an HTML form.

Description: The HTML Form's submit method submits the form to the form's target URL. It has the same effect as activating the form's Submit button. It has no arguments. Requires UniversalSendMail privilege to submit to a mailto: or news: URL.

Risk: Ensure that any sensitive data that is being submitted back to the Web server is done so in an SSL-encrypted tunnel. In nearly all cases, forms are utilized and submitted with personal customer or user information. It may be a privacy infraction to transmit that data in a insecure manner without the user realizing it's going across the wire in cleartext. Rule of Thumb: when in doubt use SSL.

Proper Usage: document.myForm.submit()

Additional Resources:
http://devedge.netscape.com/library/manuals/2000/javascript/1.3/reference/form.html#1194123

Impact: High

test

Prototype: `Boolean test(string)`

Summary: Tests whether a string matches a regular expression.

Description: The `test` method accepts a string and tests whether it matches the RegExp object's pattern. Returns `TRUE` if a match is found, `FALSE` otherwise.

Risk: All special and wildcard characters should be removed before the filename is computed on the local filesystem. Malicious filenames are interpreted differently on varying systems and as such, directory control is critical to limiting the ability of an attacker to potentially compromise files at varying levels within the application or underlying subsystem.

Additional Resources:
http://devedge.netscape.com/library/manuals/2000/javascript/1.3/reference/regexp.html#1194128

Impact: Low

toLocaleString

Prototype: `string toLocaleString()`

Summary: Converts a `Date` object to a string using the current locale and platform conventions.

Description: The `toLocaleString` method converts the `Date` object to a human-readable string. It uses the current locale and relies on the underlying platform to format the string, so the results are platform-dependant. It has no arguments.

Risk: Certain string manipulation functions to include string and character transition functions are commonly leveraged in buffer overflow attacks. At the most basic level, these functions read in data, perform analysis and execution logic, then output the data to another type of string. It is imperative that the destination string be calculated accordingly and that enough memory space is allocated. Special characters should also be stricken from the conversion where possible.

Additional Resources:
http://devedge.netscape.com/library/manuals/2000/javascript/1.5/reference/
date.html

Impact: Low

Cross Reference: toUTCString

toUTCString

Prototype: string toUTCString()

Summary: Converts a Date object to a string using universal time and platform conventions.

Description: The toUTCString method converts the Date object to a human-readable string. It uses universal time but relies on the underlying platform to format the string, so the results are platform-dependant. It has no arguments.

Risk: Certain string manipulation functions to include string and character transition functions are commonly leveraged in buffer overflow attacks. At the most basic level, these functions read in data, perform analysis and execution logic, then output the data to another type of string. It is imperative that the destination string be calculated accordingly and that enough memory space is allocated. Special characters should also be stricken from the conversion where possible.

Additional Resources:
http://devedge.netscape.com/library/manuals/2000/javascript/1.5/reference/
date.html

Impact: Low

Cross Reference: toLocaleString

JavaScript

write

Prototype: `write(string1[, string2, ..])`

Summary: Writes JavaScript expressions to the specified document.

Description: The `write` method writes the results of JavaScript expressions to the document. It takes an unspecified number of arguments, evaluates each one in turn, and writes the result to the document stream.

Risk: All inputs to this method should be thoroughly parsed to prevent the potential for cross-site scripting attacks. Input parameters should be restricted to alphanumeric characters to prevent command executions during processing.

Proper Usage: `document.write("&lt;h1&gt;Sunday Sunday Sunday!&lt;/h1&gt;")`

Additional Resources:
http://devedge.netscape.com/library/manuals/2000/javascript/1.3/reference/document.html#1221642

Impact: Medium

Cross Reference: `writeln`

writeln

Prototype: `writeln(string1[, string2, ..])`

Summary: Writes JavaScript expressions to the specified document, followed by a newline.

Description: The `writeln` method writes the results of JavaScript expressions to the document. It takes an unspecified number of arguments, evaluates each one in turn, and writes the result to the document stream. `writeln` appends a newline character at the end of its write.

Risk: All inputs to this method should be thoroughly parsed to prevent the potential for cross-site scripting attacks. Input parameters should be restricted to alphanumeric characters to prevent command executions during processing.

Additional Resources:

http://devedge.netscape.com/library/manuals/2000/javascript/1.3/reference/document.html#1194456

Impact: Medium

Cross Reference: `write`

Programmer's Ultimate Security DeskRef: JScript

compile

Prototype: `compile(pattern[, flags])`

Summary: Compiles a regular expression.

Description: The `compile` method compiles a regular expression so that it can be efficiently re-used. It accepts a pattern and optional flags. The flag is any combination of "g", "i", or "m", for global match, ignore case, or multiline search.

Risk: This function is used to compile code. Syntax errors in the string being executed can lead to errors in other areas of the code. To ensure code continues to be executed as intended it is important to guard the usage of this function carefully. Otherwise, unpredictable results may occur which can compromise the system.

Proper Usage: `compile("match[0-9]+", "g")`

Additional Resources:
http://msdn.microsoft.com/library/default.asp?url=/library/en-us/jscript7/html/jsorimethods.asp

Impact: Low

encodeURI

Prototype: `string encodeURI(string)`

Summary: Encodes a string into a URI.

Description: The `encodeURI` method encodes a string into a Uniform Resource Identifier. It accepts the string to be encoded and returns a string containing the valid URI. This method will not encode the characters ":", "/", ";", or "?".

Risk: Inputs received after encoding may need to be decoded before being processes, otherwise there is the risk that malicious or otherwise invalid strings can be passed through the application.

Additional Resources:

http://msdn.microsoft.com/library/default.asp?url=/library/en-us/jscript7/html/jsorimethods.asp

Impact: Medium

Cross Reference: `encodeURIComponent`

encodeURIComponent

Prototype: `string encodeURIComponent(string)`

Summary: Encodes a string into a URI.

Description: The `encodeURIComponent` method encodes a string into a Uniform Resource Identifier. It accepts the string to be encoded and returns a string containing the valid URI. This method will encode all characters, so be careful or you could end up with an unusable URI.

Risk: Inputs received after encoding may need to be decoded before being processes, otherwise there is the risk that malicious or otherwise invalid strings can be passed through the application.

Additional Resources:

http://msdn.microsoft.com/library/default.asp?url=/library/en-us/jscript7/html/jsorimethods.asp

Impact: Medium

Cross Reference: encodeURI

exec

Prototype: `Array exec(string)`

Summary: Executes a regular expression on a string.

Description: The exec method executes the RegExp object's pattern on a given string. The method accepts a string argument and returns a match Array if a match is found, or null otherwise. When used with the global flag, exec can be used multiple times to find successive matches. The first element of the match Array is a string containing the characters of the match found. The succeeding elements are matching parenthesized substrings from the regular expression, if any.

Risk: This function is used to compile code. Syntax errors in the string being executed can lead to errors in other areas of the code. To ensure code continues to be executed as intended it is important to guard the usage of this function carefully. Otherwise, unpredictable results may occur which can compromise the system.

Additional Resources:
http://msdn.microsoft.com/library/default.asp?url=/library/en-us/jscript7/html/jsorimethods.asp

Impact: Low

getDate

Prototype: `integer getDate()`

Summary: Returns the day of the month in a Date object.

Description: The getDate method returns the day of the month for a Date object, adjusted for local time if necessary. It has no arguments. Returns an integer between 1 and 31.

Risk: This function handles system-specific sensitive information that an attacker could leverage during a period of target reconnaissance. This function should only be utilized if it is absolutely necessary for proper execution of the application. All

JScript

analysis for the output of this function should be conducted securely within the application and never sent across the wire in cleartext.

Additional Resources:

http://msdn.microsoft.com/library/default.asp?url=/library/en-us/jscript7/html/jsoriMethodsNode.asp

Impact: Low

Cross Reference: getUTCDate

getDay

Prototype: `integer getDay()`

Summary: Returns the day of the week in a `Date` object.

Description: The `getDay` method returns an integer representation of the day of the week represented by a `Date` object, adjusted for local time if necessary. It has no arguments. Returns 0 for Sunday through 6 for Saturday.

Risk: This function handles system-specific sensitive information that an attacker could leverage during a period of target reconnaissance. This function should only be utilized if it is absolutely necessary for proper execution of the application. All analysis for the output of this function should be conducted securely within the application and never sent across the wire in cleartext.

Additional Resources:

http://msdn.microsoft.com/library/default.asp?url=/library/en-us/jscript7/html/jsoriMethodsNode.asp

Impact: Low

Cross Reference: getUTCDay

getFullYear

Prototype: `integer getFullYear()`

Summary: Returns the year in a `Date` object.

Description: The `getFullYear` method returns the 4-digit (for years between 1000 and 9999) year represented by a `Date` object, adjusted for local time if necessary. It has no arguments. Use this method instead of the `getYear` method for full Y2K compliance.

Risk: This function handles system-specific sensitive information that an attacker could leverage during a period of target reconnaissance. This function should only be utilized if it is absolutely necessary for proper execution of the application. All analysis for the output of this function should be conducted securely within the application and never sent across the wire in cleartext.

Additional Resources:

http://msdn.microsoft.com/library/default.asp?url=/library/en-us/ jscript7/html/jsoriMethodsNode.asp

Impact: Low

Cross Reference: `getUTCFullYear`

getHours

Prototype: `integer getHours()`

Summary: Returns the hour in a `Date` object.

Description: The `getHours` method returns the integer value of the hour contained in a `Date` object, adjusted to local time if necessary. It has no arguments. Returns an integer between 0 and 23.

Risk: This function handles system-specific sensitive information that an attacker could leverage during a period of target reconnaissance. This function should only be utilized if it is absolutely necessary for proper execution of the application. All analysis for the output of this function should be conducted securely within the application and never sent across the wire in cleartext.

Additional Resources:

http://msdn.microsoft.com/library/default.asp?url=/library/en-us/ jscript7/html/jsoriMethodsNode.asp

Impact: Low

Cross Reference: `getUTCHours`

JScript

getItem

Prototype: `Object getItem(index1, index2)`

Summary: Accesses items in a VBArray.

Description: The `getItem` method allows a JScript expression to access a VBArray. It accepts two indices as arguments and returns the object located at those indices.

Risk: This function handles system-specific sensitive information that an attacker could leverage during a period of target reconnaissance. This function should only be utilized if it is absolutely necessary for proper execution of the application. All analysis for the output of this function should be conducted securely within the application and never sent across the wire in cleartext.

Additional Resources:

http://msdn.microsoft.com/library/default.asp?url=/library/en-us/jscript7/html/jsorimethods.asp

Impact: Low

getTime

Prototype: `integer getTime()`

Summary: Returns the numeric value of the time in a Date, adjusted for local time if necessary.

Description: The `getTime` method returns the numeric value of a `Date` object, adjusted for local time if necessary. It has no arguments. Returns the number of milliseconds since midnight of January 1, 1970 (1 January 1970 00:00:00). Dates prior to 1970 are indicated with negative integers.

Risk: This function handles system-specific sensitive information that an attacker could leverage during a period of target reconnaissance. This function should only be utilized if it is absolutely necessary for proper execution of the application. All analysis for the output of this function should be conducted securely within the application and never sent across the wire in cleartext.

Additional Resources:
http://msdn.microsoft.com/library/default.asp?url=/library/en-us/
jscript7/html/jsoriMethodsNode.asp

Impact: Low

getTimezoneOffset

Prototype: `integer getTimezoneOffset()`

Summary: Returns the current locale's time-zone offset from GMT.

Description: The `getTimezoneOffset` method returns the offset of the current locale's time-zone from Greenwich Mean Time (GMT). It has no arguments. Returns the number of minutes, so divide the result by 60 for the number of hours. This value can change with daylight savings time. Positive integers represent offsets to the west of GMT, negative integers to the east.

Risk: This function handles system-specific sensitive information that an attacker could leverage during a period of target reconnaissance. This function should only be utilized if it is absolutely necessary for proper execution of the application. All analysis for the output of this function should be conducted securely within the application and never sent across the wire in cleartext.

Additional Resources:
http://msdn.microsoft.com/library/default.asp?url=/library/en-us/
jscript7/html/jsoriMethodsNode.asp

Impact: Low

getUTCDate

Prototype: `integer getUTCDate()`

Summary: Returns the day of the month in a `Date` object, according to universal time.

Description: The `getUTCDate` method returns the day of the month in universal time for a `Date` object, an integer between 1 and 31. It has no arguments.

JScript

Risk: This function handles system-specific sensitive information that an attacker could leverage during a period of target reconnaissance. This function should only be utilized if it is absolutely necessary for proper execution of the application. All analysis for the output of this function should be conducted securely within the application and never sent across the wire in cleartext.

Additional Resources:

http://msdn.microsoft.com/library/default.asp?url=/library/en-us/ jscript7/html/jsoriMethodsNode.asp

Impact: Low

Cross Reference: `getDate`

getUTCDay

Prototype: `integer getUTCDay()`

Summary: Returns the day of the week in a `Date` object, according to universal time.

Description: The `getUTCDay` method returns an integer representation of the day of the week represented by a `Date` object, in universal time. It has no arguments. Returns 0 for Sunday through 6 for Saturday.

Risk: This function handles system-specific sensitive information that an attacker could leverage during a period of target reconnaissance. This function should only be utilized if it is absolutely necessary for proper execution of the application. All analysis for the output of this function should be conducted securely within the application and never sent across the wire in cleartext.

Additional Resources:

http://msdn.microsoft.com/library/default.asp?url=/library/en-us/ jscript7/html/jsoriMethodsNode.asp

Impact: Low

Cross Reference: `getDay`

getUTCFullYear

Prototype: `integer getUTCFullYear()`

Summary: Returns the year in a `Date` object, according to universal time.

Description: The `getUTCFullYear` method returns the 4-digit (for years between 1000 and 9999) year represented by a `Date` object, in universal time. It has no arguments.

Risk: This function handles system-specific sensitive information that an attacker could leverage during a period of target reconnaissance. This function should only be utilized if it is absolutely necessary for proper execution of the application. All analysis for the output of this function should be conducted securely within the application and never sent across the wire in cleartext.

Additional Resources:
http://msdn.microsoft.com/library/default.asp?url=/library/en-us/jscript7/html/jsoriMethodsNode.asp

Impact: Low

Cross Reference: `getFullYear`

getUTCHours

Prototype: `integer getUTCHours()`

Summary: Returns the hour in a `Date` object, according to universal time.

Description: The `getUTCHours` method returns the integer value of the hour contained in a `Date` object, in universal time. It has no arguments. Returns an integer between 0 and 23.

Risk: This function handles system-specific sensitive information that an attacker could leverage during a period of target reconnaissance. This function should only be utilized if it is absolutely necessary for proper execution of the application. All analysis for the output of this function should be conducted securely within the application and never sent across the wire in cleartext.

JScript

Additional Resources:
http://msdn.microsoft.com/library/default.asp?url=/library/en-us/
jscript7/html/jsoriMethodsNode.asp

Impact: Low

Cross Reference: getHours

getUTCMilliseconds

Prototype: `integer getUTCMilliseconds()`

Summary: Returns the milliseconds in a `Date` object, according to universal time.

Description: The `getUTCMilliseconds` method returns the integer value of the milliseconds contained in a `Date` object. It has no arguments. Returns an integer between 0 and 999. In practice this produces the same result as `date.getMilliseconds()`.

Risk: This function handles system-specific sensitive information that an attacker could leverage during a period of target reconnaissance. This function should only be utilized if it is absolutely necessary for proper execution of the application. All analysis for the output of this function should be conducted securely within the application and never sent across the wire in cleartext.

Additional Resources:
http://msdn.microsoft.com/library/default.asp?url=/library/en-us/
jscript7/html/jsoriMethodsNode.asp

Impact: Low

Cross Reference: getMilliseconds

getUTCMinutes

Prototype: `integer getUTCMinutes()`

Summary: Returns the minutes in a `Date` object, according to universal time.

Description: The `getUTCMinutes` method returns the integer value of the minutes contained in a `Date` object. It has no arguments. Returns an integer between 0 and 59. In practice this produces the same result as `date.getMinutes()`.

Risk: This function handles system-specific sensitive information that an attacker could leverage during a period of target reconnaissance. This function should only be utilized if it is absolutely necessary for proper execution of the application. All analysis for the output of this function should be conducted securely within the application and never sent across the wire in cleartext.

Additional Resources:

http://msdn.microsoft.com/library/default.asp?url=/library/en-us/ jscript7/html/jsoriMethodsNode.asp

Impact: Low

Cross Reference: `getMinutes`

getUTCMonth

Prototype: `integer getUTCMonth()`

Summary: Returns the month of the year in a `Date` object, according to universal time.

Description: The `getMonth` method returns the integer value of the month contained in a `Date` object, in universal time. It has no arguments. Returns an integer between 0 (for January) and 11 (for December).

Risk: This function handles system-specific sensitive information that an attacker could leverage during a period of target reconnaissance. This function should only be utilized if it is absolutely necessary for proper execution of the application. All analysis for the output of this function should be conducted securely within the application and never sent across the wire in cleartext.

Additional Resources:

http://msdn.microsoft.com/library/default.asp?url=/library/en-us/ jscript7/html/jsoriMethodsNode.asp

Impact: Low

Cross Reference: `getMonth`

getUTCSeconds

Prototype: `integer getUTCSeconds()`

Summary: Returns the seconds in a `Date` object, according to universal time.

Description: The `getUTCSeconds` method returns the integer value of the seconds contained in a `Date` object. It has no arguments. Returns an integer between 0 and 59. In practice this produces the same result as `date.getSeconds()`.

Risk: This function handles system-specific sensitive information that an attacker could leverage during a period of target reconnaissance. This function should only be utilized if it is absolutely necessary for proper execution of the application. All analysis for the output of this function should be conducted securely within the application and never sent across the wire in cleartext.

Additional Resources:
http://msdn.microsoft.com/library/default.asp?url=/library/en-us/jscript7/html/jsoriMethodsNode.asp

Impact: Low

Cross Reference: `getSeconds`

getYear

Summary: Returns a 2-digit year for dates between 1900 and 1999, 4-digit years otherwise.

Description: The `getYear` method is included only for backwards compatibility with previous versions of JScript. It assumes a 2-digit year for the period 1900–1999, and a 4-digit year otherwise. It has no arguments.

Risk: This function handles system-specific sensitive information that an attacker could leverage during a period of target reconnaissance. This function should only be utilized if it is absolutely necessary for proper execution of the application. All analysis for the output of this function should be conducted securely within the application and never sent across the wire in cleartext.

Notes: Deprecated. Use `getFullYear` instead.

Impact: Low

link

Prototype: `Link link(URL)`

Summary: Creates an HTML link from a string.

Description: The `link` method accepts a URL and returns a `Link` object. The string's text becomes the contents of the Link. The URL specifies the Link's `href` attribute. Example: `"google".link("www.google.com/")` returns `&lt;a href="www.google.com/"&gt;google&lt;/a&gt;`

Risk: Inputs received after encoding may need to be decoded before being processes, otherwise there is the risk that malicious or otherwise invalid strings can be passed through the application.

Proper Usage: `document.write(someText.link(someURL))`

Additional Resources:
http://msdn.microsoft.com/library/default.asp?url=/library/en-us/ jscript7/html/jsoriMethodsNode.asp

Impact: Low

open

Prototype: `stream open([mimeType[, "replace"]])`

Summary: Opens a document stream for writing.

Description: The document's open method readies the document for writing. This can be used to create new content in a document or replace the document's current contents. A MIME type for the document may be specified. For the MIME type `text/html`, an optional `replace` argument will cause the new content to replace the old content without creating a new history entry. Returns the stream, or null if no stream could be initialized. When writing to the stream is complete, call `document.close()` to display the new content.

Risk: Any time functions are called with system access, all parameters passed to the function from user input should be carefully analyzed to prevent access to or overwriting of system files. Additionally, this function is capable of creating files on a system. Files should never be created automatically as a result of an action such as a

JScript

form submittal. Excessive submits by a malicious user can result in exhausting file nodes on the server.

Notes: I found two possibilities: `window.open` and `document.open`. I've included text for both.

Proper Usage: `document.open("text/html", "replace")`

Additional Resources:

http://msdn.microsoft.com/library/default.asp?url=/library/en-us/jscript7/html/jsoriMethodsNode.asp

Impact: Medium

Cross Reference: `reload, replace`

random

Prototype: `float random()`

Summary: Returns a pseudo-random number between 0 and 1.

Description: The `Math.random` method returns a pseudo-random number between 0 and 1. The random number seed is generated when JScript is loaded. It has no arguments.

Risk: As with most standard random functions implemented within the C and C++ libraries, this function is susceptible to bruteforce or easily guessed number-generating attacks due to a poor seed algorithm within the backend code. Amongst numerous other secure random number generating functions, Microsoft .Net has secure methods for implementing properly seeded numbers. ISAAC, designed by Bob Jenkins, is a fast cryptographic random number generator is as strong as they come. Available in multiple languages, ISAAC is a standard for many freeware and commercial solutions and should be considered the next time a random number is required within an application.

Proper Usage: `luckyNumber = Math.random()`

Additional Resources:

http://msdn.microsoft.com/library/default.asp?url=/library/en-us/jscript7/html/jsoriMethodsNode.asp

Impact: High

reverse

Prototype: `Array reverse()`

Summary: Reverses the elements of an `Array`.

Description: The `reverse` method reverses the ordering of an `Array`'s elements, so that the last element becomes the first. It returns the reversed `Array`. It has no arguments. The reversal is done in-place, so no new `Array` is created.

Risk: This function should never be utilized to obfuscate data with the goal of protecting it from prying eyes. Only industry-standard cryptography algorithms should be implemented to secure data. This function is out-of-date and should not be used!

Proper Usage: `myArray.reverse()`

Additional Resources:
http://msdn.microsoft.com/library/default.asp?url=/library/en-us/jscript7/html/jsoriMethodsNode.asp

Impact: Medium

ScriptEngineBuildVersion

Prototype: `integer ScriptEngineBuildVersion()`

Summary: Returns the build version of the current scripting engine.

Description: The `ScriptEngineBuildVersion` function returns an integer corresponding to the build version of the scripting engine in use. It is equivalent to the version information for the scripting engine's dynamic link library (DLL). It has no arguments.

Risk: This function handles system-specific sensitive information that an attacker could leverage during a period of target reconnaissance. This function should only be utilized if it is absolutely necessary for proper execution of the application. All analysis for the output of this function should be conducted securely within the application and never sent across the wire in cleartext.

Additional Resources:

http://msdn.microsoft.com/library/default.asp?url=/library/en-us/
jscript7/html/jsoriFunctions.asp

Impact: Medium

Cross Reference: `ScriptEngine`, `ScriptEngineMajorVersion`,
`ScriptEngineMinorVersion`

ScriptEngineMajorVersion

Prototype: `integer ScriptEngineMajorVersion()`

Summary: Returns the major version number of the current scripting engine.

Description: The `ScriptEngineMajorVersion` function returns an integer corresponding to the major version of the scripting engine in use. It is equivalent to the version information for the scripting engine's dynamic link library (DLL). It has no arguments.

Risk: This function handles system-specific sensitive information that an attacker could leverage during a period of target reconnaissance. This function should only be utilized if it is absolutely necessary for proper execution of the application. All analysis for the output of this function should be conducted securely within the application and never sent across the wire in cleartext.

Additional Resources:

http://msdn.microsoft.com/library/default.asp?url=/library/en-us/
jscript7/html/jsoriFunctions.asp

Impact: Medium

Cross Reference: `ScriptEngine`, `ScriptEngineBuildVersion`,
`ScriptEngineMinorVersion`

ScriptEngineMinorVersion

Prototype: `integer ScriptEngineMinorVersion()`

Summary: Returns the minor version number of the current scripting engine.

Description: The `ScriptEngineMinorVersion` function returns an integer corresponding to the minor version of the scripting engine in use. It is equivalent to the version information for the scripting engine's dynamic link library (DLL). It has no arguments.

Risk: This function handles system-specific sensitive information that an attacker could leverage during a period of target reconnaissance. This function should only be utilized if it is absolutely necessary for proper execution of the application. All analysis for the output of this function should be conducted securely within the application and never sent across the wire in cleartext.

Additional Resources:

http://msdn.microsoft.com/library/default.asp?url=/library/en-us/jscript7/html/jsoriFunctions.asp

Impact: Medium

Cross Reference: `ScriptEngine, ScriptEngineMajorVersion, ScriptEngineBuildVersion`

setDate

Prototype: `setDate(day)`

Summary: Sets the day of the month for a `Date` object.

Description: The `setDate` method sets the day of the month for a `Date` object, given in local time. Accepts an integer argument between 1 and 31. If a number out of range of the current month is given, the number of days in the current month are subtracted and the month is incremented until a valid date is reached.

Risk: This function should only be accessed and launched by administrative-level users or systems that wish to affect the underlying operating system. In nearly all cases this function is not truly required and should be removed before an application gets released as production.

Proper Usage: `theIdes.setDate(15)`

Additional Resources:

http://msdn.microsoft.com/library/default.asp?url=/library/en-us/jscript7/html/jsoriMethodsNode.asp

JScript

Impact: Medium

Cross Reference: setUTCDate

setFullYear

Prototype: setFullYear(year)

Summary: Sets the 4-digit year for a Date object.

Description: The setFullYear method sets the year for a Date object, given in local time. Four-digit years are between 1000 and 9999. Accepts an integer argument specifying the full year of the Date object.

Risk: This function should only be accessed and launched by administrative-level users or systems that wish to affect the underlying operating system. In nearly all cases this function is not truly required and should be removed before an application gets released as production.

Proper Usage: moon.setFullYear(1969)

Additional Resources:
http://msdn.microsoft.com/library/default.asp?url=/library/en-us/jscript7/html/jsoriMethodsNode.asp

Impact: Medium

Cross Reference: setUTCFullYear

setHours

Prototype: setHours(hour)

Summary: Sets the hour of the day for a Date object.

Description: The setHours method sets the hour of the day for a Date object, given in local time. Accepts an integer argument between 0 and 23. If a value greater than 23 is given, the date and all other fields are modified accordingly.

Risk: This function should only be accessed and launched by administrative-level users or systems that wish to affect the underlying operating system. In nearly all cases this function is not truly required and should be removed before an application gets released as production.

Proper Usage: `witches.setHour(0)`

Additional Resources:
http://msdn.microsoft.com/library/default.asp?url=/library/en-us/jscript7/html/jsoriMethodsNode.asp

Impact: Medium

Cross Reference: `setUTCHours`

setTime

Prototype: `setTime(milliseconds)`

Summary: Sets the exact time of a `Date` object.

Description: The `setTime` method accepts an integer parameter representing the number of milliseconds elapsed since January 1, 1970 (1 January 1970 00:00:00), given in local time.

Risk: This function should only be accessed and launched by administrative-level users or systems that wish to affect the underlying operating system. In nearly all cases this function is not truly required and should be removed before an application gets released as production.

Notes: Can be useful for storing and retrieving dates across sessions.

Additional Resources:
http://msdn.microsoft.com/library/default.asp?url=/library/en-us/jscript7/html/jsoriMethodsNode.asp

Impact: Medium

setUTCDate

Prototype: `setUTCDate(day)`

Summary: Sets the day of the month for a `Date` object.

Description: The `setUTCDate` method sets the day of the month for a `Date` object, given in universal time. Accepts an `integer` argument between 1 and 31. If a number out of range of the current month is given, the number of days in the current month are subtracted and the month is incremented until a valid date is reached.

Risk: This function should only be accessed and launched by administrative-level users or systems that wish to affect the underlying operating system. In nearly all cases this function is not truly required and should be removed before an application gets released as production.

Proper Usage: `valentine.setDate(14)`

Additional Resources:

http://msdn.microsoft.com/library/default.asp?url=/library/en-us/ jscript7/html/jsoriMethodsNode.asp

Impact: Medium

Cross Reference: `setDate`

setUTCFullYear

Prototype: `setUTCFullYear(year)`

Summary: Sets the 4-digit year for a `Date` object.

Description: The `setUTCFullYear` method sets the year for a `Date` object, given in universal time. Four-digit years are between 1000 and 9999. Accepts an `integer` argument specifying the full year of the `Date` object.

Risk: This function should only be accessed and launched by administrative-level users or systems that wish to affect the underlying operating system. In nearly all cases this function is not truly required and should be removed before an application gets released as production.

Proper Usage: `orwell.setUTCFullYear(1984)`

Additional Resources:

http://msdn.microsoft.com/library/default.asp?url=/library/en-us/ jscript7/html/jsoriMethodsNode.asp

Impact: Medium

Cross Reference: `setFullYear`

setUTCHours

Prototype: `setUTCHours(hour)`

Summary: Sets the hour of the day for a `Date` object.

Description: The `setUTCHours` method sets the hour of the day for a `Date` object, given in universal time. Accepts an `integer` argument between 0 and 23. If a value greater than 23 is given, the date and all other fields are modified accordingly.

Risk: This function should only be accessed and launched by administrative-level users or systems that wish to affect the underlying operating system. In nearly all cases this function is not truly required and should be removed before an application gets released as production.

Proper Usage: `coffee.setUTCHours(5)`

Additional Resources:
http://msdn.microsoft.com/library/default.asp?url=/library/en-us/ jscript7/html/jsoriMethodsNode.asp

Impact: Medium

Cross Reference: `setHours`

setUTCMilliseconds

Prototype: `setUTCMilliseconds(milliseconds)`

Summary: Sets the milliseconds for a `Date` object.

Description: The `setUTCMilliseconds` method sets the milliseconds for a `Date` object, given in local time. Accepts an `integer` argument between 0 and 999. In practice, this method is the same as `setMilliseconds`. If a value greater than 999 is given, the seconds are added and all other fields are modified accordingly.

Risk: This function should only be accessed and launched by administrative-level users or systems that wish to affect the underlying operating system. In nearly all cases this function is not truly required and should be removed before an application gets released as production.

Additional Resources:

http://msdn.microsoft.com/library/default.asp?url=/library/en-us/
jscript7/html/jsoriMethodsNode.asp

Impact: Medium

Cross Reference: setMilliseconds

setUTCMinutes

Prototype: setUTCMinutes(minutes)

Summary: Sets the minutes for a Date object.

Description: The setUTCMinutes method sets the minutes for a Date object, given in local time. Accepts an integer argument between 0 and 59. In practice, this method is the same as setMinutes. If a value greater than 59 is given, the hours are added and all other fields are modified accordingly.

Risk: This function should only be accessed and launched by administrative-level users or systems that wish to affect the underlying operating system. In nearly all cases this function is not truly required and should be removed before an application gets released as production.

Additional Resources:

http://msdn.microsoft.com/library/default.asp?url=/library/en-us/
jscript7/html/jsoriMethodsNode.asp

Impact: Medium

Cross Reference: setMinutes

setUTCMonth

Prototype: setUTCMonth(month)

Summary: Sets the month of the year for a Date object.

Description: The setUTCMonth method sets the month of the year for a Date object, given in universal time. Accepts an integer argument between 0 for January and 11 for December. If a value greater than 11 is given, the year is added and all other fields are modified accordingly.

Risk: This function should only be accessed and launched by administrative-level users or systems that wish to affect the underlying operating system. In nearly all cases this function is not truly required and should be removed before an application gets released as production.

Additional Resources:

http://msdn.microsoft.com/library/default.asp?url=/library/en-us/jscript7/html/jsoriMethodsNode.asp

Impact: Medium

Cross Reference: setMonth

setUTCSeconds

Prototype: setUTCSeconds(seconds[, milliseconds])

Summary: Sets the seconds for a Date object.

Description: The setUTCSeconds method sets the seconds for a Date object, given in universal time. Accepts an integer argument between 0 and 59. In practice, this method is the same as setSeconds. Optionally accepts a millisecond argument between 0 and 999, equivalent to setUTCMilliseconds. If a value greater than 59 is given, the minutes are added and all other fields are modified accordingly.

Risk: This function should only be accessed and launched by administrative-level users or systems that wish to affect the underlying operating system. In nearly all cases this function is not truly required and should be removed before an application gets released as production.

Additional Resources:

http://msdn.microsoft.com/library/default.asp?url=/library/en-us/jscript7/html/jsoriMethodsNode.asp

Impact: Medium

Cross Reference: setSeconds

setYear

Prototype: `setYear(year)`

Summary: Sets the year for a `Date` object.

Description: The `setYear` method is included only for backwards compatibility with previous versions of JScript. It assumes a 2-digit year for the period 1900-1999, and a 4-digit year otherwise. It accepts an integer year as an argument.

Risk: This function should only be accessed and launched by administrative-level users or systems that wish to affect the underlying operating system. In nearly all cases this function is not truly required and should be removed before an application gets released as production.

Notes: Deprecated. Use `setFullYear` instead.

Additional Resources:
http://msdn.microsoft.com/library/default.asp?url=/library/en-us/jscript7/html/jsoriMethodsNode.asp

Impact: Medium

toLocaleDateString

Prototype: `string toLocaleDateString()`

Summary: Returns a date string formatted to the current locale.

Description: The `toLocaleDateString` returns the date, in the current locale and time zone format, as a string. It has no arguments.

Risk: Certain string manipulation functions to include string and character transition functions are commonly leveraged in buffer overflow attacks. At the most basic level, these functions read in data, perform analysis and execution logic, then output the data to another type of string. It is imperative that the destination string be calculated accordingly and that enough memory space is allocated. Special characters should also be stricken from the conversion where possible.

Additional Resources:
http://msdn.microsoft.com/library/default.asp?url=/library/en-us/
jscript7/html/jsoriMethodsNode.asp

Impact: Medium

toLocaleLowerCase

Prototype: `string toLocaleLowerCase()`

Summary: Returns a date string formatted to the current locale, with all the letters converted to lowercase.

Description: The `toLocaleDateString` returns the date, in the current locale and time zone format, as a lower case string. It has no arguments.

Risk: Certain string manipulation functions to include string and character transition functions are commonly leveraged in buffer overflow attacks. At the most basic level, these functions read in data, perform analysis and execution logic, then output the data to another type of string. It is imperative that the destination string be calculated accordingly and that enough memory space is allocated. Special characters should also be stricken from the conversion where possible.

Additional Resources:
http://msdn.microsoft.com/library/default.asp?url=/library/en-us/
jscript7/html/jsoriMethodsNode.asp

Impact: Medium

toLocaleString

Prototype: `string toLocaleString()`

Summary: Converts a `Date` object to a string using the current locale and platform conventions.

Description: The `toLocaleString` method converts the `Date` object to a human-readable string. It uses the current locale and relies on the underlying host to format the string, so the results are platform-dependant. It has no arguments.

Risk: Certain string manipulation functions to include string and character transition functions are commonly leveraged in buffer overflow attacks. At the most basic level, these functions read in data, perform analysis and execution logic, then output the data to another type of string. It is imperative that the destination string be calculated accordingly and that enough memory space is allocated. Special characters should also be stricken from the conversion where possible.

Additional Resources:

http://msdn.microsoft.com/library/default.asp?url=/library/en-us/jscript7/html/jsoriMethodsNode.asp

Impact: Medium

Cross Reference: toUTCString

toLocaleTimeString

Prototype: string toLocaleTimeString()

Summary: Converts a Date object to a time string using the current locale and time zone.

Description: The toLocaleTimeString method converts the Date object to a human-readable string. It uses the current locale, host settings, and time zone to format the string. It has no arguments.

Risk: Certain string manipulation functions to include string and character transition functions are commonly leveraged in buffer overflow attacks. At the most basic level, these functions read in data, perform analysis and execution logic, then output the data to another type of string. It is imperative that the destination string be calculated accordingly and that enough memory space is allocated. Special characters should also be stricken from the conversion where possible.

Additional Resources:

http://msdn.microsoft.com/library/default.asp?url=/library/en-us/jscript7/html/jsoriMethodsNode.asp

Impact: Medium

toLocaleUpperCase

Prototype: `string toLocaleUpperCase()`

Summary: Returns a date string formatted to the current locale, with all the letters converted to uppercase.

Description: The `toLocaleDateString` returns the date, in the current locale and time zone format, as an upper case string. It has no arguments.

Risk: Certain string manipulation functions to include string and character transition functions are commonly leveraged in buffer overflow attacks. At the most basic level, these functions read in data, perform analysis and execution logic, then output the data to another type of string. It is imperative that the destination string be calculated accordingly and that enough memory space is allocated. Special characters should also be stricken from the conversion where possible.

Additional Resources:
http://msdn.microsoft.com/library/default.asp?url=/library/en-us/jscript7/html/jsoriMethodsNode.asp

Impact: Medium

toUTCString

Prototype: `string toUTCString()`

Summary: Converts a `Date` object to a string using universal time and platform conventions.

Description: The `toUTCString` method converts the `Date` object to a human-readable string. It uses universal time but relies on the underlying platform to format the string, so the results are host-dependant. It has no arguments.

Risk: Certain string manipulation functions to include string and character transition functions are commonly leveraged in buffer overflow attacks. At the most basic level, these functions read in data, perform analysis and execution logic, then output the data to another type of string. It is imperative that the destination string be calculated accordingly and that enough memory space is allocated. Special characters should also be stricken from the conversion where possible.

Additional Resources:

http://msdn.microsoft.com/library/default.asp?url=/library/en-us/jscript7/html/jsoriMethodsNode.asp

Impact: Medium

Cross Reference: `toLocaleString`

UTC

Prototype: `integer UTC(year, month, day[, hours[, minutes[, seconds[, milliseconds]]]])`

Summary: Returns the number of milliseconds between the supplied date and 1 January 1970 00:00:00 using universal time.

Description: The `UTC` method accepts a date in universal time and returns the number of milliseconds between that date and midnight of January 1, 1970. Zeroes are assumed for any optional arguments not specified.

Risk: Certain string manipulation functions to include string and character transition functions are commonly leveraged in buffer overflow attacks. At the most basic level, these functions read in data, perform analysis and execution logic, then output the data to another type of string. It is imperative that the destination string be calculated accordingly and that enough memory space is allocated. Special characters should also be stricken from the conversion where possible.

Additional Resources:

http://msdn.microsoft.com/library/default.asp?url=/library/en-us/jscript7/html/jsoriMethodsNode.asp

Impact: Medium

write

Prototype: `write(string1[, string2, ..])`

Summary: Writes JScript expressions to the specified document.

Description: The `write` method writes the results of JScript expressions to the document. It takes an unspecified number of arguments, evaluates each one in turn, and writes the result to the document stream.

Risk: All inputs to this method should be thoroughly parsed to prevent the potential for cross-site scripting attacks. Input parameters should be restricted to alphanumeric characters to prevent command executions during processing.

Proper Usage: `document.write("&lt;h1&gt;Sunday Sunday Sunday!&lt;/h1&gt;")`

Additional Resources:
http://msdn.microsoft.com/library/default.asp?url=/library/en-us/jscript7/html/jsoriMethodsNode.asp

Impact: Medium

Cross Reference: `writeln`

writeln

Prototype: `writeln(string1[, string2, ..])`

Summary: Writes JScript expressions to the specified document, followed by a newline.

Description: The `writeln` method writes the results of JScript expressions to the document. It takes an unspecified number of arguments, evaluates each one in turn, and writes the result to the document stream. `writeln` appends a newline character at the end of its write.

Risk: All inputs to this method should be thoroughly parsed to prevent the potential for cross-site scripting attacks. Input parameters should be restricted to alphanumeric characters to prevent command executions during processing.

Additional Resources:
http://msdn.microsoft.com/library/default.asp?url=/library/en-us/jscript7/html/jsoriMethodsNode.asp

Impact: Medium

Cross Reference: `write`

JScript

Programmer's Ultimate Security DeskRef: LISP

bit-xor

Prototype: `bit-xor 1array 2array`

Summary: This function returns TRUE if exactly one but not both of the two conditions are true

Description: This function compares two bit-arrays against an argument and returns TRUE if exactly one but not both of the two conditions are true. Deceiving by name, this function does XOR or "flip" a specified target bit.

Risk: This function is commonly misused and mistaken for a bit-flipping XOR function. Ensure that it is not being used to obfuscate data and that the allocated memory spaces are properly cleaned once this function is finished executing.

Notes: Shouldn't that be: does NOT xor or flip a target bit?

Additional Resources:
http://ugweb.cs.ualberta.ca/~c325/gcl/gcl_15.html

Impact: High

Cross References: `bit-arrays`

break

Prototype: `break &;optional format-string &;rest format-args`

Summary: This function stops execution and enters debugging mode

Description: This function stops execution and calls the debugger, allowing examination of the stack. A format string with the appropriate arguments can be used to display a message when it occurs.

Risk: The `break` function can be potentially compromised by an attacker to gain access to sensitive memory-resistant data. In many cases, memory is not effectively cleaned before the application exists if a series of break functions are encountered. It is critical to ensure that an application user may not execute this function on demand, in addition to cleaning all application data from memory before fully exiting the program.

Additional Resources: www.webweasel.com/lisp/doc/b.htm

Impact: Low

Cross References: `continue`

catch

Prototype: `catch tag {form}*`

Summary: This special form acts as the target for a Throw

Description: This acts as a return point for a `throw` function, and is specified using an object tag. `Catch` evaluates the forms of the Body and returns a value from the last Body form

Risk: While the `throw` function has minimal risk associated with using it, it is imperative that you ensure attackers do not gain the ability to call this function outside the program nor is the memory data viewable by such users.

Additional Resources: www.gnu.org/software/emacs/elisp-manual/html_node/ elisp_130.html

Impact: Low

Cross References: throw, tag

catenate

Prototype: catenate &;rest series-inputs

Summary: This function combines multiple series into a single series

Description: This function combines two or more series by appending them and is commonly utilized to add one string onto the tail or end of another string.

Risk: The input and output of the Catenate function should be controlled to the point where human users do not have the ability to call the internal function with known parameters. Attackers have been known to compromise or leverage this function in order to read a previously sensitive and private data string by attaching it to another public string.

Additional Resources: www-2.cs.cmu.edu/Groups/AI/html/cltl/clm/node353.html

Impact: Medium

Cross References: choose, split, expand, subseries, postion, mask, mingle, chunk

cell-error

Prototype: cell-error condition

Summary: This type consists of error conditions occurring when accessing a location

Description: This type consists of an error condition that occurs when accessing a location, and is a subfunction of error. It is initialized with a name, and accessible using cell-Error-Name.

LISP

Risk: System and application error messages commonly have sensitive information that an attacker could leverage to gain a foothold on a system to potentially assist in a more complicated or dangerous attack. Error information can have memory, internal configuration, function, and parameter data to include other types of data that could be sought after by a malicious user.

Additional Resources: www.cs.queensu.ca/software_docs/gnudev/gcl-ansi/gcl_601.html

Impact: Medium

Cross References: `cell-error-name`

cell-error-name

Prototype: `cell-error-name condition`

Summary: This function returns the name of an offending cell involved in the situation represented by condition.

Description: This function returns a cell name based upon a condition of type, `cell-error`.

Risk: System and application error messages commonly have sensitive information that an attacker could leverage to gain a foothold on a system to potentially assist in a more complicated or dangerous attack. Error information can have memory, internal configuration, function, and parameter data to include other types of data that could be sought after by a malicious user.

Additional Resources: www-2.cs.cmu.edu/Groups/AI/html/cltl/clm/node346.html

Impact: Medium

Cross References: `cell-error`

cerror

Prototype: `cerror continue-format-string error-format-string &;rest args`

Summary: This function signals continual errors.

Description: This function signals an error and enters the debugger, from which the error can be resolved and code execution continued, starting immediately after the `cerror` call.

Risk: System and application error messages commonly have sensitive information that an attacker could leverage to gain a foothold on a system to potentially assist in a more complicated or dangerous attack. Error information can have memory, internal configuration, function, and parameter data to include other types of data that could be sought after by a malicious user.

Additional Resources: www-2.cs.cmu.edu/Groups/AI/html/cltl/clm/node220.html

Impact: Medium

Cross References: `error`

collect-hash

Prototype: `collect-hash keys values &;key :test :size :rehash-size :rehash-threshold`

Summary: This function returns values based upon a specified series of keys and groups of corresponding valuesan association lists. This includes a property list and a hash table.

Description: This function returns values based upon a specified series of keys and groups of corresponding valuesan association lists, a property list, and a hash table. The keyword arguments of collect-hash specify attributes of the hash table produced.

Risk: Collecting hash data may allow a malicious user the ability to gain access to potentially sensitive application-stored data. In most associative arrays or hash tables, all data is not supposed to be gleaned by end users. Access control lists, human input analysis, and field protections aid in protecting arrays to ensure that only the desired and appropriate data is viewable by end users.

Additional Resources: www-2.cs.cmu.edu/Groups/AI/html/cltl/clm/node354.html

Impact: High

Cross References: `collect-alist`, `collect-plist`

compile

Prototype: `compile name &;optional definition`

Summary: This function compiles a specified interpreted function.

Description: This function produces a compiled function and requires a name for the source and compiled functions. `warnings-p`, `failure-p` returns `FALSE` if the compilation of neither is detected by the compiler.

Risk: LISP is an interpreted scripting language. The `compile` function should be controlled by internal application logic only. Restrict human input for secure usage!

Additional Resources: www.cs.queensu.ca/software_docs/gnudev/gcl-ansi/gcl_255.html

Impact: Low

Cross References: `error-output`, `compile-verbose`, `compile-print`

compiled-function-p

Prototype: `compiled-function-p object =&gt; generalized-boolean`

Summary: This function returns `true` only if the specified object is of a compiled-function.

Description: This function returns true if the specified object is of a compiled-function, and otherwise, returns false.

Risk: Utilizing an internal compiler function contains nearly all the dangers of letting an attacker control a local compiler. Such compile functions should be strictly controlled and under no circumstance should an attacker or malicious user be able to execute this function at will or control the parameters of this function. Function parameters should also be controlled whereas users do not have the ability direct a specific data stream whether internal or external to the application. This function is usually removed before an application matures to "production status."

Additional Resources: www-2.cs.cmu.edu/Groups/AI/html/cltl/clm/ node73.html

Impact: Low

Cross References: `compile, compile-file, compiled-function`

compile-file

Prototype: `compile-file input-pathname &;key :output-file :verbose :print`

Summary: This function compiles the contents of a specified input file, creating a binary output-file.

Description: This function produces a binary output-file from the compiled contents of an input-file. The verbose option can be used to display compiler messages. The print option sends the information about the file to standard-out, and external-format specifies the external file format.

Risk: Utilizing an internal compiler function contains nearly all the dangers of letting an attacker control a local compiler. Such compile functions should be strictly controlled and under no circumstance should an attacker or malicious user be able to execute this function at will or control the parameters of this function. Function parameters should also be controlled whereas users do not have the ability direct a specific data stream whether internal or external to the application. This function is usually removed before an application matures to "production status."

Additional Resources: www.lisp.org/HyperSpec/Body/fun_compile-file.html

Impact: Low

Cross References: `compile, error-output, compile-verbose, compile-print`

compile-file-pathname

Prototype: `compile-file-pathname pathname &;key :output-file`

Summary: This function returns the pathname that compile-file would write to.

Description: This function takes input-file, output-file values, returns the logical pathname. If input-file is a logical pathname, it is translated into a physical pathname as if by calling.

Risk: System path information is constantly sought after by attackers or malicious users profiling a target application or system. Path information alone can potentially identify the underlying operating system, installed applications, configurations, and in some cases user and security information. Ensure that non-alphanumeric characters are removed from the string before it is processed and that the information is only processed internally by the application. Limit the end user's ability to ascertain or traverse path information.

Additional Resources: www-2.cs.cmu.edu/Groups/AI/html/cltl/clm/ node211.html

Impact: Low

Cross References: `compile-file`, `pathname`, `logical-pathname`, `translate-logical-pathname`

compile-file-truename

Summary: This value is the physical pathname used by compile-name

Description: This value is a pathname based on the physical location a file being compiled

Risk: System path information is constantly sought after by attackers or malicious users profiling a target application or system. Path information alone can potentially identify the underlying operating system, installed applications, configurations, and in some cases user and security information. Ensure that non-alphanumeric characters are removed from the string before it is processed and that the information is only processed internally by the application. Limit the end user's ability to ascertain or traverse path information.

Additional Resources: www-2.cs.cmu.edu/Groups/AI/html/cltl/clm/node224.html

Impact: Low

Cross References: `compile-file`

compile-print

Summary: This value is a Boolean that determines whether compiler outputs input-file form data to standard-out.

Description: This Boolean is an argument of `compile-file`, and determines whether input-file form data is outputted to standard-out

Risk: Utilizing an internal compiler function contains nearly all the dangers of letting an attacker control a local compiler. Such compile functions should be strictly controlled and under no circumstance should an attacker or malicious user be able to execute this function at will or control the parameters of this function. Function parameters should also be controlled, whereas users do not have the ability direct a specific datastream whether internal or external to the application. This function is usually removed before an application matures to "production status."

Additional Resources: www-2.cs.cmu.edu/Groups/AI/html/cltl/clm/node224.html

Impact: Low

Cross References: `compile-file`

compiler-let

Prototype: `compiler-let ({var | (var value)}*) {form}*`

Summary: This special form causes processing of the body by the compiler with special variables.

Description: This special form causes processing of the body by the compiler with special variables bound to indicated values in the execution context of the compiler.

Risk: Utilizing an internal compiler function contains nearly all the dangers of letting an attacker control a local compiler. Such compile functions should be strictly controlled and under no circumstance should an attacker or malicious user be able to execute this function at will or control the parameters of this function. Function parameters should also be controlled whereas users do not have the ability direct a specific data stream whether internal or external to the application. This function is usually removed before an application matures to "production status."

Additional Resources: www-2.cs.cmu.edu/Groups/AI/html/cltl/clm/node83.html

Impact: Low

Cross References: `let`

compiler-macroexpand

Summary: This function expands compiler macro functions.

Description: This function calls a compiler macro function and expands repeatedly until it's no longer possible to expand.

Risk: Utilizing an internal compiler function contains nearly all the dangers of letting an attacker control a local compiler. Such `compile` functions should be strictly controlled and under no circumstance should an attacker or malicious user be able to execute this function at will or control the parameters of this function. Function parameters should also be controlled whereas users do not have the ability direct a specific data stream whether internal or external to the application. This function is usually removed before an application matures to "production status."

Additional Resources: www-2.cs.cmu.edu/Groups/AI/html/cltl/clm/node101.html

Impact: Low

Cross References: `macroexpand`

compiler-macroexpand1

Summary: This function expands compiler macro functions.

Description: This function calls a compiler macro function once.

Risk: Utilizing an internal compiler function contains nearly all the dangers of letting an attacker control a local compiler. Such compile functions should be strictly controlled and under no circumstance should an attacker or malicious user be able to execute this function at will or control the parameters of this function. Function parameters should also be controlled whereas users do not have the ability direct a specific data stream whether internal or external to the application. This function is usually removed before an application matures to "production status."

Additional Resources: www-2.cs.cmu.edu/Groups/AI/html/cltl/clm/node101.html

Impact: Low

Cross References: `compile-macroexpand, macroexpand`

compiler-macro-function

Prototype: `compiler-macro-function name {&;optional environ-ment} =&gt; function`

Summary: This function accesses a specified macro function.

Description: This function calls the specified macro function in an environment.

Risk: Utilizing an internal compiler function contains nearly all the dangers of letting an attacker control a local compiler. Such compile functions should be strictly controlled and under no circumstance should an attacker or malicious user be able to execute this function at will or control the parameters of this function. Function parameters should also be controlled whereas users do not have the ability direct a specific data stream whether internal or external to the application. This function is usually removed before an application matures to "production status."

Additional Resources: www-2.cs.cmu.edu/Groups/AI/html/cltl/clm/node101.html

Impact: Low

Cross References: `define-compiler-macro`

compile-verbose

Summary: This value is a Boolean that determines whether compiler displays information.

Description: This Boolean is an argument of `compile-file`, and if set to true it will cause useful information to be displayed when compiling.

Risk: Utilizing an internal compiler, function contains nearly all the dangers of letting an attacker control a local compiler. Such compile functions should be strictly controlled and under no circumstance should an attacker or malicious user be able to execute this function at will or control the parameters of this function. Function parameters should also be controlled whereas users do not have the ability direct a specific data stream whether internal or external to the application. This function is usually removed before an application matures to "production status."

Additional Resources: www-2.cs.cmu.edu/Groups/AI/html/cltl/clm/ node224.html

Impact: Medium

Cross References: `compile-file`

debugger-hook

Summary: This value is used prior to normal entry into the debugger, due to a call to invoke-debugger or automatic entry.

Description: This value is used prior to normal entry into the debugger with a condition that is not handled by `error` or `cerror`. The function can either handle the condition by transferring control or return normally, allowing the standard debugger to run.

Risk: Functions that launch or invoke system debuggers have the ability to allow local application users to view and access sensitive memory-resident data. It is critical to control these functions to disallow users from accessing these functions.

Ensure that human user input is not permitted to call these functions or directly pass data as parameters. Special characters should be stripped as a part of vetting human user input.

Additional Resources: www-2.cs.cmu.edu/Groups/AI/html/cltl/clm/ node345.html

Impact: Medium

Cross References: `invoke-debugger`, `error`, `cerror`

debug-io

Summary: This value is a stream to be used for interactive debugging purposes.

Description: This variable a standardized I/O customization variable, and can be bound or assigned in order to change the default destinations for input and/or output used by various standardized operators and facilities

Risk: Functions that launch or invoke system debuggers have the ability to allow local application users to view and access sensitive memory-resident data. It is critical to control these functions to disallow users from accessing these functions. Ensure that human user input is not permitted to call these functions or directly pass data as parameters. Special characters should be stripped as a part of vetting human user input.

Additional Resources: www-2.cs.cmu.edu/Groups/AI/html/cltl/clm/ node183.html

Impact: Medium

Cross References: `error-output`, `query-io`, `standard-input`, `standard-output`, `trace-output`

delete

Prototype: `delete item sequence &;key :from-end :test :test-not :start :end :count :key`

Summary: This function returns a sequence from which the elements that satisfy the test have been removed.

LISP

Description: This function returns a modified sequence from which elements have been removed using specified criteria. The sequence returned will be of the same data type.

Risk: In addition to the potential race condition bugs that are associated with this function, a user could also attempt to execute a denial of service attack. Ensure that only one instance of this function can be called at any given moment. All input passed to this function should be analyzed closely to ensure that only desired resources can be removed from the system. It is not uncommon for worms and viruses to exploit application-layer vulnerabilities to cause damage to files they since would not have had access to.

Additional Resources: www-2.cs.cmu.edu/Groups/AI/html/cltl/clm/node144.html

Impact: Low

Cross References: `delete-if`, `delete-if-not`, `remove`, `remove-if`, `remove-if-not`

delete-duplicates

Prototype: `delete-duplicates sequence &;key :from-end :test :test-not :start :end :key`

Summary: This function returns a modified sequence from which any element that matches another element occurring in sequence has been removed.

Description: This function returns a modified sequence from which any element matching another element occurring in same sequence has been removed. The from-end argument states which end to start from, start-end defines the sequence range, and result-sequence the modified sequence. The `Test` and `test-not` arguments are function designators for two arguments that return a Boolean.

Risk: In addition to the potential race condition bugs that are associated with this function, a user could also attempt to execute a denial of service attack. Ensure that only one instance of this function can be called at any given moment. All input passed to this function should be analyzed closely to ensure that only desired resources can be removed from the system. It is not uncommon for worms and viruses to exploit application-layer vulnerabilities to cause damage to files they since would not have had access to.

Additional Resources:
www.franz.com/support/documentation/6.2/ansicl/dictentr/remove-d.htm

Impact: Low

Cross References: `remove-duplicates`

delete-file

Prototype: `delete-file file`

Summary: This function deletes a specified file.

Description: This function deletes a file specified by the `filespec` argument, and returns true if successful.

Risk: In addition to the potential race condition bugs that are associated with this function, a user could also attempt to execute a denial of service attack. Ensure that only one instance of this function can be called at any given moment. All input passed to this function should be analyzed closely to ensure that only desired resources can be removed from the system. It is not uncommon for worms and viruses to exploit application-layer vulnerabilities to cause damage to files they since would not have had access to.

Additional Resources: www-2.cs.cmu.edu/Groups/AI/html/cltl/clm/
node216.html

Impact: Medium

Cross References: `pathname, logical-pathname`

delete-if

Prototype: `delete-if predicate sequence &;key :from-end :start :end :count :key`

Summary: This function returns a sequence from which the elements have been conditionally removed.

Description: This function returns a modified sequence with those satisfying the define conditions deleted. A sequence can be destroyed and used to construct the result.

Risk: In addition to the potential race condition bugs that are associated with this function, a user could also attempt to execute a denial of service attack. Ensure that only one instance of this function can be called at any given moment. All input passed to this function should be analyzed closely to ensure that only desired resources can be removed from the system. It is not uncommon for worms and viruses to exploit application-layer vulnerabilities to cause damage to files they since would not have had access to.

Additional Resources: www-2.cs.cmu.edu/Groups/AI/html/cltl/clm/node144.html

Impact: Low

Cross References: `delete, delete-if-not, remove, remove-if, remove-if-not`

delete-if-not

Prototype: `delete-if predicate sequence &;key :from-end :start :end :count :key`

Summary: This function returns a sequence from which the elements have been conditionally removed.

Description: This function returns a modified sequence with those satisfying the define conditions deleted. A sequence can be destroyed and used to construct the result.

Risk: In addition to the potential race condition bugs that are associated with this function, a user could also attempt to execute a denial of service attack. Ensure that only one instance of this function can be called at any given moment. All input passed to this function should be analyzed closely to ensure that only desired resources can be removed from the system. It is not uncommon for worms and viruses to exploit application-layer vulnerabilities to cause damage to files they since would not have had access to.

Additional Resources: www-2.cs.cmu.edu/Groups/AI/html/cltl/clm/node144.html

Impact: Low

Cross References: `delete`, `delete-if`, `remove`, `remove-if`, `remove-if-not`

delete-package

Prototype: `delete-package package`

Summary: This function deletes a specified package from all package system data structures.

Description: This function deletes a specified package and returns true if successful. Deleting a package causes package names and nicknames to no longer be recognized package names.

Risk: In addition to the potential race condition bugs that are associated with this function, a user could also attempt to execute a denial of service attack. Ensure that only one instance of this function can be called at any given moment. All input passed to this function should be analyzed closely to ensure that only desired resources can be removed from the system. It is not uncommon for worms and viruses to exploit application-layer vulnerabilities to cause damage to files they since would not have had access to.

Additional Resources: www-2.cs.cmu.edu/Groups/AI/html/cltl/clm/node118.html

Impact: Low

Cross References: `unuse-package`

error

Prototype: `error format-string &;rest args`

Summary: This function signals an error.

Description: This function signals a fatal error, after which it is impossible to return to the caller and continue.

Risk: System and application error messages commonly have sensitive information that an attacker could leverage to gain a foothold on a system to potentially assist in a more complicated or dangerous attack. Error information can have memory, internal configuration, function, and parameter data to include other types of data that could be sought after by a malicious user.

Additional Resources: www-2.cs.cmu.edu/Groups/AI/html/cltl/clm/node220.html

Impact: Medium

Cross References: `cerror`, `warn`, `break`

error-output

Prototype: `error-output stream`

Summary: This variable identifies a stream to which error messages are sent.

Description: This variable identifies the output stream for error messages, usually same as standard-output.

Risk: System and application error messages commonly have sensitive information that an attacker could leverage to gain a foothold on a system to potentially assist in a more complicated or dangerous attack. Error information can have memory, internal configuration, function, and parameter data to include other types of data that could be sought after by a malicious user.

Additional Resources: www-2.cs.cmu.edu/Groups/AI/html/cltl/clm/node183.html

Impact: Medium

Cross References: `standard-output`, `error`

file-author

Prototype: `file-author file`

Summary: This function returns the author of a specified file.

Description: This function returns the author name of a file as a string. The file argument can be a stream open to a file, or a filename.

Risk: This function handles system-specific sensitive information that an attacker could leverage during a period of target reconnaissance. This function should only be utilized if it is absolutely necessary for proper execution of the application. All analysis for the output of this function should be conducted securely within the application and never sent across the wire in cleartext.

Additional Resources: www-2.cs.cmu.edu/Groups/AI/html/cltl/clm/node216.html

Impact: Low

Cross References: `delete-file, file-write-date, probe-file, file-length`

file-error-pathname

Prototype: `file-error-pathname condition`

Summary: This function returns the offending pathname of a condition of type file-error.

Description: This function returns the offending pathname of a condition of type file-error.

Risk: System and application error messages commonly have sensitive information that an attacker could leverage to gain a foothold on a system to potentially assist in a more complicated or dangerous attack. Error information can have memory, internal configuration, function, and parameter data to include other types of data that could be sought after by a malicious user.

Additional Resources: www-2.cs.cmu.edu/Groups/AI/html/cltl/clm/node346.html

Impact: Low

Cross References: `file-error`

LISP

file-write-date

Prototype: `file-write-date file`

Summary: This function returns the creation of last modified date of a specified file.

Description: This function returns the creation or last written date as an integer in universal time format. The file argument can be a stream open to a file, or a file-name.

Risk: This function handles system-specific sensitive information that an attacker could leverage during a period of target reconnaissance. This function should only be utilized if it is absolutely necessary for proper execution of the application. All analysis for the output of this function should be conducted securely within the application and never sent across the wire in cleartext.

Additional Resources: www-2.cs.cmu.edu/Groups/AI/html/cltl/clm/node216.html

Impact: Low

Cross References: `delete-file`, `file-author`, `probe-file`, `file-length`

get-internal-real-time

Prototype: `get-internal-real-time`

Summary: This function returns the current time in internal time units.

Description: This function returns as an integer the current time in internal time units, relative to an arbitrary time base. The difference between the values of two calls to this function is the amount of elapsed real time between the two calls.

Risk: This function handles system-specific sensitive information that an attacker could leverage during a period of target reconnaissance. This function should only be utilized if it is absolutely necessary for proper execution of the application. All analysis for the output of this function should be conducted securely within the application and never sent across the wire in cleartext.

Additional Resources: www-2.cs.cmu.edu/Groups/AI/html/cltl/clm/node232.html

Impact: Medium

Cross References: `internal-time-units-per-second`

get-internal-run-time

Prototype: `get-internal-run-time`

Summary: This function returns the current run time in internal time units.

Description: This function returns the current run time in internal time units as an integer, and can measure real time, run time, CPU cycles, or some other quantity

Risk: This function handles system-specific sensitive information that an attacker could leverage during a period of target reconnaissance. This function should only be utilized if it is absolutely necessary for proper execution of the application. All analysis for the output of this function should be conducted securely within the application and never sent across the wire in cleartext.

Additional Resources: www-2.cs.cmu.edu/Groups/AI/html/cltl/clm/node232.html

Impact: Medium

Cross References: `internal-time-units-per-second`

get-properties

Prototype: `get-properties place indicator-list`

Summary: This function returns any of several property list entries all at once.

Description: This function searches the property list stored in place for any of the indicators in an indicator-list until it finds the first property in the property list whose indicator is one of the elements of indicator-list.

Risk: This function handles system-specific sensitive information that an attacker could leverage during a period of target reconnaissance. This function should only be utilized if it is absolutely necessary for proper execution of the application. All

analysis for the output of this function should be conducted securely within the application and never sent across the wire in cleartext.

Additional Resources: www-2.cs.cmu.edu/Groups/AI/html/cltl/clm/node108.html

Impact: Medium

Cross References: `get`, `getf`

get-universal-time

Prototype: `get-universal-time`

Summary: This function returns the time in Universal Time format.

Description: This function returns the current time as a single integer in Universal Time format. Universal Time format is represented as a non-negative integer number of seconds.

Risk: This function handles system-specific sensitive information that an attacker could leverage during a period of target reconnaissance. This function should only be utilized if it is absolutely necessary for proper execution of the application. All analysis for the output of this function should be conducted securely within the application and never sent across the wire in cleartext.

Additional Resources: www-2.cs.cmu.edu/Groups/AI/html/cltl/clm/node232.html

Impact: Low

Cross References: `decode-universal-time`, `encode-universal-time`

hash-table-rehash-threshold

Prototype: `hash-table-rehash-threshold hash-table`

Summary: This function returns the current rehash threshold of hash-table

Description: This function returns the current rehash threshold of a hash-table, suitable for use in a call to make-hash-table in order to produce a hash table with state corresponding to the current state of the hash-table.

Risk: Hash tables or associative arrays can be utilized to store large amounts of information. It is critical to control human user access to such data structures. Human user input should be analyzed and vetted, user access control put on the tables, and output restricted to certain public information. Since this function passes potentially sensitive memory information as its output, it should be mandatory to only use this function were necessary.

Additional Resources: www-2.cs.cmu.edu/Groups/AI/html/cltl/clm/ node155.html

Impact: Medium

Cross References: `make-hash-table`, `hash-table-rehash-size`

host-namestring

Prototype: `host-namestring pathname`

Summary: This function returns the host name portion of a pathname.

Description: This function takes a pathname value and returns the host name.

Risk: This function handles system-specific sensitive information that an attacker could leverage during a period of target reconnaissance. This function should only be utilized if it is absolutely necessary for proper execution of the application. All analysis for the output of this function should be conducted securely within the application and never sent across the wire in cleartext.

Additional Resources: www-2.cs.cmu.edu/Groups/AI/html/cltl/clm/ node214.html

Impact: Medium

Cross References: `truename`, `merge-pathnames`, `pathname`, `logical-pathname`

import

Prototype: `import symbols &;optional package`

Summary: This function adds a single symbol or symbols to the package.

Description: This function adds a single symbol or symbols to the package, and checks for name conflicts with existing symbols.

Risk: All special and wildcard characters should be removed before the filename is computed on the local filesystem. Malicious filenames are interpreted differently on varying systems and as such, directory control is critical to limiting the ability of an attacker to potentially compromise files at varying levels within the application or underlying subsystem.

Additional Resources: www-2.cs.cmu.edu/Groups/AI/html/cltl/clm/node118.html

Impact: Low

Cross References: `shadow, export`

invoke-debugger

Prototype: `invoke-debugger condition`

Summary: This function invokes the debugger.

Description: This function attempts interactive handling of its argument, which must be a condition by invoking the debugger.

Risk: Functions that launch or invoke system debuggers have the ability to allow local application users to view and access sensitive memory-resident data. It is critical to control these functions to disallow users from accessing these functions. Ensure that human user input is not permitted to call these functions or directly pass data as parameters. Special characters should be stripped as a part of vetting human user input.

Additional Resources: www-2.cs.cmu.edu/Groups/AI/html/cltl/clm/node345.html

Impact: High

Cross References: `error, break`

lisp-implementation-type

Prototype: `lisp-implementation-type`

Summary: This function returns the name of the current Lisp implementation.

Description: This function returns a string identifying the name of the particular implementation in use.

Risk: This function handles system-specific sensitive information that an attacker could leverage during a period of target reconnaissance. This function should only be utilized if it is absolutely necessary for proper execution of the application. All analysis for the output of this function should be conducted securely within the application and never sent across the wire in cleartext.

Additional Resources: www-2.cs.cmu.edu/Groups/AI/html/cltl/clm/node233.html

Impact: High

Cross References: `lisp-implementation-version`

lisp-implementation-version

Prototype: `lisp-implementation-version`

Summary: This function returns the version number of the current Lisp implementation.

Description: This function returns a string identifying the version number of the particular implementation in use.

Risk: This function handles system-specific sensitive information that an attacker could leverage during a period of target reconnaissance. This function should only be utilized if it is absolutely necessary for proper execution of the application. All analysis for the output of this function should be conducted securely within the application and never sent across the wire in cleartext.

Additional Resources: www-2.cs.cmu.edu/Groups/AI/html/cltl/clm/node233.html

Impact: High

Cross References: `lisp-implementation-name`

make-random-state

Prototype: `make-random-state &;optional state`

Summary: This function returns an new random-state value.

Description: This function returns a fresh object of type random-state, suitable for use as the value of random-state. If the state is a random state object, the new-state is a copy of that object. If state is nil, the new-state is a copy of the current random state. If state is t, the new-state is a fresh random state object that has been randomly initialized by some means.

Risk: As with most standard random functions implemented within the programming and scripting libraries, this function is susceptible to bruteforce or easily guessed number generating attacks due to a poor seed algorithm within the backend code. Amongst numerous other secure random number generating functions, Microsoft .Net has secure methods for implementing properly seeded numbers. ISAAC, designed by Bob Jenkins, is a fast cryptographic random number generator is as strong as they come. Available in multiple languages, ISAAC is a standard for many freeware and commercial solutions and should be considered the next time a random number is required within an application.

Additional Resources: www-2.cs.cmu.edu/Groups/AI/html/cltl/clm/node133.html

Impact: High

Cross References: `random, random-state`

mapping

Prototype: `mapping ({({var | ({var}*)} value)}*) {declaration}* {form}*`

Summary: This macro helps specify uses of map-fn.

Description: This macro helps specify uses of map-fn where type is t and the function is a literal lambda. he binding list specifies zero or more variables that are bound in parallel to successive values of series. The value part of each pair is an expression that must produce a series. The declarations and forms are treated as the body of a lambda expression that is mapped over the series values. A series of the first values returned by this lambda expression is returned as the result of mapping.

Risk: Ensure that the output of this function is viewable only by the appropriate human-user parties and that output geared for internal application usage is vetted directly after parsing.

Additional Resources: www-2.cs.cmu.edu/Groups/AI/html/cltl/clm/ node351.html

Impact: Low

Cross References: `let`

nreverse

Prototype: `nreverse sequence`

Summary: This function returns a sequence of the same kind as a specified sequence, containing the same elements, but in reverse order.

Description: This function can modify and return a new sequence of the same kind as a sequence containing the same elements, but in reverse order. The new sequence

Risk: This function should never be utilized to obfuscate data with the goal of protecting it from prying eyes. Only industry-standard cryptography algorithms should be implemented to secure data. This function is out-of-date and should not be used!

Additional Resources: www-2.cs.cmu.edu/Groups/AI/html/cltl/clm/ node142.html

Impact: Low

Cross References: `reverse`

open

Prototype: `open filename &;key :direction :element-type :if-exists :if-does-not-exist :external-format`

Summary: This function creates, opens, and returns a file stream to the specified file.

Description: This function creates, opens, and returns a file stream connected to the specified file. The keyword arguments specify the characteristics of the file stream that is returned, and how to handle errors

Risk: All special and wildcard characters should be removed before the filename is computed on the local filesystem. Malicious filenames are interpreted differently on varying systems and as such, directory control is critical to limiting the ability of an attacker to potentially compromise files at varying levels within the application or underlying subsystem.

Additional Resources: www-2.cs.cmu.edu/Groups/AI/html/cltl/clm/node215.html

Impact: Low

Cross References: `with-open-file`, `close`, `pathname`, `logical-pathname`

open-stream-p

Prototype: `open-stream-p stream`

Summary: This function returns a Boolean value if the specified stream is open.

Description: This function returns true if a specified stream is an open stream, and otherwise returns false. Streams are open until they have been explicitly closed with close, or until they are implicitly closed.

Risk: Human users should not have the ability to execute this function at will. Control the output of this function as it may pass information to an attacker who could use it to determine targeted network and filesystem information.

Additional Resources: www-2.cs.cmu.edu/Groups/AI/html/cltl/clm/node185.html

Impact: Low

Cross References: `close`, `with-output-to-string`, `with-open-file`, `with-input-from-string`, `with-open-stream`

output-stream-p

Prototype: `output-stream-p stream`

Summary: This function returns a Boolean value if the specified stream is an output stream.

Description: This function returns `TRUE` if stream is an output stream, and otherwise returns `FALSE`.

Risk: Human users should not have the ability to execute this function at will. Control the output of this function as it may pass information to an attacker who could use it to determine targeted network and filesystem information.

Additional Resources: www-2.cs.cmu.edu/Groups/AI/html/cltl/clm/node185.html

Impact: Low

Cross References: `input-stream-p`

pathname

Prototype: `pathname pathname`

Summary: This function returns a pathname from the supplied pathname.

Description: This function returns a pathname from the supplied argument, which can be a string, symbol or stream. Pathname represents the name used to access a file. Valid pathnames consist of a host, device, directory, name, type, and version.

Risk: System path information is constantly sought after by attackers or malicious users profiling a target application or system. Path information alone can potentially identify the underlying operating system, installed applications, configurations, and in some cases user and security information. Ensure that non–alphanumeric characters are removed from the string before it is processed and that the information is only processed internally by the application. Limit the end-user's ability to ascertain or traverse path information.

Additional Resources: www-2.cs.cmu.edu/Groups/AI/html/cltl/clm/node214.html

Impact: Low

Cross References: `pathname-device`, `pathname-directory`, `pathname-host`, `pathname-match-p`, `pathname-name`, `pathname-type`, `pathname-version`, `pathnamep`

pathname-device

Prototype: `pathname-device pathname`

Summary: This function returns pathname device component from the supplied pathname.

Description: This function returns the pathname device component from the supplied pathname argument which can be a string, symbol, or stream.

Risk: System path information is constantly sought after by attackers or malicious users profiling a target application or system. Path information alone can potentially identify the underlying operating system, installed applications, configurations, and in some cases user and security information. Ensure that non-alphanumeric characters are removed from the string before it is processed and that the information is only processed internally by the application. Limit the end-user's ability to ascertain or traverse path information.

Additional Resources: www-2.cs.cmu.edu/Groups/AI/html/cltl/clm/node214.html

Impact: Low

Cross References: `pathname`, `pathname-directory`, `pathname-host`, `pathname-match-p`, `pathname-name`, `pathname-type`, `pathname-version`, `pathnamep`

pathname-directory

Prototype: `pathname-directory pathname`

Summary: This function returns the directory component from the supplied pathname.

Description: This function returns the pathname directory component from the supplied pathname argument, which can be a string, symbol, or stream.

Risk: System path information is constantly sought after by attackers or malicious users profiling a target application or system. Path information alone can potentially identify the underlying operating system, installed applications, configurations, and in some cases user and security information. Ensure that non-alphanumeric characters are removed from the string before it is processed and that the information is only processed internally by the application. Limit the end-user's ability to ascertain or traverse path information.

Additional Resources: www-2.cs.cmu.edu/Groups/AI/html/cltl/clm/node214.html

Impact: Low

Cross References: `pathname-device`, `pathname`, `pathname-host`, `pathname-match-p`, `pathname-name`, `pathname-type`, `pathname-version`, `pathnamep`

pathname-host

Prototype: `pathname-host pathname`

Summary: This function returns the host component from the supplied pathname.

Description: This function returns the pathname host component from the supplied pathname argument which can be a string, symbol or stream.

Risk: System path information is constantly sought after by attackers or malicious users profiling a target application or system. Path information alone can potentially identify the underlying operating system, installed applications, configurations, and in some cases user and security information. Ensure that non-alphanumeric characters are removed from the string before it is processed and that the information is only

processed internally by the application. Limit the end user's ability to ascertain or traverse path information.

Additional Resources: www-2.cs.cmu.edu/Groups/AI/html/cltl/clm/node214.html

Impact: Low

Cross References: `pathname-device`, `pathname-directory`, `pathname`, `pathname-match-p`, `pathname-name`, `pathname-type`, `pathname-version`, `pathnamep`

pathname-match-p

Prototype: `pathname-match-p pathname wildname`

Summary: This function returns true if a pathname matches a supplied argument.

Description: This function returns `TRUE` if a supplied wildcard and pathname arguments match, and `FALSE` otherwise.

Risk: System path information is constantly sought after by attackers or malicious users profiling a target application or system. Path information alone can potentially identify the underlying operating system, installed applications, configurations, and in some cases user and security information. Ensure that non–alphanumeric characters are removed from the string before it is processed and that the information is only processed internally by the application. Limit the end user's ability to ascertain or traverse path information.

Additional Resources: www-2.cs.cmu.edu/Groups/AI/html/cltl/clm/node207.html

Impact: Low

Cross References: `pathname-device`, `pathname-directory`, `pathname-host`, `pathname`, `pathname-name`, `pathname-type`, `pathname-version`, `pathnamep`

pathname-name

Prototype: `pathname-name pathname &;key :case`

Summary: This function returns the name component from the supplied path-name.

Description: This function returns the pathname name component from the supplied pathname argument which can be a string, symbol or stream.

Risk: System path information is constantly sought after by attackers or malicious users profiling a target application or system. Path information alone can potentially identify the underlying operating system, installed applications, configurations, and in some cases user and security information. Ensure that non-alphanumeric characters are removed from the string before it is processed and that the information is only processed internally by the application. Limit the end-user's ability to ascertain or traverse path information.

Additional Resources: www-2.cs.cmu.edu/Groups/AI/html/cltl/clm/node214.html

Impact: Low

Cross References: `pathname-device`, `pathname-directory`, `pathname-host`, `pathname-match-p`, `pathname`, `pathname-type`, `pathname-version`, `pathnamep`

pathnamep

Prototype: `pathnamep object`

Summary: This function returns TRUE if an object is a valid pathname.

Description: This function returns TRUE if an object is a valid pathname, otherwise FALSE.

Risk: System path information is constantly sought after by attackers or malicious users profiling a target application or system. Path information alone can potentially identify the underlying operating system, installed applications, configurations, and in some cases user and security information. Ensure that non-alphanumeric characters are removed from the string before it is processed and that the information is only

processed internally by the application. Limit the end-user's ability to ascertain or traverse path information.

Additional Resources: www-2.cs.cmu.edu/Groups/AI/html/cltl/clm/ node214.html

Impact: Low

Cross References: `pathname-device, pathname-directory, pathname-host, pathname-match-p, pathname-name, pathname-type, pathname-version`

pathname-type

Prototype: `pathname-type pathname &;key :case`

Summary: This function returns the type component from the supplied pathname argument.

Description: This function returns the pathname type component from the supplied pathname argument which can be a string, symbol or stream.

Risk: System path information is constantly sought after by attackers or malicious users profiling a target application or system. Path information alone can potentially identify the underlying operating system, installed applications, configurations, and in some cases user and security information. Ensure that non-alphanumeric characters are removed from the string before it is processed and that the information is only processed internally by the application. Limit the end user's ability to ascertain or traverse path information.

Additional Resources: www-2.cs.cmu.edu/Groups/AI/html/cltl/clm/ node214.html

Impact: Low

Cross References: `pathname-device, pathname-directory, pathname-host, pathname-match-p, pathname-name, pathname, pathname-version, pathnamep`

pathname-version

Prototype: `pathname-version pathname`

Summary: This function returns the version component from the supplied pathname argument.

Description: This function returns the pathname version component from the supplied pathname argument which can be a string, symbol or stream.

Risk: System path information is constantly sought after by attackers or malicious users profiling a target application or system. Path information alone can potentially identify the underlying operating system, installed applications, configurations, and in some cases user and security information. Ensure that non-alphanumeric characters are removed from the string before it is processed and that the information is only processed internally by the application. Limit the end user's ability to ascertain or traverse path information.

Additional Resources: www-2.cs.cmu.edu/Groups/AI/html/cltl/clm/node214.html

Impact: Low

Cross References: `pathname-device`, `pathname-directory`, `pathname-host`, `pathname-match-p`, `pathname-name`, `pathname-type`, `pathname`, `pathnamep`

random

Prototype: `random number &;optional state`

Summary: This function returns a random number.

Description: This function returns a pseudo-random number between zero and a supplied number.

Risk: As with most standard random functions implemented within the programming and scripting libraries, this function is susceptible to bruteforce or easily guessed number-generating attacks due to a poor seed algorithm within the backend code. Amongst numerous other secure random number generating functions, Microsoft .Net has secure methods for implementing properly seeded numbers. ISAAC,

LISP

designed by Bob Jenkins, is a fast cryptographic random number generator is as strong as they come. Available in multiple languages, ISAAC is a standard for many freeware and commercial solutions and should be considered the next time a random number is required within an application.

Additional Resources: www-2.cs.cmu.edu/Groups/AI/html/cltl/clm/node133.html

Impact: High

Cross References: `random-state, random-state-p`

random-state

Summary: This type of object contains state information used by the random number generator.

Description: This object is used to maintain the state of the random-number generator and is altered when a random operation occurs.

Risk: As with most standard random functions implemented within the programming and scripting libraries, this function is susceptible to bruteforce or easily guessed number-generating attacks due to a poor seed algorithm within the backend code. Amongst numerous other secure random number generating functions, Microsoft .Net has secure methods for implementing properly seeded numbers. ISAAC, designed by Bob Jenkins, is a fast cryptographic random number generator is as strong as they come. Available in multiple languages, ISAAC is a standard for many freeware and commercial solutions and should be considered the next time a random number is required within an application.

Additional Resources: www-2.cs.cmu.edu/Groups/AI/html/cltl/clm/node133.html

Impact: High

Cross References: `random, random-state-p`

remove

Prototype: `remove item sequence &;key :from-end :test :test-not :start :end :count :key`

Summary: This function returns a sequence without the elements satisfying the specified test.

Description: This function returns a sequence without the elements satisfying the specified test.

Risk: In addition to the potential race condition bugs that are associated with this function, a user could also attempt to execute a denial of service attack. Ensure that only one instance of this function can be called at any given moment. All input passed to this function should be analyzed closely to ensure that only desired resources can be removed from the system. It is not uncommon for worms and viruses to exploit application-layer vulnerabilities to cause damage to files they since would not have had access to.

Additional Resources: www-2.cs.cmu.edu/Groups/AI/html/cltl/clm/node144.html

Impact: Low

Cross References: `delete, delete-duplicates, delete-if, delete-if-not, delete-package, delete-file`

shadow

Prototype: `shadow symbols &;optional package`

Summary: This function assures symbols with names specified by symbol-names are present in the package.

Description: This function assures that symbols with names given by symbol-names are present in the package. Any missing symbol is created and inserted into the package as an inserted-symbol.

Risk: Under no circumstance should shadow functions be utilized to obfuscate sensitive information. Only industry-standard cryptography algorithms should be implemented to secure data. This function is out-of-date and should not be used! It is recommended that a commercially accepted encryption algorithm be utilized for any type of encryption. These types of implementations include DES, AES, Blowfish, or RSA to mention a few.

Additional Resources: www-2.cs.cmu.edu/Groups/AI/html/cltl/clm/ node118.html

Impact: High

Cross References: `package-shadowing-symbols`

shadowing-import

Prototype: `shadowing-import symbols &;optional package`

Summary: This function inserts symbols into a package as an internal symbol.

Description: This function inserts symbols into a package as an internal symbol, but does not signal an error even if the importation of a symbol would shadow some symbol already accessible in the package.

Risk: Under no circumstance should shadow functions be utilized to obfuscate sensitive information. Only industry-standard cryptography algorithms should be implemented to secure data. This function is out-of-date and should not be used! It is recommended that a commercially accepted encryption algorithm be utilized for any type of encryption. These types of implementations include DES, AES, Blowfish, or RSA to mention a few.

Additional Resources: www-2.cs.cmu.edu/Groups/AI/html/cltl/clm/ node118.html

Impact: High

Cross References: `import, unintern, package-shadowing-symbols`

software-type

Prototype: `software-type`

Summary: This function returns the name of any supporting software.

Description: This function returns a string containing the generic name of any relevant supporting software.

Risk: This function handles system-specific sensitive information that an attacker could leverage during a period of target reconnaissance. This function should only be utilized if it is absolutely necessary for proper execution of the application. All analysis for the output of this function should be conducted securely within the application and never sent across the wire in cleartext.

Additional Resources: www-2.cs.cmu.edu/Groups/AI/html/cltl/clm/node233.html

Impact: Medium

Cross References: `software-version`

software-version

Prototype: `software-version`

Summary: This function returns the version information for any supporting software.

Description: This function returns a string containing the version information for any relevant supporting software.

Risk: This function handles system-specific sensitive information that an attacker could leverage during a period of target reconnaissance. This function should only be utilized if it is absolutely necessary for proper execution of the application. All analysis for the output of this function should be conducted securely within the application and never sent across the wire in cleartext.

Additional Resources: www-2.cs.cmu.edu/Groups/AI/html/cltl/clm/node233.html

Impact: Medium

Cross References: `software-type`

warn

Prototype: `warn format-string &;rest args`

Summary: This function signals a condition or situation.

Description: This function signals a mild error with the supplied arguments.

Risk: Warning messages commonly have sensitive information that an attacker could leverage to gain a foothold on a system to potentially assist in a more complicated or dangerous attack. Language-internal warning functions are out-of-date and should not be utilized in production or publicly accessible applications.

Additional Resources: www-2.cs.cmu.edu/Groups/AI/html/cltl/clm/node343.html

Impact: Low

Cross References: `warning`

warning

Summary: This type consists of all types of warnings.

Description: This type consists of all types of warnings and is a subtype of condition.

Risk: Warning messages commonly have sensitive information that an attacker could leverage to gain a foothold on a system to potentially assist in a more complicated or dangerous attack. Language-internal warning functions are out-of-date and should not be utilized in production or publicly-accessible applications.

Additional Resources: www-2.cs.cmu.edu/Groups/AI/html/cltl/clm/node346.html

Impact: Low

Cross References: `warn, condition`

ArrayDeleteAt

Prototype: `ArrayDeleteAt(array, position)`

Summary: This function deletes an element from an array.

Description: The function attempts to delete the element located at a given position. The function has two input variables: the array and the position. The function will return TRUE if successful, and FALSE if not. The function will recalculate the indexing, as well, when deleting the member of the array. Thus, when deleting multiple elements, this fact must be considered.

Risk: Elements in an array are common targets of SQL injection and manipulation attacks in addition to cross-site scripting (CSS/XSS) attacks. These data elements are commonly stored and allowed to pass through weakly vetted input streams and during analysis within the program are executed thereby potentially putting additional data at risk. Restrict all input data for arrays that is human generated.

Impact: Low

Cross References: `ArrayInsertAt, ArrayNew, ArrayToList`

chdir

Prototype: `chdir EXPR, chdir`

Summary: This function changes the current, active directory.

Description: The function attempts to change the working directory of the active process. The function can handle one argument: the new target directory. However, if the user does not specify, the function will attempt to change the directory to the user's home directory. The function returns a Boolean value upon completion: `TRUE` for success, `FALSE` for failure.

Risk: This function poses minimal risk but the result of the changed directory should be limited to a set of directories for the desired resource—in other words, application users should not be able to point this function at any directory on the underlying subsystem. Execution and binary-residing directories are the most common targets.

Additional Resources: www.perl.org/docs.html

Impact: High

chmod

Prototype: `chmod LIST`

Summary: This function changes the permissions of a file.

Description: This function attempts to change the permissions of a list of files. The first entry of the list is the mode to which the function will change the permissions. The function will then read the list of files that follow. The function will attempt to change the permissions and will return an integer value ranging from zero to the total count of files. The function will not count in the return value any files that failed. Possible reasons for failure is not having the proper access to change the permissions of a file.

Risk: In addition to the potential race condition vulnerability that is associated with this function it also handles potentially sensitive information. The function is inherently flawed if two processes try to access and modify the permissions of a single file simultaneously, one function could receive the overriding permissions from the other. If the application is transmitting this information over the wire, it should utilize strong point-to-point encryption to ensure that an attacker could not ascertain the filename, path, old permissions, or new permissions.

Additional Resources: www.perl.org/docs.html

Impact: High

chown

Prototype: chown LIST

Summary: This function changes the owner/group associations of a file.

Description: This function attempts to change the owner of a list of files. The first entries of the list are the user ID number and group ID number for the function to use. The function will then read the list of files that follow. The function will attempt to change the ownership and will return an integer value ranging from zero to the total count of files. The function will not count in the return value any files that failed. Possible reasons for failure are not having the proper access to change the ownership of a file.

Risk: The chown function is susceptible to multiple race condition attacks whereas an attacker could attempt to modify the permissions of a file multiple times simultaneously. In addition to the race condition attacks, the chown function should only be executed on files from a local perspective due to the sensitive nature of the information required. If the application is designed to run in a distributed matter, it is pertinent that you encrypt all session data between the systems communicating, since filenames and permissions are both included.

Additional Resources: www.perl.org/docs.html

Impact: High

chroot

Prototype: `chroot DIRNAME, chroot`

Summary: This function changes the root directory of a process.

Description: The function attempts to change the root directory of the current process. The function will attempt to set the root to the path indicated in the input argument. If no argument is given, the function will attempt to set root as the user's home directory. There is no way to undo this function call, and it requires superuser access is required.

Risk: The `chroot` function is susceptible to race condition attacks thereby you must ensure that only one instance of this function can be called at any given point in time. Additionally, the `chroot` function is commonly targeted by attackers to see if they can change the root directory of a target server to that of an Internet-accessible directory. Internet accessible directories would include /public, /incoming, /ftp/public, etc. It is critical that you verify that users do not have direct access to the parameters taken by this function.

Note: This function was written for Unix-based systems.

Additional Resources: www.perl.org/docs.html

Impact: High

connect

Prototype: `connect SOCKET, NAME`

Summary: This function connects to another process.

Description: The function attempts to connect to another active process in the system. It takes two input arguments: the socket to connect to and the name of the address to connect to. The function call will expect the process it is attempting to connect to to be in a state of "accept." The function returns TRUE if successful, FALSE if not.

Risk: Processes that connect to externally available or other processes should be considered highly dangerous. Unless the goal of the application is to ascertain output from another process then that process output and direction should either not be used or called again from within the application.

Additional Resources: www.perl.org/docs.html

Impact: Low

eval

Prototype: eval STRING, eval BLOCK, eval

Summary: This function handles exceptions.

Description: The function is an overloaded form for exception handling. The function, in one form, catches errors and keeps the program running. The second form actually can compile bits of code and catch the exceptions in that. The second version is a more generalized version of the first, but is much slower. The function returns the value of the last correctly evaluated statement.

Risk: Error and exception handling could stop numerous attacks against your application gained from data ascertained from sensitive error information. All error information should be suppressed for end users and written in backend logs for administrators or developers only.

Additional Resources: www.perl.org/docs.html

Impact: Low

exec

Prototype: `exec COMMAND`

Summary: This function terminates the current Perl script and executes a command.

Description: The function executes a command given by the string `COMMAND`. The function, however, shuts down the current Perl script, and thus, can not be recovered.

Risk: This function is utilized to execute system-level commands from within an application. Executing system-level commands are one of the most dangerous types of operations that an application can hardcode into its backend logic. Multiple vectors for potential attacks are available and must be addressed to secure your application. User input should be reviewed and all non-alphanumeric characters removed. Additionally, the directory structure should be limited to include only the directory or directories where the desired executables reside. As an example, you would restrict users to running commands or executables in /user/local/bin or c:/documents and settings/userX/programs/. Lastly, all output for the application should be captured within the subprocess that has launched the executable. `Fork`, `CreateProcess`, or `CreateThread` are examples of additional functions that can be used to contain output.

Note: This function was written for Unix-based systems.

Additional Resources: www.perl.org/docs.html

Impact: High

Cross References: `system`

fcntl

Prototype: `fcntl FILEHANDLE, FUNCTION, ARG`

Summary: This function executes a file control function.

Description: The function attempts to execute a file control function on a given file. The function takes three input arguments: the file to open, the function to use, and the way in which to access the file (given as a scalar constant). The function requires (obviously) that the file control function be implemented and will cause an error if not. The function will return a value corresponding to the Unix-based function `fcntl` that gets called from within the Perl function.

Risk: Functions that execute control functions are commonly called within applications derived from static application logic. The output should be controlled and human users should be restricted from executing this function at all times!

Note: This function was written for Unix-based systems.

Additional Resources: www.perl.org/docs.html

Impact: High

Cross References: `ioctl`

fork

Prototype: `fork`

Summary: This function spawns a child process.

Description: The function spawns a new child process. This child process will be the active process until it is killed off somehow (usually with exit). The script then returns to the original process. The function will return the ID for the child process to the parent and a zero to the child.

Risk: Fork can leveraged in an attack in multiple ways and is especially common in launching Denial-of-Service attacks against the underlying operating system. Deny human users from accessing or launching this function or from controlling any type of execution for this function. Additionally, you should close all processes as soon as their execution logic is complete while being aware that it is extremely risky to ever launch a subprocess within an over-arching process.

Note: This function was written for Unix-based systems.

Additional Resources: www.perl.org/docs.html

Impact: Low

getc

Prototype: `getc FILEHANDLE, getc`

Summary: This function retrieves a character from a stream.

Description: The function attempts to retrieve a character from a stream. The function will read the next character in the stream from a file pointed to with a handle given in the input argument or if no handle is given, the standard I/O stream. It returns the value of the character captured.

Risk: This function parses input blindly. Additionally, logic should be incorporated into the application to ensure that human supplied input does not contain potentially malicious content. Data streams that are attached to external sources must first verify the integrity of those sources before interpreting and implementing the data. The destination buffer should be verified before any data is copied into memory or another data stream as to minimize the risk for an attack against a buffer overflow.

Additional Resources: www.perl.org/docs.html

Impact: Low

gethostbyaddr

Prototype: `gethostbyaddr ADDR, ADDRTYPE`

Summary: This function gets a host's name from its fully qualified address.

Description: The function attempts to get a host's name from its fully qualified address. The function has two input arguments: the address and the address type. The function is used mostly with IP addresses, and will default to that if the address type is omitted. The function returns a list containing the name, aliases, and so on associated with the address.

Risk: This function handles system-specific sensitive information that an attacker could leverage during a period of target reconnaissance. This function should only be utilized if it is absolutely necessary for proper execution of the application. All analysis for the output of this function should be conducted securely within the application and never sent across the wire in cleartext.

Additional Resources: www.perl.org/docs.html

Impact: Low

Cross References: `gethostbyname`

gethostbyname

Prototype: `gethostbyname NAME`

Summary: This function gets a host's address from its fully qualified name.

Description: The function attempts to get a host's address from its fully qualified name. The function has one input argument: the name. The function returns a list containing the address, aliases, and so on associated with the host name.

Risk: This function handles system-specific sensitive information that an attacker could leverage during a period of target reconnaissance. This function should only be utilized if it is absolutely necessary for proper execution of the application. All analysis for the output of this function should be conducted securely within the application and never sent across the wire in clear-text.

Additional Resources: www.perl.org/docs.html

Impact: Low

Cross References: `gethostbyaddr`

Perl

glob

Prototype: `glob EXPR`

Summary: This function expands a file name.

Description: The function expands a filename (taking care of wildcards, etc.). The function returns the value of the expanded name. This is the internal function that implements the '*' operator.

Risk: All special and wildcard characters should be removed before the filename is computed on the local filesystem. Malicious filenames are interpreted differently on varying systems and as such, directory control is critical to limiting the ability of an attacker to potentially compromise files at varying levels within the application or underlying subsystem.

Additional Resources: www.perl.org/docs.html

Impact: Low

ioctl

Prototype: `ioctl FILEHANDLE, FUNCTION, ARG`

Summary: This function executes an I/O control function.

Description: The function attempts to execute an I/O control function on a given file. The function takes three input arguments: the file to open, the function to use, and the way in which to access the file (given as a scalar constant). The function requires (obviously) that the I/O control function be implemented and will cause an error if not. The function will return a value corresponding to the Unix-based function `ioctl` that gets called from within the Perl function.

Risk: Functions that execute control functions are commonly called within applications derived from static application logic. The output should be controlled and human users should be restricted from executing this function at all times!

Note: This function was written for Unix-based systems.

Additional Resources: www.perl.org/docs.html

Impact: Low

Cross References: `fcntl`

kill

Prototype: `kill SIGNAL, LIST`

Summary: This function sends kill signals to processes of process groups.

Description: The function sends kill signals to a list of processes. The function has two input arguments: the signal to send and the list of processes to send it to. If the signal is negative, the function kills process groups and not just processes. The function return value is undefined.

Risk: This function can be leveraged an attack by a local user to cause disruptions in normal execution of the application. Ensure that human users do not have the ability to modify the parameters for this function nor the ability to launch this function at will. It is commonly utilized in localized Denial-of-Service attacks.

Additional Resources: www.perl.org/docs.html

Impact: Low

link

Prototype: `link OLDFILE, NEWFILE`

Summary: This function creates a link between two files.

Description: The function creates a file and links it to another file. It has two input arguments: the old file (the one to which the link will point) and the new file. The old file should be on the same file system as the new one. The function returns TRUE for success, and FALSE for failure.

Risk: Characters used in the filenames should be restricted to the alphanumeric base or less depending on the underlying operating platform. Ensure that all links are removed before the program executes or are cleaned up before program execution, in the case where a program crashes or exits unexpectedly. The link function is commonly targeted in Denial-of-Service attacks attempting to consume all of the local CPU or memory resources.

Perl

Note: This function was written for Unix-based systems.

Additional Resources: www.perl.org/docs.html

Impact: Low

Cross References: `symlink, unlink`

mkdir

Prototype: `mkdir FILENAME, MODE`

Summary: This function creates a new directory.

Description: The function attempts to create a new directory. The function has two input arguments: the new directory's name and the mode in which to create it. The function will return `TRUE` if successful, `FALSE` if not.

Risk: Users should not be given free reign with this function and should be restricted to only create directories from a desired list provided by the development team. Also limit the parent directory of the new directory to a predefined or static source thereby minimizing your risk of enabling an attacker to control your underlying operating system.

Additional Resources: www.perl.org/docs.html

Impact: Low

open

Prototype: `open FILEHANDLE, MODE, LIST`

Summary: This function opens a file.

Description: The function attempts to open a file. The function has three arguments: the filehandle to associate to the file, the mode in which to open it, and the path to the file (given by `EXPR`). The function will open the file if successful. If completed with success, the function returns a non-zero value.

Risk: All special and wildcard characters should be removed before the filename is computed on the local filesystem. Malicious filenames are interpreted differently on varying systems and as such, directory control is critical to limiting the ability of an attacker to potentially compromise files at varying levels within the application or underlying subsystem.

Additional Resources: www.perl.org/docs.html

Impact: Low

rand

Prototype: `rand EXPR`

Summary: This function generates a random number.

Description: The function attempts to generate a random number. The function has an input argument: a maximum number or ceiling for the random number. However, if an input argument is omitted, the function defaults to 1. The function produces a floating point number between 0 and the ceiling (or 1) and returns it.

Risk: As with most standard random functions implemented within the C and C++ libraries, this function is susceptible to brute-force or easily guessed number generating attacks due to a poor seed algorithm within the backend code. Amongst numerous other secure random number generating functions, Microsoft .Net has secure methods for implementing properly seeded numbers. ISAAC, designed by Bob Jenkins, is a fast cryptographic random number generator is as strong as they come. Available in multiple languages, ISAAC is a standard for many freeware and commercial solutions and should be considered the next time a random number is required within an application.

Additional Resources: www.burtleburtle.net/bob/rand/isaacafa.html, www.perl.org/docs.html

Impact: Medium

Cross References: `srand`

read

Prototype: read FILEHANDLE, $VAR, LENGTH, OFFSET

Summary: This function reads a string of data into a variable.

Description: The function will read a string a data from a file into a new variable. The function takes the file's handle, the variable to save the string to, and the length as its primary arguments. An optional offsetting argument exists (allowing the function to read into the middle of the variable). The function will return the number of bytes read, or 0 if at the end-of-file.

Risk: This function parses input blindly. Additionally, logic should be incorporated into the application to ensure that human supplied input does not contain potentially malicious content. Data streams that are attached to external sources must first verify the integrity of those sources before interpreting and implementing the data. The destination buffer should be verified before any data is copied into memory or another data stream as to minimize the risk for an attack against a buffer overflow.

Additional Resources: www.perl.org/docs.html

Impact: Low

readdir

Prototype: readdir DIRHANDLE

Summary: This function reads directory entries.

Description: The function attempts to read directory entries. The function takes the directory handle in as the input argument. It will then read the directory entries (mostly file names, etc.). It returns the entries in a LIST format, unless there are no entries, and the list is empty.

Risk: This function handles system-specific sensitive information that an attacker could leverage during a period of target reconnaissance. This function should only

be utilized if it is absolutely necessary for proper execution of the application. All analysis for the output of this function should be conducted securely within the application and never sent across the wire in cleartext.

Additional Resources: www.perl.org/docs.html

Impact: Low

rmdir

Prototype: rmdir FILENAME

Summary: This function removes an empty directory

Description: The function attempts to remove a directory. The function takes the directory name in as its input argument. The function will fail if the directory is not empty. The function returns TRUE if successful, FALSE if not.

Risk: In addition to the potential race condition bugs that are associated with this function, a user could also attempt to execute a Denial-of-Service attack. Ensure that only one instance of this function can be called at any given moment. All input passed to this function should be analyzed closely to ensure that only desired resources can be removed from the system. It is not uncommon for worms and viruses to exploit application-layer vulnerabilities to cause damage to files they since would not have had access to.

Additional Resources: www.perl.org/docs.html

Impact: Low

setpgrp

Prototype: setpgrp PID, PGRP

Summary: This function changes the active process group of a specific process.

Description: The function attempts to change the process group of a process. The function has two input arguments: the process ID and the new process group. The function requires the system call setpgrp is actually implemented, as well. The function will return TRUE if successful, FALSE if not.

Risk: Ensure that only administrative-users can modify the group of a system-level or application process.

Additional Resources: www.perl.org/docs.html

Impact: Low

setpriority

Prototype: `setpriority WHICH, WHO, PRIORITY`

Summary: This function sets the priority of a process, process group, or user.

Description: The function attempts to change the priority of a process, process group, or user. The function has three input arguments: an identifier flag (telling the function if it is changing a process, process group, or user), the ID number of the target, and the new priority. The function has set values to use for the priority. The function will return TRUE if successful, FALSE if not.

Risk: Ensure that only administrative-users can increase the priorities of a system-level or application process.

Additional Resources: www.perl.org/docs.html

Impact: Low

srand

Prototype: `srand EXPR`

Summary: This function seeds the random number generator.

Description: The function sets the seed for the random number generator `rand`. The function can handle an input argument to help set the seed. However, if omitted, the function will use a default value it takes from the kernel. The function can use the time, process ID, and so on to help facilitate the randomness of the function `rand`.

Risk: As with most standard random functions implemented within the C and C++ libraries, this function is susceptible to brute-force or easily guessed number generating attacks due to a poor seed algorithm within the backend code. Amongst numerous other secure random number generating functions, Microsoft .Net has secure methods for implementing properly seeded numbers. ISAAC, designed by Bob Jenkins, is a fast cryptographic random number generator is as strong as they come. Available in multiple languages, ISAAC is a standard for many freeware and commercial solutions and should be considered the next time a random number is required within an application.

Additional Resources: www.perl.org/docs.html

Impact: Medium

Cross References: rand

symlink

Prototype: symlink OLDFILE, NEWFILE

Summary: This function creates a symbolic link between two files.

Description: The function creates a file and symbolically links it to another file. It has two input arguments: the old file (the one to which the link will point) and the new file. The old file should be on the same file system as the new one. The function returns TRUE for success, and FALSE for failure.

Risk: Ensure that users do not have the ability to specify which files are linked together and that application logic drives this function.

Note: This function was written for Unix-based systems.

Additional Resources: www.perl.org/docs.html

Impact: Low

Cross References: link, unlink

syscall

Prototype: `syscall LIST`

Summary: This function makes a system call.

Description: The function attempts to make a system call. The function has a `LIST` input argument. The first member of the list must be the system call to use. The remaining members of the list (which are be optional) are arguments for the system call. The function returns the value that the system call returns.

Risk: This function is utilized to execute system-level commands from within an application. Executing system-level commands are one of the most dangerous types of operations that an application can hardcode into its backend logic. Multiple vectors for potential attacks are available and must be addressed to secure your application. User input should be reviewed and all non-alphanumeric characters removed. Additionally, the directory structure should be limited to include only the directory or directories where the desired executables reside. As an example, you would restrict users to running commands or executables in /user/local/bin or c:/documents and settings/userX/programs/. Lastly, all output for the application should be captured within the subprocess that has launched the executable. `Fork`, `CreateProcess`, or `CreateThread` are examples of additional functions that can be used to contain output.

Additional Resources: www.perl.org/docs.html

Impact: High

sysread

Prototype: `sysread FILEHANDLE, SCALAR, LENGTH, OFFSET`

Summary: This function reads data into a variable.

Description: The function will read a string a data from a file into a new variable. The function takes the file's handle, the variable to save the string to, and the length as its primary arguments. An optional `offsetting` argument exists (allowing the function to read into the middle of the variable). The function will return the number of bytes read, or 0 if at the end-of-file. This function is distinct from the

Perl function read because it uses the lower-level system call read in the implementation.

Risk: All special and wildcard characters should be removed before the filename is computed on the local filesystem. Malicious filenames are interpreted differently on varying systems and as such, directory control is critical to limiting the ability of an attacker to potentially compromise files at varying levels within the application or underlying subsystem.

Additional Resources: www.perl.org/docs.html

Impact: Low

system

Prototype: system COMMAND

Summary: This function executes a command.

Description: The function is practically identical to the function exec. However, the function does not kill the Perl script; it calls a fork before execution. The function takes the system command to execute in as input, and returns the exit status of the call. If the return value is wanted, there are a variety of ways to capture that.

Risk: This function is utilized to execute system-level commands from within an application. Executing system-level commands are one of the most dangerous types of operations that an application can hardcode into its backend logic. Multiple vectors for potential attacks are available and must be addressed to secure your application. User input should be reviewed and all non-alphanumeric characters removed. Additionally, the directory structure should be limited to include only the directory or directories where the desired executables reside. As an example, you would restrict users to running commands or executables in /user/local/bin or c:/documents and settings/userX/programs/. Lastly, all output for the application should be captured within the subprocess that has launched the executable. Fork, CreateProcess, or CreateThread are examples of additional functions that can be used to contain output.

Additional Resources: www.perl.org/docs.html

Impact: High

Cross References: exec

truncate

Prototype: `truncate FILEHANDLE, LENGTH`

Summary: This function truncates a file.

Description: The function attempts to truncate a given file. The function has two input arguments. The file handle of the target file is used, and the length bytes to allow (i.e., where to truncate the file). The function requires that an equivalent system call be implemented. The function returns TRUE if successful, and is undefined otherwise.

Risk: All special and wildcard characters should be removed before the filename is computed on the local filesystem. Malicious filenames are interpreted differently on varying systems and as such, directory control is critical to limiting the ability of an attacker to potentially compromise files at varying levels within the application or underlying subsystem.

Additional Resources: www.perl.org/docs.html

Impact: Low

umask

Prototype: `umask EXPR`

Summary: This function sets the umask for the process.

Description: The function changes the umask for the current process. The function takes an input argument: the new umask. The function returns the old umask if successful. It is undefined if the function fails.

Risk: Setting the umask for any file could adversely affect other applications utilizing that file. Unless this function was designed as a greater part of a umask application the function should not be used!

Additional Resources: www.perl.org/docs.html

Impact: Medium

unlink

Prototype: `unlink LIST`

Summary: This function deletes a list of files.

Description: The attempts to remove a list of files. The function will follow linked files if in a Unix-based system, and no other links point to the target. The function's only input is the list of files to delete. The function returns the number of files successfully deleted.

Risk: This function can be leveraged an attack by a local user to cause disruptions in normal execution of the application. Ensure that human users do not have the ability to modify the parameters for this function nor the ability to launch this function at will. It is commonly utilized in localized Denial-of-Service attacks.

Additional Resources: www.perl.org/docs.html

Impact: Low

Cross References: `link, symlink`

basename

Prototype: `string basename ( string path [, string suffix])`

Summary: This function is used to strip path information and file extensions from a filename.

Description: The basename function is used to remove directory information and optionally file extension from a path string for a file. The first parameter is used to determine the full path of the file. All directory names in the path defined by a "/" or "\" are removed leaving only the filename. Additionally, a suffix may be used (file extension) which will be removed from the end of the name. For example, the string variable `$path="/var/www/html/index.html"` would return `index.html` when run through basename as follows `basename($path)`. If `.html` was added as the suffix, then only `index` would be returned.

Risk: basename allows for imprecise file instructions to be sent to the systems processing. When using basename as a means to normalize filenames it is possible to interpret two different files with identical names that exist in different directory structures. This can lead to file corruption and unintentional disclosure of data. When using this function it is imperative that directory structures are not ignored.

Additional Resources: www.php.net/manual/en/function.basename.php

Impact: Low

Cross References: dirname

bzopen

Prototype: resource bzopen (string filename, string mode)

Summary: Similar to fopen, this function is used to open bzip2 files.

Description: The bzopen function is used in a manner similar to fopen, to open a bzip2 file (.bz2) These files can be opened and assigned to a resource (file pointer) with read or write capabilities which are determined based on the characters "r" and "w". The "r" stands for read and the "w" stands for write.

Risk: Anytime functions are called with system access, all parameters passed to the function from user input should be carefully analyzed to prevent access to or overwriting of system files. Additionally, this function is capable of creating files on a system. Files should never be created automatically as a result of an action such as a form submittal. Excessive submits by a malicious user can result in exhausting file nodes on the server.

Additional Resources: www.php.net/manual/en/function.bzopen.php, http:/www.php.net/manual/en/function.fopen.php

Impact: Medium

Cross References: bzread, fopen

bzread

Prototype: `string bzread ( resource bz [, int length])`

Summary: `bzread` is a function designed to read bzip2 files in a binary safe manner.

Description: The `bzread` function is used in a manner similar to `fread`, to open and read a bzip2 file (.bz2) These files can be read and assigned to a resource (file pointer) up to an integer length of bytes or the end of file character depending on which occurs first.

Risk: Anytime functions are called with system access, all parameters passed to the function from user input should be carefully analyzed to prevent access to or over-writing of system files.

Additional Resources: www.php.net/manual/en/function.bzread.php, www.php.net/manual/en/function.fread.php

Impact: Medium

Cross References: `bzopen`, `fread`

chmod

Prototype: `bool chmod ( string filename, int mode)`

Summary: Changes the mode on system files permissions.

Description: Similar to the `chmod` function found in Unix, this function allows PHP to manipulate file properties such as readable, writable, executable, etc. Note the number passed as the mode change must be represented as a 4-digit octal beginning with a zero. Unlike the Unix version of `chmod`, the PHP `chmod` function can not be interpreted.

Risk: When embedded into server functionality utilizing client input, this function allows the Web client to modify file permissions. In instances where a file is actually a symbolic link pointing to a file, the file being pointed to will change permissions, and not the symbolic link.

Additional Resources: www.php.net/manual/en/function.chmod.php

Impact: High

chown

Prototype: `bool chown ( string filename, mixed user)`

Summary: Changes ownership properties of a file.

Description: Similar to the chown function found in Unix, this function allows PHP to manipulate file properties such as user and group owner ship of a file. Note: Web servers depend on ownership of files to display content, therefore changes to file ownership may prevent files from being displayed by the Web server.

Risk: When embedded into server functionality utilizing client input, this function allows the web client to modify file ownership. In instances where a file is actually a symbolic link pointing to a file, the file being pointed to will change ownership, and not the symbolic link. Most Web servers require ownership of files in order to display their contents. Changing file ownership properties could prevent accessibility.

Additional Resources: www.php.net/manual/en/function.chown.php

Impact: High

chroot

Prototype: `bool chroot ( string directory)`

Summary: Changes the root directory.

Description: chroot changes the root directory of the current active process. This new directory is will then be used for all relative paths in execution and file access.

Risk: Allowing web users to access chroot command statements via inputs provided to the browser may allow commands in a public directory to be executed with server access permissions. Public directories are often writable, this in effect allows a malicious user to execute to execute externally written code on the system.

Additional Resources: www.php.net/manual/en/function.chroot.php

Impact: High

dirname

Prototype: `string dirname ( string path)`

Summary: Returns the directory name from a path.

Description: The `dirname` function takes an input string containing the path of a file and returns the directory containing the file from the path. In essence this function strips out the file name from the path and returns the remainder.

Risk: When parsing input data to obtain pathing for output, It is important to ensure user input does not contain strings such as `../../` which is commonly used to gain access to restricted files.

Additional Resources: www.php.net/manual/en/function.dirname.php

Impact: Low

Cross References: `basename`

eval

Prototype: `mixed eval ( string code_str)`

Summary: Executes a string as a PHP command.

Description: Takes a string containing valid PHP code and executes it. This allows administrators to store commands in a database or file and use at later times in the code. The string given to `eval` must be in proper PHP syntax including all terminating characters, or else the script will error and cause problems during execution. Additionally, any variables or other data modified as a result of the evaluation will be maintained after execution having the same scope as the calling function. On exit, this function will return null unless the execution string tells it to return another value.

Risk: This function is used to execute PHP code. Syntax errors in the string being executed can lead to errors in other areas of the code. To ensure code continues to be executed as intended it is important to guard the usage of this function carefully. Otherwise, unpredictable results may occur which can compromise the system.

Additional Resources: www.php.net/manual/en/function.eval.php

Impact: Medium

exec

Prototype: `string exec ( string command [, array &amp;output [, int &amp;return_var]])`

Summary: Executes an external command.

Description: Executes a string containing a system command or external program. The last line of the results is returned by the function. Additionally an array passed in as the second parameter will store all lines of the command's output. This information will be appended to the array the array if it is already populated.

Risk: This function executes external commands or programs with the access privileges provided by the calling user. In most cases the Web server. Anytime external code is executed on a server, restrictions need to be implemented to prevent unauthorized user access. If a user can execute custom code, it will become possible for that user to gain unauthorized access to the system.

Additional Resources: www.php.net/manual/en/function.exec.php

Impact: High

Cross References: `system`, `passthru`

fgets

Prototype: `string fgets ( resource handle [, int length])`

Summary: Return a string comprised of a line from a file.

Description: Pulls a string up to 1024 characters as a line unless otherwise specified by the length argument. The function will continue to read a line up to length characters, or until it encounters a new line/EOF character. Note if the file pointer is currently in the middle of a line, the `fgets` function will begin reading the next complete line and ignore the current line.

Risk: Results read from a file should be carefully parsed before used as program inputs. Otherwise, improper formatting can lead to data corruption in the output.

Additional Resources: www.php.net/manual/en/function.fgets.php

Impact: Low

Cross References: `fgetss`

fgetss

Prototype: `string fgetss ( resource handle [, int length [, string allowable_tags]])`

Summary: Return a string comprised of a line from a file with HTML tags taken out.

Description: Pulls a string up to 1024 characters as a line unless otherwise specified by the length argument. The function will continue to read a line up to length characters, or until it encounters a new line/EOF character. Note that if the file pointer is currently in the middle of a line, the `fgets` function will begin reading the next complete line and ignore the current line. Additionally, all html tags will be stripped from the resulting string.

Risk: Results read from a file should be carefully parsed before used as program inputs. Otherwise improper formatting can lead to data corruption in the output.

Additional Resources: www.php.net/manual/en/function.fgetss.php

Impact: Low

Cross References: `fgets`

file

Prototype: `array file ( string filename [, int use_include_path [, resource context]])`

Summary: Reads a file into an array.

Description: This function reads an entire file from a string containing the file name, into an array. Each element of the array contains the information of each line of the file, including its new line character. If file() is unable to open or otherwise access the file, it will return false. If it successfully reads the file, it will return an array containing the file data.

Risk: Results read from a file should be carefully parsed before used as program inputs. Otherwise improper formatting can lead to data corruption in the output.

Additional Resources: www.php.net/manual/en/function.file.php

Impact: Medium

filegroup

Prototype: `int filegroup ( string filename)`

Summary: Returns the group ownership of a file.

Description: Returns the file group ID of a file specified by the filename string. All file groups are returned in numerical format so you must use another function such as `posix_getgrgid()` to resolve group names.

Risk: Reveals unnecessary file information to an external user when results are passed to output screen. Additionally, may result in lower system security since it may be used to override privileges. Instead, programmers should implement system and server authentication methods.

Additional Resources: www.php.net/manual/en/function.filegroup.php

Impact: Low

Cross References: `fileowner, fileperms`

fileowner

Prototype: `int fileowner ( string filename)`

Summary: Return the owner of a file.

Description: Returns the file owner ID of a file specified by the filename string. All file owner is returned in numerical format so you must use another function such as `posix_getpwuid()` to resolve owner names.

Risk: Reveals unnecessary file information to an external user when results are passed to output screen. Additionally, may result in lower system security since it may be used to override privileges. Instead, programmers should implement system and server authentication methods.

Additional Resources: www.php.net/manual/en/function.fileowner.php

Impact: Low

Cross References: `filegroup, fileperms`

fileperms

Prototype: `int fileperms ( string filename)`

Summary: Returns permissions for a file.

Description: Returns the permissions on a file, or false if unable to obtain file access.

Risk: Reveals unnecessary file information to an external user when results are passed to output screen. Additionally, may result in lower system security since it may be used to override privileges. Instead programmers should implement system and server authentication methods.

Additional Resources: www.php.net/manual/en/function.fileperms.php

Impact: Medium

Cross References: `fileowner, filegroup`

fopen

Prototype: `resource fopen ( string filename, string mode [, bool use_include_path [, resource zcontext]])`

Summary: Opens a file or URL as a file pointer.

Description: Similar to `fopen` found in C, this function binds a file or URL to a file pointer with read or write capabilities which are determined based on the characters as follows:

'r' Open for reading only; place the file pointer at the beginning of the file.

'r+' Open for reading and writing; place the file pointer at the beginning of the file.

'w' Open for writing only; place the file pointer at the beginning of the file and truncate the file to zero length. If the file does not exist, attempt to create it.

'w+' Open for reading and writing; place the file pointer at the beginning of the file and truncate the file to zero length. If the file does not exist, attempt to create it.

'a' Open for writing only; place the file pointer at the end of the file. If the file does not exist, attempt to create it.

'a+' Open for reading and writing; place the file pointer at the end of the file. If the file does not exist, attempt to create it.

'x' Create and open for writing only; place the file pointer at the beginning of the file. If the file already exists, the `fopen()` call will fail by returning `FALSE` and generating an error of level `E_WARNING`. If the file does not exist, attempt to create it.

'x+' Create and open for reading and writing; place the file pointer at the beginning of the file. If the file already exists, the `fopen()` call will fail by returning `FALSE` and generating an error of level `E_WARNING`. If the file does not exist, attempt to create it.

Risk: Anytime functions are called with system access, all parameters passed to the function from user input should be carefully analyzed to prevent access to or over-writing of system files. Additionally, this function is capable of creating files on a system. Files should never be created automatically as a result of an action such as a form submittal. Excessive submits by a malicious user can result in exhausting file nodes on the server.

Additional Resources: www.php.net/manual/en/function.fopen.php

Impact: Low

Cross References: `bzopen`, `bzread`

fread

Prototype: `string fread ( resource handle, int length)`

Summary: Reads up to length bytes from a file pointer.

Description: Pulls a string up to 1024 characters from a file unless otherwise specified by the length argument. The function will continue to read a file up to length characters, or until it encounters a new line/EOF character.

Risk: Anytime functions are called with system access, all parameters passed to the function from user input should be carefully analyzed to prevent access to or overwriting of system files.

Additional Resources: www.php.net/manual/en/function.fread.php

Impact: Low

Cross References: `bzopen`, `bzread`

fscanf

Prototype: `mixed fscanf ( resource handle, string format [, mixed &amp;...])`

Summary: Reads a file and parses input based on c-style `scanf` formatting.

Description: This function is similar to the `fscanf` function found in C. It is used to read input from a file in a specified format. The format string is composed of zero or more directives: ordinary characters (excluding %) that are copied directly to the result, and conversion specifications, each of which results in fetching its own parameter. The following are the types of directives usable by `fscanf`.

% A literal percent character. No argument is required.

b The argument is treated as an integer, and presented as a binary number.

c The argument is treated as an integer, and presented as the character with that ASCII value.

d The argument is treated as an integer, and presented as a (signed) decimal number.

e The argument is treated as scientific notation (e.g., 1.2e+2).

u The argument is treated as an integer, and presented as an unsigned decimal number.

f The argument is treated as a float, and presented as a floating-point number.

o The argument is treated as an integer, and presented as an octal number.

s The argument is treated as and presented as a string.

x The argument is treated as an integer and presented as a hexadecimal number (with lowercase letters).

X The argument is treated as an integer and presented as a hexadecimal number (with uppercase letters).

Risk: Results read from a file should be carefully parsed before used as program inputs. Otherwise, improper formatting can lead to data corruption in the output.

Additional Resources: www.php.net/manual/en/function.fscanf.php

Impact: Low

Cross References: `bzopen`, `bzread`, `fopen`, `fread`

fsockopen

Prototype: `resource fsockopen ( string target, int port [, int &amp;errno [, string &amp;errstr [, float timeout]]])`

Summary: Opens a network socket connection.

Description: Creates a socket connection and returns a file pointer to the socket on success. If the connection fails, then `fsockopen` returns a false.

Risk: Opens a network socket which may be used by an attacker to gain access to the system. When using sockets, one should carefully regulate all incoming and outgoing data traffic.

Additional Resources: www.php.net/manual/en/function.fsockopen.php

Impact: High

Cross References: `pfsockopen`

getallheaders

Prototype: `array getallheaders ( void )`

Summary: Gets all HTTP request headers.

Description: `Getallheaders()` returns an associative array of all the HTTP headers in the current request. This is only supported when PHP runs as an Apache module. It is essentially an alias of `apache_request_headers()`.

Risk: When used to process all headers in the array as a whole, malicious users could pass custom headers to pass to the server for processing. Instead of retrieving all headers one should query specific headers for information.

Additional Resources: www.php.net/manual/en/function.getallheaders.php

Impact: Medium

getenv

Prototype: `string getenv ( string varname)`

Summary: Returns an environment variable.

Description: Returns the value of the environment variable requested as a string `varname`, or `FALSE` if there is an error.

Risk: May reveal sensitive system information that can lead to further understanding and ability to gain control of a system.

Additional Resources: www.php.net/manual/en/function.getenv.php

Impact: Medium

gzfile

Prototype: `array gzfile ( string filename [, int use_include_path])`

Summary: Reads a gzip file into an array.

Description: This function reads an entire file from a string containing the file name, into an array. Each element of the array contains the information of each line of the file, including its new line character. If file() is unable to open or otherwise access the file, it will return false. If it successfully reads the file, it will return an array containing the file data.

Risk: Results read from a file should be carefully parsed before used as program inputs. Otherwise improper formatting can lead to data corruption in the output.

Additional Resources: www.php.net/manual/en/function.gzfile.php

Impact: Low

Cross References: gzgetc, gzgets, gzgetss, gzopen, gzread

gzgetc

Prototype: `string gzgetc ( resource zp)`

Summary: Read a character from a gzip file pointer.

Description: Reads a single uncompressed character at a time from a gzip-compressed file. The file pointer must be a gz file pointer handling gzip file.

Risk: Results read from a file should be carefully parsed before used as program inputs. Otherwise, improper formatting can lead to data corruption in the output.

Additional Resources: www.php.net/manual/en/function.gzgetc.php

Impact: Low

Cross References: gzfile, gzgets, gzgetss, gzopen, gzread

gzgets

Prototype: `string gzgets ( resource zp, int length)`

Summary: Reads a line from a gzip file.

Description: Pulls a string up to 1024 characters as a line unless otherwise specified by the length argument from a gzip file. The function will continue to read a line up to length characters, or until it encounters a new line/EOF character. Note if the file pointer is currently in the middle of a line, the fgets function will begin reading the next complete line and ignore the current line.

Risk: Results read from a file should be carefully parsed before used as program inputs. Otherwise improper formatting can lead to data corruption in the output.

Additional Resources: www.php.net/manual/en/function.gzgets.php

Impact: Low

Cross References: gzgetc, gzfile, gzgetss, gzopen, gzread

gzgetss

Prototype: string gzgetss (resource zp, int length [, string allowable_tags])

Summary: Reads a line from a file while stripping HTML tags.

Description: Pulls a string up to 1024 characters as a line unless otherwise specified by the length argument from a gzip file. The function will continue to read a line up to length characters, or until it encounters a new line/EOF character. Note if the file pointer is currently in the middle of a line, the fgets function will begin reading the next complete line and ignore the current line. Additionally all html tags will be stripped from the resulting string.

Risk: Results read from a file should be carefully parsed before used as program inputs. Otherwise, improper formatting can lead to data corruption in the output.

Additional Resources: www.php.net/manual/en/function.gzgetss.php

Impact: Low

Cross References: gzgetc, gzgets, gzfile, gzopen, gzread

gzopen

Prototype: resource gzopen (string filename, string mode [, int use_include_path])

Summary: Opens a gzip file.

Description: The gzopen function is used in a manner similar to fopen, to open a gzip file (.gz) These files can be opened and assigned to a resource (file pointer)

PHP

with read or write capabilities which are determined based on the characters "r" and "w". The "r" stands for read and the "w" stands for write.

Risk: Anytime functions are called with system access, all parameters passed to the function from user input should be carefully analyzed to prevent access to or over-writing of system files. Additionally, this function is capable of creating files on a system. Files should never be created automatically as a result of an action such as a form submittal. Excessive submits by a malicious user can result in exhausting file nodes on the server.

Additional Resources: www.php.net/manual/en/function.gzopen.php

Impact: Low

Cross References: `gzgetc, gzgets, gzgetss, gzfile, gzread`

gzread

Prototype: `string gzread ( resource zp, int length)`

Summary: Read up to length bytes from a gzip file.

Description: The `gzread` function is used in a manner similar to `fread`, to open and read a gzip file (.gz). These files can be read and assigned to a resource (file pointer) up to an integer length of bytes or the end of file character depending on which occurs first.

Risk: Anytime functions are called with system access, all parameters passed to the function from user input should be carefully analyzed to prevent access to or over-writing of system files.

Additional Resources: www.php.net/manual/en/function.gzread.php

Impact: Low

Cross References: `gzgetc, gzgets, gzgetss, gzopen, gzfile`

Highlight_file

Prototype: `mixed highlight_file ( string filename [, bool return])`

Summary: Outputs a file with syntax highlights.

Description: Reads in the file addressed by the string `filename` and outputs it with highlighted syntax information for code contained in the file. When the second argument is set to true, the highlighted code will be returned as a string instead of being sent to output.

Risk: May be used by a malicious user to gain further understanding on how to use a particular function or file in the server path.

Additional Resources: www.php.net/manual/en/function.highlight_file.php, www.php.net/manual/en/function.show_source.php

Impact: Low

is_dir

Prototype: `bool is_dir ( string filename)`

Summary: Determines whether a file is a directory.

Description: Checks to see if a file exists and is a directory. If these conditions are true, it will return true, otherwise it will return false.

Risk: `Is_dir` can be used to determine file properties which may help an attacker determine vital information about a specific file, which may assist in an attack.

Additional Resources: www.php.net/manual/en/function.is_dir.php

Impact: Low

Cross References: `is_executable`, `is_file`, `is_link`, `is_readable`, `is_writable`, `is_writeable`

is_executable

Prototype: `bool is_executable ( string filename)`

Summary: Determines whether a file is an executable

Description: Checks to see if a file exists and is executable. If these conditions are true it will return true, otherwise it will return false.

Risk: is_executable can be used to determine file properties which may help an attacker determine vital information about a specific file, which may assist in an attack.

Additional Resources: www.php.net/manual/en/function.is_executable.php

Impact: Low

Cross References: is_dir, is_file, is_link, is_readable, is_writable, is_writeable

is_file

Prototype: bool is_file (string filename)

Summary: Determines whether a file is a regular file.

Description: Checks to see if a file exists and is an actual file. If these conditions are true, it will return true, otherwise it will return false.

Risk: is_file can be used to determine file properties that may help an attacker determine vital information about a specific file, which may assist in an attack.

Additional Resources: www.php.net/manual/en/function.is_file.php

Impact: Low

Cross References: is_executable, is_dir, is_link, is_readable, is_writable, is_writeable

is_link

Prototype: bool is_link (string filename)

Summary: Determines whether a file is a link.

Description: Checks to see if a file exists and is a link. If these conditions are true it will return true, otherwise it will return false.

Risk: is_link can be used to determine file properties that may help an attacker determine vital information about a specific file, which may assist in an attack.

Additional Resources: www.php.net/manual/en/function.is_link.php

Impact: Low

Cross References: is_executable, is_file, is_dir, is_readable, is_writable, is_writeable

is_readable

Prototype: bool is_readable (string filename)

Summary: Determines whether a file is readable.

Description: Checks to see if a file exists and is a readable. If these conditions are true, it will return true, otherwise it will return false.

Risk: is_readable can be used to determine file properties that may help an attacker determine vital information about a specific file, which may assist in an attack.

Additional Resources: www.php.net/manual/en/function.is_readable.php

Impact: Low

Cross References: is_executable, is_file, is_link, is_dir, is_writable, is_writeable

is_writable

Prototype: bool is_writable (string filename)

Summary: Determines whether a file is writable.

Description: Checks to see if a file exists and is writable. If these conditions are true, it will return true, otherwise it will return false.

Risk: is_writable can be used to determine file properties that may help an attacker determine vital information about a specific file, which may assist in an attack.

Additional Resources: www.php.net/manual/en/function.is_writable.php, www.php.net/manual/en/function.is_writeable.php

Impact: Low

Cross References: is_executable, is_file, is_link, is_readable, is_dir, is_writeable

is_writeable

Prototype: bool is_writeable (string filename)

Summary: Determines whether a file is writeable.

Description: An alias of is_writable(). Checks to see if a file exists and is writable. If these conditions are true, it will return true, otherwise it will return false.

Risk: is_writeable can be used to determine file properties that may help an attacker determine vital information about a specific file, which may assist in an attack.

Additional Resources: www.php.net/manual/en/function.is_writeable.php, www.php.net/manual/en/function.is_writable.php

Impact: Low

Cross References: is_executable, is_file, is_link, is_readable, is_writable, is_dir

leak

Prototype: void leak (int bytes)

Summary: Leaks a specific amount of memory.

Description: Used to dump out leaked memory before the memory manager has a chance to clean up leaked memory.

Risk: When using dynamic memory, it is possible to lose sensitive information in memory. If this memory is then leaked to an outside source, information can be exposed to a malicious user.

Additional Resources:
http://aspn.activestate.com/ASPN/docs/PHP/function.leak.html

Impact: High

PHP

link

Prototype: `bool link ( string target, string link)`

Summary: Creates a hard link to a target.

Description: Creates a hard link to a file; returning TRUE on success and FALSE on failure.

Risk: Creating links to files may allow users to gain access to information while simultaneously overriding file permissions. Since the link can have different access rights than the file, users unauthorized to access the file may still access the link. Additionally, this function is capable of creating files on a system. Files should never be created automatically as a result of an action such as a form submittal. Excessive submits by a malicious user can result in exhausting file nodes on the server.

Additional Resources: www.php.net/manual/en/function.link.php

Impact: Low

Cross References: `unlink`

lstat

Prototype: `array lstat ( string filename)`

Summary: Provides statistics for a file.

Description: Returns the status of a file or symbolic link. Nearly identical to `stat()` except it does not follow the link and display target file info, it returns status of the link itself.

Risk: May reveal sensitive system information that can lead to further understanding and ability to gain control of a system.

Additional Resources: www.php.net/manual/en/function.lstat.php

Impact: Low

Cross References: `stat`

mkdir

Prototype: `bool mkdir ( string pathname [, int mode [, bool recursive [, resource context]]])`

Summary: Creates a directory.

Description: Similar to the `mkdir` command in Unix, this function creates a directory with the 0777 permission set. This allows full access to the directory by all users. File permissions can be set in the second argument as a 4-digit octal number with leading zero.

Risk: Anytime functions are called with system access, all parameters passed to the function from user input should be carefully analyzed to prevent access to or over-writing of system files. Additionally, this function is capable of creating files on a system. Files should never be created automatically as a result of an action such as a form submittal. Excessive submits by a malicious user can result in exhausting file nodes on the server.

Additional Resources: www.php.net/manual/en/function.mkdir.php

Impact: Low

Cross References: `opendir`, `rmdir`

opendir

Prototype: `resource opendir ( string path)`

Summary: Opens a directory handle.

Description: Opens a directory to be read from and later closed. Is only affective if directory permissions allow access.

Risk: Anytime functions are called with system access, all parameters passed to the function from user input should be carefully analyzed to prevent access to or over-writing of system files. Additionally, this function is capable of creating files on a system. Files should never be created automatically as a result of an action such as a form submittal. Excessive submits by a malicious user can result in exhausting file nodes on the server.

Additional Resources: www.php.net/manual/en/function.opendir.php

Impact: Low

Cross References: `mkdir`, `rmdir`

passthru

Prototype: `void passthru ( string command [, int &amp;return_var])`

Summary: Executes an external command and displays raw output.

Description: A binary safe execution command similar to `exec` and `system`. This function executes external commands and returns output to display.

Risk: This function executes external commands or programs with the access privileges provided by the calling user. In most cases the Web server. Anytime external code is executed on a server, restrictions need to be implemented to prevent unauthorized user access. If a user can execute custom code, it will become possible for that user to gain unauthorized access to the system.

Additional Resources: www.php.net/manual/en/function.passthru.php

Impact: High

Cross References: `system`, `exec`

pfsockopen

Prototype: `resource pfsockopen ( string hostname, int port [, int &amp;errno [, string &amp;errstr [, int timeout]]])`

Summary: Open a persistent network socket.

Description: Opens a network socket connection similar to `fsockopen`. Unlike `fsockopen`, this connection is persistent and is maintained even after script completion.

Risk: Opens a persistent network socket that maybe used by an attacker to gain access to the system. When using sockets, one should carefully regulate all incoming and outgoing data traffic.

Additional Resources: www.php.net/manual/en/function.pfsockopen.php

Impact: High

Cross References: `fsockopen`

popen

Prototype: `resource popen ( string command, string mode)`

Summary: Creates a file pointer to a process fork.

Description: Opens a special file pointer, which serves as a unidirectional communication pipe to a forked command process.

Risk: Anytime functions are called with system access, all parameters passed to the function from user input should be carefully analyzed to prevent access to or overwriting of system files. Additionally, this function is capable of creating files on a system. Files should never be created automatically as a result of an action such as a form submittal. Excessive submits by a malicious user can result in exhausting file nodes on the server.

Additional Resources: www.php.net/manual/en/function.popen.php

Impact: Low

posix_getlogin

Prototype: `string posix_getlogin (void)`

Summary: Returns the login name for the current process owner.

Description: Returns the login name for the owner of the current running process. Usually the process executing the PHP file.

Risk: May reveal sensitive system information that can lead to further understanding and ability to gain control of a system.

Additional Resources: www.php.net/manual/en/function.posix_getlogin.php

Impact: Medium

Cross References: `posix_mkfifo`, `posix_ttyname`

posix_mkfifo

Prototype: `bool posix_mkfifo ( string pathname, int mode)`

Summary: Creates a named bidirectional pipe.

Description: Creates a special FIFO file which serves as a bidirectional communication pipe for different process. Permissions can be set on this file with the second mode argument, which is comprised of a 4-digit octal with a leading zero.

Risk: Opens a bidirectional communication pipe that maybe used by an attacker to gain access to the system. When using FIFOs, one should carefully regulate all incoming and outgoing data traffic.

Additional Resources: www.php.net/manual/en/function.posix_mkfifo.php

Impact: Medium

Cross References: `posix_getlogin`, `posix_ttyname`

posix_ttyname

Prototype: `string posix_ttyname ( int fd)`

Summary: Returns the terminal device name.

Description: Returns the terminal device name of the current process.

Risk: May reveal sensitive system information that can lead to further understanding and ability to gain control of a system.

Additional Resources: www.php.net/manual/en/function.posix_ttyname.php

Impact: Medium

Cross References: `posix_mkfifo`, `posix_getlogin`

readfile

Prototype: `int readfile ( string filename [, bool use_include_path [, resource context]])`

Summary: Outputs a file.

PHP

Description: Reads a file and prints it to the output buffer then returns the number of bytes read if successful.

Risk: Results read from a file should be carefully parsed before used as program inputs. Otherwise, improper formatting can lead to data corruption in the output.

Additional Resources: www.php.net/manual/en/function.readfile.php

Impact: Low

rename

Prototype: `bool rename ( string oldname, string newname [, resource context])`

Summary: Renames a file or directory.

Description: Renames a file directly from the old name to a new name specified by the first and second arguments respectively.

Risk: If malicious users are able to discern file execution based on paths, he may be able to move malicious code into it the execution path using this function to rename directories or files.

Additional Resources: www.php.net/manual/en/function.rename.php

Impact: Low

rmdir

Prototype: `bool rmdir ( string dirname [, resource context])`

Summary: Deletes a directory.

Description: Removes a directory of the provided name if the directory is empty. If the directory is not empty, it returns false and does not remove the directory. Otherwise it returns true and removes the directory.

Risk: Since this function is capable of deleting directories from the system, usage of this function should be carefully controlled to prevent the accidental or malicious deletion of critical files.

Additional Resources: www.php.net/manual/en/function.rmdir.php

Impact: Low

Cross References: `opendir`, `mkdir`

show_source

Prototype: `mixed show_source ( string filename [, bool return])`

Summary: Outputs a file with syntax highlights

Description: An alias for `highlight_file`. Reads in the file addressed by the string `filename` and outputs it with highlighted syntax information for code contained in the file. When the second argument is set to true, the highlighted code will be returned as a string instead of being sent to output.

Risk: Maybe be used by a malicious user to gain further understanding on how to use a particular function or file in the server path.

Additional Resources: www.php.net/manual/en/function.show_source.php, www.php.net/manual/en/function.highlight_file.php

Impact: Low

stat

Prototype: `array stat ( string filename)`

Summary: Returns information about a file.

Description: Creates an array of statistical information about a file. If the file is actually a symbolic link, it will create statistics on the file pointed to by the link.

Numeric	Associative	Description
0	dev	device number
1	ino	inode number
2	mode	inode protection mode
3	nlink	number of links
4	uid	userid of owner
5	gid	groupid of owner

PHP

6	rdev	device type, if inode device★
7	size	size in bytes
8	atime	time of last access (Unix timestamp
9	mtime	time of last modification (Unix timestamp)
10	ctime	tine of last inode change (Unix timestamp
11	clksize	blocksize of filesystem IO★
12	blocks	number of blocks allocated

Risk: May reveal sensitive system information which can lead to further understanding and ability to gain control of a system.

Additional Resources: www.php.net/manual/en/function.stat.php

Impact: Medium

Cross References: lstat

symlink

Prototype: `bool symlink ( string target, string link)`

Summary: Creates a symbolic link.

Description: Much like the `syslink` command in Unix, this function creates a symbolic link with a specifiable name to a target file or directory.

Risk: Creating links to files may allow users to gain access to information while simultaneously overriding file permissions. Since the link can have different access rights than the file, users unauthorized to access the file may still access the link. Additionally, this function is capable of creating files on a system. Files should never be created automatically as a result of an action such as a form submittal. Excessive submits by a malicious user can result in exhausting file nodes on the server.

Additional Resources: www.php.net/manual/en/function.symlink.php

Impact: High

Cross References: link, unlink

system

Prototype: `string system ( string command [, int &amp;return_var])`

Summary: Executes an external command and displays program output.

Description: This function executes an external command. The results of the program will then be output to the screen unless output to a file or written to a variable. The PHP script will wait for program completion if output is sent directly to the display.

Risk: This function executes external commands or programs with the access privileges provided by the calling user. In most cases the Web server. Anytime external code is executed on a server, restrictions need to be implemented to prevent unauthorized user access. If a user can execute custom code, it will become possible for that user to gain unauthorized access to the system.

Additional Resources: www.php.net/manual/en/function.system.php

Impact: High

Cross References: `exec`, `passthru`

unlink

Prototype: `bool unlink ( string filename [, resource context])`

Summary: Deletes a file.

Description: Used to delete a file from the system. Returns a Boolean value signifying true for success and false for failure.

Risk: Since this function is capable of deleting files from the system, usage of this function should be carefully controlled to prevent the accidental or malicious deletion of critical files.

Additional Resources: www.php.net/manual/en/function.unlink.php

Impact: Low

Cross References: `link`, `symlink`

Programmer's Ultimate Security DeskRef: Python

betavariate

Prototype: `betavariate(alpha, beta)`

Summary: This function draws a pseudo-random number from a beta distribution.

Description: The function generates a pseudo-random number from the beta probability distribution. The function requires two input arguments: the alpha and beta parameters for the distribution. To generate the Beta distribution, both `alpha` and `beta` must be less than -1. The function returns a number between 0 and 1.

Risk: As with most standard random functions implemented within the C and C++ libraries, this function is susceptible to brute-force or easily guessed number generating attacks due to a poor seed algorithm within the backend code. Amongst numerous other secure random number generating functions, Microsoft .Net has secure methods for implementing properly seeded numbers. ISAAC, designed by Bob Jenkins, is a fast cryptographic random number generator is as strong as they come. Available in multiple languages, ISAAC is a standard for many freeware and commercial solutions and should be considered the next time a random number is required within an application.

Additional Resources: www.burtleburtle.net/bob/rand/isaacafa.html, www.python.org/doc/

Impact: Medium

chmod

Prototype: chmod(path, mode)

Summary: This function is used to change the permissions of a file.

Description: The function attempts to change the permissions of a file. The function requires two input arguments: the path to the file and the accessibility to change it to. The function returns a Boolean value depending on the success of the change. The function returns a 1 if successful and 0 if not.

Risk: In addition to the potential race condition vulnerability that is associated with this function it also handles potentially sensitive information. The function is inherently flawed if two processes try to access and modify the permissions of a single file simultaneously, one function could receive the overriding permissions from the other. If the application is transmitting this information over the wire, it should utilize strong point-to-point encryption to ensure that an attacker could not ascertain the filename, path, old permissions, or new permissions.

Additional Resources: www.python.org/doc/

Impact: Medium

choice

Prototype: choice(seq)

Summary: This function is used to draw a random element from a given sequence.

Description: This function is used to simulate a random choice from a sequence. The function requires only one input argument: the sequence to choose the value from. The function can choose from any sequence. It returns the "chosen" value.

Risk: As with most standard random functions implemented within the C and C++ libraries, this function is susceptible to brute-force or easily guessed number generating attacks due to a poor seed algorithm within the backend code. Amongst numerous other secure random number generating functions, Microsoft .Net has secure methods for implementing properly seeded numbers. ISAAC, designed by Bob Jenkins, is a fast cryptographic random number generator is as strong as they come. Available in multiple languages, ISAAC is a standard for many freeware and commercial solutions and should be considered the next time a random number is required within an application.

Additional Resources: www.python.org/doc/

Impact: Medium

chown

Prototype: chown(path, uid, gid)

Summary: This function is used to change the ownership of a file.

Description: The function attempts to change the ownership of a given file. It can attempt to change the individual and group ownership associated with the file. The function requires three input values: the path to the file, the user identification for the new owner, and the group identifier. The function will return a 1 upon completion, and a 0 in the event of failure.

Risk: The chown function is susceptible to multiple race condition attacks whereas an attacker could attempt to modify the permissions of a file multiple times simultaneously. In addition to the race condition attacks, the chown function should only be executed on files from a local perspective due to the sensitive nature of the information required. If the application is designed to run in a distributed matter, it is pertinent that you encrypt all session data between the systems communicating, since filenames and permissions are both included.

Additional Resources: www.python.org/doc/

Impact: High

compile

Prototype: `compile(string, filename, kind[, flags[, dont_inherit]])`

Summary: This function is used to compile a code object.

Description: This function is used to compile code into an executable code object. The function takes three input parameters: the string for compilation, the filename, and the kind of code to compile. The function also takes two optional input arguments: a set of flags for the compiler and a tag for whether to inherit those flags. The function returns a `1` if successful, and `0` if not.

Risk: Python is an interpreted scripting language. The `compile` function should be controlled by internal application logic only. Restrict human input for secure usage!

Additional Resources: www.python.org/doc/

Impact: Medium

cunifvariate

Prototype: `cunifvariate(mean, arc)`

Summary: This function draws a pseudo-random number from a circular-uniform distribution.

Description: The function generates a pseudo-random number from the circular-uniform probability distribution. The function requires two input arguments: the mean angle and arc (range of motion) parameters for the distribution. To generate the distribution, both mean and arc must be between 0 and pi. The function returns a normalized value between 0 and pi.

Risk: As with most standard random functions implemented within the C and C++ libraries, this function is susceptible to brute-force or easily guessed number generating attacks due to a poor seed algorithm within the backend code. Amongst numerous other secure random number generating functions, Microsoft .Net has secure methods for implementing properly seeded numbers. ISAAC, designed by Bob Jenkins, is a fast cryptographic random number generator is as strong as they

come. Available in multiple languages, ISAAC is a standard for many freeware and commercial solutions and should be considered the next time a random number is required within an application.

Additional Resources: www.burtleburtle.net/bob/rand/isaacafa.html, www.python.org/doc/

Impact: Medium

eval

Prototype: `eval(expression[, globals[, locals]])`

Summary: This function is used to evaluate an expression in the shell.

Description: The function attempts to evaluate a given expression in the shell. It has one required input argument: the expression. However, the function can handle lists of global and local parameters to be used in the shell. These lists are both optional. The function will return the value that the shell receives from the evaluated expression.

Risk: This function is utilized to execute system-level commands from within an application. Executing system-level commands are one of the most dangerous types of operations that an application can hardcode into its backend logic. Multiple vectors for potential attacks are available and must be addressed to secure your application. User input should be reviewed and all non-alphanumeric characters removed. Additionally, the directory structure should be limited to include only the directory or directories where the desired executables reside. As an example, you would restrict users to running commands or executables in /user/local/bin or c:/documents and settings/userX/programs/. Lastly, all output for the application should be captured within the subprocess that has launched the executable. `Fork`, `CreateProcess`, or `CreateThread` are examples of additional functions that can be used to contain output.

Additional Resources: www.python.org/doc/

Impact: High

execfile

Prototype: `execfile(filename[, globals[, locals]])`

Summary: This function is used to execute a file in the shell.

Description: The function attempts to execute a given file in the shell. It has one required input argument: the filename. However, the function can handle lists of global and local parameters to be used in execution in the shell. These lists are both optional. The function will return the value that the shell receives from the executed program/file.

Risk: This function has the ability to execute a file on the local system. Attackers commonly target functions similar to this since they have the ability to launch potentially dangerous or malicious executables with differing privileges. It is imperative that you filter all input and never allow a user direct access to passing variables as the parameters for this function. Ensure that all special characters are stripped before the data is parsed and passed in addition to limiting access to only the desired executables. Lastly, require that all executable output is controlled within a forked or spawned process within the local application to ensure the integrity of the outputted data. If possible, avoid calling dynamic programs from within applications. Static program execution is more secure.

Additional Resources: www.python.org/doc/

Impact: High

execl

Prototype: `execl (path, arg0, ...)`

Summary: This function is used to execute a command.

Description: The function will execute a file pointed to by the argument `path`, which contains the path to file to be executed. The other input arguments (`arg0`, `arg1, ..., argN`) are command-line parameters to be used in the execution of the file. Ideally, the function does not return a value, as it does not return to the calling process.

Risk: This function is utilized to execute system-level commands from within an application. Executing system-level commands are one of the most dangerous types of operations that an application can hardcode into its backend logic. Multiple vectors for potential attacks are available and must be addressed to secure your application. User input should be reviewed and all non-alphanumeric characters removed. Additionally, the directory structure should be limited to include only the directory or directories where the desired executables reside. As an example, you would restrict users to running commands or executables in /user/local/bin or c:/documents and settings/userX/programs/. Lastly, all output for the application should be captured within the subprocess that has launched the executable. `Fork`, `CreateProcess`, or `CreateThread` are examples of additional functions that can be used to contain output.

Additional Resources: www.python.org/doc/

Impact: High

execle

Prototype: `execle ( path, arg0, … , envp )`

Summary: This function executes a file with control given over the environmental parameters.

Description: The function will execute a file pointed to by the argument `path`, which contains the path to file to be executed. The second set of input arguments (`arg0`, `arg1`, ..., `argN`) are command-line parameters to be used in the execution of the file. The final input argument is the array of pointers to environmental parameters needed for file execution. Like `_execl`, the function does not return a value unless an error occurs, as it does not return to the calling process. However, upon an error, a value of -1 is returned and the global variable ERRNO is set.

Risk: This function has the ability to execute a file on the local system. Attackers commonly target functions similar to this since they have the ability to launch potentially dangerous or malicious executables with differing privileges. It is imperative that you filter all input and never allow a user direct access to passing variables as the parameters for this function. Ensure that all special characters are stripped before the data is parsed and passed in addition to limiting access to only the desired executables. Lastly, require that all executable output is controlled within a forked or spawned process within the local application to ensure the integrity of the outputted data. If possible, avoid calling dynamic programs from within applications. Static program execution is more secure.

Additional Resources: www.python.org/doc/

Impact: High

execlp

Prototype: `execlp( filename, arg0, ... )`

Summary: This function executes a file from within the current shell, searching for it from the `PATH` environment variable.

Description: The function will execute a file pointed to by the argument `file-name`, searching in the system's `PATH` for the file. The other input arguments (`arg0`, `arg1`, ..., `argN`) are command-line parameters to be used in the execution of the file. Ideally, the function does not return a value, as it does not return to the calling process. However, upon an error, a value of `-1` is returned and the global variable `ERRNO` is set.

Risk: This function has the ability to execute a file on the local system. Attackers commonly target functions similar to this since they have the ability to launch potentially dangerous or malicious executables with differing privileges. It is imperative that you filter all input and never allow a user direct access to passing variables as the parameters for this function. Ensure that all special characters are stripped before the data is parsed and passed in addition to limiting access to only the desired executables. Lastly, require that all executable output is controlled within a forked or spawned process within the local application to ensure the integrity of the outputted data. If possible, avoid calling dynamic programs from within applications. Static program execution is more secure.

Additional Resources: www.python.org/doc/

Impact: High

execv

Prototype: `execv( path, argv )`

Summary: This function executes a file with an array of pointers to be passed to the command line.

Description: The function will execute a file pointed to by the argument `path`, which contains the path to file to be executed. The other input argument, `argv`, is an array command-line parameter used in the execution of the file. Ideally, the function does not return a value, as it does not return to the calling process. However, upon an error, a value of -1 is returned and the global variable ERRNO is set.

Risk: This function has the ability to execute a file on the local system. Attackers commonly target functions similar to this since they have the ability to launch potentially dangerous or malicious executables with differing privileges. It is imperative that you filter all input and never allow a user direct access to passing variables as the parameters for this function. Ensure that all special characters are stripped before the data is parsed and passed in addition to limiting access to only the desired executables. Lastly, require that all executable output is controlled within a forked or spawned process within the local application to ensure the integrity of the outputted data. If possible, avoid calling dynamic programs from within applications. Static program execution is more secure.

Additional Resources: www.python.org/doc/

Impact: High

execve

Prototype: `execve( path, argv, envp )`

Summary: This function executes a file with an array of pointers to be passed to the command line, keeping control over the environmental parameters.

Description: The function will execute a file pointed to by the argument `path`, which contains the path to file to be executed. The next input argument, `argv`, is an array command-line parameter used in the execution of the file. The final input argument is an array of environmental parameters for file execution. Ideally, the function does not return a value, as it does not return to the calling process. However, upon an error, a value of −1 is returned and the global variable ERRNO is set.

Risk: This function has the ability to execute a file on the local system. Attackers commonly target functions similar to this since they have the ability to launch potentially dangerous or malicious executables with differing privileges. It is imperative that you filter all input and never allow a user direct access to passing variables as the parameters for this function. Ensure that all special characters are stripped before the data is parsed and passed in addition to limiting access to only the desired executables. Lastly, require that all executable output is controlled within a forked or spawned process within the local application to ensure the integrity of the outputted data. If possible, avoid calling dynamic programs from within applications. Static program execution is more secure.

Additional Resources: www.python.org/doc/

Impact: High

execvp

Prototype: execvp(filename, argv)

Summary: This function executes a file with an array of pointers to be passed to the command line using the environment variable PATH to find the file.

Description: The function will execute a file pointed to by the argument filename, searching for it using the environmental variable PATH. The other input argument, argv, is an array command-line parameter to be used in the execution of the file. Ideally, the function does not return a value, as it does not return to the calling process. However, upon an error, a value of −1 is returned and the global variable ERRNO is set.

Risk: This function has the ability to execute a file on the local system. Attackers commonly target functions similar to this since they have the ability to launch potentially dangerous or malicious executables with differing privileges. It is imperative that you filter all input and never allow a user direct access to passing variables as the parameters for this function. Ensure that all special characters are stripped before the data is parsed and passed in addition to limiting access to only the desired executables. Lastly, require that all executable output is controlled within a forked or spawned process within the local application to ensure the integrity of the outputted data. If possible, avoid calling dynamic programs from within applications. Static program execution is more secure.

Additional Resources: www.python.org/doc/

Impact: High

expovariate

Prototype: `expovariate(lambd)`

Summary: This function generates a pseudo-random number from the exponential distribution.

Description: This function is used to generate a pseudo-random number from the exponential probability distribution. The function requires only the parameter `lambd` be passed to it. This parameter is the reciprocal of the desired mean of the distribution. The function returns a value between 0 and infinity (i.e., the largest number representable on the machine).

Risk: As with most standard random functions implemented within the C and C++ libraries, this function is susceptible to brute-force or easily guessed number generating attacks due to a poor seed algorithm within the backend code. Amongst numerous other secure random number generating functions, Microsoft .Net has secure methods for implementing properly seeded numbers. ISAAC, designed by Bob Jenkins, is a fast cryptographic random number generator is as strong as they come. Available in multiple languages, ISAAC is a standard for many freeware and commercial solutions and should be considered the next time a random number is required within an application.

Additional Resources: www.burtleburtle.net/bob/rand/isaacafa.html, www.python.org/doc/

Impact: Medium

fork

Prototype: `fork()`

Summary: This function creates a child process.

Description: The function creates a child process off of the master. The function does not require any input arguments. It returns a zero to the child process, signaling a good call. The function also returns to the parent program the ID of the child process.

Risk: `Fork` can be leveraged in an attack in multiple ways and is especially common in launching Denial-of-Service attacks against the underlying operating system. Deny human users from accessing or launching this function or from controlling any type of execution for this function. Additionally, you should close all processes as soon as their execution logic is complete while being aware that it is extremely risky to ever launch a subprocess within an over-arching process.

Additional Resources: www.python.org/doc/

Impact: Low

gammavariate

Prototype: `gammavariate(alpha, beta)`

Summary: This function generates a pseudo-random number using the Gamma distribution.

Description: The function attempts to generate a pseudo-random number using the Gamma probability distribution. The function requires two input values: the alpha and beta parameters of the distribution. Both of these parameters must be greater than zero. The function returns only the random number.

Risk: As with most standard random functions implemented within the C and C++ libraries, this function is susceptible to brute-force or easily guessed number generating attacks due to a poor seed algorithm within the backend code. Amongst numerous other secure random number generating functions, Microsoft .Net has secure methods for implementing properly seeded numbers. ISAAC, designed by Bob Jenkins, is a fast cryptographic random number generator is as strong as they

come. Available in multiple languages, ISAAC is a standard for many freeware and commercial solutions and should be considered the next time a random number is required within an application.

Additional Resources: www.burtleburtle.net/bob/rand/isaacafa.html, www.python.org/doc/

Impact: Medium

gauss

Prototype: `gauss(mu, sigma)`

Summary: This function generates a pseudo-random number from the Gaussian distribution.

Description: The function draws a pseudo-random number from the Gaussian probability distribution. The function requires two input values: the parameters mu and sigma of the distribution (mean and the standard deviation). The mean has no restrictions on it, but the standard deviation should be greater than zero. The function returns the random number, whose only restriction is the numbers that a machine can represent in binary.

Risk: As with most standard random functions implemented within the C and C++ libraries, this function is susceptible to brute-force or easily guessed number generating attacks due to a poor seed algorithm within the backend code. Amongst numerous other secure random number generating functions, Microsoft .Net has secure methods for implementing properly seeded numbers. ISAAC, designed by Bob Jenkins, is a fast cryptographic random number generator is as strong as they come. Available in multiple languages, ISAAC is a standard for many freeware and commercial solutions and should be considered the next time a random number is required within an application.

Additional Resources: www.python.org/doc/

Impact: Medium

gethostbyaddr

Prototype: `gethostbyaddr(ip_address)`

Summary: This function retrieves a host's name information from the IP address.

Description: The function attempts to retrieve a given host's information based on an IP address. The function takes only one input argument: the IP address. The function returns a triplet of information. The triplet contains the host name, a list of possible aliases, and a list of other IP addresses associated with the host name. The second and third parts of the triplet will many times give little new information.

Risk: This function handles system-specific sensitive information that an attacker could leverage during a period of target reconnaissance. This function should only be utilized if it is absolutely necessary for proper execution of the application. All analysis for the output of this function should be conducted securely within the application and never sent across the wire in cleartext.

Additional Resources: www.python.org/doc/

Impact: Low

gethostbyname

Prototype: `gethostbyname(hostname)`

Summary: This function translates a hostname into the IP address associated with it.

Description: The function attempts to resolve a hostname and return the associated IP address. The function requires only the hostname as an input parameter. The function returns only the IP address in single quotes.

Risk: This function handles system-specific sensitive information that an attacker could leverage during a period of target reconnaissance. This function should only be utilized if it is absolutely necessary for proper execution of the application. All analysis for the output of this function should be conducted securely within the application and never sent across the wire in cleartext.

Additional Resources: www.python.org/doc/

Impact: Low

gethostbyname_ex

Prototype: `gethostbyname_ex(hostname)`

Summary: This function collects a host's information using its hostname.

Description: The function attempts to resolve a hostname and return the associated information. The function requires only the hostname as an input parameter. The function returns a triplet of information. The triplet contains the host name, a list of possible aliases, and a list of other IP addresses associated with the host name. The second and third parts of the triplet will many times give little new information.

Risk: Temporary filenames are often created with static and easily guessable algorithms such as the system time or application name appended with the day, month, and year. If at all possible, do not use this function and instead store temporary information in a secure memory space. If a temporary file is necessary, ensure that it is removed upon exiting the program or in the case where a program exits unexpectedly is removed upon program relaunch. Consider utilizing a random number generator such as ISAAC for creating secure random filenames.

Additional Resources: www.python.org/doc/

Impact: Low

getlogin

Prototype: `getlogin( )`

Summary: This function retrieves the name of the user logged onto the controlling process.

Description: This function attempts to resolve the user name associated with the current (i.e., controlling) process. The function does not require any input arguments. The function returns the requested user name when completed. In the event of failure, the function returns an empty string.

Risk: This function handles system-specific sensitive information that an attacker could leverage during a period of target reconnaissance. This function should only be utilized if it is absolutely necessary for proper execution of the application. All analysis for the output of this function should be conducted securely within the application and never sent across the wire in cleartext.

Additional Resources: www.python.org/doc/

Impact: High

getstate

Prototype: `getstate( )`

Summary: This function is used to retrieve the state of the random number generator.

Description: The function is used to retrieve the internal state of the random number generator. The function does not require any input arguments. The function returns an object describing the state. This object is passable to the function `setstate` for the reclamation of a previous state.

Risk: As with most standard random functions implemented within the C and C++ libraries, this function is susceptible to brute-force or easily guessed number generating attacks due to a poor seed algorithm within the backend code. Amongst numerous other secure random number generating functions, Microsoft .Net has secure methods for implementing properly seeded numbers. ISAAC, designed by Bob Jenkins, is a fast cryptographic random number generator is as strong as they come. Available in multiple languages, ISAAC is a standard for many freeware and commercial solutions and should be considered the next time a random number is required within an application.

Additional Resources: www.burtleburtle.net/bob/rand/isaacafa.html, www.python.org/doc/

Impact: Medium

input

Prototype: `input([command])`

Summary: This function executes a Python command.

Description: This function is used similarly to the `eval` function. It is used to evaluate Python-capable commands. The function will work without an input argument (though it will do nothing). Otherwise, it uses a string to be issued as a command. The function returns the value that the command issued returns.

Risk: This function is utilized to execute system-level commands from within an application. Executing system-level commands are one of the most dangerous types of operations that an application can hardcode into its backend logic. Multiple vectors for potential attacks are available and must be addressed to secure your application. User input should be reviewed and all non-alphanumeric characters removed. Additionally, the directory structure should be limited to include only the directory or directories where the desired executables reside. As an example, you would restrict users to running commands or executables in /user/local/bin or c:/documents and settings/userX/programs/. Lastly, all output for the application should be captured within the subprocess that has launched the executable. `Fork`, `CreateProcess`, or `CreateThread` are examples of additional functions that can be used to contain output.

Additional Resources: www.python.org/doc/

Impact: High

jumpahead

Prototype: `jumpahead(n)`

Summary: This function is used to change the internal state of the random number generator.

Description: The function attempts to change the internal state of the random number generator. The function requires a number "n" used to alter the state. The function does not return any values. This function can be used to alter the states of several incarnations of the random number generator to distinct states.

Risk: As with most standard random functions implemented within the C and C++ libraries, this function is susceptible to brute-force or easily guessed number generating attacks due to a poor seed algorithm within the backend code. Amongst numerous other secure random number generating functions, Microsoft .Net has secure methods for implementing properly seeded numbers. ISAAC, designed by Bob Jenkins, is a fast cryptographic random number generator is as strong as they come. Available in multiple languages, ISAAC is a standard for many freeware and commercial solutions and should be considered the next time a random number is required within an application.

Additional Resources: www.burtleburtle.net/bob/rand/isaacafa.html, www.python.org/doc/

Impact: High

link

Prototype: link(src, dst)

Summary: This function is used to create a linker file.

Description: The function creates a linker file. The function requires two input arguments: the source file (path) and the name of the new linker file. The function creates a hard-wired link from the destination file pointing to the source file. The function returns a Boolean value signaling success with a 1 and failure with a 0.

Risk: Characters used in the filenames should be restricted to the alphanumeric base or less depending on the underlying operating platform. Ensure that all links are removed before the program executes or are cleaned up before program execution, in the case where a program crashes or exits unexpectedly. The link function is commonly targeted in Denial-of-Service attacks attempting to consume all of the local CPU or memory resources.

Additional Resources: www.python.org/doc/

Impact: Low

listdir

Prototype: `listdir(path)`

Summary: This function retrieves a list of the contents of a directory.

Description: The function attempts to resolve the contents of a given directory. The function takes only one input argument: the path to the directory in question. The function returns a list of the contents of that directory. The list is in no particular order and does not contain the linker files "." and "..".

Risk: Attackers commonly seek out the contents of a directory to see where potentially powerful or vulnerable files are located. Ensure that the only the desired directory's contents is viewable and that wildcards and special characters are removed from the passed string.

Additional Resources: www.python.org/doc/

Impact: Low

lognormvariate

Prototype: `lognormvariate(mu, sigma)`

Summary: This function generates a pseudo-random number from the log-normal distribution.

Description: The function attempts to retrieve a pseudo-random number by drawing from the log-normal probability distribution. The function is basically the exponential of the normal distribution (i.e., taking the natural logarithm of this distribution results in the normal distribution). The function thus requires the same parameters as the normal distribution: the mean (mu) and standard deviation (sigma). The function returns a pseudo-random number.

Risk: As with most standard random functions implemented within the C and C++ libraries, this function is susceptible to brute-force or easily guessed number generating attacks due to a poor seed algorithm within the backend code. Amongst numerous other secure random number generating functions, Microsoft .Net has secure methods for implementing properly seeded numbers. ISAAC, designed by Bob Jenkins, is a fast cryptographic random number generator is as strong as they

come. Available in multiple languages, ISAAC is a standard for many freeware and commercial solutions and should be considered the next time a random number is required within an application.

Additional Resources: www.burtleburtle.net/bob/rand/isaacafa.html, www.python.org/doc/

Impact: Medium

lstat

Prototype: `lstat(path)`

Summary: This function retrieves information on an object in the given path.

Description: The function attempts to resolve the information in the structure `stat` for an object in the given path. The function requires only the path of the object in question. The function does not follow links (both symbolic and hard-wired), unlike the `stat` function. This function returns an object of the `stat` structure containing the requested information.

Risk: The `stat` function output should be restricted to trusted administrative-level users or the internal workings of the application. `stat` output contains sensitive information that an attacker could leverage to advance an attack scenario.

Additional Resources: www.python.org/doc/

Impact: Low

mkdir

Prototype: `mkdir(path[, mode])`

Summary: This function is used to create a directory.

Description: The function attempts to create a new directory. The function requires only one input value: the path for the new directory. However, a second, optional argument can be handled. It is a permissions creation mode. The function returns 1 upon successful completion, a 0 in the event of failure.

Risk: Users should not be given free reign with this function and should be restricted to only create directories from a desired list provided by the development team. Also limit the parent directory of the new directory to a predefined or static source thereby minimizing your risk of enabling an attacker to control your underlying operating system.

Additional Resources: www.python.org/doc/

Impact: Low

mkfifo

Prototype: mkfifo(path[, mode])

Summary: This function is used to create a new FIFO pipe.

Description: The function attempts to create a new pipe in the file system. The function requires only one input parameter: the path of the new pipe. It also can handle an additional, optional argument. That optional parameter is a mode-creation handle. The function returns a 1 if completed successfully, a 0 if not.

Risk: In 2002, a myriad of vulnerabilities were identified in Microsoft pipes; however, the implementation and exploitation of these vulnerabilities is not strictly limited to Microsoft Windows operating systems. Similar to socket-level vulnerabilities, the pipe vulnerabilities exploit trusts between the clients and server on the ends of the connection. Ensure that your compiler is up-to-date and that all parameters passed to this function are derived from internal system information and not human data. Human data should be scrubbed and presented with options for selections if this function must be utilized.

Additional Resources: www.python.org/doc/

Impact: Low

normalvariate

Prototype: normalvariate(mu, sigma)

Summary: This function generates a pseudo-random number from the normal distribution.

Description: The function attempts to retrieve a pseudo-random number by drawing from a normal probability distribution. The function requires two input parameters: the mean (mu) and standard deviation (sigma) of the distribution. The parameter mu can be any value, while the parameter sigma should be greater than zero. The function returns the number when completed.

Risk: As with most standard random functions implemented within the C and C++ libraries, this function is susceptible to brute-force or easily guessed number generating attacks due to a poor seed algorithm within the backend code. Amongst numerous other secure random number generating functions, Microsoft .Net has secure methods for implementing properly seeded numbers. ISAAC, designed by Bob Jenkins, is a fast cryptographic random number generator is as strong as they come. Available in multiple languages, ISAAC is a standard for many freeware and commercial solutions and should be considered the next time a random number is required within an application.

Additional Resources: www.burtleburtle.net/bob/rand/isaacafa.html, www.python.org/doc/

Impact: Medium

open

Prototype: `open(filename[, mode[, bufsize]])`

Summary: This function is used to open a given file.

Description: The function attempts to open a file for use in the program. The function requires only one input value: the filename (and/or path to it). However, there are two optional parameters: the mode in which to open the file (defaults to 'r') and the buffer size to use with the file (defaults to system's choice). The function returns address of the location of the file (i.e., the handle).

Risk: All special and wildcard characters should be removed before the filename is computed on the local filesystem. Malicious filenames are interpreted differently on varying systems and as such, directory control is critical to limiting the ability of an attacker to potentially compromise files at varying levels within the application or underlying subsystem.

Additional Resources: www.python.org/doc/

Impact: Low

paretovariate

Prototype: `paretovariate(alpha)`

Summary: This function is used to draw a pseudo-random number from a `Pareto` distribution.

Description: The function generates a pseudo-random number from the Pareto probability distribution. The function requires only one input value: the shape parameter of the distribution. The function's input value `alpha` will affect the mean and standard deviation and should be chosen with care. The function returns the number when completed.

Risk: As with most standard random functions implemented within the C and C++ libraries, this function is susceptible to brute-force or easily guessed number generating attacks due to a poor seed algorithm within the backend code. Amongst numerous other secure random number generating functions, Microsoft .Net has secure methods for implementing properly seeded numbers. ISAAC, designed by Bob Jenkins, is a fast cryptographic random number generator is as strong as they come. Available in multiple languages, ISAAC is a standard for many freeware and commercial solutions and should be considered the next time a random number is required within an application.

Additional Resources: www.burtleburtle.net/bob/rand/isaacafa.html, www.python.org/doc/

Impact: Medium

pathconf

Prototype: `pathconf(path, name)`

Summary: This function is used to retrieve configuration information for a file.

Description: The function attempts to resolve configuration information given a path to a file in question. The function requires two input parameters: the path of the file and the name of the information wanted. The function's response to the name parameter varies according to the system running it. The function returns the requested information when completed.

Risk: System path information is constantly sought after by attackers or malicious users profiling a target application or system. Path information alone can potentially identify the underlying operating system, installed applications, configurations, and in some cases user and security information. Ensure that non-alphanumeric characters are removed from the string before it is processed and that the information is only processed internally by the application. Limit the end-user's ability to ascertain or traverse path information.

Additional Resources: www.python.org/doc/

Impact: Low

popen

Prototype: `popen(filename [, mode[, bufsize]])`

Summary: This function is used to open a pipe.

Description: The function attempts to open a given pipe. The function requires only one input command: the pipe name. The function can handle two additional, optional arguments: the mode in which to open the file and the buffer size. The mode defaults to "r" when not specified and the buffer size choice defaults to the operating system's default. The function returns the handle for the opened pipe when completed.

Risk: In 2002, a myriad of vulnerabilities were identified in Microsoft pipes; however, the implementation and exploitation of these vulnerabilities is not strictly limited to Microsoft Windows operating systems. Similar to socket-level vulnerabilities, the pipe vulnerabilities exploit trusts between the clients and server on the ends of the connection. Ensure that your compiler is up-to-date and that all parameters passed to this function are derived from internal system information and not human data. Human data should be scrubbed and presented with options for selections if this function must be utilized.

Additional Resources: www.python.org/doc/

Impact: Low

randint

Prototype: `randint(a, b)`

Summary: The function generates a pseudo-random integer from a given range.

Description: The function attempts to draw a pseudo-random integer from a range specified by the user. The function requires two input parameters: the lower and upper bounds of the range (inclusive). The function draws an integer from the range [a, b]. The integer is returned when completed.

Risk: As with most standard random functions implemented within the C and C++ libraries, this function is susceptible to brute-force or easily guessed number generating attacks due to a poor seed algorithm within the backend code. Amongst numerous other secure random number generating functions, Microsoft .Net has secure methods for implementing properly seeded numbers. ISAAC, designed by Bob Jenkins, is a fast cryptographic random number generator is as strong as they come. Available in multiple languages, ISAAC is a standard for many freeware and commercial solutions and should be considered the next time a random number is required within an application.

Additional Resources: www.burtleburtle.net/bob/rand/isaacafa.html, www.python.org/doc/

Impact: Medium

random

Prototype: `random( )`

Summary: This function generates a random number.

Description: The function attempts to create a random number in the range [0, 1]. The function uses the internal state of the random number generator to draw the number. It does not require any input parameters. The function returns the random number when complete.

Risk: As with most standard random functions implemented within the C and C++ libraries, this function is susceptible to brute-force or easily guessed number generating attacks due to a poor seed algorithm within the backend code. Amongst numerous other secure random number generating functions, Microsoft .Net has secure methods for implementing properly seeded numbers. ISAAC, designed by Bob Jenkins, is a fast cryptographic random number generator is as strong as they come. Available in multiple languages, ISAAC is a standard for many freeware and commercial solutions and should be considered the next time a random number is required within an application.

Additional Resources: www.burtleburtle.net/bob/rand/isaacafa.html, www.python.org/doc/

Impact: Medium

randrange

Prototype: `randrange([start,] stop[, step])`

Summary: This function is used to pick an object from a range of numbers.

Description: The function attempts to grab a pseudo-random element from a generated range. The function is best used with three input parameters: the start and stopping points of the range and the step size to take. The function temporarily generates the range object, picks one element at random, destroys the range object, and then returns randomized element.

Risk: As with most standard random functions implemented within the C and C++ libraries, this function is susceptible to brute-force or easily guessed number generating attacks due to a poor seed algorithm within the backend code. Amongst numerous other secure random number generating functions, Microsoft .Net has secure methods for implementing properly seeded numbers. ISAAC, designed by Bob Jenkins, is a fast cryptographic random number generator is as strong as they come. Available in multiple languages, ISAAC is a standard for many freeware and commercial solutions and should be considered the next time a random number is required within an application.

Python

Additional Resources: www.burtleburtle.net/bob/rand/isaacafa.html, www.python.org/doc/

Impact: Medium

raw_input

Prototype: `raw_input([prompt])`

Summary: This function is used to write to standard output and read the subsequent standard input.

Description: The function is used to write a prompt to the standard output and then read any input from the user up to a new line. The function does not require any input arguments, though a prompt is recommended. The function outputs the prompt (if used) and waits for the user input to finish with a new line character. The function then saves the input and returns it.

Risk: Raw network data received from a socket has the potential to be malicious in nature due to the great number of attacks that are designed to be executed remotely. Packet fragmentations can cause serious disruptions to the application and underlying operating system. If at all possible, packet reassembly should be conducted at the OS-layer.

Additional Resources: www.python.org/doc/

Impact: Medium

read

Prototype: `read(file, n)`

Summary: This function is used to read data from a file.

Description: The function attempts to read a given amount of data from a file. The function requires two input parameters: the file handle and the maximum number of bytes to read from the file. The function will read the file until an EOF is encountered or the maximum number of bytes is reached. The function returns the data as a string.

Risk: All special and wildcard characters should be removed before the filename is computed on the local filesystem. Malicious filenames are interpreted differently on varying systems and as such, directory control is critical to limiting the ability of an attacker to potentially compromise files at varying levels within the application or underlying subsystem.

Additional Resources: www.python.org/doc/

Impact: Low

recv

Prototype: `recv(bufsize[, flags])`

Summary: This function is used to receive information from an open socket.

Description: The function is used to read incoming information from an open socket. The function has only one required input parameter: the buffer size for the incoming data to be read to. There is an additional argument (optional) that can be tripped to include several flags (see the Unix Man pages for more details on what these can be). The function returns the buffer of data read from the incoming data stream.

Risk: Raw network data received from a socket has the potential to be malicious in nature due to the numerous amounts of attacks that are designed to be executed remotely. Packet fragmentations can cause serious disruptions to the application and underlying operating system. If at all possible, packet reassembly should be conducted at the OS-layer.

Additional Resources: www.python.org/doc/

Impact: Low

recvfrom

Prototype: `recvfrom(bufsize[, flags])`

Summary: This function is used to receive information from an open socket.

Description: The function is used to read incoming information from an open socket. The function has only one required input parameter: the buffer size for the incoming data to be read to. There is an additional argument (optional) that can be tripped to include several flags (see the Unix Man pages for more details on what these can be). The function returns the buffer of data read from the incoming data stream as well as the address for the source of the incoming data.

Risk: Raw network data received from a socket has the potential to be malicious in nature due to the great number of attacks that are designed to be executed remotely. Packet fragmentations can cause serious disruptions to the application and underlying operating system. If at all possible, packet reassembly should be conducted at the OS-layer.

Additional Resources: www.python.org/doc/

Impact: Low

remove

Prototype: `remove(path)`

Summary: This function is used to remove file.

Description: The function attempts to delete a file in a given path. The function has only one input argument: the path of the file in question. The function deletes the file, and if successful returns a `0`. In the event of failure, the function returns a `-1`.

Risk: In addition to the potential race condition bugs that are associated with this function, a user could also attempt to execute a Denial-of-Service attack. Ensure that only one instance of this function can be called at any given moment. All input passed to this function should be analyzed closely to ensure that only desired resources can be removed from the system. It is not uncommon for worms and viruses to exploit application-layer vulnerabilities to cause damage to files they since would not have had access to.

Additional Resources: www.python.org/doc/

Impact: Low

rename

Prototype: `rename(source, dest)`

Summary: This function is used to rename a given file.

Description: The function attempts to change the name of a given file. The function requires two input arguments: the path of the source file and the new name (destination path). The function requires that the user have the file permissions to achieve the name change. The function returns a `0` if completed successfully, and a `-1` if not.

Risk: In addition to the potential race condition bugs that are associated with this function, a user could also attempt to execute a Denial-of-Service attack. Ensure that only one instance of this function can be called at any given moment. All input passed to this function should be analyzed closely to ensure that only desired resources can be removed from the system. It is not uncommon for worms and viruses to exploit application-layer vulnerabilities to cause damage to files they since would not have had access to by renaming all files within an operating system or renaming files and directories to those that are commonly executed upon system boot.

Additional Resources: www.python.org/doc/

Impact: Low

rmdir

Prototype: `rmdir(path)`

Summary: This function is used to remove a given directory.

Description: The function attempts to remove a given directory. The function requires only the path to directory in question. The target directory must be empty to complete the operation. The function returns a `0` when successful, and a `-1` if not.

Risk: In addition to the potential race condition bugs that are associated with this function, a user could also attempt to execute a Denial-of-Service attack. Ensure that only one instance of this function can be called at any given moment. All input passed to this function should be analyzed closely to ensure that only desired resources can be removed from the system. It is not uncommon for worms and viruses to exploit application-layer vulnerabilities to cause damage to files they since would not have had access to.

Additional Resources: www.python.org/doc/

Impact: Low

seed

Prototype: `seed([x])`

Summary: This function is used to "seed" the general random number generator.

Description: The function attempts to seed the random number generator for future use. The function does not require any input parameters (as it will use the current system time). However, any hashable object can be passed to the function to use as a seed. The function does not return any values.

Risk: As with most standard random functions implemented within the C and C++ libraries, this function is susceptible to brute-force or easily guessed number generating attacks due to a poor seed algorithm within the backend code. Amongst numerous other secure random number generating functions, Microsoft .Net has secure methods for implementing properly seeded numbers. ISAAC, designed by Bob Jenkins, is a fast cryptographic random number generator is as strong as they come. Available in multiple languages, ISAAC is a standard for many freeware and commercial solutions and should be considered the next time a random number is required within an application.

Additional Resources: www.burtleburtle.net/bob/rand/isaacafa.html, www.python.org/doc/

Impact: High

setstate

Prototype: `setstate(state)`

Summary: This function is used to set the state of the random number generator.

Description: The function attempts to set the current state of the random generator. The function requires one input argument: a state structure to use to set the random number generator. The function is used in conjunction with the get-state function to duplicate results. The function returns a Boolean value dependent on successful completion.

Risk: As with most standard random functions implemented within the C and C++ libraries, this function is susceptible to brute-force or easily guessed number generating attacks due to a poor seed algorithm within the backend code. Amongst numerous other secure random number generating functions, Microsoft .Net has secure methods for implementing properly seeded numbers. ISAAC, designed by Bob Jenkins, is a fast cryptographic random number generator is as strong as they come. Available in multiple languages, ISAAC is a standard for many freeware and commercial solutions and should be considered the next time a random number is required within an application.

Additional Resources: www.python.org/doc/

Impact: Medium

shuffle

Prototype: shuffle(x[, random])

Summary: This function is used to permute a list.

Description: The function attempts to randomize a given list. The function requires only one input value: the list in question. The function can handle an additional input argument: a function requiring no input parameters that returns a float in the range [0,1.0]. This is used to set the state for the permutations. The function returns the shuffled list when complete.

Risk: The shuffle function should never be utilized to obfuscate data with the goal of protecting it from prying eyes. Only industry-standard cryptography algorithms should be implemented to secure data. Do not use this function!

Additional Resources: www.python.org/doc/

Impact: High

signal

Prototype: `signal(signalnum, handler)`

Summary: This function sets the handler for a given signal.

Description: The function attempts to change the handler name for a given signal. The function requires two input parameters: the signal and the new handler name. The function can only be called from the main thread when using multiple threads. The function returns the previous signal handler name when complete.

Risk: Functions that handle or pass data to signals could be open for attacks to race condition bugs found within your logic. Ensure that only one instance of the signal function can be called at any given period of time and that if utilized in multiple locations within an application, a time delay routine be implemented to monitor the function usage.

Additional Resources: www.python.org/doc/

Impact: Low

stat

Prototype: `stat(path)`

Summary: This function retrieves information on an object in the given path.

Description: The function attempts to resolve the information in the structure `stat` for an object in the given path. The function requires only the path of the object in question. The function does will follow links (both symbolic and hard-wired), unlike the `lstat` function. This function returns an object of the `stat` structure containing the requested information.

Risk: The stat function output should be restricted to trusted administrative-level users or the internal workings of the application. `stat` output contains sensitive information that an attacker could leverage to advance an attack scenario.

Additional Resources: www.python.org/doc/

Impact: Low

system

Prototype: `system(command)`

Summary: This function executes a command in the shell.

Description: The function is used to execute a command in the system's shell. The function requires only one input argument: the command. The function executes the command in a new shell. When complete, the function returns the output of the command run in the shell.

Risk: This function is utilized to execute system-level commands from within an application. Executing system-level commands are one of the most dangerous types of operations that an application can hardcode into its backend logic. Multiple vectors for potential attacks are available and must be addressed to secure your application. User input should be reviewed and all non-alphanumeric characters removed. Additionally, the directory structure should be limited to include only the directory or directories where the desired executables reside. As an example, you would restrict users to running commands or executables in /user/local/bin or c:/documents and settings/userX/programs/. Lastly, all output for the application should be captured within the subprocess that has launched the executable. `Fork`, `CreateProcess`, or `CreateThread` are examples of additional functions that can be used to contain output.

Additional Resources: www.python.org/doc/

Impact: High

tmpfile

Prototype: `tmpfile( )`

Summary: This function is used to create a temporary file.

Description: The function creates a new file to use as a temporary source of information. The function does not require any input arguments. It creates the file, sets the creation to the "update" mode, and will delete it when it is "closed." The function returns the file descriptor (ID).

Risk: Temporary filenames are often created with static and easily guessable algorithms such as the system time or application name appended with the day, month, and year. If at all possible, do not use this function and instead store temporary information in a secure memory space. If a temporary file is necessary, ensure that it is removed upon exiting the program or in the case where a program exits unexpectedly is removed upon program relaunch. Consider utilizing a random number generator such as ISAAC for creating secure random filenames.

Additional Resources: www.python.org/doc/

Impact: Low

tmpnam

Prototype: `tmpnam( )`

Summary: This function is used to create a unique name for a temporary file.

Description: The function attempts to create a unique, temporary file name. The function does not require any input arguments, and returns a string containing the new file name. There is no automatic cleaning associated with this file, unlike the function `tmpfile`.

Risk: Temporary file names are often created with static and easily guessable algorithms such as the system time or application name appended with the day, month, and year. If at all possible, do not use this function and instead store temporary information in a secure memory space. If a temporary file is necessary, ensure that it is removed upon exiting the program or in the case where a program exits unexpectedly is removed upon program relaunch. Consider utilizing a random number generator such as ISAAC for creating secure random filenames.

Additional Resources: www.python.org/doc/

Impact: Medium

ttyname

Prototype: `ttyname( file )`

Summary: This function is used to determine the device associated with a file.

Description: The function attempts to resolve the device associated with a particular file. The function requires one input parameter: the file handle (descriptor). The function returns the device associated with the file in question.

Risk: This function handles system-specific sensitive information that an attacker could leverage during a period of target reconnaissance. This function should only be utilized if it is absolutely necessary for proper execution of the application. All analysis for the output of this function should be conducted securely within the application and never sent across the wire in cleartext.

Additional Resources: www.python.org/doc/

Impact: Low

uniform

Prototype: `uniform(a, b)`

Summary: This function generates a pseudo-random number from an interval.

Description: The function attempts to generate a random number from a given interval. The function will choose a number using the given interval boundaries. It requires two input parameters: the lower and upper bounds, respectively. The function uses the uniform distribution, so each number has equally likely weight. It returns the chosen number when complete.

Risk: As with most standard random functions implemented within the C and C++ libraries, this function is susceptible to brute-force or easily guessed number generating attacks due to a poor seed algorithm within the backend code. Amongst numerous other secure random number generating functions, Microsoft .Net has secure methods for implementing properly seeded numbers. ISAAC, designed by Bob Jenkins, is a fast cryptographic random number generator is as strong as they come. Available in multiple languages, ISAAC is a standard for many freeware and commercial solutions and should be considered the next time a random number is required within an application.

Additional Resources: www.python.org/doc/

Impact: Medium

unlink

Prototype: `unlink(path)`

Summary: This function is used to remove a file.

Description: The function attempts to remove a given file. The function requires only input value: the path of the file in question. The function will return a modified Boolean value when completed. It returns a 0 if successful, a -1 if not.

Risk: The `unlink` function can be leveraged to cause a Denial-of-Service attack on the target application. If improperly secured, an attacker could unlink multiple files required by the application to function thereby disrupting normal execution. Ensure that human input is passed as a parameter for this function.

Additional Resources: www.python.org/doc/

Impact: Low

vonmisesvariate

Prototype: `vonmisesvariate(mu, kappa)`

Summary: This function generates a pseudo-random number using the Von Mises distribution.

Description: The function attempts to generate a random number using the Von Mises probability distribution. The function requires two input parameters: the mean angle (mu) and the concentration index (kappa). The parameter mu should be in radians coming from the interval [0, 2*pi), while the parameter kappa should be greater than or equal to zero. The function returns the random number when completed.

Risk: As with most standard random functions implemented within the C and C++ libraries, this function is susceptible to brute-force or easily guessed number generating attacks due to a poor seed algorithm within the backend code. Amongst numerous other secure random number generating functions, Microsoft .Net has secure methods for implementing properly seeded numbers. ISAAC, designed by Bob Jenkins, is a fast cryptographic random number generator is as strong as they come. Available in multiple languages, ISAAC is a standard for many freeware and

commercial solutions and should be considered the next time a random number is required within an application.

Additional Resources: www.python.org/doc/

Impact: Medium

weibullvariate

Prototype: `weibullvariate(alpha, beta)`

Summary: This function generates a pseudo-random number using the Weibull distribution.

Description: The function attempts to generate a random number using the Weibull probability distribution. The function requires two input parameters: the scale (`alpha`) and shape (`beta`) parameters of the distribution. The distribution requires that both parameters be greater than zero. The function returns the random number when completed.

Risk: As with most standard random functions implemented within the C and C++ libraries, this function is susceptible to brute-force or easily guessed number generating attacks due to a poor seed algorithm within the backend code. Amongst numerous other secure random number generating functions, Microsoft .Net has secure methods for implementing properly seeded numbers. ISAAC, designed by Bob Jenkins, is a fast cryptographic random number generator is as strong as they come. Available in multiple languages, ISAAC is a standard for many freeware and commercial solutions and should be considered the next time a random number is required within an application.

Additional Resources: www.python.org/doc/

Impact: Medium

whseed

Prototype: `whseed([x])`

Summary: This function is used to seed the internal state of the random number generator.

Description: The function attempts to seed the internal state of the random number generator. It does not require any input parameters, as it will default to using the system clock to set the state. However, any number may be passed to set the state. The function returns the previous state of the random number generator when finished. This function is obsolete.

Risk: As with most standard random functions implemented within the C and C++ libraries, this function is susceptible to brute-force or easily guessed number generating attacks due to a poor seed algorithm within the backend code. Amongst numerous other secure random number generating functions, Microsoft .Net has secure methods for implementing properly seeded numbers. ISAAC, designed by Bob Jenkins, is a fast cryptographic random number generator is as strong as they come. Available in multiple languages, ISAAC is a standard for many freeware and commercial solutions and should be considered the next time a random number is required within an application.

Additional Resources: www.python.org/doc/

Impact: High

Programmer's Ultimate Security DeskRef: VBA

AddFile

Prototype: `object.AddFile (ByVal pathname As String, [relateddocument As Boolean]) As VBComponent`

Summary: This method is used to return a newly added component to a VBComponent object.

Description: The `AddFile` method is a part of the `VBComponents collection`, and is used to add a file to a VBComponent object. This method takes two parameters, one required and the other optional. The first parameter is the `pathname`; it is a path and filename of a file to open as a template. The second optional parameter is the `relateddocument`; it's a Boolean expression specifying whether the file is to be treated as a standard module or a document.

Risk: All parameters passed to the function from user input should be carefully analyzed to prevent access to or overwriting of components. Invalid adds into the collection class can result in data corruption or unauthorized execution of code.

Additional Resources:

http://msdn.microsoft.com/library/default.asp?url=/library/en-us/vbext98/html/vbmthaddfilemethod.asp

Impact: Medium

BuildPath

Prototype: `object.BuildPath(path, name)`

Summary: This method is used to append a name to an existing path for a `FileSystemObject` object.

Description: The `BuildPath` method is a part of the `FileSystemObject` object, it is used to append a name to an existing path. This method takes two required parameters. The first parameter is the path; it is a path to which the name parameter is to be appended. The second parameter is the name that needs to be appended to the existing path.

Risk: When parsing input data to obtain pathing for output, It is important to ensure user input does not contain strings commonly used to gain access to restricted files, such as "../../".

Additional Resources:

http://msdn.microsoft.com/library/default.asp?url=/library/en-us/vbenlr98/html/vamthbuildpath.asp

Impact: Medium

Command

Prototype: `Public Function Command() As String`

Summary: This function is used to gather all switches that follow a VB application when run on a command line.

Description: The `Command` function is used to gather all the arguments that follow a VB application when it is run from the command line. The `Command` function has no input arguments. The function returns a string containing all requested information following the executable when run from the command line.

Risk: When using the command function it is important to carefully parse the input arguments provided, otherwise invalid arguments can be passed on to the program and cause program errors. Visual Basic applications are typically not run from the command line therefore, debugging arguments that are used by developers to test functionality create unnecessary risk based on the developer assumptions of security through obscurity.

Additional Resources:

http://msdn.microsoft.com/library/default.asp?url=/library/en-us/vblr7/html/vafctcommand.asp

Impact: High

CreateObject

Prototype: CreateObject(class,[servername])

Summary: This function creates and returns a reference to an ActiveX object.

Description: This function creates a reference to an ActiveX object and then returns it. The CreateObject function has two parameters, one required and the other optional. The first parameter is a string containing the application name and object name, the two separated by a " . ". The second optional parameter is a string containing the location of the ActiveX object, if left blank it is defaulted to the local machine. The returned value is reference to the created ActiveX object.

Risk: The CreateObject function permits the creation of or access to any object available on any machine accessible. This function is available in VBScript and used in Web pages and html-enabled e-mail and is very frequently used in cross-site scripting to give a user access to data manipulation capabilities not intended for users.

Additional Resources:

http://msdn.microsoft.com/library/default.asp?url=/library/en-us/vbenlr98/html/vafctCreateObject.asp

Impact: Low

VBA

CurDir

Prototype: `Public Overloads Function CurDir([ ByVal Drive As Char ]) As String`

Summary: This function returns the current drive and letter.

Description: The `CurDir` function returns the current directory and drive. This function has one optional string parameter, when left empty the function returns the current drive and current directory. When the parameter contains a letter that corresponds with an existing drive letter that drive letter with its current directory is returned. The returned value is a string containing the current directory.

Risk: Unchecked, this function has the ability to disclose the current execution path to the user. This functions use should be restricted to the application and carefully controlled when output is being passed to the user. The results of this function may give an attacker a better understanding of the system architecture.

Additional Resources:

http://msdn.microsoft.com/library/default.asp?url=/library/en-us/vblr7/html/vafctcurdir.asp

Impact: Low

Date

Prototype: `Public Function Date() As Date`

Summary: This function is used to retrieve the current date.

Description: The `Date` function is used to retrieve the current date. There are no parameters associated with the `Date` function. It returns the date as a `Date` object.

Risk: The `Date` function relies on the system clock; accordingly, applications that depend on the `Date` function to control trail licenses and other control elements can be fooled by simply resetting the system clock.

Additional Resources:

http://msdn.microsoft.com/library/default.asp?url=/library/en-us/script56/html/vsfctdate.asp

Impact: Low

VBA

Dir

Prototype: `Public Overloads Function Dir() As String -OR-`
`Public Overloads Function Dir( Optional ByVal PathName As`
`String, Optional ByVal Attributes As FileAttribute =`
`FileAttribute.Normal ) As String`

Summary: This function is used to gain a file, directory, or folder that matches a set of parameters.

Description: This function returns a file, directory or folder based on a specified pattern, file attribute, or the volume label of a drive. It contains two parameters both are optional. The first optional parameter is a string containing a path name to be searched. The second optional parameter is a `FileAttribute`. The returned value is a string containing the file, directory or folder that matches the request.

Risk: The `Dir` function can be used to obtain directory listing and file properties similar to the `dir` command in DOS. When used in an application, input should be carefully parsed to prevent a user from gaining access to the file system structures and layout that may assist an attacker in gaining unnecessary understanding of the application or system.

Additional Resources:

http://msdn.microsoft.com/library/default.asp?url=/library/en-us/vblr7/
html/vafctdir.asp

Impact: Medium

DoEvents

Prototype: `DoEvents()`

Summary: This function hands over execution to the operating system so that it can process events.

Description: The `DoEvents` function stops the controlling process. It provides control of the program to the operating system so that the OS can process other open events. The `DoEvents` function has no parameters and returns an integer stating the number of forms open.

Risk: If the DoEvents function is used it can cause a denial of service condition to take place. If the procedure is executed again from a different point in the application it could cause unpredictable results to take place. Because of the dated nature and lack of current support it is advised to refrain from using the DoEvents function in server applications.

Additional Resources:

http://msdn.microsoft.com/library/default.asp?url=/library/en-us/vbenlr98/html/vafctdoevents.asp

Impact: Medium

DriveExists

Prototype: object.DriveExists(drivespec)

Summary: This method is used to determine if a FileSystemObject object drive exists.

Description: The DriveExists method is a part of the FileSystemObject object. It is used to determine if a drive exists. This method takes a single required parameter: the drive letter or a complete path specification. The function returns a Boolean TRUE if the drive exists, and FALSE if not.

Risk: Can be used to determine file properties that may help an attacker determine vital information about a specific file, which may assist in an attack.

Additional Resources:

http://msdn.microsoft.com/library/default.asp?url=/library/en-us/vbenlr98/html/vamthdriveexists.asp

Impact: Medium

Environ

Prototype: Overloads Function Environ(ByVal Expression As Integer) As String -OR- Overloads Function Environ(ByVal Expression As String) As String

Summary: This function is used to return operating system environment variables.

Description: The Environ function is used to gain operating system environment variables. The Environ function is an overloaded function that takes one parameter, either an integer or a string. When an integer is provided as a parameter the string occupying that environment variable is returned. When a string is provided as a parameter a string value of the occupying number of that environment variable is returned.

Risk: This function may reveal sensitive information about the operating system. It is possible that when used in a server application, a remote user could access this function and cause an unintentional information disclosure. In general, environment information should be restricted to program internals for access to libraries or other objects.

Additional Resources:
http://msdn.microsoft.com/library/default.asp?url=/library/en-us/vblr7/html/vafctenviron.asp

Impact: High

EOF

Prototype: `Public Function EOF(ByVal FileNumber As Integer) As Boolean`

Summary: This function is used to determine if the end of the file has been reached.

Description: The EOF function or "End of File" function is used to determine if the end of the file has been reached. The EOF function contains a required integer parameter; this integer should be any valid file number. The EOF function returns a Boolean true if the end of the file has been reached, and false if not.

Risk: This function should be used to ensure errors do not occur from going past the last record.

Additional Resources:
http://msdn.microsoft.com/library/default.asp?url=/library/en-us/vblr7/html/vafcteof.asp

Impact: Low

EstablishConnection

Prototype: `object.EstablishConnection( prompt, readonly, options )`

Summary: This method is used to establish a connection for a `RemoteDataObject` object.

Description: The `EstablishConnection` method is a part of the `RemoteDataObject` object, it is used to make a connection to an ODBC server. This method takes three optional parameters. The first parameter is the `prompt`; it is an integer value indicating ODBC prompting characteristic. The second parameter is a Boolean value for whether it should be a read-only connection. The third parameter is the options value; it's an integer value indicating connections options.

Risk: Opens a network connection to a ODBC Server which maybe used by an attacker to gain access to the system. When using external, one should carefully regulate all incoming and outgoing data traffic. An attacker could perform a man in the middle attack to intercept traffic to the database and provide altered content.

Additional Resources:
http://msdn.microsoft.com/library/default.asp?url=/library/en-us/rdo98/html/rdmthestablishconnection.asp

Impact: High

Execute

Prototype: `Sub Execute( ByVal path As String)`

Summary: This method is used to execute the current page using another page.

Description: The `Execute` method is a part of the `HttpServerUtility` object. It is used to execute the current page using another page at the specified URL path. This method takes one parameter: the URL path of the new page.

Risk: This method relies on external servers to execute internal content. The external server may manipulate the content of the current object causing users to enter invalid or unintended results. This method is subject to cross-site scripting attacks. All results passed to this function should be carefully controlled.

Additional Resources:

http://msdn.microsoft.com/library/default.asp?url=/library/en-us/cpref/html/
frlrfsystemwebhttpserverutilityclassexecutetopic1.asp

Impact: High

FileExists

Prototype: `object.FileExists(filespec)`

Summary: This method is used to determine if a `FileSystemObject` object exists.

Description: The `FileExists` method is a part of the `FileSystemObject` object. It is used to determine if a file exists at a specific location. This method takes a single required parameter: the complete path to the requested object. The function returns a Boolean `TRUE` if it exists, and `FALSE` if not.

Risk: Can be used to determine file properties that may help an attacker determine vital information about a specific file, which may assist in an attack.

Additional Resources:

http://msdn.microsoft.com/library/default.asp?url=/library/en-us/
vbenlr98/html/vamthfileexists.asp

Impact: Medium

FreeFile

Prototype: `FreeFile() As Integer`

Summary: This function returns an integer for the next available file number.

Description: The `FreeFile` function provides the next available unused file number. The `FreeFile` function has an optional argument stipulating the range from which to draw the next file number. The function returns the integer value for the next file to open.

Risk: When calling this function it is important to regulate user input that may result in a call to the `FreeFile` function. Unchecked, users could exhaust the file numbers and cause errors in the application process.

Additional Resources:

http://msdn.microsoft.com/library/default.asp?url=/library/en-us/vblr7/html/
vafctfreefile.asp

Impact: Low

GetAbsolutePathName

Prototype: `object.GetAbsolutePathName(pathspec)`

Summary: This method is used to return a complete and unambiguous path for
`FileSystemObject` object.

Description: The `GetAbsolutePathName` method is a part of the
`FileSystemObject` object. It is used to retrieve a complete and unambiguous
path. This method takes a single required parameter: a path specification that needs
to be changed to a complete and unambiguous path. The function returns the absolute path name as a string.

Risk: If results are directed to user output, an attacker can use the information contained in the absolute path to gain an understanding of system architecture that will
assist him in performing system attacks.

Additional Resources:

http://msdn.microsoft.com/library/default.asp?url=/library/en-us/vbenlr98/
html/vamthgetabsolutepathname.asp

Impact: Medium

GetAllSettings

Prototype: `Public Function GetAllSettings(ByVal AppName As
String, ByVal Section As String) As String(,)`

Summary: This function returns a list of key settings and their values.

Description: The `GetAllSettings` function returns a list of key settings from an
application's entries into the Windows Registry. It contains two required argument
inputs and returns a string value. The first parameter is a string containing the applications name. The second parameter is a string containing the section of which key
settings being acquired.

Risk: This function reveals sensitive information about the Registry entries. Applications should avoid authorizing users access to results. When using this function for application internals is necessary, it is important to parse user input to prevent access to restricted files and restricted Registry entries.

Additional Resources:
http://msdn.microsoft.com/library/default.asp?url=/library/en-us/vblr7/html/vafctgetallsettings.asp

Impact: Medium

GetAttr

Prototype: `Public Function GetAttr(ByVal PathName As String) As FileAttribute`

Summary: This function returns the attributes of a file, directory or folder.

Description: The `GetAttr` function provides information about the attributes of a file, directory or folder. The attributes revealed include: `Normal`, `ReadOnly`, `Hidden`, `System`, `Directory`, `Archive`, and `Alias`. It contains one required parameter the `PathName`. The `PathName` is a string that specifies a file, directory or folder name. The returned value is a `FileAttribute` constant.

Risk: This function reveals sensitive information about the files and permissions. Applications should avoid authorizing users access to results. When using this function for application internals is necessary, it is important to parse user input to prevent access to restricted files.

Additional Resources:
http://msdn.microsoft.com/library/default.asp?url=/library/en-us/vblr7/html/vafctgetattr.asp

Impact: Medium

GetAutoServerSettings

Prototype: `object.GetAutoServerSettings([progid], [clsid])`

Summary: This function returns information about the state of an ActiveX component's registration.

Description: The `GetAutoServerSettings` function returns information about an ActiveX components registration, specifically whether or not its registered locally and if not local the name of the server it is registered on. This function must be run against an ActiveX object and has two optional parameters. The first parameter is the `progid` that must evaluate to Programmatic Identifier for the component. The second parameter is the `clsid`, which must evaluate to a class ID for the component.

Risk: This function reveals sensitive information about the ActiveX components. Applications should avoid authorizing users access to this function's results. This function should be used to ensure ActiveX components being processed are from the proper machine to avoid the execution of malicious ActiveX components.

Additional Resources:

http://msdn.microsoft.com/library/default.asp?url=/library/en-us/vb98/html/vbfctgetautoserversettingsfunction.asp

Impact: Medium

GetDrive

Prototype: `object.GetDrive drivespec`

Summary: This method is used to return the `drive` object for a specified path.

Description: The `GetDrive` method is a part of the `FileSystemObject` object. It is used to retrieve the `drive` object for a specified path. This method takes a single required parameter: a drive letter (`c`), a drive letter with a colon (`c:`), a drive letter with a colon and path separator appended (`c:\`), or any network share specification. The function will

Risk: If results are directed to user output, an attacker can use the information contained in the absolute path to gain an understanding of system architecture that will assist him in performing system attacks.

Additional Resources:
http://msdn.microsoft.com/library/default.asp?url=/library/en-us/vbenlr98/
html/vamthgetdrive.asp

Impact: Medium

GetDriveName

Prototype: `object.GetDriveName(path)`

Summary: This method is used to return the name of the drive for a specified
path.

Description: The `GetDriveName` method is a part of the `FileSystemObject`
object. It is used to retrieve the drive for a specified path. This method takes a single
required parameter: a string specifying the path to a component whose drive name
is to be returned.

Risk: If results are directed to user output, an attacker can use the information contained in the absolute path to gain an understanding of system architecture that will
assist him in performing system attacks.

Additional Resources:
http://msdn.microsoft.com/library/default.asp?url=/library/en-us/vbenlr98/html/
vamthgetdrivename.asp

Impact: Medium

GetExtensionName

Prototype: `object.GetExtensionName(path)`

Summary: This method is used to return the extension name for the last component in the path.

Description: The `GetExtensionName` method is a part of the
`FileSystemObject` object. It is used to retrieve the last component in a path.
This method takes a single required parameter. It is a string specifying the path for
the component whose extension name is to be returned.

Risk: Access to files based on file extensions may result in corrupt data or the execution otherwise restricted processes. Data returned via the `GetExtensionName` should be verified to insure integrity.

Additional Resources:

http://msdn.microsoft.com/library/default.asp?url=/library/en–us/vbenlr98/html/vamthgetextensionname.asp

Impact: Low

GetFile

Prototype: `object.GetFile(filespec)`

Summary: This method is used to return the file object of the file in a specified path.

Description: The `GetFile` method is a part of the `FileSystemObject` object. It is used to retrieve the file object of the file in a specified path. This method takes a single required parameter. It is a string used to specify the path to a file.

Risk: If control of inputs is not carefully regulated, users may gain access to otherwise privileged files. When parsing input data to obtain pathing for output, It is important to ensure user input does not contain strings commonly used to gain access to restricted files, such as "../../".

Additional Resources:

http://msdn.microsoft.com/library/default.asp?url=/library/en–us/script56/html/jsmthgetfile.asp

Impact: High

GetFileName

Prototype: `object.GetFileName(pathspec)`

Summary: This method is used to return the last component of the specified path.

Description: The `GetFileName` method is a part of the `FileSystemObject` object. It is used to retrieve the last component in a path that is not part of the drive specification. This method takes a single required parameter. It is a string to specify the path to a file.

Risk: The basename function is used to remove directory information and optionally file extension from a path string for a file. The first parameter is used to determine the full path of the file. All directory names in the path defined by a '/' or '\' are removed leaving only the filename. Additionally, a suffix may be used (file extension) which will be removed from the end of the name. For example, the string variable `$path="/var/www/html/index.html"` would return `"index.html"` when run through basename as follows `basename($path)`. If `.html` were added as the suffix, then only `"index"` would be returned.

Additional Resources:

http://msdn.microsoft.com/library/default.asp?url=/library/en-us/vbenlr98/html/vamthgetfilename.asp

Impact: Medium

GetObject

Prototype: `Public Function GetObject( Optional ByVal PathName As String = Nothing, Optional ByVal Class As String = Nothing ) As Object`

Summary: This function returns an object provided by a COM component.

Description: The GetObject function returns an object provided by a COM component for use by an application. It has two string parameters, however only one of the two may be omitted. The first optional string parameter is the path name of a target object, if left blank the second parameter is required. The second parameter is the class parameter that has a format of "name of the application" dot "object type it supports". The return value is an object that can be used in an application.

Risk: The GetObject function is available in VB script and used in Web pages and html enabled email. When used in by malicious users as a Web page or html enabled email it is possible for outside attackers to view files on a remote system.

Additional Resources:

http://msdn.microsoft.com/library/default.asp?url=/library/en-us/vblr7/html/vafctgetobject.asp

Impact: Medium

GetSetting

Prototype: `Public Function GetSetting( ByVal AppName As String, ByVal Section As String, ByVal Key As String, Optional ByVal Default As String = "" ) As String`

Summary: This function is used to retrieve the key setting value from an applications Windows Registry entry.

Description: The `GetSetting` function is used to retrieve the key setting value created by an application that resides in the Windows Registry. It possesses four parameters, three required and the fourth optional. The first parameter is a string value for the application or project which key setting is being requested. The second parameter is the section in which the key setting can be found. The third parameter is the name of the key setting that is being returned. The fourth optional parameter is the default setting; this is what gets returned if no key is discovered in that location.

Risk: This function reveals sensitive information about the Registry entries. Applications should avoid authorizing users access to results. When using this function for application internals is necessary, it is important to parse user input to prevent access to restricted files and restricted Registry entries.

Additional Resources:

http://msdn.microsoft.com/library/default.asp?url=/library/en-us/vblr7/html/vafctgetsetting.asp

Impact: Medium

GetTempName

Prototype: `object.GetTempName`

Summary: This method is used to return a randomly generated temporary file or folder.

Description: The GetTempName method provides a name for a temporary file or folder. The GetTempName function has no parameters. It returns a string containing the name to use. It does not create the file.

Risk: This method is used for temporary files and folders that are intended for deletion once an application terminates it is important to delete these files and folder along with any other forms of caching after they become no longer necessary, in order to restrict access to sensitive information. In general, sensitive information should not be placed in these files and folder since temporary files tend to have lower access restrictions.

Additional Resources:

http://msdn.microsoft.com/library/default.asp?url=/library/en-us/
vbenlr98/html/vamthgettempname.asp

Impact: Low

GetText

Prototype: object.GetText (format)

Summary: This method is used to return a text string from a Clipboard object.

Description: The GetText method is a part of the Clipboard object. It is used to retrieve a text string from a Clipboard object. This method takes a single optional parameter, a flag signifying the Clipboard object format.

Risk: The Clipboard object is not restricted to the calling program. This makes it possible for users to manipulate data in the clipboard and potentially corrupt expected results.

Additional Resources:

http://msdn.microsoft.com/library/default.asp?url=/library/en-us/
vb98/html/vbmthgettext.asp

Impact: Low

Hide

Prototype: `objMMC.Hide`

Summary: This method is used to set the visible property of any Microsoft Management Console (MMC) applications.

Description: The `Hide` method is a part of any Microsoft Management Console (MMC) application and is used to set the visible property. Applications that have their visible property set to hide are still running, however. The functions run in the background. This method has no input parameters and does not return any values.

Risk: Malicious applications often have visible properties set to hide in order to prevent users from seeing they are running. Hidden application will still show up in the task manager.

Additional Resources:

http://msdn.microsoft.com/library/default.asp?url=/library/en-us/mmc/mmc/application_hide.asp

Impact: High

Insert

Prototype: `Insert( int index, string item)`

Summary: This method adds an item to a `collection` object.

Description: The `Insert` method adds an item to a specific location to a `collection` object. It takes two parameters. The first parameter is an integer indicating the index that will be its location in the collection. The second parameter is a string that is the item to be added to the collection.

Risk: All parameters passed to the function from user input should be carefully analyzed to prevent access to or overwriting of system files. Invalid inserts into the collection class can result in data corruption or unauthorized execution of code.

Additional Resources:

http://msdn.microsoft.com/library/default.asp?url=/library/en-us/mwsdk/html/mwlrfinsertmethod.asp

Impact: Low

InsertFile

Prototype: `expression.InsertFile(FileName, Range, ConfirmConversions, Link, Attachment)`

Summary: This method is used to insert a file into a `Word` object.

Description: The `InsertFile` method is apart of the `Word` object; it is used to insert a file into a `Word` object. This method has five parameters. The first and only required parameter is a string; this is the file name and location of the file that is intended on being inserted. If no path is provided, `Word` will work from the current folder. The second parameter, which is optional, is a variant for the range; if the file is a Word document this parameter is a bookmark. The third parameter which is optional is a variant; it is the `ConfirmConversion` when set to "TRUE", it will prompt you to confirm conversion when inserting files in formats other then the Word Document format. The fourth parameter is the link. This is optional. If set to "TRUE", it will insert the file by using the `INCLUEDTEXT` field. The fifth parameter is a variant; this is optional. If set to "TRUE", it will insert the file as an attachment to an e-mail message.

Risk: All parameters passed to the function from user input should be carefully analyzed to prevent access to or overwriting of system files. Additionally, this method is capable of creating files on a system. Files should never be created automatically as a result of an action such as a form submittal. Excessive submits by a malicious user can result in exhausting file nodes on the server.

Additional Resources:

http://msdn.microsoft.com/library/default.asp?url=/library/en-us/vbawd11/html/womthinsertfile1.asp

Impact: Medium

IMEStatus

Prototype: `IMEStatus() as Integer`

Summary: This function returns the Input Method Editor (IME) mode. (This function is only available in east-Asian versions only.)

Description: This function returns the value of the current Input Method Editor (IME) mode. This function has no input arguments. It returns an integer value indicating what the IME the system is currently using.

Risk: This function contains no known vulnerabilities. Because of the nature of this function is revealing sensitive information about the operating system it is possible that when used in a server application a remote user could access this function and cause an unintentional information disclosure.

Additional Resources:

http://msdn.microsoft.com/library/default.asp?url=/library/en-us/vbenlr98/html/vafctimestatus.asp

Impact: Medium

Import

Prototype: `object.Import(filename)`

Summary: This function is used to add a component to an existing project.

Description: The `Import` function is part of the `VBComponents` object. The function has one input parameter: the path/name of the file to add to the current project. It can be used to add a component, form, module, class, etc... The function returns the name of the file that was added to the project.

Risk: When using this function to add components to projects, it is important to verify the integrity of the component being imported. Developers often rely on third party components without fully understanding the details of the components design. As a result developers can unintentionally build in malicious or poorly written code.

Additional Resources:

http://msdn.microsoft.com/library/default.asp?url=/library/en-us/vb98/html/vbmthKillDoc.asp

Impact: High

Input

Prototype: `Public Sub Input( FileNumber As Integer, ByRef Value As Object )`

Summary: This function reads data from a sequential file into an application.

Description: The `input` function reads data from a sequential file and loads those values into variables. It contains two required input arguments. The first argument is the `FileNumber`; it is an integer of a valid file. The second input argument is the `value`; this is an object variable that is assigned the values that are read from the file.

Risk: The `input` function poses a security risk when it is used to determine the content of a file. When reading a file, do not make decisions about the file type based on the file extension type. Doing so can lead to unintended programs or files being executed that are mistakenly and/or deliberately mislabeled. Syntax used for input values should be carefully parsed to prevent the malicious execution of code or data corruption.

Additional Resources:
http://msdn.microsoft.com/library/default.asp?url=/library/en-us/vblr7/html/vastminputdata.asp

Impact: Medium

InputBox

Prototype: `Public Function InputBox( ByVal Prompt As String, Optional ByVal Title As String = "", Optional ByVal DefaultResponse As String = "", Optional ByVal XPos As Integer = -1, Optional ByVal YPos As Integer = -1 ) As String`

Summary: This function is used to gain input from a user.

Description: This function creates an input box to retrieve data from a user. The function has one required and five optional input arguments. The required input (which can be NULL) is a string containing the prompt for the user. The optional arguments control the title, size, and location of the input box, as well as the help file location. The function returns a string containing the user's input.

Risk: The return value of the `InputBox` function is a string; VB strings are of variable length. Thus the length of the user supplied input while it will not affect the InputBox this input can be potentially dangerous if supplied to a non VB string or if passed to another application. Syntax used for input should be carefully parsed to prevent the malicious execution of code or data corruption.

Additional Resources:
http://msdn.microsoft.com/library/default.asp?url=/library/en-us/vblr7/html/vafctinputbox.asp

Impact: Medium

KillDoc

Prototype: `object.KillDoc`

Summary: This method is used to terminate the current print job of a `printer` object.

Description: The `KillDoc` method is a part of the `printer` object. It is used to terminate the current print job that a `printer` object may be working on. This method has no parameters.

Risk: Usage of this method should be carefully regulated to prevent users from accidental or malicious usage. Unchecked a malicious user could effectively denial of service a printer by continuously canceling print jobs.

Additional Resources:
http://msdn.microsoft.com/library/default.asp?url=/library/en-us/vb98/html/vbmthkilldoc.asp

Impact: Medium

Listen

Prototype: `Public Sub Listen( ByVal backlog As Integer )`

Summary: This method is used to place a `socket` object into a listening state.

Description: The Listen method is a part of the socket object, and is used to place the socket object into a listening state. This method takes a single required parameter; it is for the backlog which is the maximum length of the pending connections queue.

Risk: Opens a network socket that maybe used by an attacker to gain access to the system. When using sockets, one should carefully regulate all incoming and outgoing data traffic to prevent malicious data from compromising a system.

Additional Resources:
http://msdn.microsoft.com/library/default.asp?url=/library/en-us/cpref/html/frlrfsystemnetsocketssocketclasslistentopic.asp

Impact: High

LoadFile

Prototype: `Overloads Public Sub LoadFile( ByVal path As String )`

Summary: This method is used to load Text Format (RTF) or standard ASCII text into a RichTextBox control.

Description: The LoadFile method is a part of the RichTextBox control. It is used to load the contents of the text file into the text property of the RichTextBox. This method has a single required parameter; it is a string containing the name and location of the file to load into the control.

Risk: Any time functions are called with system access, all parameters passed to the function from user input should be carefully analyzed to prevent access to restricted or unprivileged system files.

Additional Resources:
http://msdn.microsoft.com/library/default.asp?url=/library/en-us/cpref/html/frlrfsystemwindowsformsrichtextboxclassloadfiletopic1.asp

Impact: High

LoadPicture

Prototype: `LoadPicture(picturename)`

Summary: This function is used to display pictures to the screen.

Description: The `LoadPicture` function is used to convert a number of graphics file types into a picture object recognized by most VB components. The `LoadPicture` function has a several parameters, including a string indicating the path/name of the picture file needed to be loaded, as well as optional size arguments for the picture. Other optional arguments are for the depth of the color field to use and a separate size control.

Risk: Any time functions are called with system access, all parameters passed to the function from user input should be carefully analyzed to prevent access to restricted or unprivileged system files.

Additional Resources:

http://msdn.microsoft.com/library/default.asp?url=/library/en-us/script56/html/vsfctloadpicture.asp

Impact: Medium

LoadResData

Prototype: `LoadResData(index, format)`

Summary: This function loads the contents of a resource (.res) file and returns a byte array.

Description: The `LoadResData` function loads the contents of a resource (.res) file and returns a byte array. The function contains two required input arguments. The first argument is the index; it is an integer or string specifying the identifier of data in a resource file. The second input argument is the format; this value could be one of many types, including bitmap.

Risk: Any time functions are called with system access, all parameters passed to the function from user input should be carefully analyzed to prevent access to restricted or unprivileged system data.

VBA

Additional Resources:

http://msdn.microsoft.com/library/default.asp?url=/library/en-us/vb98/html/vbmthloadresdata.asp

Impact: High

LoadResPicture

Prototype: `LoadResPicture(index, format)`

Summary: This function loads an image file into an application.

Description: The `LoadResPicture` loads icons, bitmap and cursor images into an application for use by a form or control to use. It contains two input arguments. The first argument is the index; it is an integer or string specifying the identifier of data in a resource file. The second input argument is the format; this value could be one of many types including bitmap.

Risk: Any time functions are called with system access, all parameters passed to the function from user input should be carefully analyzed to prevent access to restricted or unprivileged system files.

Additional Resources:

http://msdn.microsoft.com/library/default.asp?url=/library/en-us/vb98/html/vbmthloadrespicture.asp

Impact: High

LoadResString

Prototype: `LoadResString(index)`

Summary: This function loads a string from a resource (.res) file.

Description: The `LoadResString` loads a string into an application from a resource (.res) file in order to improve performance and facilitates easier localization of an application. It contains one input argument. The argument is the index; it is an integer or string specifying the identifier of data in a resource file.

Risk: Any time functions are called with system access, all parameters passed to the function from user input should be carefully analyzed to prevent access to restricted or unprivileged system files.

Additional Resources:
http://msdn.microsoft.com/library/default.asp?url=/library/en-us/vb98/html/vbmthloadresstring.asp

Impact: Low

LOF

Prototype: `Public Function LOF(ByVal FileNumber As Integer) As Long`

Summary: This function is used to get the length of a file in bytes.

Description: The `LOF` function or "Length of File" function is used to gain the length of a file opened with the `FileOpen` function. The `LOF` function has a single parameter an integer value that is the `FileNumber` of the file. The function returns the length of the file (in bytes) as Long integer.

Risk: This function should be used to ensure errors do not occur from going past the last character in a record.

Additional Resources:
http://msdn.microsoft.com/library/default.asp?url=/library/en-us/vblr7/html/vafctlof.asp

Impact: Low

MsgBox

Prototype: `Public Function MsgBox( ByVal Prompt As Object, Optional ByVal Buttons As MsgBoxStyle = MsgBoxStyle.OKOnly, Optional ByVal Title As Object = Nothing ) As MsgBoxResult`

Summary: This function is used to display a common message box to the user.

Description: This function posts a simple message box to the screen to accommodate a number of common situations. It contains three format input arguments. The first required argument is the prompt; this is the body of the message box. The second parameter is a flag for the buttons, an optional integer value that indicates the number of buttons, default selection and also what icon gets displayed in the message box. The third option is also optional; it is a string value for the title. Omission of this value results in the title bar displaying the name of the project. The return value is an integer value indicating which button was selected.

Risk: ActiveX objects allowed by the `MsgBox` can be triggered by a local user or by a cross-site scripting attack that has the `MsgBox` function available to them. These objects can be used to display information with server application privileges that are higher then that of the user who called the ActiveX object.

Additional Resources:

http://msdn.microsoft.com/library/default.asp?url=/library/en-us/vblr7/html/vafctmsgbox.asp

Impact: High

Now

Prototype: `Public Function Now() As Date`

Summary: This function is used to retrieve the current date.

Description: The Now function is used to retrieve the current date and time. There are no parameters associated with the now function. This function returns the requested information in a modified `Date` object.

Risk: The Now function relies on the system clock; accordingly, applications that depend on the `Date` function to control trail licenses and other control elements can be fooled by simply resetting the system clock.

Additional Resources:

http://msdn.microsoft.com/library/default.asp?url=/library/en-us/script56/html/vsfctnow.asp

Impact: Low

RandomDataFill

Prototype: `object.RandomDataFill`

Summary: This method fills a data grid with random values for a `DataGrid` object.

Description: The `RandomDataFill` is a method of the `DataGrid` object. It is used to fill a data grid with random values. This method has no parameters.

Risk: Since this method can be used to generate random data fields it is important to carefully control objects this function is executed on. Otherwise, there is a potential to overwrite sensitive data or corrupt the data flow of an application.

Additional Resources:

http://msdn.microsoft.com/library/default.asp?url=/library/en-us/mschrt/html/vbmthrandomdatafillmethod.asp

Impact: High

RandomFillColumns

Prototype: `object.RandomFillColumns (column, count)`

Summary: This method fills a number of data grid columns with random values for a `DataGrid` object.

Description: The `RandomFillColumns` is a method of the `DataGrid` object. It is used to fill a number of data grid columns associated with a chart with random values. This method takes two parameters, both required. The first parameter is the `column`; it is an integer value and identifies the first column you wish to fill. The second parameter is the `count`; it is an integer value specifying the number of columns you wan to fill with random data.

Risk: Since this method can be used to generate random data fields it is important to carefully control objects this function is executed on. Otherwise, there is a potential to overwrite sensitive data or corrupt the data flow of an application.

Additional Resources:

http://msdn.microsoft.com/library/default.asp?url=/library/en-us/mschrt/html/vbmthrandomfillcolumnsmethod.asp

Impact: High

RandomFillRows

Prototype: `object.RandomFillRows (row, count)`

Summary: This method fills a number of data grid rows with random values for a `DataGrid` object.

Description: The `RandomFillRows` is a method of the `DataGrid` object, it is used to fill a number of data grid rows associated with a chart with random values. This method takes two parameters, both required. The first parameter is the `row`; it is an integer value and identifies the first row you wish to fill. The second parameter is the `count`; it is an integer value specifying the number of rows you wan to fill with random data.

Risk: Since this method can be used to generate random data fields it is important to carefully control objects this function is executed on. Otherwise, there is a potential to overwrite sensitive data or corrupt the data flow of an application.

Additional Resources:

http://msdn.microsoft.com/library/default.asp?url=/library/en-us/mschrt/html/vbmthrandomfillrowsmethod.asp

Impact: High

ReadAll

Prototype: `object.ReadAll`

Summary: This method is used to read an entire TextStream file from a `TextStream` object.

Description: The `ReadAll` method is a member of the `TextStream` object. It is used to read an entire TextStream file from a `TextStream` object. This method does not take any parameters.

Risk: For large files, using the `ReadAll` method wastes memory resources and could be the source of a denial of service condition if applied to a server. Other techniques should be used to input a file, such as reading a file line by line.

Additional Resources:
http://msdn.microsoft.com/library/default.asp?url=/library/en-us/vbenlr98/html/vamthreadall.asp

Impact: Low

ReadFromFile

Prototype: `object.ReadFromFile filenumber`

Summary: This method loads an object form a data file.

Description: The `ReadFromFile` loads an object from a data file created using the `SaveToFile` method. This method takes one required parameter; a numeric expression specifying the file number used when loading an object. This number must correspond to an open, binary file.

Risk: Any time functions are called with system access, all parameters passed to the function from user input should be carefully analyzed to prevent access to restricted or unprivileged system files.

Additional Resources:
http://msdn.microsoft.com/library/default.asp?url=/library/en-us/vb98/html/vbmthreadfromfile.asp

Impact: Medium

ReadProperty

Prototype: `object.ReadProperty(DataName[, DefaultValue])`

Summary: This method returns a saved value from a `PropertyBag` object.

Description: The `ReadProperty` method is a part of the `PropertyBag` object, it is used to return the saved value. This method takes two parameters. The first parameter is the `DataName`; it is a string expression that represents a data value in

VBA

the property bag. The second optional parameter is the `DefaultValue`; this is the value to be returned if no value is present.

Risk: All inputs property requests passed to this method should be carefully parsed to prevent access to sensitive information about property data for other data members in the `PropertyBag` object.

Additional Resources:
http://msdn.microsoft.com/library/default.asp?url=/library/en-us/vb98/html/vbmthreadpropertymethod.asp

Impact: Medium

ReleaseInstance

Prototype: `object.ReleaseInstance`

Summary: This method is used to release an instance of a `Webclass` object.

Description: The `ReleaseInstance` method is used by `Webclass` objects to destroy a specific instance that has been kept alive across HTTP requests. This method has no parameters.

Risk: Calls to this method should be carefully controlled to prevent accidental deletion of necessary `Webclass` objects owed by the user, or malicious deletion of other user's objects.

Additional Resources:
http://msdn.microsoft.com/library/default.asp?url=/library/en-us/vb98/html/vbmthsetcompletemethod_x.asp

Impact: High

Reload

Prototype: `expression.Reload`

Summary: This method is used to reload a cached document for a `Document` object.

Description: The `Reload` method is used by the `Document` object by reloading the cached document resolving hyperlinks to the document and downloading it. This method has no parameters.

Risk: The `Reload` method takes place asynchronously, thus procedures following the `Reload` command may execute before the reload is complete and may cause unexpected results. All data processed after a `reload` method call should be treated as if it was from the original load to prevent corruption of data as a result of document cache tampering.

Additional Resources:

http://msdn.microsoft.com/library/default.asp?url=/library/en-us/vbawd11/html/womthreload1.asp

Impact: Medium

Rnd

Prototype: `Rnd[(number)]`

Summary: This function is used to produce a random number.

Description: The `Rnd` function is used to generate random numbers. This function takes one optional numeric parameter, a flag for determining how the random number will be generated. The returned value is a random single-precision floating-point number.

Risk: In order for the numbers produced by the `Rnd` function to be random a call to the `Randomize` statement with no arguments must be made. Since this function can be used to generate random encryption keys it is important that the numbers be random, failure to use randomize will result in easily decipherable keys.

Additional Resources:

http://msdn.microsoft.com/library/default.asp?url=/library/en-us/script56/html/vsfctrnd.asp

Impact: High

Replace

Prototype: `Public Function Replace( ByVal Expression As String, ByVal Find As String, ByVal Replacement As String, Optional ByVal Start As Integer = 1, Optional ByVal Count As Integer = -1, Optional ByVal Compare As CompareMethod = CompareMethod.Binary) As String`

Summary: This function is used to parse out and replace a piece of a string from a larger string.

Description: This function returns a string where a substring has been replaced by another string a certain number of times. It contains six input arguments, three required and three optional. The first argument is required and it is the expression string or the larger string which contains a smaller string that needs replacement. The next expression also required is the find string, this is the substring that needs to be searched out and replaced. The third expression is required and is the replacement string; this is the string that will be in the place of the searched out substring. The fourth argument is the start point; this is optional and will default to 1 if not stated. The start point is a numeric value to indicate where to start the search for the substring. The fifth argument is an optional parameter; it is the count vector that indicates how many times the replacement substring should be done. This value defaults to -1, which indicates it must replace every occurrence of the substring. The final parameter is the `compare` argument; this can be either a binary comparison or a textual comparison.

Risk: The `replace` function is one of many forbidden functions that can provide a malicious Web site the ability to inflict harm to visitors. Most Web browsers limit the permissions and scope of the VB Script version of the `replace` function that could pose a problem when it is employed in a Web application. Content filtering should be employed if a user has any access to the values for the `replaced` parameter, `string` parameter, or `find` parameter. This could provide a means for a malicious user to write to areas of a file or string that the user is not intended to write to.

VBA

VBA

Additional Resources:

http://msdn.microsoft.com/library/default.asp?url=/library/en-us/vblr7/html/vafctreplace.asp

Impact: High

Shell

Prototype: `Shell(pathname[,windowstyle])`

Summary: This function is used to run executable programs.

Description: This function runs an executable program and returns a double value that is the program's task ID, if an error occurs it returns zero. Shell contains two parameters, one required and one optional. The first parameter is the `pathname`; this is a string value that contains the name of the executable file with switches of applicable, drive, and folder. The second optional parameter is the window style; this is an integer value that will default to minimize with focus.

Risk: The `Shell` function has the ability to run any executable on a system with the same privileges as the executing user. Any time external code is executed on a server, restrictions need to be implemented to prevent unauthorized user access. If a user can execute custom code, it will become possible for that user to gain unauthorized access to the system.

Additional Resources:

http://msdn.microsoft.com/library/default.asp?url=/library/en-us/vbenlr98/html/vafctShell.asp

Impact: Medium

Time

Prototype: `Public Function Time() As Date`

Summary: This function is used to retrieve the current time.

Description: The `Time` function is used to retrieve the current time. There are no parameters associated with the `time` function. The time is returned in a modified `Date` object.

Risk: The Time function relies on the system clock; accordingly, applications that depend on the Date function to control trail licenses and other control elements can be fooled by simply resetting the system clock. For instance a program which uses the time function to restrict the execution of elements to an hour in order to prevent overload, could cause a system overload when someone resets there time for daylight savings or similar events.

Additional Resources:

http://msdn.microsoft.com/library/default.asp?url=/library/en-us/script56/html/vsfcttime.asp

Impact: Medium

Programmer's Ultimate Security DeskRef: VBScript

Date

Prototype: `Date`

Summary: This function returns the current system date.

Description: The VBScript `Date` function returns the current local time and date of the underlying operating system in its native format. As with most VBScript functions, `Date` is a reserved word that takes no parameters nor does it first need to be prototyped or initialized.

Risk: The local server time could be utilized to ascertain geography-specific information on a cyber target. This information could then be leveraged to advance an attack. Ensure that it is acceptable to release the system's time and date settings to external parties before outputting the results of this function to human users.

Note: In general, this function was written for Microsoft Windows-based operating systems.

Additional Resources:

http://msdn.microsoft.com/library/default.asp?url=/library/en-us/
script56/html/vtoriVBScript.asp

Impact: Low

Cross References: Now, Time, Cdate

Debug.write

Prototype: debug.write(string1, string2,… stringX)

Summary: This function sends a string to the Microsoft script debugger.

Description: The Write method is extended from the VBScript Debug object. The VBScript Write method sends strings to the active script debugger. While there is no limitation on the number of strings that can be sent to the debugger for contextual analysis, it is a function that has the potential to put a lag on system resources. In most cases, it's beneficial to enable just-in-time (JIT) debugging when utilizing this method.

Risk: Methods that utilize a backend debugger are in danger of putting underlying executables and applications at risk when that debugger is called. It is not uncommon for bugs or vulnerabilities to be identified in closed source applications to include Microsoft applications. Once launched, the application will send datastreams to the debugger for execution. All transmitted data should be analyzed and stripped of potentially malicious content.

Note: In general, VBScript functionality is geared for Microsoft operating systems only.

Additional Resources:

http://msdn.microsoft.com/library/default.asp?url=/library/en-us/
script56/html/vtoriVBScript.asp

Impact: Medium

Cross References: debug.writeline

Debug.writeline

Prototype: `debug.writeline(string1, string2,… stringX)`

Summary: This function sends a string to the Microsoft script debugged with an appended newline character.

Description: The `Writeline` method is extended from the VBScript `Debug` object. The VBScript `Writeline` method sends strings followed by a newline character "/n" to the active script debugger. While there is no limitation on the number of strings that can be sent to the debugger for contextual analysis, it is a function that has the potential to put a lag on system resources. In most cases, it's beneficial to enable just-in-time (JIT) debugging when utilizing this method.

Risk: Methods that utilize a backend debugger are in danger of putting underlying executables and applications at risk when that debugger is called. It is not uncommon for bugs or vulnerabilities to be identified in closed source applications to include Microsoft applications. Once launched, the application will send datas-treams to the debugger for execution. All transmitted data should be analyzed and stripped of potentially malicious content.

Note: In general, VBScript functionality is geared for Microsoft operating systems only.

Additional Resources:

http://msdn.microsoft.com/library/default.asp?url=/library/en-us/script56/html/vtoriVBScript.asp

Impact: Medium

Cross References: `debug.write`

GetLocale

Prototype: `GetLocale()`

Summary: This function returns the current system Locale.

Description: The `GetLocale` function returns the value of the locale ID for the current system. In general the locale can contain information to include local user configurations and settings, country, or even keyboard layout. The returned value is a 32-bit number that can be cross-referenced with Microsoft's Locale ID chart.

Risk: Output of this function could be enough to field an educated attack on a vulnerable system. This function handles highly sensitive system-specific sensitive information that an attacker could leverage during a period of target reconnaissance. This function should only be utilized if it is absolutely necessary for proper execution of the application. All analysis for the output of this function should be conducted securely within the application and never sent across the wire in cleartext.

Note: In general, VBScript functionality is geared for Microsoft operating systems only.

Additional Resources:

http://msdn.microsoft.com/library/default.asp?url=/library/en-us/script56/html/vsmsclcid.asp,

http://msdn.microsoft.com/library/default.asp?url=/library/en-us/script56/html/vtoriVBScript.asp

Impact: Medium

Cross References: SetLocale

InputBox

Prototype: InputBox(prompt, title, default, xpos, ypos, helpfile, context)

Summary: This function is utilized to create an input box for gathering human user input.

Description: The VBScript InputBox prompts a user with a custom-crafted Web-based dialog box. This box usually requires action before it removed from the foremost position on the screen that usually happens to be human user input text or the acknowledged click of a button. If a text box is used, then the text would be returned, while buttons usually return Boolean or whole integer numbers. The function can take up to seven parameters as seen in the prototype.

Risk: Input boxes are commonly misused for password and other types of sensitive information storage. Sensitive information should never be transmitted from clients to servers via Web page input boxes. In addition, SSL should be implemented when transferring sensitive data. Lastly, ensure that all user input is fully scrutinized whereas non-alphanumeric characters are removed where possible.

Note: In general, VBScript functionality is geared for Microsoft operating systems only.

Additional Resources:
http://msdn.microsoft.com/library/default.asp?url=/library/en-us/script56/html/vtoriVBScript.asp

Impact: Low

LoadPicture

Prototype: `LoadPicture(name_of_picture)`

Summary: This function is utilized to load a picture with VBScript controls.

Description: The `LoadPicture` function takes one parameter that is utilized to house the name of the picture that is to be uploaded to an application. This function is commonly utilized for Web browser functionality to load pictures to a Web site. By default, the `LoadPicture` function supports bitmap, enhanced metafiles, GIF, icon, JPEG, run-length encoded, and windows metafiles.

Risk: Access controls should be implemented to restrict users from loading files that are not pictures. Additionally, consider adding or plugging in a malicious content filter such as that offered by McAfee. These types of anti-virus additions are becoming more and more popular in the software development industry.

Note: In general VBScript functionality is geared for Microsoft operating systems only.

Additional Resources:
http://msdn.microsoft.com/library/default.asp?url=/library/en-us/script56/html/vtoriVBScript.asp

Impact: Low

Now

Prototype: Now

Summary: This function returns the current system time.

Description: The Now function returns the current system's date and time. Both of these variables are stored into a single string variable upon execution and no parameters are necessary to run this function.

Risk: This function handles system-specific sensitive information that an attacker could leverage during a period of target reconnaissance. This function should only be utilized if it is absolutely necessary for proper execution of the application. All analysis for the output of this function should be conducted securely within the application and never sent across the wire in cleartext.

Note: In general, VBScript functionality is geared for Microsoft operating systems only.

Additional Resources:

http://msdn.microsoft.com/library/default.asp?url=/library/en-us/script56/html/vtoriVBScript.asp

Impact: Low

Cross References: Time, Date

Replace

Prototype: Replace

Summary: This function returns a final string after it's replace with string is implemented.

Description: The replace function takes six parameters. The first three are required while the last three are optional additions. The expression parameter contains the value that you are searching and replacing within, whereas the find is the string you are looking for, and the replacement is the string that's going to replace the find value. The start parameter is utilized if you wish to start searching at a specific location within a certain string. The count parameter defines how many times a replacement will be made, while compare defines whether it's a binary or text-based compare algorithm that should be utilized.

Risk: The `replace` function is commonly poorly implemented, whereas attackers obtain the ability to replace data within sensitive files or datastreams. It is critical to ensure that human users cannot call this function nor pass random variables to the `replace` function.

Note: In general, VBScript functionality is geared for Microsoft operating systems only.

Additional Resources:
http://msdn.microsoft.com/library/default.asp?url=/library/en-us/
script56/html/vtoriVBScript.asp

Impact: Low

Rnd

Prototype: `Rnd (number)`

Summary: This function returns a random number.

Description: The `Rnd` function returns a quasi-random number generated by an internal VBScript system function. The `(number)` parameter that the `Rnd` function accepts helps determine what kind of random number is generated. A number less than zero will use the same seed every time, whereas a number greater than zero will return the next random number in the sequence.

Risk: As with most standard random functions implemented within the C and C++ libraries, this function is susceptible to brute force or easily guessed number generating attacks due to a poor seed algorithm within the backend code. Amongst numerous other secure random number generating functions, Microsoft .Net has secure methods for implementing properly seeded numbers. ISAAC, designed by Bob Jenkins, is a fast cryptographic random number generator is as strong as they come. Available in multiple languages, ISAAC is a standard for many freeware and commercial solutions and should be considered the next time a random number is required within an application.

Note: In general, VBScript functionality is geared for Microsoft operating systems only.

Additional Resources:

http://msdn.microsoft.com/library/default.asp?url=/library/en-us/script56/html/vtoriVBScript.asp

Impact: High

ScriptEngineBuildVersion

Prototype: ScriptingEngineBuildVersion

Summary: This function returns the complete build version for the current scripting engine.

Description: In most applications that must determine if a certain scripting engine is running, they must first detect the engine type then build information of the engine. The ScriptingEngineBuildVersion function returns the complete build version of the scripting engine to include both the major and minor version numbers.

Risk: This function handles system-specific sensitive information that an attacker could leverage during a period of target reconnaissance. This function should only be utilized if it is absolutely necessary for proper execution of the application. All analysis for the output of this function should be conducted securely within the application and never sent across the wire in cleartext.

Note: In general, VBScript functionality is geared for Microsoft operating systems only.

Additional Resources:

http://msdn.microsoft.com/library/default.asp?url=/library/en-us/script56/html/vtoriVBScript.asp

Impact: Medium

ScriptEngineMajorVersion

Prototype: `ScriptingEngineMajorVersion`

Summary: This function returns the major version for the current scripting engine.

Description: In most applications that must determine if a certain scripting engine is running, they must first detect the engine type then build information of the engine. The `ScriptingEngineMajorVersion` function returns the major build version of the scripting engine.

Risk: This function handles system-specific sensitive information that an attacker could leverage during a period of target reconnaissance. This function should only be utilized if it is absolutely necessary for proper execution of the application. All analysis for the output of this function should be conducted securely within the application and never sent across the wire in cleartext.

Note: In general, VBScript functionality is geared for Microsoft operating systems only.

Additional Resources:

http://msdn.microsoft.com/library/default.asp?url=/library/en-us/ script56/html/vtoriVBScript.asp

Impact: Medium

ScriptEngineMinorVersion

Prototype: `ScriptingEngineMinorVersion`

Summary: This function returns the minor version of the current scripting engine.

Description: In most applications that must determine if a certain scripting engine is running, they must first detect the engine type then build information of the engine. The `ScriptingEngineMinorVersion` function returns the minor build version of the scripting engine.

Risk: This function handles system-specific sensitive information that an attacker could leverage during a period of target reconnaissance. This function should only

be utilized if it is absolutely necessary for proper execution of the application. All analysis for the output of this function should be conducted securely within the application and never sent across the wire in cleartext.

Note: In general, VBScript functionality is geared for Microsoft operating systems only.

Additional Resources:
http://msdn.microsoft.com/library/default.asp?url=/library/en–us/ script56/html/vtoriVBScript.asp

Impact: Medium

ScriptingEngine

Prototype: ScriptingEngine

Summary: This function returns a character-based string with the current scripting language in use.

Description: Microsoft operating systems currently support multiple scripting engines that can be running dormant in the background. The ScriptEngine function returns a string detailing what engine is currently being utilized. The three most common strings returned are Jscript, VBA, or VBScript.

Risk: This function handles system-specific sensitive information that an attacker could leverage during a period of target reconnaissance. This function should only be utilized if it is absolutely necessary for proper execution of the application. All analysis for the output of this function should be conducted securely within the application and never sent across the wire in cleartext.

Note: In general, VBScript functionality is geared for Microsoft operating systems only.

Additional Resources:
http://msdn.microsoft.com/library/default.asp?url=/library/en–us/ script56/html/vtoriVBScript.asp

Impact: Medium

SetLocale

Prototype: `SetLocale(lcid)`

Summary: This function is utilized to set the system global locale.

Description: The `SetLocale` function permits the application end-user to set the local environment variables. In general, the locale can contain information to include local user configurations and settings, country, or even keyboard layout. The returned value is a 32-bit number that can be cross-referenced with Microsoft's Locale ID chart.

Risk: Output of this function could be enough to field an educated attack on a vulnerable system. This function handles highly sensitive system-specific sensitive information that an attacker could leverage during a period of target reconnaissance. This function should only be utilized if it is absolutely necessary for proper execution of the application. All analysis for the output of this function should be conducted securely within the application and never sent across the wire in cleartext.

Note: In general, VBScript functionality is geared for Microsoft operating systems only.

Additional Resources:

http://msdn.microsoft.com/library/default.asp?url=/library/en-us/
script56/html/vsmsclcid.asp,
http://msdn.microsoft.com/library/default.asp?url=/library/en-us/
script56/html/vtoriVBScript.asp

Impact: High

Cross References: `GetLocale`

Time

Prototype: Time

Summary: This function returns the current system's time.

Description: The Time function does not require any parameters and only returns the system's current time as opposed to date and time. The system time is returned in a single string.

Risk: This function handles system-specific sensitive information that an attacker could leverage during a period of target reconnaissance. This function should only be utilized if it is absolutely necessary for proper execution of the application. All analysis for the output of this function should be conducted securely within the application and never sent across the wire in cleartext.

Note: In general, VBScript functionality is geared for Microsoft operating systems only.

Cross References: Date, Now

Additional Resources:
http://msdn.microsoft.com/library/default.asp?url=/library/en-us/script56/html/vtoriVBScript.asp

Impact: Low

Timer

Prototype: Timer

Summary: This function returns the time that has passed since midnight in seconds.

Description: The Timer function does not require any parameters and returns the time that has elapsed passed the most recently 12:00 A.M. according to local system time. The retrieved number is the total number of seconds past midnight.

Risk: This function handles system-specific sensitive information that an attacker could leverage during a period of target reconnaissance. This function should only be utilized if it is absolutely necessary for proper execution of the application. All

analysis for the output of this function should be conducted securely within the application and never sent across the wire in cleartext.

Note: In general, VBScript functionality is geared for Microsoft operating systems only.

Additional Resources:
http://msdn.microsoft.com/library/default.asp?url=/library/en–us/ script56/html/vtoriVBScript.asp

Impact: Low

Cross References: Time, Date, Now

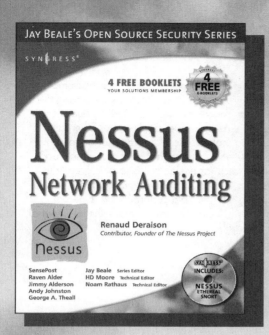

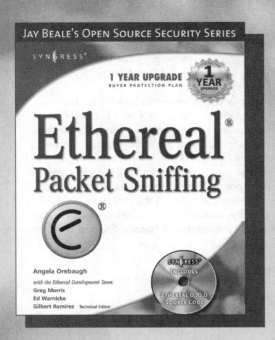
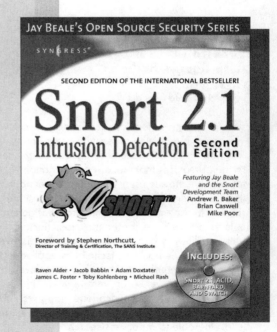

Inside the SPAM Cartel

Spammer X

Authored by a former spammer, this is a methodical, technically explicit expose of the inner workings of the SPAM economy. Readers will be shocked by the sophistication and sheer size of this underworld. "Inside the Spam Cartel" is a great read for people with even a casual interest in cyber-crime. In addition, it includes a level of technical detail that will clearly attract its core audience of technology junkies and security professionals.

ISBN: 1932266-86-0

Price: $49.95 US   72.95 CAN

Microsoft Log Parser Toolkit

Gabriele Giuseppini
and Mark Burnett

Do you want to find Brute Force Attacks against your Exchange Server? Would you like to know who is spamming you? Do you need to monitor the performance of your IIS Server? Are there intruders out there you would like to find? Would you like to build user logon reports from your Windows Server? Would you like working scripts to automate all of these tasks and many more for you? If so, "Microsoft Log Parser Toolkit" is the book for you...

ISBN: 1-932266-52-6

Price: $39.95 USA $57.95 CAN

SYNGRESS®

Syngress: *The Definition of a Serious Security Library*

Syn·gress (sin–gres): *noun, sing.* Freedom from risk or danger; safety. See *security*.

WarDriving: Drive, Detect, Defend A Guide to Wireless Security

Mark Burnett

The act of driving or walking through urban areas with a wireless-equipped laptop to map protected and un-protected wireless networks has sparked intense debate amongst lawmakers, security professionals, and the telecommunications industry. This first ever book on WarDriving is written from the inside perspective of those who have created the tools that make WarDriving possible.

ISBN: -1932266-65-8

Price: $59.95 US $79.95 CAN

Stealing the Network: How to Own a Continent

131ah, Russ Rogers, Jay Beale, Joe Grand, Fyodor, FX, Paul Craig, Timothy Mullen (Thor), Tom Parker, Ryan Russell, Kevin D. Mitnick

The first book in the *"Stealing the Network"* series was called a "blockbuster" by Wired magazine, a "refreshing change from more traditional computer books" by Slashdot.org, and "an entertaining and informative look at the weapons and tactics employed by those who attack and defend digital systems" by Amazon.com. This follow-on book once again combines a set of fictional stories with real technology to show readers the danger that lurks in the shadows of the information security industry... Could hackers take over a continent?

ISBN: 1-931836-05-1

Price: $49.95 US $69.95 CAN

The Mezonic Agenda: Hacking the Presidency

Dr. Herbert H. Thompson and Spyros Nomikos

The Mezonic Agenda: Hacking the Presidency is the first Cyber-Thriller that allows the reader to "hack along" with both the heroes and villains of this fictional narrative using the accompanying CD containing real, working versions of all the applications described and exploited in the fictional narrative of the book. The Mezonic Agenda deals with some of the most pressing topics in technology and computer security today including: reverse engineering, cryptography, buffer overflows, and steganography. The book tells the tale of criminal hackers attempting to compromise the results of a presidential election for their own gain.

ISBN: 1-931836-83-3

Price: $34.95 U.S. $50.95 CAN

SYNGRESS